*Introduction
to the Administration of Justice*

Administration of Justice Series

INTRODUCTION TO THE ADMINISTRATION OF JUSTICE
Robert E. Blanchard, Volume Coordinator
Riverside City College and the American Justice Institute

PRINCIPLES AND PROCEDURES IN THE ADMINISTRATION OF JUSTICE
Harry W. More, Volume Coordinator
San Jose State University, San Jose

LAW AND THE ADMINISTRATION OF JUSTICE
Vernon Rich, Volume Coordinator
Southern Illinois University, Carbondale

EVIDENCE AND PROCEDURE IN THE ADMINISTRATION OF JUSTICE
Kenneth Katsaris, Volume Coordinator
Tallahassee Community College, Tallahassee

COMMUNITY RELATIONS AND THE ADMINISTRATION OF JUSTICE
David P. Geary, Volume Coordinator
University of Wisconsin, Milwaukee

Introduction to the Administration of Justice

ROBERT E. BLANCHARD
Volume Coordinator
Riverside City College
and
American Justice Institute

John Wiley & Sons, Inc.
New York London Sydney Toronto

Credits for Photographs

The South Carolina Department of Corrections, Columbia, South Carolina, Ken Sturgeon, Special Projects Officer: Figures 6-3, 6-4, 6-5, and 11-4.

The Federal Bureau of Prisons, Washington, D.C.: Figures 6-2, 11-5, and 15-3.

New York City Police Department, Bureau of Public Information: Figures 9-3 and 15-2.
Spring 3100: Figures 4-1 and 8-4a.

Los Angeles County Sheriff's Department: Figures 4-3 and 13-1. The Police Academy: Figure 13-3.

Ken Heyman: Figures 3-1 and 7-1.

Mark Quieto: Figures 9-1 and 9-2.

United Press International: Figures 2-6, 3-2, and 15-1.

Roger Malloch–Magnum: Figure 4-2.

Bob Adelman–Magnum: Figure 8.4b.

Geoffrey Gove–Ralpho-Guillumette: Figure 8-1.

Cornell Capa–Magnum: Figure 11-2.

Copyright © 1975, by John Wiley & Sons, Inc.

All rights reserved. Published simultaneously in Canada.

No part of this book may be reproduced by any means, nor transmitted, nor translated into a machine language without the written permission of the publisher.

Library of Congress Cataloging in Publication Data:

Blanchard, Robert, E. 1938-
   Introduction to the administration of justice.

   (Administration of justice series)
   Includes bibliographies.
   1. Criminal justice, Administration of—United States. I. Title. II. Series
KF9223.B54   364   74-5283
ISBN 0-471-07936-7

Printed in the United States of America

10 9 8 7 6 5 4

Contributors

Volume Coordinator:
Robert E. Blanchard

Carl Ball
*Commission for Peace Officers Standards and Training
Sacramento, California*

Erik Beckman
Saginaw Valley College

Ben Clark
Riverside County Sheriff's Department, California

Frank Dell'Apa
Western Interstate Commission for Higher Education, Boulder, Colorado

Jack D. Foster
Youngstown State University

Jon Howington
MacComb County Community College

James C. Kane
University of Omaha

Jack Kuykendall
San Jose State University

Arthur A. Kingsbury
MacComb County Community College

Don Mathews
San Jose State University

Argel E. Roberts
Commission on Law Enforcement Standards, Austin, Texas

Jack L. Ryle
Commission on Law Enforcement Standards, Austin, Texas

Joseph L. Schott
Tarrant County Junior College

G. Roy Sumpter
Youngstown State University

William Tafoya
Pacifica, California

Peter Unsinger
San Jose State University

Richard Ward
John Jay College of Criminal Justice, New York, New York

Introduction to the Series

Wiley has undertaken a significantly different approach to the development of five textbooks. The "Administration of Justice" series responds to the belief that teachers should be given an opportunity to state their textbook needs and to define how the organization and contents of a textbook can best serve these needs. Although teachers are generally asked to react to a book after it is published, we sought advice before final decisions were made.

Traditional textbook publishing has assumed that an author is all-knowing about the content of his book and how the content should be organized. The results often have been disappointing for the following reasons.

1. Some books are very long because they attempt to ensure that there will be something for everyone in the text.
2. Some books are written with one type of student or one section of the United States in mind.
3. Other books reflect an author's strengths and weaknesses; they are sound in some areas (where the author is strong) and superficial in other areas.

We began by working with five tentative outlines that were sent to hundreds of educators and professionals within the criminal justice system. Feedback on the outlines—on how they could be strengthened and improved—was excellent and encouraged us to sponsor a series of meetings throughout the United States. Many participants helped us to synthesize the comments received on the outlines, and each participant prepared revised outlines based on the responses evoked by questionnaires. We especially thank the participants. The books could not have been produced without the help and enthusiasm of Bernard Barry, Scott Bennett, Bob Blanchard, John Boyd, Wordie Burrow, Tom Cochee, Bill Cusack, Stan Everett, Matt Fitzgerald, Ed Flint, Jack Foster, George Gaudette, Dave Geary, Henry Guttenplan, Karl Hutchinson, Keith Jackson, Ken Katsaris, Art Kingsbury, Roger Kirvan, Martha Kornstein, Harry More, and Vern Rich.

Several sets of new outlines resulted from the regional meetings, and these outlines were further expanded and refined at a final meeting. Responsibility for the final outlines was placed with the following educators, who managed the process of evolving the outlines into books with great care, professionalism, and perseverance.

Robert E. Blanchard, Riverside City College and the American Justice Institute, *Introduction to the Administration of Justice.*

Harry W. More, San Jose State University, *Principles and Procedures in the Administration of Justice*

Vernon Rich, Southern Illinois University, *Law and the Administration of Justice.*

Kenneth Katsaris, Tallahassee Community College, *Evidence and Procedure in the Administration of Justice.*

David P. Geary, University of Wisconsin, Milwaukee, *Community Relations and the Administration of Justice.*

Volume coordinators identified leading national figures whose area of particular competence is represented by a chapter in each volume. Specialists throughout the United States brought their insight and experience to bear on the writing of individual chapters, which met the goals and requirements of our advisory groups. These chapter authors are listed on page v. Thus, five highly authoritative, highly current, exceptionally interesting textbooks have resulted.

Individual chapters were examined by the volume coordinator and then were assigned to professional writers. Joseph Schott, Jim George, Charlotte Shelby, Irvin Lee, and Betty Bosarge worked hard and well on homogenizing the volumes. In addition to the responsibility of rewriting two volumes, Charlotte Shelby devoted considerable effort, imagination, and skill to enhancing the clarity and excitement of the other volumes.

Our approach to the development of this series, I believe, has resulted in five important textbooks. It will be for the students and instructors to determine how well we have done. Write to me and tell me how the books might be made even more useful to you.

Alan B. Lesure, Editor
John Wiley & Sons, Inc.

Preface

During the past few years, presidential crime commissions and numerous other authorities representing a cross section of interests have concluded that education for persons aspiring to be a part of the justice system should be based on two elementary premises. First, that subsystem members are no longer provided the luxury of functioning in a vacuum, disregarding other system members or lacking concern for the impact that one subsystem had on the other; and second, that all members of the system have a sincere sensitivity and deep understanding of human beings and the society in which they live. This knowledge should include not only the origin and styles of delinquent behavior but also contemporary theories and techniques of dealing with and treating human frailties.

Encompassed within the functional areas of the criminal justice system, the student usually will find (1) police and related enforcement agencies, responsible for investigation and apprehension; (2) prosecution and defense, charged with trying and protecting; (3) the courts, exercising complete jurisdiction over all criminal matters; (4) probationary staff, assisting the courts in determining method of punishment; (5) correctional institutions, for confinement and making ready for reentry; and (6) parole, concerned with compliance of obligations after release from custody.

The term "system," used in connection with criminal justice, denotes a sequence of functions and they are all part of the whole—a rational series of events with regular interaction or interdependence with each other. These functions represent a cooperative venture that depends on each participant actively fulfilling its responsibilities to accomplish the system's objectives.

The student actually should view the current system more as a "nonsystem," even though the term system is used throughout the text. This series of subsystems generally works independently, strives toward diverse objectives, and possesses a variety of responsibilities and authority that frequently overlap and are highly competitive.

As an academic field of study, the system of criminal justice education is relatively new. Only within the last few years has any progress been made toward viewing the system as a whole and not merely as a random collection of subsystems. The major rationale for the existence of this field of study is twofold. First, to prepare the student to enter the system of justice and to staff its current operation, thus stimulating him to rethink the status quo in order to develop realistically imaginative approaches to resolving the crime issue; and second, to consider personnel already performing the responsibilities of the system and recharge their enthusiasm, creativity, and dedication to the success of the system.

The substance of this text is presented in a careful sequence. Chapter 1 gives a broad overview of the total system of justice and how each subsystem fits into the overall process of American criminal justice. Chapter 2 surveys the nature and degree to which criminal acts are committed. Chapter 3 focuses on the numerous theories of criminal behavior. It provides a historical and contemporary view of causal theories. Chapters 4 to 6 outline the historical development of each of the major subsystems of justice: police, courts, and corrections. Chapter 7 deals with the various levels of enforcement agencies on a nationwide basis. Chapter 8 examines the styles of policing techniques. Chapter 9 gives an overview of the many roles and responsibilities of a policing agency. Chapter 10 outlines the primary function of the court system and its various levels. Chapter 11 discusses the theory and contemporary practice of corrections. Chapter 12 deals with the matter of presenting a basic understanding of professionalism for criminal justice system personnel. Chapter 13 gives an overview of education and training concepts for personnel of the criminal justice system. Chapter 14 examines the interview process as a management tool for entrance level and promotional opportunities within the justice system. Chapter 15 points out possible future trends in concepts and priorities of the justice system.

Two important factors distinguish this textbook from others within this field of study.

1. Here, numerous authors, with the most recognizable credentials, were commissioned to write chapters in the areas of their expertise. Several reviewing editors, representing community colleges and four-year institutions from a wide geographic area, screened each chapter and checked its accuracy and currency—with the student's viewpoint as their primary concern. Too often, textbooks are written for the benefit of another instructor and not for a student or inexperienced practitioner within the system.

2. Each chapter begins with a set of objectives, which graphically directs the student to the chapter information that contains the author's most critical points. These performance goals define clearly what the student should do, know, and remember. They explain the nature of each chapter and make it easier for him to complete the required work satisfactorily. They are parameters and guideposts for both the student and the instructor, and they create a fairer examination process for the student. This fairness doctrine is always a critical issue in student–instructor relationships. I believe that the performance goals will enhance and maintain these relationships.

Bob Blanchard

Contents

PART ONE	INTRODUCTION TO THE ADMINISTRATION OF JUSTICE	1
1	Overview of the Criminal Justice System	3
2	Survey of the Crime Problem	25
3	Explanations for Criminal Actions	47
PART TWO	EVOLUTION OF THE JUSTICE SYSTEM	71
4	The Police	73
5	The Courts	93
6	Corrections	111
PART THREE	ROLES OF COMPONENTS OF THE JUSTICE SYSTEM	131
7	Primary Functions of the Police	133
8	Styles of Policing	171
9	Overview of Police Services	197
10	Primary Functions of the Courts	229
11	Corrections	249
PART FOUR	PROFESSIONALISM WITHIN THE JUSTICE SYSTEM	281
12	Canons of Ethical Conduct	283
13	Education and Training Concepts	297
14	Preparation for Employment	321
PART FIVE	THE FUTURE	335
15	Trends in the Administration of Justice System	337
	Glossary	359
	Subject Index	387

*Introduction
to the Administration of Justice*

Part One

Introduction to the Administration of Justice

The study of this chapter will enable you to:

1. Outline the system of criminal justice.
2. Define the basic responsibilities of each subsystem.
3. Cite examples of how each subsystem relates organizationally to each other.
4. Describe examples of "people" problems within the system.
5. Suggest possible solutions for the problem areas cited.

1
Overview of the Criminal Justice System

This book is concerned with a system in our society that may be compared to a tunnel through a mountain. The tunnel through it joins a series of connecting rooms: the institutions of the American criminal justice system.

In this first chapter we will use the word institution in two different ways: first, as a general term describing a long-established organization made up of people with many inherited ideas and procedures dedicated to, or established for, the purpose of public service. The second (and specific) definition is that of penal institutions—buildings where people are locked up to serve out sentences imposed by courts.

Most people in our society never enter the criminal justice system, but they see the inhabitants of its institutions every day: uniformed police officers directing traffic, black-robed judges and lawyers carrying briefcases at the courthouses, and guards on the watch towers of penitentiaries. Law-abiding citizens who never enter the system know few true facts about what goes on in the connecting rooms. Even some of the people who have made the journey through the tunnel from one side of the mountain to the other emerge confused, unable to comprehend what exactly happened to them.

The criminal justice system is merely one of the many institutional systems that make up our environment. Our world is a mass of systems; educational systems, religious systems, governmental systems, economic systems, and many others. Observing an institution of a system on an everyday basis and not understanding its inner workings nor its relationship with the other institutions of the overall system is not unusual. A bank, for example, is one of the most prevalent, visible, and publicly frequented institutions. Yet most people do not know what a bank really

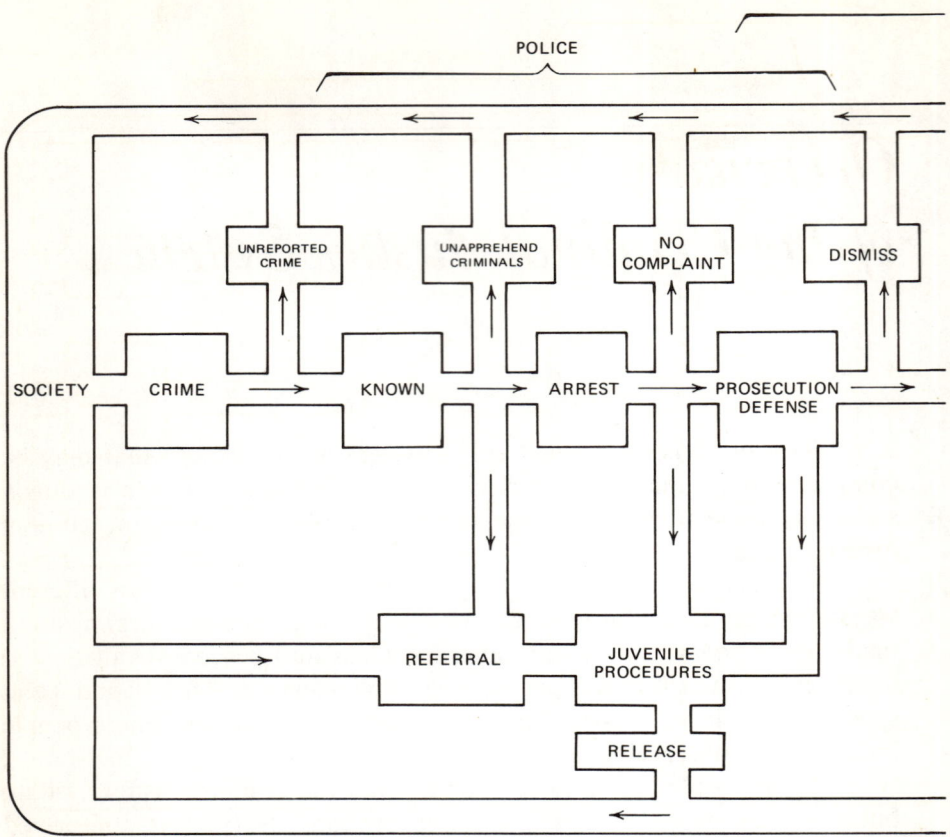

Figure 1-1. The criminal justice flow.

does and what its many functions are as an institution of the monetary and credit system. This lack of exact knowledge of institutional roles and goals prevails widely in criminal justice, one of the most fundamental and all-encompassing systems of our society.

The Chronology of the System

Let us walk through the criminal justice tunnel as if we were observers, look at what goes on in each room, and try to understand how the hap-

4   *introduction to the administration of justice*

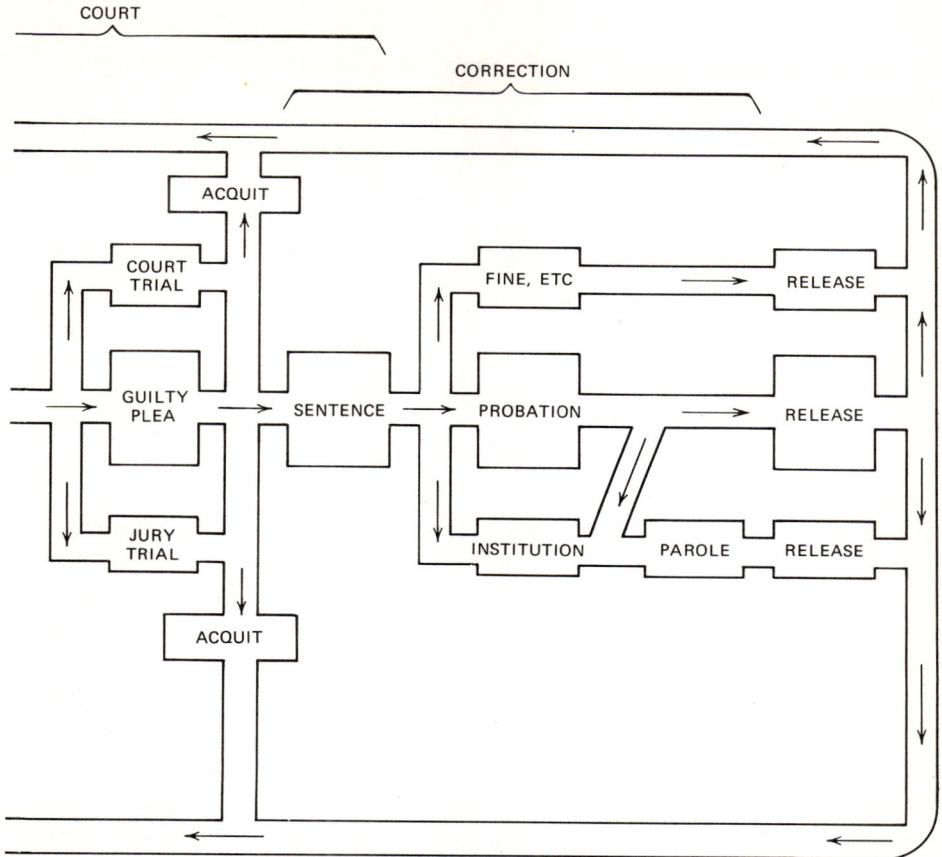

penings in each relate to the others and to the whole system (Figure 1-1). Remember that the rooms are institutions of the general definition: long-established organizations made up of people with a lot of inherited ideas and procedures dedicated to, or established for, the purpose of public service. Keep in mind that for a person caught in the tunnel, each room has one or more escape hatches leading back to daylight. The person enters (or is pulled into) the tunnel because he is believed guilty of some violation of the law. If he is found innocent as he passes through the first two rooms, he may be shown an exit. Or if he is lucky enough or shrewd enough he may find a legal exit in these first two rooms for himself and never reach the third room. If the person reaches the third room, his only real exit lies at the end of the tunnel on the other side of the mountain. If the person finds no legal escape hatch, he will proceed in

overview of the criminal justice system   5

chronological order, with a certain amount of institutional overlapping, through the following:
1. Police
2. Courts
   a. Judge
   b. Prosecutor
   c. Defender
3. Corrections
   a. Probation
   b. Confinement
   c. Parole

Public Attitudes and Myths
In the beginning we should make a few general statements about the public's attitudes toward each of these institutions. Novels, movies, and television shows have created a mythology about them that is difficult to dispel. Much of the fiction about police, for example, has glorified the role of detectives, creating the impression that they are the most important members of police departments. This is certainly not so. Most police work is done by patrolmen. Patrolmen usher many more lawbreakers to the criminal justice tunnel entrance than do detectives. Other mythology: fictional lawyers, such as Perry Mason, have glorified defense attorneys and have spread a lot of false information regarding courtroom procedures and the adversary encounters we call criminal trials. Generally speaking, the fictional trend has been to portray defense attorneys as heroes, and prosecutors as unrelenting, unscrupulous characters who will resort to any means to convict a defendant, guilty or not. Judges have been diversely portrayed, ranging from weak, ignorant, corrupt, or even comic characters to white-haired, godlike figures who dispense justice with divine authority. Corrections as a whole has been badly defamed in fiction. Probation and parole officers are generally ignored, but popular literature—from *I Was a Fugitive from a Georgia Chain Gang* in the 1930s to *Cool Hand Luke* of the late 1960s—abounds with sadistic wardens and prison guards.

More realistic fiction about police is now being written, however. Joseph Wambaugh's *The New Centurions* and *The Blue Knight*, Robin Moore's *The French Connection,* and George V. Higgins' *The Friends of Eddie Coyle* are examples of this new trend.

One of the purposes of this book is to help dispel some of the myths that cloud the operation of our criminal justice system and prevent reform or constructive change by obscuring the strengths and weaknesses of its institutions. With this end in mind, let us "walk" an individual through the tunnel from beginning to end and show what he experiences as he passes through the connecting institutions. Then we will describe and explain why the individual institutions occasionally seem to be in conflict with each other.

Notice that the institutional order followed presumes that the accused person is an adult or a juvenile being processed as an adult, a procedure possible in some states. We will learn later that the institutional order for juveniles being processed as juveniles is somewhat different.

The Police

The police stand at the criminal justice tunnel entrance. If a policeman observes a person committing what appears to be a violation of the law, he may arrest him immediately and book him into jail on a charge. If the crime has been observed and reported by another person, the policeman may arrest the person so charged at once, or he may perform an additional investigation prior to making an arrest.

Crimes fall into two broad categories: felonies and misdemeanors, rated according to their seriousness as judged by the penalties attached to them by law. A felony is generally defined as an offense that is punishable by death or by imprisonment in a state (or federal) prison. Felonies punishable by death are traditionally referred to as capital offenses. The general definition of a misdemeanor is that it is any offense that is not a felony. Misdemeanors, therefore, are minor crimes with minor penalties attached.

As a matter of law in most jurisdictions, anyone (either an officer or a private citizen) can make an arrest without a warrant for a felony or a misdemeanor attempted or committed in his presence, or for a felony committed outside of his presence on receipt of reliable information that a felony has been committed. We will not discuss the subject of citizens' arrest powers here because such arrests are exceptions rather than the rule. Almost all arrests are made by professional law enforcement officers who presumably have the training and experience necessary to make legal arrests.

overview of the criminal justice system

Whenever an officer interferes with a citizen's individual personal freedom by detaining him even briefly or by arresting him, it is a serious matter; the officer must have a reason for doing so *before* he stops the individual. But an innocent citizen stopped and questioned and even frisked on the street by an officer and then released should not presume that the officer has done something illegal, something that has violated the citizen's civil rights. The officer may have a valid reason for being suspicious that the citizen is unaware of; if so, he can legally perform a sufficient investigation to confirm or eliminate the suspicion because police have *investigative* as well as *arrest* powers. After stopping a suspicious person, the officer, if he has reason to believe the person stopped might perform an act of violence, may frisk him by patting him down in order to feel for a weapon and may detain him to ask questions. Of course, this type of action on the street is an intrusion on the right to privacy, but generally courts have held that the right to privacy must yield when police are drawn into a lawful "threshold" inquiry because they have reason to suspect unlawful conduct.

The citizen has been stopped, questioned, perhaps frisked, and then released. If this is all that happens, he does not enter the tunnel. He has lingered briefly at the entrance, but he has not entered.

Arrest. On the other hand, the officer may arrest the citizen. Arrest is a procedure defined by our laws and is basically uniform in all the 50 states as well as in the federal government's criminal procedures. There is nothing new about it. Our law of arrest, based on the British common law, has not varied significantly in over 300 years.

Arrest is defined as follows: "The apprehending or restraining of one's person in order to be forthcoming to answer an alleged or suspected crime."[1]

Police should, whenever possible, obtain an arrest warrant prior to arresting a person. Arrest warrants are written documents obtained from an impartial judicial officer who demands a sworn statement of incriminating actions or circumstances called probable cause. But in most cases time will not permit this. Legal arrests without warrants can therefore be made in emergency situations requiring immediate police action.

A police officer making an arrest for a felony or misdemeanor,

---

[1] *Blackstone Commentaries* 289, p. 1679 (1897 ed.).

with or without a warrant, should warn the suspect of his constitutional rights—the so-called Miranda Warning[2] as follows:

1. You have a constitutional right to remain silent and say absolutely nothing. If you do make a statement, you may stop at any time.
2. Anything you say can and will be used against you later.
3. You can have a lawyer here to help you while we ask you questions.
4. If you don't have a lawyer, one will be appointed for you if you want one now.

After arresting a person, the police officer will book him at the police department. The arrested person is photographed, fingerprinted, and asked questions relating to his background and identity. These administrative procedures do not violate a person's constitutional rights if he has been legally arrested. Also, if the person has been legally arrested, the police, if they suspect intoxication by alcohol or narcotics, may obtain blood samples from him without violating his Fifth Amendment rights against self-incrimination, provided that proper medical procedures are followed.

After a brief period of detention the police may release the person without filing formal charges. A victim may decline to press charges or a witness may decide not to testify. Release after brief police detention is the first of the legal exits in the tunnel.

Courts

If retained in custody, the person should be taken before a judicial officer without undue delay. This step, called an initial appearance in some jurisdictions, a first appearance in others, is the arrested person's first contact with the institution of the courts. The judicial officer—magistrate, justice of the peace, or commissioner—formally notifies the arrested person of the charges against him and advises him of his constitutional rights. If this judicial officer finds the charge or the arrest defective in some way, he may release the arrested person. This is another legal escape hatch. If the charges are not dismissed, the judicial officer will generally set bond for his reappearance at a later date for a preliminary hearing. In petty offenses a summary trial may be held against the arrested person at this stage without further processing and his case disposed of, by release if found not guilty and probably by the

---

[2] Miranda v. Arizona, 384 U.S. 436 (1966).

payment of a fine if found guilty. If found guilty, the person pays his fine and is released. If he is indigent (without money), he may have to serve a short sentence in jail instead of the fine.

As noted in the Miranda Warning, an accused person is entitled to have a lawyer present at any time he is questioned by the police about any crime he allegedly committed. If indigent, the judicial officer may appoint a private attorney to represent him. In jurisdictions that support a public defender's office, indigent defendants are represented by the public defender. If the defendant has funds, he must retain his own attorney.

Bail Bond. After any judicial officer sets a bond, the accused must post it in cash, property of equivalent value, or he must hire a professional bondsman to post the bond for him, at a fee amounting to 10 percent or more of the bond. This fee, dependent on the restrictions imposed by state laws and the bondsman's opinion of the degree of risk he is assuming, is not returnable to the defendant. If the accused person has no money for bond or bondsman, he may have to wait in jail during the period of time he is working his way through the system.

Posting a bail bond is the method traditionally used in our criminal court system to ensure the defendant's appearance in a designated court *instanter* (when summoned) or at a designated time on a designated date. If the defendant does not appear, the bond may be forfeited —impounded—by the court and an additional charge of bond default may be filed against the defendant. In later chapters, we will discuss the criticism of the practice of requiring money or property bonds for release of person awaiting judicial action, which obviously discriminates against the poor.

Release or Jail. It is becoming a common practice that judges, especially in the federal courts, release defendants on personal recognizance, or own recognizance, to await further judicial action, rather than requiring them to remain in jail because of lack of funds. Release on recognizance generally is granted when the defendant has no prior criminal record, or a minor one, and the judge believes that he will not flee the jurisdiction to avoid trial. So, if the defendant makes bond in any form, he has found an exit from the tunnel, a temporary one to be sure, since the bond acts as a string to bring him back when he is wanted.

However, if the defendant does not have the money for bond and has a background that causes the judge to believe he will probably flee if released on recognizance, the judge will send him to jail to await the disposition of his case. When this occurs, the defendant, generally through his attorney, may file an appeal to reduce what he considers to be an excessively high bond and may be successful in having the bond reduced to an amount that he can afford.

Usually, between the time of arrest and court appearance for trial on a serious charge, the accused will ask for and be granted a preliminary hearing or examining trial. The defendant will request this to find out in advance as much as he can about the evidence gathered against him and to attempt to legally suppress (prohibit the use of) as much of the evidence as possible. This is the first critical adversary encounter between the prosecutor and the defense counsel. The procedure often determines whether a trial will be held at all. If the defendant is successful in obtaining a judicial ruling suppressing most of the evidence against him, the charges may be dropped and the defendant freed, or the charges may be reduced. So it may possibly create an escape hatch. But even if it does not, it tests the evidence and gives the defendant a much better idea of the strength of the case against him.

In felony cases the accused will be brought before the trial court for his first formal appearance, called an *arraignment*, by the issuance of a document called an *information* or one called an *indictment*. Both are formal, written accusations of crime. An information is prepared by a prosecutor on the basis of information submitted by police or citizens. An indictment is prepared by a grand jury.

Grand Jury. A grand jury is defined as follows:
> *A jury of inquiry who are summoned and returned by the sheriff (or U. S. Marshal in federal procedure) to each session of the criminal courts, and whose duty is to receive complaints and accusations in criminal cases, hear the evidence adduced on the part of the state (or federal government), and find bills of indictment in cases where they are satisfied a trial ought to be had. They are first sworn by the court. They vary in size in various jurisdictions.*[3]

A grand jury meets in secret session, hearing witnesses and examining evidence, and the defendant has no right to appear before it without the grand jury's permission. If the grand jury decides there is sufficient

---

[3] Henry Campbell Black, *Black's Law Dictionary*, 4th ed. (St. Paul, Minn.: West Publishing Co. 1951).

evidence to warrant a trial, it issues a "true bill" resulting in the defendant being indicted. If the grand jury decides that the evidence is insufficient, it issues a "no bill," which results in the charges against the defendant being dropped. Thus, a "no bill" can be another ecape hatch for the defendant. Some states have no grand jury systems; others seldom use it. Grand juries practically never hear misdemeanors, only felonies. Even in jurisdictions where grand juries are widely used, misdemeanors are almost always brought into court by the use of informations.

Arraignment. After the issuance of an information or indictment, the defendant is arraigned. He makes a formal appearance in his trial court to hear the charge against him read and to enter a plea. A possible temporary escape hatch may open here if his defense counsel can find something technically wrong with the formal charge, information or indictment, as presented. If nothing is found wrong with the charge, then he must make a choice; he must decide whether to plead guilty or not guilty to the charge.

If the defendant enters a plea of guilty and "throws himself on the mercy of the court," the judge sentences him then and there, or at a later date, to a term of probation or institutional confinement. A plea of guilty immediately ushers the defendant into the third room of the tunnel: corrections.

Plea of Not Guilty. If the defendant enters a plea of not guilty and demands a trial, it is possible for him in rare instances to be tried before a judge without a jury, but this is the exception rather than the rule in felony cases. We will assume a jury trial. This means that a *petit* (trial) jury, usually consisting of 12 persons must be selected from a larger group of citizenry called a panel of veniremen assembled in the courtroom. In picking the jury, the prosecutor and the defense counsel are given the opportunity to question the panel generally, individually, or both generally and individually, in order to come up with 12 people acceptable to both. Each side has a designated number of "strikes"—rights to bar certain individuals of the panel from serving on the trial jury. In some jurisdictions two or three extra alternate jurors are chosen, in addition to the basic 12. These alternates sit in the jury box during the trial and listen to the proceedings, but they do not become jurors, entering into deliberations and voting on the verdict unless they replace one or more of the regular jurors who die, become disabled, or are excused during the course of the trial.

In America, court trials are conducted as adversary proceedings. A trial can be compared to a boxing match between a professional and an amateur who is allowed to hire the services of a professional to fight for him. The prosecution has the district attorney or one of his assistants as its champion. The defendant, generally a nonattorney, must hire an attorney, accept one appointed by the court, or seek the aid of the public defender. While the attorneys carry on their legal battle, the judge acts as an impartial referee, carefully watching, ready to intervene if he observes any illegalities or encroachments on the rights of the defendant. The philosophy behind the adversary proceeding is that the contest between the two trained legal champions, fought in the presence of an impartial referee, will cause justice to prevail: the guilt or innocence of the defendant will be established beyond a reasonable doubt and the jury will return a just verdict based on this proven guilt or innocence.

At the conclusion of the trial, if the jury does find the defendant not guilty, he is freed. He has found a legal exit. If the jury cannot come to a unanimous verdict as to guilt or innocence and deadlocks, the judge may declare a mistrial. Then the defendant will have to be tried again on the same charge, probably before a different jury, or the prosecutor may decide his case is not strong enough to win and will request that the charge be dropped. Thus, a mistrial may or may not be a legal exit for the defendant.

Corrections

If the jury finds the defendant guilty, the judge or the jury, depending on the laws of the state, will set the penalty and the defendant will be relegated to corrections. On being sentenced to corrections the defendant faces two possibilities: probation or institutionalization. Here we use the specialized definition of institution, as a prison or reformatory where the convicted person is confined.

If the sentence is probation, the defendant leaves the courtroom in the custody of a probation officer. The probation officer has already made an investigation of the defendant's background and has probably expressed the opinion in open court that he considers the defendant to be "probation material," someone who can be salvaged for society's benefit without being sentenced to confinement.

The probation officer generally has more people in his (or her) caseload than can be adequately supervised. His attitudes may be stern or sympathetic: his background may be in sociology or social work, or he may be a retired law enforcement officer with or without any academic background. He will state the rules regulating his client's conduct during the prescribed period of probation, the types of places where the probationer can and cannot work or live, and the types of persons with whom he cannot associate. The probation officer's supervision extends to seeing that the probationer adheres to any special requirements imposed by the court, such as financial restitution to a party injured by the probationer. A reporting schedule is arranged; the probationer will be required to contact the probation officer in person or in writing at stated intervals. The probation officer may make surprise visits to the probationer's residence or his place of employment to verify that he lives where he says he does, works where he says he does, is not associating with criminals, and is complying with all special requirements.

If the probationer completes his sentence successfully, the probation officer meets with him for a final interview. If the probationer does not live up to the standard of conduct imposed, the probation officer will have the defendant brought back before the judge and, in most instances, the judge will revoke the person's probation and send him to an institution.

Let us return briefly to the termination of a trial in which the defendant has been found guilty and the court has not sentenced the defendant to probation but to a term in a penal institution. The defendant will be transported to an institution without delay to begin serving his sentence, unless he files an appeal of some sort, which may or may not become an escape hatch.

The subject of penal institutions will be covered in detail in later chapters. Even the most lenient and comfortable of them are unhappy places for the inmates, some of whom break rules, which causes them to lose time off for good behavior and serve their entire terms in prison. Others may commit additional crimes in prison and receive additional prison sentences. Most inmates, however, obtain an earlier release than their sentences specify because of good behavior. These inmates serve a supervised period of parole or conditional release outside the institution prior to the full expiration of their sentences.

During this period they are supervised in much the same way as are probationers. In fact, federal probationers and conditional releasees are supervised by the same federal probation officers. Supervision practices vary throughout the different state jurisdictions; some states use the same staffs for both probationers and parolees and others use separate agencies.

When the person completes his period of parole successfully, he is in the same situation as the probationer who has successfully completed his probation. Both have paid their debts to society for breaking the law, and both have emerged into the daylight at the opposite end of the criminal justice tunnel.

Friction within the System
This route we have described through the justice system seems easy enough to follow with all exits clearly marked, but problems arise along the way because of frictions between the institutions involved. In many cases their institutional roles and goals seem to oppose each other. The adversary system of the courtroom, although certainly not perfect, seems to be the best method yet devised to ensure a fair trial, but unfortunately the adversary system within the criminal justice process as a whole is not confined to the courtroom. It pervades the entire criminal justice system, causing on many occasions the individual institutions—police, courts, and corrections—to become adversaries rather than colleagues in the overall quest for justice. Why? Mainly because of "people" problems. Let us examine some of them.

First, the police. Police departments tend to be closely knit, paramilitary organizations with strong group ties. Generally, policemen think of themselves as policemen rather than as individuals who happen to be employed by police departments.

The police institution is situated alongside the courts institution. Courts are dominated by lawyers in all component parts: judge, prosecutor, and defender. In their education and training, lawyers are taught to think of themselves more as individuals than the police. We mentioned earlier that in court lawyers are professional adversaries. Both the prosecutor and the defender think of themselves that way. The judge himself, although not an adversary in the trial setting, is an attorney appointed or elected to his post from their ranks. Judges maintain their individuality and generally resist being organized into a tightly knit system. You might say that lawyers and judges tend to be soloists who resist playing together as an orchestra.

Here we have the police institution with its tendency toward group thinking connected as a feeder device to the courts, an institution made up generally of self-assertive individuals. These two institutions are expected to cooperate very closely in the operation of the criminal justice system, but because of their basic compositional differences it is easy to see why they do not always do so.

A police officer arrests an individual for a crime, and his investigation convinces him that the individual is guilty. When he presents his case to an assistant district attorney, he may be put off by the prosecutor's seemingly skeptical attitude. The prosecutor is "testing" the strength of the case, but his searching, sometimes brusque questions on such points as probable cause, legality of search, or use of physical force may offend the officer and put him on the defensive. The officer may receive the impression that the prosecutor thinks he is lying or that he did something wrong. The officer may have had to make his arrest in a tense, dangerous situation amid uproar and confusion; and now, in the quiet of the office, this lawyer seems to be trying to hindsight him by asking all sorts of questions about why he did this and why he did not do that, concentrating on legal details rather than on the important fact that the arrested person is guilty of a crime and deserves punishment.

Then, after the assistant district attorney authorizes or accepts prosecution, the case finally goes to trial. The officer takes the stand and testifies as a witness for the prosecution and the defense attorney, on cross-examination, harasses him with all sorts of questions—some intentionally insulting—intended to shake his credibility and composure. The officer may feel that he is being unfairly attacked by the defense counsel and that the prosecutor and judge are doing nothing to help him. In fact, the prosecutor and the judge may ask the officer some rather searching and unexpected questions themselves if the defense counsel during his cross-examination uncovers some investigative error on the part of the officer. Perspiring under the limelight of the witness stand, the officer concludes that all three members of the court's institution—prosecutor, defense counsel, and judge—are all after him instead of the defendant.

What the officer should learn early in his career is that he must know the rules of criminal procedure better than the prosecutor and the judge. He must learn them; they must be ready for his use at all times. In the midst of an altercation on the street he cannot call for a short recess to research a legal point in his office or library. He must make quick, sure legal decisions on short notice. When the officer does learn the procedures well and gains confidence in following them, he can sit solidly in the witness box and ride out the barrage of questions without losing his composure.

Then the trial is over. The jury goes out to deliberate its verdict. Three things can happen as a result of their deliberations, and two of them are bad as far as the police and prosecution are concerned:
1. The defendant is found guilty.
2. The defendant is found not guilty.
3. The jury deadlocks and a mistrial results.

If the jury finds the defendant guilty, the police officer and prosecutor congratulate each other on their victory. But if the probation officer makes a report recommending probation, both may become irritated at the probation officer for being "weak-kneed" or "soft on criminals." Institutional friction. If the judge accepts the recommendation and puts the defendant on probation, then the prosecutor and the officer are irritated at the judge as well as the probation officer. More institutional friction. On the other hand, if the judge does not accept the probation officer's recommendation, this irritates the probation officer, the representative of corrections. He has made his investigation and believes the defendant to be probation material, or he would not have so recommended. In the estimation of the probation officer, the judge has no heart; he is a "hanging judge." Still more institutional friction.

If the jury finds the defendant not guilty, the officer and prosecutor are downcast, and the defense counsel and the defendant are flushed with victory. The defendant, carried away with emotion, may hug his champion, the defense counsel, and shake hands with the members of the jury, congratulating them on their fairness and their intelligence in seeing through the false charges of the prosecution. To the chagrin of the officer, the defendant (whom the officer is sure is guilty) swaggers from the courtroom scot-free. To the chagrin of the prosecutor, defense counsel may favor him with a superior smile and say something like, "Better luck next time, Charlie."

After a mistrial or a not guilty verdict comes a period of meditation and reflection for both the officer and the prosecutor. Rationalization enters the process.

The policeman goes back to the police station and explains to his fellow officers that the prosecutor or the judge lost the case; he wants to make it very clear that losing the case was not his fault. His fellow officers, who have been through the same experience, may not be impressed by his explanations and may banter him unmercifully about his "defeat." The officer may learn something constructive from his experience and do a better job next time, or he may become permanently bitter toward the institution of the courts.

The prosecutor's rationalized meditation on the cause of the verdict or nonverdict will generally result in a different opinion than the officer's. He may feel that the case was lost because of faulty investigation or the hostile attitude of the judge.

Another potential source of friction between police and prosecutor is plea bargaining prior to trial. The prosecutor has a heavy caseload. Acting on the facts set forth in a police investigative report, he has charged a defendant with first degree murder. Looking over the reports of later investigation, he can see that the trial will be lengthy and complicated and perhaps difficult to prove beyond a reasonable doubt. Defense counsel comes to him with a proposition. The defendant will enter a plea to murder in the second degree, a lesser charge, if the prosecutor will not contest it and will not recommend the maximum sentence. To avoid a lengthy trial with a dubious outcome, the prosecutor will agree. This decision may irritate the police officer who has spent a lot of time on the case and who believes that such a deal allows the defendant to "get off too light."

Both the prosecution and the police appear united in the belief that, as a general rule, people convicted of crimes are not locked up often enough or given long enough sentences when they are. This vindictive attitude irritates the inhabitants of the corrections institution who generally think of themselves as social workers rather than avengers of wrongs. A majority of corrections people stress the undeniable fact that there is no uniformity in the sentencing for comparable crimes, and they allege that prejudice, discrimination, racial bias, and poverty are often the deciding factors in determining who gets the longest prison sentences. They charge that the police and courts are mainly interested in "warehousing" lawbreakers rather than in rehabilitating them. They charge further that the police and courts are primarily interested in punishment and not in eliminating the causes of crime.

Over the years corrections has experimented with four major philosophies of handling convicted persons: restraint, reform, rehabilitation, and reintegration. None has proved especially successful. The philosophies will be described in detail later.

The criminal justice process described until now assumed that the offender was an adult, or a juvenile being tried as an adult, a procedure possible in some jurisdictions. In cases involving juveniles being processed as juveniles, the same institutions are involved—police, courts, and corrections—but the juvenile may make contact with them in a different order than an adult.

Juveniles in the Criminal Justice System

An important point to keep in mind is that in America, since the turn of the century, the basic attitude of the criminal justice system has been that juveniles are children to be helped rather than punished whenever possible. This philosophy has been one of the main sources of institutional friction within the criminal justice system as far as the processing of juveniles is concerned.

Most cases involving juveniles come to the attention of the police first. A patrolman apprehends a juvenile for an offense and turns him over to the juvenile unit of his department or to a juvenile probation officer at a detention or intake center. If he is turned over to the police department juvenile unit, that unit may hold an informal hearing and release the juvenile to his parents, dismissing or adjusting the charges without further processing. If they do not release the juvenile to his parents or guardian, the police will take him to a juvenile detention center where he will be interviewed by an intake officer who will determine whether or not to request court action. This interview is generally called an intake hearing. As a result of his interview, the intake officer may make "nonadjudicatory disposition" of the case by referring the juvenile to a welfare agency or social service for counseling, medical care, or some other form of aid. If the intake officer believes the case warrants it, he will refer the matter to the juvenile court for adjudication. A point to remember is that juveniles are not "tried" in juvenile court; their cases are "adjudicated" there.

Generally, the intake officer will refer cases to the court for adjudication when one of the following conditions is present:
1. The juvenile is dangerous to others.
2. The juvenile is dangerous to himself.
3. The juvenile should be protected from some part of society; he is in danger from others.

The court may release the juvenile at the adjudicatory hearing or may go through full adjudication, a legal process very like a trial in which the juvenile is represented by legal counsel. As a result of adjudication, the court may place the juvenile on probation or sentence him to a term of confinement in a juvenile institution. As in the case of adults, juvenile probation may be revoked if the client does not follow the general or specific terms of probation and, as a result, the client may be sent to serve time in a juvenile institution. Also, the juvenile may be afforded early release from confinement on parole in a manner similar to the procedure followed by adults.

Many of the same "people" problems arise in the institutions of the juvenile criminal justice system as in the adult system. An additional source of friction may appear within the police institution, between the juvenile unit and the line units of the police department. Regular patrolmen and detectives may develop the feeling that the members of their own department in the juvenile unit are too soft on juveniles who commit crimes.

The use of community auxiliary agencies is growing in the field of juvenile criminal justice. More and more delinquent juveniles are being referred, or diverted, to these community agencies—some of them volunteer—for supervision, foster care, and counseling, in order to keep them from being processed by the criminal justice system and acquiring a criminal record.

Many of the agencies, such as Alcoholics Anonymous and drug treatment facilities, are also available to adult offenders. The quality of the services offered by the auxiliary agencies varies from community to community, and institutional friction frequently develops among these agencies themselves and between the auxiliary agencies and the institutions of the criminal justice system. So it goes, adversary relationships arise from conflicts of roles and goals, and valuable time is wasted—time that could be more profitably spent in achieving our goal of universal justice by unified action of our institutions.

Summary

This chapter has compared the American criminal justice system to a tunnel through a mountain, a tunnel connecting the individual institutions and subinstitutions of the system. An adult offender entering the tunnel progresses through institutions in the following order: police, courts (judge, prosecutor, and defender), and corrections (probation, institutionalization, and parole).

Each of the institutions has one or more legal exits if the traveler can find them. Most of these exits are in the institution of the courts and require professional legal guidance to find. After reaching corrections, the only exit remaining is the other end of the tunnel.

"People" problems arise between the institutions because each follows inherited codes and procedures that often conflict. This institutional conflict hampers the functioning of the overall system.

Juveniles charged with delinquent acts contact the same institutions, but in different order than do the adults, generally making contact with a probation officer (a member of the corrections institution) prior to going to court. Also, juvenile cases are "adjudicated" rather than "tried." The underlying philosophy is that they should be helped when possible rather than punished.

Student Checklist

1. Can you list the entire system of criminal justice?
2. Are you able to define the basic responsibilities of each subsystem?
3. Can you cite examples of how each subsystem relates to each other?
4. Can you describe some examples of "people" problems within the system?
5. Can you suggest possible solutions for the problem areas cited?

Topics for Discussion

1. Discuss the organizational structure of the criminal justice system.
2. Discuss the various responsibilities that each subsystem is charged with.

ANNOTATED BIBLIOGRAPHY

Arnold, William R. *Juveniles on Parole: A Sociological Perspective*. New York: Random House, 1970. Presents case studies of individual juveniles on probation and parole and the degrees of success achieved in rehabilitation. The theme is that the juveniles almost invariably return to delinquency after adjudication because probation or parole almost invariably returns them to the environment that was the original main causal factor of their delinquency.

Asch, Sidney H. *Police Authority and the Rights of the Individual*. New York: Arco, 1968. A description of specific examples of the use and misuse of police discretion as applied to the preservation and violation of the constitutional rights of the individual citizen.

Bassiouni, M. Cherif. *Criminal Law and Its Processes: The Law of Public Order*. Springfield, Ill.: Charles C. Thomas, 1969. Criminal procedures, in the United States, as they may be applied in a constitutionally correct manner to the maintenance of public order, especially in the face of civil disorders and riotous behavior.

Bittner, Egon. *The Functions of Police in Modern Society*. Chevy Chase, Md.: National Institute of Mental Health, 1970. A sociological analysis of the police role in our society. Stresses also the psychological concept of self-image on the part of the individual policeman and its relationship to the public image.

Dressler, David. *Practice and Theory of Probation and Parole*. New York: Columbia University Press, 1970. A review, past and present, of the prevailing practices and leading theories of probation and parole since its inception during the mid-nineteenth century.

Eldefonso, Edward. *Youth Problems and Law Enforcement*. Englewood Cliffs, N.J.: Prentice-Hall, 1972. An introductory college text setting forth standard police practices and procedures in dealing with juvenile delinquents. Outlines specific police problems in dealing with juveniles and attempts to offer viable solutions.

Inbau, Fred E., and James R. Thompson. *Administration of Criminal Justice*. Mineola, N. Y.: Foundation Press, 1970. An introductory college text describing the workings of the individual institutions of the U.S. criminal justice system and their relationship to each other.

President's Commission on Law Enforcement and Administration of Justice. *Challenge of Crime in a Free Society*. Washington, D.C.: U.S. Government Printing Office, 1967. Introductory volume to the exhaustive study of the criminal justice system. The material in this volume is supported by individual Task Force Reports.

Probation/Parole, Vol. 1. Washington, D.C.: U.S. Government Printing Office, 1969. A review of the federal procedures relating to probation and parole current *circa* 1969.

U.S. Department of Health, Education and Welfare. National Institute of Mental Health. *The Juvenile Court: A Status Report*. Public Health Service Publication No. 2132, 1971. Washington, D.C.: U.S. Government Printing Office. A review of procedures in various juvenile courts throughout the United States current *circa* 1969. Points out different procedures followed by courts in different areas.

U.S. Department of Justice. *Correctional Institutions*, Vol. 2. Washington, D.C.: U.S. Government Printing Office, 1969. Sets forth data obtained from studies made of various penal institutions throughout the United States, pertaining to administration, rehabilitation facilities, and general institutional conditions.

The study of this chapter will enable you to:

1. Cite the legal definition of crime.
2. Explain the sociological definition of crime.
3. Cite examples justifying the existence of the criminal justice system.
4. Explain the strengths and weaknesses of the federal crime statistics.
5. Explain constitutional factors supporting the criminal justice system.
6. Explain nationwide crime trends.

2

Survey of the Crime Problem

Crime is more and more becoming a concern of the American public. As people's awareness becomes more evident, the criminal justice system continues to attempt to deal with this problem. Law enforcement, courts, and the correctional systems have been given increased resources in the form of funds, manpower, and equipment.

What is a Crime?

Before looking into the crime problem further, it will be helpful to define the term crime.

The legal definition of crime is an intentional act or omission to act in violation of law without justification, to which a penalty is attached. We see then that a crime cannot only be an overt act, such as murder, robbery, or assault; but that failure to act can also constitute a crime. For example, failure to file an income tax return, refusal to assist a police officer upon demand, or failure to stop after a traffic accident and identify oneself and render aid to the injured are all omissions that constitute crimes.

Crimes are classified as felonies and misdemeanors. (In some states, infractions are considered crimes.) A felony is a serious crime for which a defendant can be imprisoned in the state prison, and a misdemeanor is any other crime, which may result in imprisonment in the county or city jail. A few states, such as Michigan, are exceptions to this rule in that a few serious misdemeanors may result in a short term in the state prison.

Crimes can be violations of local, city, or county ordinances, the state penal code, or, in the case of federal offenses, violations of the United States Penal Code. Some criminal acts may violate state as well as federal laws. For example, the robbery of a bank or theft of merchandise in an interstate shipment can be prosecuted either under the state law where the offense occurred or by the federal government. In such cases local police and the Federal Bureau of Investigation have what is called overlapping jurisdiction.

Although legal definitions of crime are specific, sociological definitions are much broader and encompass any act harmful to society. This includes many problems not traditionally viewed as criminal. Those who subscribe to the broad sociological definitions of crime charge that air pollution, water pollution, the failure to educate, or the denial of equal opportunities in housing and employment are, in fact, so harmful that they can be included in the category of crime. It is difficult to deny that the severe smog in some of our cities is, indeed, more harmful and dangerous to the lives of millions of Americans than is, for example, a simple assault.

We have, in recent years, begun to transfer some harmful activities from the category of "sociological crime" into the category covered by the legal definition. For example, some cities have begun to provide criminal penalties for industrial pollution. However, enforcement and punishment have often failed to act as a significant deterrent. For example, one oil company that was cited for unlawful air pollution for the fifth time in one year received a fine of $250!

Arguments can be made that those situations and conditions truly harmful to human life should receive greater attention from the agencies of criminal justice. There is a reluctance, however, to move in that direction because we have become accustomed to accept many such activities or conditions as traditional and normal. Official and public apathy is further compounded by the fact that the perpetrators of these activities are seen as "respectable" and powerful. Mike Royko, a *Chicago Daily News* columnist, once commented that if militant radicals were responsible for the polluted Chicago air, then city, state, and federal forces would have moved immediately to correct the situation and punish those responsible.

In addition to the transfer into the criminal statutes of harmful acts not previously considered criminal, consideration should also be given to the legalization of some conduct currently prohibited by law, in which no one suffers an injury. These acts, often referred to as crimes without victims, include homosexuality and other private sexual behavior, noncommercial gambling, prostitution, and abortion.[1] This reevaluation of criminal behavior may be particularly justified in view of the fact that the police and the courts are already overburdened with cases.[2]

The Need for Laws, Regulations, Regulators

Whether human beings live in a primitive setting or in a highly complex society, they are interdependent and must cooperate for their mutual benefit and survival. They must engage in a variety of social, economic, political, and occupational relationships. This interaction must be covered by rules of conduct. Studies of primitive tribes in ancient as well as contemporary times have shown that, even in the absence of written rules, the conduct of the individual member is regulated for the welfare of the group. Anarchy, or the total absence of rules, cannot be tolerated if the group is to maintain its stability and that of subsequent generations.

Each society, therefore, is engaged in the process known as social control, by which society or the group prescribes (directs) or proscribes (forbids) certain behavior on the part of its members to insure the success and survival of the group with a minimum of friction. Broom and Selznick comment:

> *The individual gains much from his involvement in social organization, but he always pays a price. That price is the acceptance of restraints, of limitations on the freedom to do as he pleases.*[3]

Berger and Berger explain:

> *Social order is maintained by enforced compliance with the social norms and rules that are thought to insure the effective operation of the particular society. . . . There are a variety of devices of social control, varying from physical force to mild psychological pressure, that are supposed to protect and enforce these norms and rules.*[4]

---

[1] See Edwin M. Schur, *Crimes Without Victims* (Englewood Cliffs, N.J.: Prentice-Hall, 1965).
[2] For discussion of a police look at related social problems, see Daniel B. Kennedy and Bruce Kennedy, *Applied Sociology for Police* (Springfield, Ill.: Charles C. Thomas, 1972), pp. 29-42.
[3] Leonard Broom and Philip Selznick, *Sociology* (New York: Harper & Row, 1968), p. 20.
[4] Peter L. Berger and Brigitte Berger, *Sociology: A Biographical Approach* (New York: Basic Books, 1972), p. 277.

Although the rules of required behavior have developed from cultural customs through the system of common law, the United States relies upon various written laws created by cities, counties, states, and the federal government. These written laws spell out the obligations placed upon our citizens as well as specify which conduct is unacceptable.

The law, however, is not a dead collection of rules; it is a living instrument. New laws are passed based upon new and changing needs, other laws are amended or repealed, and decisions from higher courts constantly refine the law.

While new laws are often placed on the books with relative ease as an answer to a given problem, we have experienced difficulties and reluctance on the part of lawmakers to modify or eliminate existing laws in response to our changing society. The term institutional lag is the label used to describe this delay in governmental response.

This highly refined system of law is administered by our criminal justice personnel, the three main components of which are police, courts, and corrections. Without professional personnel assigned to the system, the law would have little value.

When the law is broken or peace is threatened, we rely on police agencies to take appropriate action. *Municipal Police Administration* describes the police mission as "maintenance of social order within carefully prescribed ethical and constitutional restrictions."[5]

A growing field also concerned with providing protection is private and industrial security. "The need for providing protection for property and private interest, over and above those which government can provide, have never been more in demand."[6]

While law enforcement duties include investigation and arrest, adjudication must always and without exception be the province of the courtroom presided over by a judge. The judge should carefully rule on the law and insure that justice is rendered to both society and the defendant, a challenge that is placing increasingly high demands on the judiciary.

Correctional officials face a particularly difficult challenge. They are responsible not only for the security of their institutions, but for the

---

[5] George D. Eastman, ed., *Municipal Police Administration* (Washington, D.C.: International City Management Association, 1969), p. 3.
[6] Richard S. Post and Arthur A. Kingsbury, *Security Administration* (Springfield, Ill.: Charles C. Thomas, 1970), p. 3.

rehabilitation of the convicted offenders, who must be returned to society with the expectation that they will not again commit criminal acts.[7]

The quality of justice depends strongly on the quality of the personnel administrating the system of justice. The people who have dedicated themselves to such a career are devoting their energies on a full-time basis to what is the responsibility of all of us. Given this great responsibility, American society must attract and train, retain and support, the best men and women in the criminal justice system.

The Justification for the System

Reference is often made to the criminal justice system as though it is a single unit. It does, however, consist of several subunits, whose functions and responsibilities differ, and whose success in protecting society from crime and criminals depend upon society's efforts toward total cooperation. The system functions much like a revolving door; the prisoner released on parole returns to the society from which the police officer arrested him.

Ideally, the criminal justice system must function to insure an orderly, organized, just, professional, and constitutional approach to the serious problem of crime in America, each unit offering the best it has to offer the total criminal justice system.

As so responsibly demonstrated in *The Challenge of Crime in a Free Society*, all the agencies of criminal justice suffer from imperfections and share a common need to reform in order to earn greater public confidence.[8]

Constitutional Factors and Considerations

The Constitution of the United States was adopted in 1789. It was created in part out of a sense of understanding that government can become

---

[7] For a commentary on resocialization of the convicted offender, see Daniel B. Kennedy and August Kerber, *Resocialization: An American Experiment* (New York: Behavioral Publications, 1973), pp. 85-114.

[8] The President's Commission on Law Enforcement and Administration of Justice, *The Challenge of Crime in a Free Society* (Washington, D.C.: U. S. Government Printing Office, 1967).

survey of the crime problem   **29**

tyrannical and that provisions must exist for limiting and restraining governmental power. In 1791, ten amendments to the Constitution were adopted which specifically limit and restrict the actions that the government may take against the people.

Today not all of these amendments are of equal significance or practical importance to the criminal justice practitioner. The amendments that do hold special significance include the First Amendment, which prohibits the government from abridging the freedom of speech or press or the right of the people to peaceably assemble. This amendment places a special responsibility upon police to protect those who wish to speak in public, pass out literature, and hold assemblies. This is a particularly important responsibility placed upon American law enforcement because such assemblies are often controversial and attract persons of opposing views, thereby creating a potential for a display of emotionalism and even violence. Nevertheless, the responsibility of law enforcement to protect those who wish to exercise their rights under the First Amendment is clearly provided for.

The Fourth Amendment insures the right of people to be secure in their persons and houses against unreasonable searches and seizures. In other words, police can search for evidence only under certain specific circumstances supported by a search warrant or probable cause. Evidence seized under unreasonable circumstances may not be used against a defendant. Prior to the 1961 *Mapp* v. *Ohio* decision, 367 U.S. 643 (1961), some state courts had been routinely admitting evidence even when it was illegally seized.

The Fifth Amendment prohibits the placing of a person in double jeopardy, and that he need not be a witness against himself. The effect of this amendment upon American law enforcement was spelled out in the 1966 case of *Miranda* v. *Arizona*, in which the Supreme Court held that, before the police can interrogate a suspect, they must advise him of his right to remain silent, that anything he says can be used against him in court, that he has the right to have an attorney present before answering any questions, and that in the event that he cannot afford an attorney, the court will provide one free of charge. Many American police officers denounced this court decision in the belief that a great number of guilty persons would go free. However, as a practical matter, the *Miranda* decision appears to have had little or no effect upon the rate of confessions obtained by police officers.

The Seventh Amendment guarantees the right to a jury trial. In the past a unanimous decision by a jury was required for conviction, but some recent efforts had been made toward conviction by a jury that is not necessarily unanimous. This is a questionable trend in view of the legal tradition that holds that a defendant must be proven guilty beyond reasonable doubt, a condition that would appear not to exist if all jurors cannot vote for conviction.

The Eighth Amendment provides that excessive bail shall not be required, and that cruel and unusual punishment may not be inflicted. Some police officials have difficulty understanding that the sole purpose of bail is to insure appearance in court and that bail may not be set as a means of inflicting punishment. The cruel and unusual punishment prohibition has recently led the Supreme Court to remand several cases (which would have led to the death penalty) back to the states to rewrite statutes according to guidelines set by the Supreme Court, so that there would be no discriminating practices (*Furman* v. *Georgia*, 33 L. Ed., 2nd, 346).

The United States functions under a majority rule but with minority rights. In other words, the majority of the American people can exercise their right to vote for certain political candidates and on a variety of issues. However, the Constitution does limit what the majority can do. It cannot interfere with the basic rights of a minority of people. Those who hold unpopular political views, those who print material disliked by the majority, those who belong to an obscure religious group, and those who express opinions that make the majority uncomfortable are all entitled to the protection of the Constitution, despite the fact that the majority of the citizens would prefer to see them conform to the standards of the majority. As expressed by Germann:

> *We cannot be for the Bill of Rights for ourselves and for our friends. The application of constitutional protection does not fluctuate according to our political, social, economic and religious preferences. It is all or nothing. No man's rights are safe unless all men's rights are respected.*[9]

It is the freedom and respect for others guaranteed by the Constitution that provides us with particular pride in the administration of American justice.

---

[9] A. C. Germann, Frank D. Day, and Robert R. J. Gallati, *Introduction to Law Enforcement and Criminal Justice* (Springfield, Ill.: Charles C. Thomas, 1970), p. 71.

Overview of the Crime Problem Nationwide

Criminal justice practitioners and teachers, legislators, members of the judiciary, and others concerned with crime trends in America often rely on the crime statistics collected and published annually by the Federal Bureau of Investigation. The statistics for the year 1972 were released in August 1973 under the title, *Crime in the United States*.[10]

To measure the trends in crime, seven types of offenses, known as the index crimes, have been selected:

1. Murder and nonnegligent manslaughter
2. Forcible rape
3. Robbery
4. Aggravated assault
5. Burglary
6. Larceny over $50
7. Auto theft

Figure 2-1 shows that these seven index crimes have increased 55 percent between 1967 and 1972.

Breaking the offenses down into violence categories (murder, forc-

Figure 2-1. Crime and population, 1967-1972. Percent change over 1967. FBI chart.

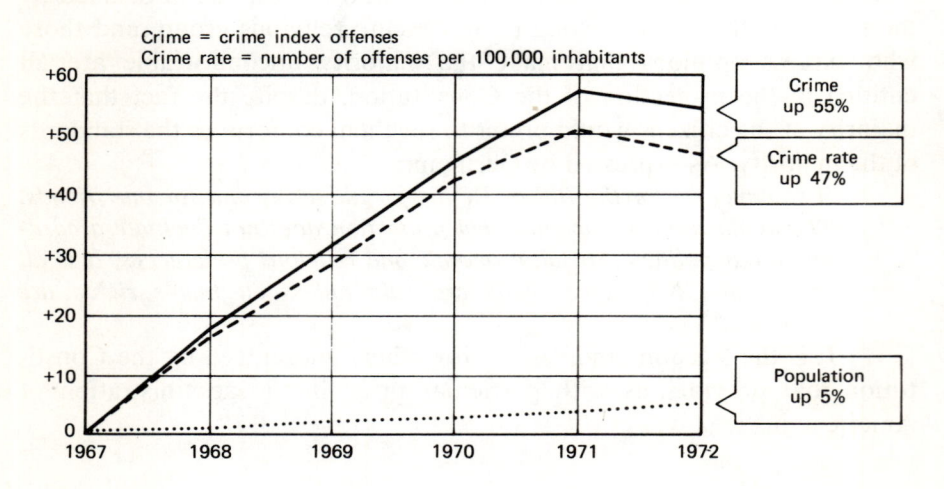

Crime = crime index offenses
Crime rate = number of offenses per 100,000 inhabitants

Crime up 55%
Crime rate up 47%
Population up 5%

[10] Clarence M. Kelley, *Crime in the United States* (Washington, D.C.: U.S. Government Printing Office, 1973).

ible rape, robbery, and aggravated assault) versus crimes against property (burglary, larceny over $50, and auto theft), it will be noted from Figures 2-2 and 2-3 that crimes of violence have increased 67 percent while property crimes have increased 53 percent in the 1967 to 1972 time period.

Expressed in numbers, there were 5,891,900 index crimes reported in 1972, which represents a 2 percent decrease in the index crimes reported in 1971.

It must be recognized, however, that the majority of the reported crimes are crimes against property (86 percent) compared with crimes of violence (14 percent).

Figures 2-1, 2-2, and 2-3 show not only a crime increase but also a crime rate. To understand the difference, let us first examine the Crime Index. The Crime Index is simply the number of reported index crimes from the seven categories per 100,000 population. If we can imagine a city with exactly a 100,000 population that has 10 reported index crimes occurring in a given period, then the Crime Index in that city for that period will be 10. This means that the risk of becoming a victim of one of the index crimes is 10 per 100,000 people.

It is this risk factor expressed in Figures 2-1, 2-2, and 2-3 by the expression, "crime rate." In other words, the crime increase lists only the

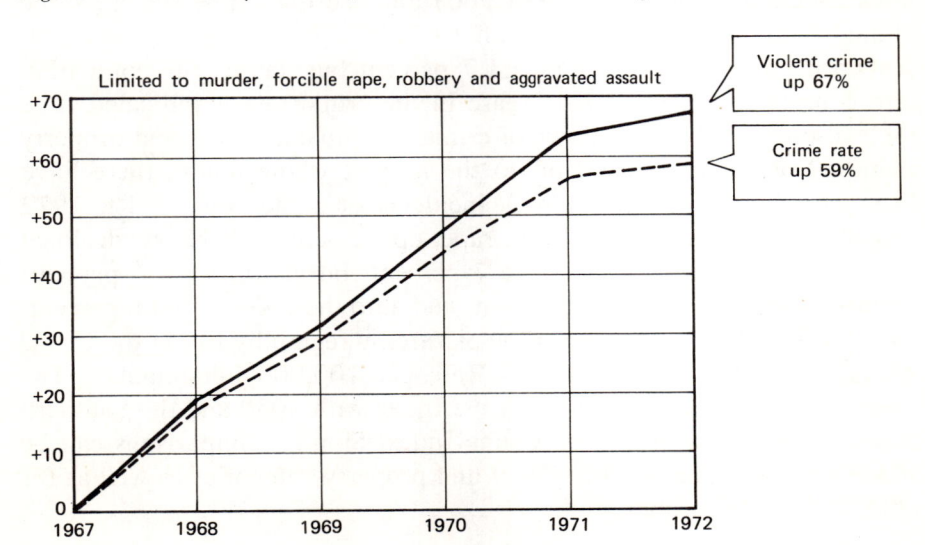

Figure 2-2. Crimes of violence, 1967-1972. Percent change over 1967. FBI chart.

survey of the crime problem

Figure 2-3. Crimes against property, 1967-1972. Percent change over 1967. FBI chart.

Limited to burglary, larceny $50 and over, and auto theft

Property crime up 53%

Crime rate up 45%

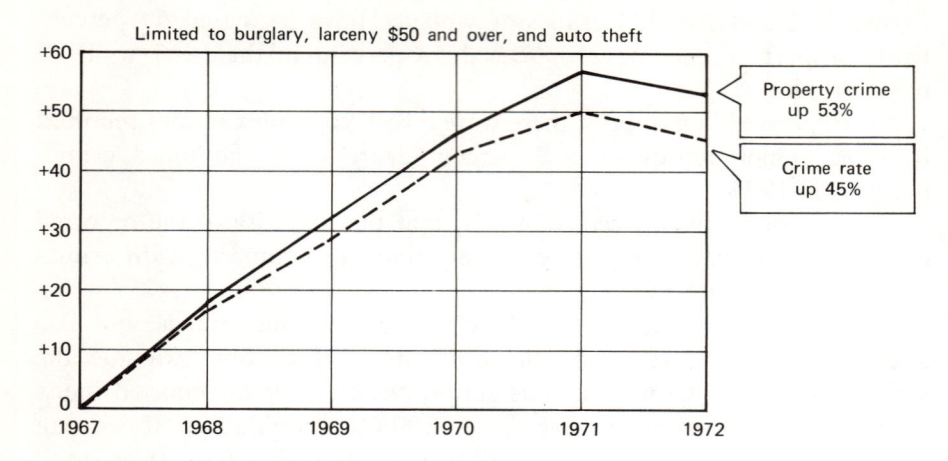

rise in crime, although the crime rate takes into account any change in population.

The Crime Index for the United States (the number of index crimes per 100,000 population) was 2830 in 1972, a −2.7 percent decrease from the previous year.

Table 2-1 gives us a more detailed picture of the specific criminal offenses. Note that under the heading, Estimated crime 1972, we find not only the total number (5,891,900) but also the Crime Index for the United States (2829.5 rounded off to 2830). Numerically, this represents a decrease from 1971 of −1.7 percent but, taking the population into consideration, a −2.7 decrease in the crime rate is indicated. The table also shows the breakdown of crime into violent crimes and property crimes. Note that, rounded off to the nearest whole figure, there have been increases and decreases in the incidence of crime from 1971 to 1972 as follows: murder, up 5 percent; rape, up 11 percent; robbery, declined 3 percent; aggravated assault, up 7 percent; burglary, down 1 percent; larceny over $50, declined 2 percent; and auto theft, decreased 6 percent.

Table 2-2 explains the crime picture by region by listing the Crime Index (described in the table as Rate per 100,000 inhabitants). The Western states have the highest Crime Index with 4030 and the Southern states the lowest with a 2463 Crime Index. Similar comparisons can be made from this chart in the violent and property categories as well as for each of the index crimes.

TABLE 2-1. National Crime Rate and Percent Change

Crime Index Offenses	Estimated crime 1972 Number	Rate per 100,000 inhabitants	Percent change over 1971 Number	Rate	Percent change over 1967 Number	Rate	Percent change over 1960 Number	Rate
Total	5,891,900	2,829.5	− 1.7	− 2.7	+ 54.6	+ 46.9	+191.7	+151.2
Violent	828,150	397.7	+ 2.2	+ 1.3	+ 67.1	+ 58.8	+189.6	+149.3
Property	5,063,800	2,431.8	− 2.3	− 3.3	+ 52.7	+ 45.1	+192.1	+151.6
Murder	18,520	8.9	+ 5.0	+ 4.7	+ 52.6	+ 45.9	+105.0	+ 78.0
Forcible rape	46,430	22.3	+10.8	+ 9.9	+ 69.6	+ 61.6	+172.6	+134.7
Robbery	374,560	179.9	− 2.9	− 3.8	+ 85.5	+ 76.2	+248.9	+200.3
Aggravated assault	388,650	186.6	+ 6.6	+ 5.5	+ 52.9	+ 45.2	+154.7	+119.3
Burglary	2,345,000	1,126.1	− 1.0	− 1.9	+ 45.6	+ 38.3	+160.4	+124.3
Larceny $50 and over	1,837,800	882.6	− 2.0	− 2.9	+ 75.1	+ 66.4	+262.3	+212.0
Auto theft	881,000	423.1	− 6.4	− 7.3	+ 34.5	+ 27.8	+170.3	+132.9

survey of the crime problem   35

TABLE 2-2. **Crime Rate by Region, 1972**

	[Rate per 100,000 inhabitants]			
Crime Index Offenses	North-eastern states	North Central states	Southern states	Western states
Total	2840.6	2480.7	2462.7	4030.3
Violent	449.8	334.6	391.4	438.0
Property	2390.9	2146.1	2071.3	3592.3
Murder	7.3	6.8	12.6	7.7
Forcible rape	17.1	20.2	21.6	34.1
Robbery	263.5	165.2	129.9	177.6
Aggravated assault	161.9	142.3	227.2	218.6
Burglary	1074.6	954.7	1005.8	1687.2
Larceny $50 and over	775.2	808.4	770.9	1349.8
Auto theft	541.0	383.1	294.6	555.3

Not reflected in this regional table, however, but nevertheless reported by the FBI elsewhere is the observation that index crimes decreased 7 percent in the Northeastern states, increased 2 percent in the Western states, and decreased 1 percent in the Southern and North Central states from 1971 to 1972.

Table 2-3 gives breakdowns of crime similar to these categories listed in the regional table except that the information provided here is based on an area analysis (large cities, suburbs, and rural areas). The Crime Index is a very high 4948 in the large cities, lower in the suburbs with 2364, and lowest in the rural areas with a 1084 Crime Index.

Although not evident from the table, the respective increase percentages from 1971 to 1972 may be of particular interest to those who are students of the urban problems of decaying cities and the flight to the suburbs.

Although crime in the large cities still remains the major problem, a shift is now in progress. Crime in cities with a 250,000 population decreased 8 percent from 1971 to 1972. The suburban crime rate increased 2 percent over the same period and rural crime, 4 percent!

One may speculate that crime control and prevention efforts in the large cities have become increasing factors of deterrence for the criminal. Adding to this changing picture may be that much wealth is moving to the suburbs, that the suburbanites have not yet learned through experi-

TABLE 2-3. **Crime Rate by Area, 1972**

	\multicolumn{4}{c}{Area [Rate per 100,000 inhabitants]}
Crime Index Offenses	Total U.S.	Cities over 250,000	Suburban	Rural
Total	2,829.5	4,947.9	2,363.6	1,084.4
Violent	397.7	998.6	221.7	143.6
Property	2,431.8	3,949.3	2,141.9	940.8
Murder	8.9	10.7	4.6	7.4
Forcible rape	22.3	47.1	17.1	11.2
Robbery	179.9	578.8	72.3	16.1
Aggravated assault	186.6	353.0	127.8	109.0
Burglary	1,126.1	1,877.5	963.1	507.5
Larceny $50 and over	882.6	1,104.6	890.5	363.6
Auto theft	423.1	967.2	288.3	69.7

ence to be security conscious, and that growing freeway networks also assist the criminal in his travels.

Figure 2-4, referred to as the FBI Crime Clock, lists the frequency of occurrence of various crimes. The Crime Clock is a popular teaching tool in many police academy training programs. Its weakness is that it does not reflect any changes in population.

Police departments clear crimes when they arrest and charge the offender; when the offender is identified, but some circumstances beyond police control prevent prosecution; or when the police establish the fact that the reported crime did, in fact, not occur ("unfounded").

On the national average, police departments "unfound" 4 percent of the crime reports, ranging from a low of 2 percent in the case of larceny reports to a high of 15 percent of forcible rape reports.

American law enforcement cleared 21 percent of the reported index crimes. Figure 2-5 illustrates the various degrees of success in clearing (solving by arrest) the index offenses. It is of interest to note that police have a much greater success rate in clearing crimes against the person than in clearing crimes against property. This may be because police are able to devote greater time and manpower to crimes of violence, and also that such offenses are witnessed more frequently by others than are thefts and other property offenses.

survey of the crime problem

Figure 2-4. Crime Clocks, 1972. FBI chart.

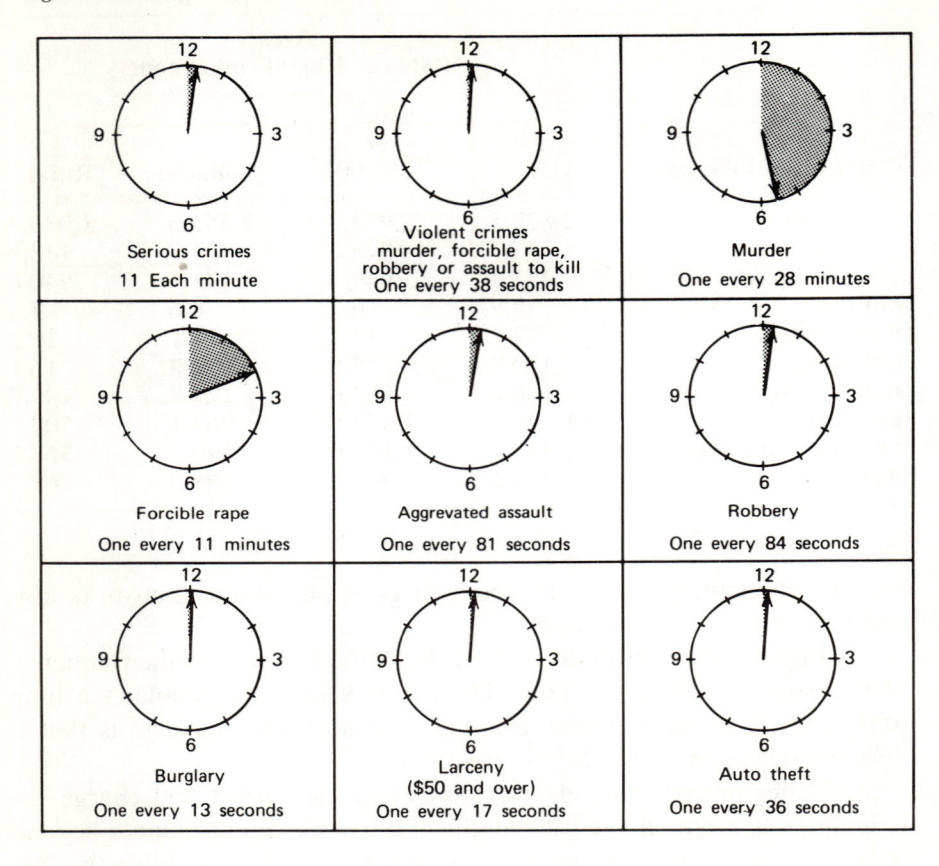

Serious crimes 11 Each minute	Violent crimes murder, forcible rape, robbery or assault to kill One every 38 seconds	Murder One every 28 minutes
Forcible rape One every 11 minutes	Aggravated assault One every 81 seconds	Robbery One every 84 seconds
Burglary One every 13 seconds	Larceny ($50 and over) One every 17 seconds	Auto theft One every 36 seconds

Of the people arrested in 1972 for crime index offenses, 83 percent were prosecuted, and of those, 71 percent were convicted of the original charge or a lesser offense.

The analyses that we have presented in this section are based on the 1972 *Crime in the United States: Uniform Crime Reports*, published by the FBI. Although the data have great value in understanding America's crime problem, they should nevertheless be seen in perspective.

First, not all crime is reported to the police and is, therefore, not counted in the FBI statistics. Second, police departments are not required to report their crime statistics to the FBI. Even the law enforcement

Figure 2-5. Crimes cleared by arrest, 1972.

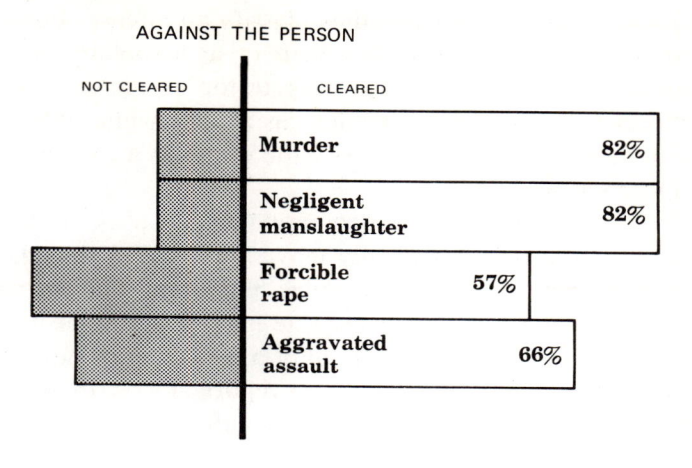

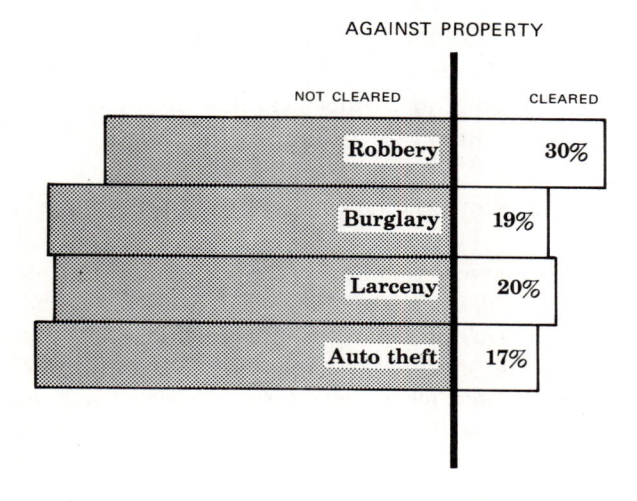

AGAINST THE PERSON

NOT CLEARED	CLEARED	
	Murder	82%
	Negligent manslaughter	82%
	Forcible rape	57%
	Aggravated assault	66%

AGAINST PROPERTY

NOT CLEARED	CLEARED	
	Robbery	30%
	Burglary	19%
	Larceny	20%
	Auto theft	17%

agencies that do submit the proper forms to the FBI may be reporting less than accurately.

Incidents can be classified by police in a variety of ways. For example, when a police department has to approach its city council for an increased budget, it may be tempted to count certain incidents in categories more likely to make the city council sympathetic to the needs

survey of the crime problem

of police. Furthermore, whether the police have a suspect in custody or not may influence the way they classify an offense. For example, a purse snatch may be classified as a theft or as a robbery depending upon the degree of force used by the perpetrator. If no suspect is known, some officers will classify the incident as a theft while, if a suspect is known or in custody, they may classify the crime as a robbery, thereby clearing a more serious crime.

Crime increase or decrease must also be viewed with care. A decrease in crime statistically may simply mean that the citizens have a lowered confidence level in police and simply do not report crimes. On the other hand, a rising crime rate may be a sign of increased quality in community relations, the arrival of a new chief of police, or other factors that suddenly bring the public to report more crimes as a manifestation of a new-found faith and trust in law enforcement.

We must also caution against seeing the FBI statistics as reflecting all types of crime. Press releases often refer to the seven index crimes as "serious crime," but it must be recognized that although some of those crimes are indeed serious (murder, rape, and others), included in the index crimes are the offenses of larceny over $50 and auto theft, and excluded are arson, the sale of heroin, and other acts that are dangerous or have greater potential harm than, for example, the theft of an automobile.

Former Attorney General Ramsey Clark maintains that "crime has many faces," and speaks of:

> White-collar crime (which) converts billions of dollars annually in tax evasion, price fixing, embezzlement, swindling, and consumer fraud. Organized crime reaps hundreds of millions in gambling, loansharking, drug traffic, extortion, and prostitution, corrupting officials and resorting to force, including murder when necessary, to accomplish its purposes. . . . Corruption in public office—bribes, payoffs, fixes, conflicts of interest—occurs in every branch of government, legislative executive, judicial, administrative, and at every level, federal, state, and local.[11]

Ramsey Clark's message is clear: There is much serious crime that never finds its way into the FBI's Crime Index.

The study of crime and crime trends can be approached in a

---

[11] Ramsey Clark, *Crime in America* (New York: Simon and Schuster, 1970), pp. 35, 36.

Figure 2-6. Crime has many faces. This white-collar crime caught the attention of an incredulous public when the author, Clifford Irving, and his wife were indicted and sentenced on charges ranging from mail fraud to forgery in connection with the discredited "autobiography" of Howard Hughes.

variety of ways depending on the information desired. Some criminologists have made in-depth studies of variables in crime, such as age, sex, race, ecological factors, and seasonal variations.[12]

[12] For studies into these issues, see Richard D. Knudten, *Crime in a Complex Society* (Homewood, Ill.: Dorsey Press, pp. 58-86).

Crime is complex. Just as the reasons for crime are complex, so are the solutions. Let us beware of those who have simplistic explanations. Let us be wary of those whose vocabulary regarding offenders is limited to "laziness," "no character," and "anyone can make it." Let us also be wary of those who see as solutions simply more police, more armamentarium, 50-year prison sentences for everyone, and bigger and better jails and prisons.

Let us listen to those in our society who see the need for improving the quality of life by improving education, housing, clothing, food, and medical care—the necessities of life.

Summary

In this chapter we have seen that crimes can be viewed in a strictly legal sense or in the broader sociological view. In a complex society such as ours, we must have laws ("social contracts") enforced by the police, subject to adjudication by the courts, and sanctions against the offenders by the correctional system.

We must recognize that all the agencies of the criminal justice system suffer from varying degrees and types of imperfection that, in the interest of increased efficiency and intercooperation, must be corrected.

Although efficiency is important, and even though our country is generally governed by majority right, we have observed how the minority (religious, political, or whatever) must nevertheless be afforded constitutional protections. Unless these protections are afforded to even the most unpopular group, they lose both value and meaning.

This chapter has discussed crime statistics, particularly the statistics issued by the FBI, and their values as well as their shortcomings were noted.

Finally, it was suggested that America's crime problem is too complicated to be solved by more police, more severe sentences, and bigger and better jails. We must look to the causes of crime, to the basic quality of life in order to understand the behavior of our fellow citizens.

Student Checklist

1. Can you define the legal definition of crime?
2. Are you able to explain the sociological definition of crime?
3. Can you explain the rationale for the existence of the criminal justice system?
4. Can you explain the strengths and weaknesses of federal crime statistics?
5. Can you explain the constitutional considerations supporting the justice system?
6. Can you define the nationwide crime trend?

Topics for Discussion

1. Discuss the concept of what crime is.
2. Discuss the need for laws and regulations governing society.
3. Discuss the constitutional amendments that support the existence of criminal law sanctions.

ANNOTATED BIBLIOGRAPHY

Berger, Peter L., and Brigitte Berger. *Sociology: A Biographical Approach*. New York: Basic Books, 1972. Describes the discipline of sociology, the process of socialization; discusses various institutions, social control, and a variety of sociological problems.

Broom, Leonard, and Philip Selznick. *Sociology*. New York: Harper & Row, 1968. Covers extensively sociology, social organization, culture, the means of socialization, and social stratification. Discusses in detail various institutions, including religion, education, and selected political considerations.

Clark, Ramsey. *Crime in America*. New York: Simon & Schuster, 1970. An idealistic and compassionate commentary on the nature and causes of crime, a critical review of the criminal justice system, and a discussion of the balance between security and constitutional considerations.

Eastman, George D., ed. *Municipal Police Administration*. Washington, D.C.: International City Management Association, 1969. A comprehensive, authoritative text dealing with police organization, management, and a variety of police operations.

Germann, A. C.; Frank D. Day; and Robert R. J. Gallati. *Intrdoduction to Law Enforcement and Criminal Justice*. Springfield, Ill.; Charles C. Thomas, 1970. A text describing the history and the constitutional and philosophical aspects of criminal justice, concluding with an evaluation of American justice. There is some emphasis on philosophical considerations.

Gray, L. Patrick III. *Crime in the United States*. Washington, D.C.; Federal Bureau of Investigation, 1972. A statistical analysis of the trends of crime in the United States, arrests, clearances; some information is broken down into geographical data.

Kennedy, Daniel B., and Bruce Kennedy. *Applied Sociology for Police*. Springfield, Ill.; Charles C. Thomas, 1972. An introductory text in sociology particularly suited for the law enforcement officer. In addition to covering such areas as the family, understanding crime, probation, and parole, the authors introduce the reader to such specialized topics as the police officer in a social system; enforcement and minority groups; the police officer and the city; and other areas of sociology that are of particular interest to those employed in law enforcement.

Kennedy, Daniel B., and August Kerber. *Resocialization: An American Experiment*. New York: Behavioral Publications, 1973. Describes the nature of resocialization, and investigates resocialization in three main areas: compensatory education; criminal rehabilitation; and training for the unemployed. Discusses techniques and success rates in the resocialization of individuals.

Knudten, Richard D. *Crime in a Complex Society*. Homewood, Ill.: Dorsey Press, 1970. A comprehensive text exploring crime, criminology, theoretical origins of delinquency, systems of social control, and the justice system and its dispositions. Rich with theories and statistical information.

Post, Richard S., and Arthur A. Kingsbury. *Security Administration: An Introduction.* Springfield, Ill.: Charles C. Thomas, 1970. Background, components, and programming security. The authors point out that the private segment is necessary, in addition to official law enforcement, to participate in loss prevention.

President's Commission on Law Enforcement and Administration of Justice. *The Challenge of Crime in a Free Society.* Washington, D.C.: U.S. Government Printing Office, 1967. An official evaluation made by a presidential commission of the agencies of criminal justice and their numerous responsibilities. A very responsible document containing numerous specific recommendations for change.

Schur, Edwin M. *Crimes Without Victims.* Englewood Cliffs, N.J.: Prentice-Hall, 1965. A discussion of deviance and public policy, particularly as related to abortion, homosexuality, and drug addiction. Discusses policy reform in relation to these acts and, by implication, similar "crimes without victims."

The study of this chapter will enable you to:

1. Explain the administrative and legislative theory for crime causation.
2. Identify at least three historical authors in the study of causal theories.
3. Explain the biophysical theory of crime causation.
4. Define socioeconomic determinism as used in crime causation.
5. Understand contemporary theories of crime causation.
6. Outline the future of criminology as reviewed in this chapter.

3

Explanations for Criminal Actions

All societies, however backward, have considered specific forms of human conduct undesirable. Some actions are more severely forbidden than others, but the acts most frowned upon are those identified as "criminal." People caught engaging in criminal acts are treated with public contempt; they may be temporarily or permanently removed from the rest of society, and they are generally punished for their transgression. The punishers have been mobs, priests, kings, public executioners or prosecutors, and the like, depending upon the structure of the society, but there has been no society that has not devised some method of attempting to force its members to observe its taboos.

In modern times, people have sought to understand what causes a person to violate the laws of his society. The assumption seems to be that people should want to observe the law as a matter of course, and if they do not, there must be a reason—something has gone wrong. However, to this day, no general cause of crime has been found, although the search has been based on many different attitudes. Much information has been gathered in recent years on crimes and criminals, but the cause of criminal behavior has eluded us.

In the pages that follow you will read about some of the major theories of the causes of crime. Your familiarity with these ideas will prevent you from being misled into the belief that there is some simple solution to the "crime problem."

Historically, crime has been attributed to environmental conditions, such as slums, poverty, poor family life; to some defect, such as mental illness, physical disability, or biochemical deficiency in the person who commits the crime; to the interpersonal influences of bad companions, gang activities, or unhappy school experiences; or finally, social structural factors, such as inability to get good jobs, alienation from the norms of the society, prejudice, and other social forces that prevent a person from obtaining his goals through legitimate means.

Curiously, several basic approaches to the explanation of crime have developed or evolved parallel to each other. There has not been any clear evolutionary development of a single theory of crime similar to the way theory has developed in other fields. In physics or biology, for example, there is often a breakthrough in research that confirms some basic propositions of a major theory out of which new research and knowledge grows. Unfortunately, in the field of criminology, we are unable to point to similar achievements.

Crime is as old as man himself, so attempts to explain it go back to the time when man first began to recognize the transgressions of his brother. Modern explanations of crime are generally traced to the mid-eighteenth century when the first efforts at a scientific explanation were attempted. But many of them can be traced back farther to a few central ideas that are centuries old. These same ideas resurface sometimes with a new element that captures the imagination of the public and creates the notion that a new theory of crime is born. The purpose of this chapter is to describe some of the more prominent theories that have cropped up during the last century or so, and to organize them in such a way that you will be able to see their common threads.

Administrative and Legislative Theories

One of the oldest explanations for crime finds the reason in the law itself. Without criminal law there would be no crime, and obviously no criminals. Crime is therefore a matter of social definition as manifested in the criminal statutes of that society. This theory emphasizes the process by which certain behavior comes to be labeled criminal rather than what causes crime. Let us begin with the position expounded by one of the best known of the classical criminologists—Cesare Bonesana, Marchese de Beccaria (1738–94)—an Italian social philosopher whose influence extends into the twentieth century.[1]

---

[1] Cesare Beccaria, *On Crimes and Punishment*, English trans. (Indianapolis: Bobbs-Merrill, 1963).

Beccaria and his British contemporary, Jeremy Bentham (1748–1832),[2] were disturbed that the jurists of their day were permitted both to define which behavior was "criminal" and to assign whatever penalty they felt appropriate. Beccaria felt that this was often done in a capricious and injust manner, without the benefit of legislative control. He believed that the people of the society should define what was criminal rather than an individual jurist, and that legislature, representative of the people, should be the source of criminal law and its penalties, not the judges.

The major reforms proposed by Beccaria and Bentham concentrated on what would constitute an appropriate penalty system. It is only at this point that we gain some insight into how they explained crime. The penalty system they proposed was built upon a hedonistic principle which assumes that people weigh alternative behaviors in terms of the relative pleasure or pain they will produce. If the pain outweighs the anticipated pleasure, a person will be afraid to perform the act. They further believed that the most effective deterrent to criminal conduct was swift and sure punishment with penalties severe enough to outweigh any possible gain from the act. These penalties would be written into the criminal law so that they would be known in advance and could be taken into consideration when a criminal act was contemplated. Beccaria and Bentham believed that the amount of crime a society experiences is determined by the effectiveness of its social control mechanisms—such as the threat of pain—in deterring crime.

Emile Durkheim (1858–1917), a French sociologist, said that crime can be found in every society and suggested that it might be necessary for the well-being of society.[3] Crimes were useful, he said, to mark the moral boundaries of a society. A society without crime would be inconceivable and undesirable, according to Durkheim, since there would always be a minority of people who would try to innovate, thus testing the limits of society's moral conscience in an effort to change the rules. In his view, most crimes were committed by people residing on the moral fringe of a society.

Not only did Durkheim consider crime a normal condition in a healthy society, but also that crimes were relative in nature. What might

---

[2] Jeremy Bentham, *Theory of Punishments and Rewards* (London: Pickering, 1873).
[3] Emile Durkheim, *The Rules of Sociological Method*, 8th ed., English trans. (New York: Free Press, 1950).

explanations for criminal actions

be criminal in one society might not be in another; what was criminal was a matter of where a particular society decided to draw the line. Criminal behavior was not in itself sick or unnatural, he said. Criminals were really innovators who were ahead of their time in a sense. They were labeled criminals for behavior that the next generation might very well accept as legal or normal behavior.

An American sociologist of this century, Thorsten Sellin,[4] agreed with Durkheim that crime is a relative thing; but Sellin went further to point out that much crime is a result of cultural conflict within a society caused by a minority's attempt to impose universal rules of behavior on all members of society. Crimes increase when there is doubt in many minds that the behavior forbidden by the criminal law is really criminal. American society—made up of many cultures and ethnic groups—is especially susceptible to culture conflict and, therefore, can expect a higher crime rate than other societies.

The contemporary theory closest to the views of these men is offered by Richard Quinney.[5] He maintains that crime is primarily a matter of social belief as expressed in the criminal code, so without criminal law there would be no crime. Quinney sees crime as a reflection of the moral and social concerns of the people who make the laws of a society or those people who have substantial influence over legislators or the legislative process. The kinds of behavior that come to be defined as crime and the emphasis of enforcement are heavily weighted against the politically powerless. Conduct engaged in by influential people that may be more socially costly or threatening escapes similar treatment in the criminal code. This occurs because they (the politically powerful) control the process that both defines and enforces the criminal code. They are able to get legal restraints effectively applied against those whose crimes arouse their indignation; they can prevent their own misconduct from being labeled criminal; or, failing this, they can effectively defend themselves against the application of criminal charges.

Perhaps the best documentation of Quinney's position came about 30 years ago in research conducted by Edwin Sutherland on what was then called white-collar crime.[6] Sutherland was attempting to make the

---

[4] Thorsten Sellin, *Culture Conflict and Crime* (New York: Social Science Research Council, 1938).
[5] Richard Quinney, *The Social Reality of Crime* (Boston: Little, Brown, 1970).
[6] Edwin Sutherland, *White-Collar Crime* (New York: Dryden Press, 1949).

point that many crimes were committed by persons of respectability and high social status in the course of their occupations. He contended that such crimes are widespread, but that an index of their frequency is not found in police reports. He maintained that prosecution for this kind of crime frequently was avoided because of (1) the political or financial power of the parties concerned, (2) the apparent triviality of the crimes, or (3) the difficulty of securing evidence sufficient for prosecution, particularly in the case of crimes by corporations.[7]

In summary, these theorists have maintained that crime is a normal product of the conflict between the definers of crime and those whose conduct is defined as crime. Crime is not caused by any personality or biological defects, nor is it the product of overpowering social forces working upon an individual, forcing him to embark upon a criminal career. Crime is inevitable so long as there are strong differences of opinion among segments of a society about human conduct and acceptable means for reaching one's goals. These theorists believe that the volume of crime in any given society is proportionate to the amount of effort put forth by those in control of the society to deter or suppress it.

Biophysical Theories

In direct contrast to the theories just described other opinions hold that man is not a self-determining creature who is able to choose between alternatives, but rather man is a being whose behavior is determined or "caused" by certain biological or physiological conditions. This position was first put forth as a scientific approach by Cesare Lombroso in the last half of the nineteenth century.[8] He maintained that there were three major classes of criminals: born criminals, insane criminals, and criminaloids. He considered born criminals as throwbacks to a lower, more primitive evolutionary form of man and believed that about one-third of all offenders were born criminals. According to Lombroso, insane criminals included such persons as idiots, imbeciles, or psychiatric cases;

---

[7] Edwin Sutherland, "White-Collar Criminality," *Am. Soc. Rev.*, 5 (February, 1940).
[8] Cesare Lombroso, *Crime, Its Causes and Remedies* (Boston: Little, Brown, 1911).

criminaloids were a large catchall class of those not having any of the physical characteristics of the born criminal but whose mental or emotional makeup caused them, under certain circumstances, to indulge in vicious and criminal behavior.

Lombroso's theory was later proved incorrect, but he is generally recognized as the first person to attempt a purely scientific explanation of crime. He consistently emphasized the need for a direct study of the individual criminal, using precise measurements and statistical methods. His major contribution to the study of crime may well have been his persistent emphasis on a scientific approach to the subject.

Interest in the biological or genetic approach to crime did not die with Lombroso. Several other outstanding attempts have been made to find a biological basis for criminal behavior. In America, perhaps the most noted studies have been those by Ernst Hooton, William Sheldon, and Eleanor Glueck.

In 1939, Ernest Hooton stirred a great deal of controversy with the publication of *Crime and the Man*[9] in which he argued on behalf of his belief in physical determinism. Hooton had made 107 anthropometric measurements (anthropometry is the science of measuring the human body and its parts) of 14,477 convicts and compared these measurements with a control group consisting of 3203 noncriminals. He concluded that the criminals appeared to be distinctly physically inferior to the noncriminals. In addition, he stated that there was a relationship between specific types of body build and particular offenses such as murder, assault, robbery, and sex offenses.

Other scientists, like William Sheldon and the Gluecks, have reached different conclusions. Unlike Hooton, they have maintained that delinquents are actually physically superior to the normal population, if superiority is defined as the athletic type of body build—muscular, tightly knit, and physically solid. William Sheldon developed an elaborate scheme by which he classified individuals according to body build and temperament.[10] His research on 16 delinquent youths identified among the 200 residents of the Hayden Goodwill Inn in South Boston (a private treatment institution) indicated that they were, with-

---

[9] Ernest A. Hooton, *The American Criminal: An Anthropological Study* (Cambridge: Harvard University Press, 1939).

[10] William H. Sheldon, *Varieties of Delinquent Youth: An Introduction to Constitutional Psychiatry* (New York: Harper & Bros., 1949).

out exception, boys with an endomorphic-mesomorph body build; that is, a body build generally associated with the stereotype of an athlete.

Using Sheldon's classification of body types, the Gluecks reported: (1) the boys who were mesomorph (muscular) in constitution were found to be members of delinquent groups in much higher proportion than in nondelinquent groups; (2) delinquent groups have a much smaller proportion of ectomorphs (lean, thin body build); and (3) ectomorphs and endomorphs (round, plump body build) and balanced types are decidedly subordinate among the delinquents.[11]

The work of H. J. Eysenck probably represents the most recent theory based on biological factors.[12] He has developed a complex theory of the biological basis for personality, one portion of which attempts to explain criminal behavior. In essense, he maintains that criminals are people with unstable, extroverted personalities. Instability is seen as a biological condition in which a person is highly sensitive to stimuli around him and is, therefore, very emotional in nature. Extroverts show a strong tendency to cortical fatigue, a condition that retards the development of the inhibitions that usually control behavior. The criminal is a person who has unusual difficulty in learning from his experiences, so he continues to behave in ways that others disapprove of in spite of the penalties that he receives as a consequence of his behavior.

Eysenck probably offers the best general biological theory currently under study today, but there is considerable research being carried out that examines the possible link between specific physiological or genetic factors and specific types of crimes. It now seems clear that such things as blood-sugar level, imbalances in body hormones secreted by the ductless glands, brain tumors, and the like are closely associated with highly aggressive violent behavior.

The much-publicized XYY chromosome and its relationship to crime is another example of a genetic factor currently being investigated as a possible explanation of crime. Studies concerning chromosomal deviation have been based on the finding that there are males, and only males, who have an extra male chromosome, called the Y gonosome; that is, they display an XYY combination rather than the usual XY.

---

[11] Sheldon and Eleanor Glueck, *Physique and Delinquency* (New York: Harper & Bros., 1956).
[12] H. J. Eysenck, *Crime and Personality* (New York: Houghton Mifflin, 1964).

Although it is true that there have been varied and conflicting results from the various studies looking into this deviation, there are some suggestive conclusions that seem consistent throughout. Among criminals, it has been found that the chance of possessing an extra Y gonosome is up to 60 times greater than for the general population. On the whole, the XYY physique is taller and thinner than members of control groups. There is a tendency toward a higher frequency of aggressive and disturbed behavior. Higher rates of violent crime are found among men with an extra Y gonosome, and they begin their criminal activity at a relatively early age. While it is clear that a greater proportion of criminals than noncriminals exhibit the XYY syndrome, the link between this syndrome and criminal behavior is not yet clearly demonstrated nor understood.[13]

Socioeconomic Determinism

With the beginning of the twentieth century, a strong movement developed that blamed all major social problems on the economic system of society. This theory, often referred to as economic determinism, cites the economic inequalities within society as a major cause of crime. William Bonger, a Dutch criminologist, strongly supported this view.[14] He maintained that the capitalistic economic system was particularly effective in creating crime because it placed such an extraordinary emphasis upon the acquisition of wealth.

There does seem to be one clear relationship between economic concerns and crime: the more value a society places upon property, the more criminal laws it develops to protect that property. The number of laws in the United States that deal with property far outnumber the laws that deal with crimes against the person. It is also true that crimes committed against property are more than 10 times greater in number than the crimes of murder, assault, and rape. The great volume of crimes

---

[13] M. Amir and Y. Berman, "Chromosomal Deviation and Crime," *Federal Probation* (September 1969).
[14] William Bonger, *Criminality and Economic Conditions* (Boston: Little, Brown, 1916).

committed involving property or money would seem to support the contention that much crime in America has an economic base.

The economic determinists have had difficulty in demonstrating exactly how economic variables influence crime. Studies of the statistical relationship between crime rates and business cycles have indicated that crimes against property tend to increase during times of prosperity rather than depression, as one might predict. If crime is indeed a product of economic need, it should be most frequent when economic conditions are at their worst.

The fact that official crime statistics show that disproportionately large numbers of the poor are found guilty of crime has been offered as evidence that poverty causes crime. However, critics of the economic determinists contend that the statistics merely reflect the fact that the crimes of the poor are more socially visible than the crimes of middle-class and upper-class people (white-collar crimes), and the poor are less able to defend themselves against criminal prosecution as successfully as those with more money and education.

Some theorists have suggested that prosperity that is unequally shared aggravates the feelings of economic deprivation among the poor by increasing the social distance between the "haves" and the "have-nots." Robert Merton, in a discussion of the sources of crime, noted that motivation for most crime can be traced to frustration felt by members of society who have been taught to want social prestige and economic affluence, but who have been deprived of a legitimate means of attaining these goals.[15] The criminal social structure provides an alternative "ladder to success" for people who have been denied full participation in the legitimate economic and social system of the society. Crime is committed as a means of satisfying a desire for those material things that are held out for all to see—rich and poor alike—disregarding the fact that substantial differences exist in the economic means available to acquire them. Crime is seen as a response to overstimulation of economic needs rather than actual poverty or economic destitution.

Donald Taft agrees with Merton and argues that the American emphasis upon competition and materialism has been the major source

---

[15] Robert K. Merton, *Social Theory and Social Structure* (New York: Free Press, 1957).

of criminal motivation in the society.[16] The inconsistency between what is promised and what can be achieved legitimately by "have-nots" creates feelings of economic discrimination that encourage economically deprived people to use criminal means to obtain the things they want and are unable to obtain through legitimate means.

In the 1950s a new direction was taken in the attempt to relate economic variables to crime. The emphasis turned away from pure economic need to the *social* implications of being poor in an affluent society. Since delinquency was thought to be most prevalent in poverty-stricken neighborhoods, some theorists tried to explain the relationship between poverty and delinquency. Albert Cohen contended that delinquency was the lower-class boy's path to success since he could not compete in the school system, where the rewards were closely tied to middle-class standards of performance. The lower-class boy suffered from what Cohen called "status frustration."[17]

Cohen maintained that being unable to succeed in the schools forced the lower-class boys to seek recognition on the street. Lower-class boys, he thought, grouped together in defense against their rejection in school, and street gangs emerged that had a subculture (sometimes called a contraculture) that was built upon rejection of the major values of the middle-class system. Since the middle class valued neatness, property, education, and postponement of immediate gratification in favor of long-term goals, the lower-class boy adopted a value system that was pleasure-oriented, "now"-oriented, and malicious and destructive in nature. Boys turned to delinquency as a means to social success rather than economic success, but they did so as a result of the socioeconomic conditions related to being lower class.

Cohen's writings stimulated much research and discussion regarding the relationship between social class and crime or delinquency. Some alternative ideas have since been advanced in response to Cohen's explanation. Walter B. Miller, an anthropologist, agreed with Cohen that the lower-class boy who finds himself unable to cope with the middle-class bias in the public schools ultimately drops out of school. However, Miller does not think that this is what leads to delinquency. He believes that the

---

[16] Donald Taft, *Criminology*, 3rd ed. (New York: Macmillan, 1956).
[17] Albert K. Cohen, *Delinquent Boys: The Culture of the Gang* (Glencoe, Ill.: Free Press, 1955).

lower class has developed certain responses to poverty, which he calls "focal concerns," that eventually lead the lower-class child into conflict with the legal authorities. He views delinquency as the product of well-established cultural traditions of lower-class life, rather than the result of a conflict with middle-class values.[18]

Richard Cloward and Lloyd Ohlin agree with Merton on those socioeconomic factors among the poor that contribute to delinquency. Whereas Cohen emphasized the issue of alienation of the lower-class boy from the middle-class oriented school system, Cloward and Ohlin feel that his legitimate avenues to success are blocked and that he must accept illegitimate alternatives. They see the delinquent boy using crime as an alternate route to success. He finds in his neighborhood many opportunities for gain through criminal activity. They note, however, that the opportunities for gainful criminal behavior are also unequally distributed in society. There are lower-class neighborhoods too poor to make robbery worthwhile; therefore, gainful criminal opportunity is limited. Here a different kind of response is found—a conflict response. Violence and alienation are characteristic of this response, but unlike gainful criminal activity, it seldom leads to social success. It merely illustrates that the boy is striking out at a society that he holds responsible for his frustration.[19]

Crime as Learned Behavior

An approach held at the beginning of the twentieth century maintains that criminal behavior is learned like any occupational skill, often from others engaged in similar escapades. Gabriel Tarde, a French jurist and social psychologist, said that criminal behavior is learned from others through "imitation or suggestion" just as one learns to play a sport or an apprentice learns a skill.[20] Tarde saw street gangs as the training ground

---

[18] Walter B. Miller, "Lower-Class Culture as a Generating Milieu of Gang Delinquency," *J. Social Issues 33* (September, 1959).

[19] Richard Cloward and Lloyd Ohlin, *Delinquency and Opportunity* (Glencoe, Ill.: Free Press, 1961).

[20] Gabriel Tarde, *Penal Philosophy*, trans. Rapelje Howell (Boston: Little, Brown, 1912).

for most delinquency since it was on the street that boys shared with each other the specific details about crime.

Although Tarde's ideas were not accepted by many people at the time, his basic idea was restated in a more sophisticated form by Edwin Sutherland in what later came to be known as the theory of differential association. In a classic work on professional theft, Sutherland developed the idea that crime and criminal values are transmitted from one person to another. His book, *The Professional Thief*,[21] describes young thieves learning both techniques and justifications for theft from professional thieves. Criminal behavior occurs, he said, when the person believes that there are more reasons for violating the law than observing it. According to this theory, criminal behavior is socially acquired by contact with others who are disposed to crime, and this influence is most evident in delinquent gangs.

Frederic Thrasher, in his study of more than a thousand gangs in Chicago, concluded that street gangs make chronic truants and delinquents out of street boys and mold them into finished criminals. It is through the gang that a young prospective criminal makes his first contact with older professionals, such as "fences" who buy stolen property. Also, the intense loyalty generated within the gang membership encourages the delinquent's participation in the gang's criminal enterprises and provides him with moral support when he gets into trouble with the law.[22]

Environmental Influences

Criminality has been traced by some theorists to social environmental conditions, such as slums, overcrowding, lack of recreational facilities, or family and community disorganization. A group of sociologists at the University of Chicago conducted numerous studies from the 1920s through the 1940s that examined the relationship between man's social environment and the incidence of broad social problems, such as divorce,

---

[21] Edwin Sutherland. *The Professional Thief* (Chicago: University of Chicago Press, 1937).
[22] Frederick M. Thrasher, *The Gang* (Chicago: University of Chicago Press, 1927).

unemployment, suicide, and crime. Their research indicated a correlation between crime rates and the distance one lived from the central city. They noted that cities evolved over time and, in this process of evolution, the central city deteriorated and became a socially and physically unhealthy place to live. Statistical studies based upon court and police data showed that crime rates were highest in the slum areas of the city and steadily declined as one moved out to the commuter zone or suburbs.

The work of the Chicago sociologists indicated that all major social problems, including crime and delinquency, were closely associated with the ecology of one's residence. Clifford Shaw and Henry McKay sought to identify the specific conditions characteristic of the high crime areas.[23] They were able to show that high-crime-rate neighborhoods were deteriorated, transient, dirty, and crowded, but they were not able to clearly show how or why these conditions produced crime. They were unable to explain why many people who grew up under these slum conditions did not resort to crime, and others who grow up in good neighborhoods did resort to crime.

Walter Reckless and Simon Dinitz thought there might be some kind of internal personality factor that "insulated" some slum children against delinquency in spite of their exposure to delinquency-generating environmental conditions.[24] They wanted to explain why some children, and not others, succumbed to delinquency and crime in the slum neighborhood. Their research on the self-concept (the kind of person one believes himself to be) of both delinquent and nondelinquent boys indicated that children with good self-concepts were much less likely to get involved with the police or court than children whose perceptions of themselves were poor. Amos suggested that the poor self-concept of a delinquent may develop from his lack of a father image.[25] The delinquent may have rejected his father as a model for his image or he may have been reared in a fatherless home. In either case, the lack of a family

---

[23] Clifford R. Shaw and Henry D. McKay, *Juvenile Delinquency and Urban Areas* (Chicago: University of Chicago Press, 1942).

[24] Walter C. Reckless, Simon Dinitz, and Barbara Kay, "The Self Component in Potential Delinquency and Potential Nondelinquency," *American Soc. Rev.,* 22 (October 1957).

[25] W. E. Amos, "A Study of Self-concept: Delinquent Boy's Accuracy in Selected Self-evaluation," *Genetic Psychology Monographs* 67 (1967).

Figure 3-1. An historic explanation for crime; an explanation that is still valid today is that high-crime neighborhoods are deteriorated, transient, dirty, and crowded.

Figure 3-2. But crime cannot always be explained by slum conditions. A building completed in 1956 is demolished deliberately by dynamite in 1972, as one city's solution for a fierce crime-ridden community. The Pruitt-Igoe housing project in St. Louis became a haven for vandals, addicts, rapists, and others.

explanations for criminal actions

masculine image with which to identify could cause him, according to Amos, to rely on the delinquent group for a masculine image. The development of a positive (good) self-concept appeared to be closely linked to strong two-parent family relationships characterized by warmth, cohesiveness, and positive rewards for conformity.

In a similar vein, other theorists point to the widespread family disorganization among slum residents as the real cause of their high crime and delinquency rates. These theorists point to volumes of statistical data that show that the majority of persistent offenders come from homes that are broken, either in reality or psychologically, as evidence that the family is the real source of criminal behavior. Everything from discipline to type of toilet training used by families has been examined in an effort to isolate the specific characteristics of family life that are responsible for crime.

The most recent theory using environmental factors tries to relate crime to a combination of external environmental factors and internal personal factors. Its central idea is that crime occurs when there is a breakdown in the controls on behavior. Containment theory, as proposed by Walter Reckless, is based on the assumption that there exists in man an outer and an inner control system or "buffers."[26] Outer containment consists of the "holding" power or capability of society, groups, organizations, and communities to keep persons within the desired norms of society. Inner containment is defined by Reckless as the ability on the part of the individual to respect and follow the norms of society. The main force behind inner containment is a favorable self-image or concept that results from successful socialization, primarily within the family. He also recognizes three other components of inner containment: goal orientation, frustration tolerance, and retention of norms and standards.

Reckless believes that if an individual possessing a high degree of inner containment finds himself in highly containing groups or organizations, the likelihood of his becoming involved in delinquency or crime is almost nonexistent. However, the chances of criminal and delinquent involvement are maximized when both inner and outer containment are either absent or weak. They are not able to effectively operate as "buffers" against deviancy and thus restrain the person from crime.

---

[26] Walter C. Reckless, *The Crime Problem* (New York: Appleton-Century-Crofts, 1967).

The major difficulty confronting those who take the environmental approach is tracing crime to any identifiable set of environment factors. Although it seems true that crime is most prevalent where social environmental conditions are poorest, how these conditions cause human beings to commit crime is still not clearly understood.

Psychoanalysis and Crime

There have been many theories suggested to explain crime in terms of its relationship to the individual's psychological makeup. Specifically, they hold that early childhood experiences leave an indelible imprint upon the child's unconscious mind which, in turn, affects later behavior. The criminal is seen as an individual who is mentally ill, driven by unconscious motivation over which he has little or no control.

Psychoanalytic theory, conceived by Sigmund Freud (1856–1939), assumes that all human behavior is motivated and, hence, goal-oriented in character. However, neither the motives nor the purposes of any given act can be understood by observing the overt act itself. Behavior can be understood only in terms of the subjective meanings and significances that the person himself attaches to his action.

Freud believed that the structure of the personality consisted of three basic components: the id, ego, and superego. The id represents the pleasure principle and is primarily aimed at avoiding pain and obtaining pleasure. The id is the basic source of motivation for human behavior. The superego is the internal representative of the traditional values and ideas of society as interpreted to the child by his parents: it functions as the conscience of the person. It is the moral arm of the personality, representing the ideal rather than the real, and it strives for perfection rather than for pleasure. The ego is said to obey the reality principle, and its chief function is mediating between the id and superego.

Freud had little to say concerning crime, but some of those who adhere to his psychoanalytical principles have written at great length about crime and its cause. Psychoanalytic theories of crime tend to fall into three major categories or groups. The first group sees criminality as a form of neurosis. A neurotic individual may be characterized as suffering from guilt and anxiety brought about because of the overactivity of the superego with its relentless demand for perfection. Generally, it is

explanations for criminal actions   **63**

believed that the criminal neurotic suffers from a compulsive need for punishment to alleviate his unconscious guilt, so he commits crime in order to gain this punishment.

The second group describes the criminal as an antisocial person who has either a poorly developed superego or no superego at all. He is unable to cope properly with the restrictions of his society. He also lacks adequate internal controls, thus allowing the id to go unchecked. His sole basis for judging any act, then, is one of pleasure and pain.

The third group sees criminality as a product of faulty family relationships. Criminal activity is carried out to gratify needs that would usually be met and fulfilled within the family—such needs as security, recognition, acceptance, status, and self-esteem. Instead, the criminal directs his activity into illegal channels of delinquency and crime as a means of securing substitute satisfactions for his faulty family situation.

Abrahamsen, a noted psychoanalyst, believed that basically an instability of three factors leads a man to crime: criminalistic tendencies, mental resistance, and situation.[27] By criminalistic tendencies are meant the individual's subconscious desires, phobias, compulsions, and obsessions that wait for the right moment to emerge from the subconscious mind and to be acted out. He emphasizes the theory of unconscious guilt as in the neurotic, and feels that only by penetrating into the deepest layers of the human mind are we able to trace the motives that link the criminal to the past; motives of which he himself has been unaware.

Through socialization, repression, and inhibition, a person develops mental resistance that, in turn, prevents criminalistic tendencies from becoming criminal behavior. Furthermore, the more the person leans toward crime (low resistance), the weaker the precipitating events would have to be to bring it out; the less the criminal leanings, the greater the precipitating events needed to call it forth. These precipitating events Abrahamsen calls the situation. We must consider all three aspects simultaneously in order to explain crime and the individual's interaction with it.

It seems plausible that some people commit crimes because they are emotionally or psychologically unstable or defective. Occasionally one reads in the newspapers about some bizarre killing or sex crime

---

[27] David Abrahamsen, *Crime and the Human Mind* (New York: Columbia University Press, 1969).

committed by a person who is clearly mentally deranged. However, many studies of the personalities of criminals have shown that most of them are psychologically normal.[28] Furthermore, psychiatrists have often given conflicting diagnoses of criminals who have pled insanity as a defense against criminal culpability.[29]

At the present time there is no generally accepted psychological explanation for crime. The vast majority of persons defined as mentally ill are not criminals, and the majority of criminals are not mentally ill. Whatever relationships may exist between crime and mental illness must involve factors other than the mental state of the criminal. Otherwise all criminals would be mentally ill and vice versa.

The Future of Criminology

This brief review of a wide variety of explanations for crime has perhaps confused you. As we said at the beginning of this chapter, no specific causes of crime have been found, although the search has been conducted from many different points of view. The study of crime and criminals goes on at a faster pace than ever before, but there is little evidence that we are any nearer to the understanding of crime than we were one hundred years ago. One possible reason for this lack of progress may be found in the kinds of assumptions that have been made by those who have proposed explanations for crime. Almost all of the theories that we have examined have assumed that man naturally conforms to social order. In other words, they all assume that man is basically good (non-criminal) by nature. If he commits a crime, it must be because something must have gone wrong with him. His wrongdoing has been variously blamed on his mental state, his biological condition, his social environment, or his associations with others.

Perhaps the time has come for us to challenge this assumption. What kind of theory of crime would we develop if we assumed that man

---

[28] Karl R. Schuesssler and Donald R. Cressey, "Personality Characteristics of Criminals," *Am. J. Sociol.* (March 1950).

[29] See Michael Hakeem, "A Critique of the Psychiatric Approach to Delinquency and Crime," *Law and Contempt. Problems* (Autumn 1958) and Thomas J. Meyers, "The Riddle of Legal Insanity," *J. Crim. L., Crimin, and Police Sc.* 44 (1953).

was essentially *nonconforming*, and that he conformed only under certain conditions that could be personal or social in nature? The whole focus of our research would have to shift from an attempt to understand crime to an attempt to understand why there is not more crime. What keeps the majority of people from committing crime? If we knew the answer to this, we might know more about "deterrence" and "crime control"—concepts that we hear much about but so little understand.

The idea that crime is normal behavior has been suggested by a number of theorists over the years. As Merton and others have suggested, the central issue to the motivation of crime is the inability on occasion to find legitimate means to legitimate ends. They see most crime as the result of someone resorting to these illegitimate means to achieve otherwise legitimate objectives. One might assume that most of us would resort to the most efficient means available to us, legal or not, were it not for certain restraints put upon us by ourselves or others. Criminologists of the future may emphasize more research on the social-control process that keeps people within the boundaries society has set for the conduct of its members, rather than looking for causes of behavior that the law happens to define as crime.

Another assumption that has dominated criminological theory is "determinism." Determinism may be defined here as the belief that every human act and decision is the inevitable consequence of antecedents (prior events or conditions) such as traumatic (damaging) events or physical, psychological, or environmental conditions, which are independent of the human will. Until recently, most theories of crime have assumed that a particular criminal act could be explained by tracing it back to these guilty antecedents, which might be an unhappy home life, slums, alienation from school, or physical or mental defects, to name a few. Every person is a product of his antecedents; every criminal, a victim of them, forced to commit crimes by factors beyond his control. This theory held that the events or conditions that preceded the criminal act made the act itself inevitable; in the same sense that dropping a stone from a window made it inevitable the stone would fall to the ground.

Today, some contemporary theorists are challenging the deterministic view of human behavior by asserting that man is a determiner of his own future.[30] These people believe that an individual knows that his

---

[30] See David Matza, *Becoming Deviant* (Englewood Cliffs, N.J.: Prentice-Hall, 1969).

action is legally considered a crime, and is aware of the consequences if he is caught. He makes the choice of his own free will to take the risk involved in committing the crime in order to achieve his goals more effectively or efficiently than he can by legal means. This view seems to fit the world as we know it better than the complex theories that try to link criminal behavior with many complicated "causal" factors. The theory agrees that crimes may be committed on impulse, but even then they are committed with full awareness that society will punish the doer if he is found out.

In the past, the most influential theory of criminal behavior has been the "medical" model, that is, the belief that the criminal was a sick person who needed treatment in the same way as did the person with an organic illness. According to this theory, the sickness produced the criminality, and since it made no sense to punish a sick person, subscribers to this theory placed great emphasis on treatment and rehabilitation rather than on punishment. To illustrate this trend, we might point to the sharp decline in the use of punishment as a tool of social control during the past century, and the rise of counseling, therapy, and physical treatments ranging from brain surgery (lobotomies) to tranquilizers (chemotherapy).

In recent years, however, more emphasis has been placed upon considering the criminal to be a perfectly normal human being, completely responsible for his actions. Even after the conviction of a crime, a person is often allowed to continue as a free member of society, on probation. This is called reality therapy and puts the responsibility for correction on the individual himself rather than upon society. This change may indicate that we are now beginning to abandon the medical model in favor of a personal responsibility (existential) model of human behavior. This would challenge still another assumption of the past that has perhaps slowed our progress toward the control of crime.

Summary

For centuries, theories have been proposed to explain a specific cause of crime, theories based on economical factors or individual defects, such as mental illness or physical disibility. Society as a whole is often blamed because of prejudices that will not allow attainment of legitimate goals.

The studies have provided a great deal of information, but they have not given a cause for crime.

The theories have covered many different areas. Some of them are (1) administrative and legislative, (2) biophysical, (3) socioeconomic determinism, (4) crime as learned behavior, (5) environmental influences, and (6) psychoanalysis.

The study of crime and criminals goes on at a faster pace than ever before, but there is little evidence that we are nearer to understanding crime then before. The theories to date assume that man is a conforming creature; theories that assume a nonconformity may tell us more about crime.

Another assumption that has dominated criminology is determinism, which is now being challenged, as well as is the medical model.

We can make no definitive statements about the kind of theories of criminal behavior that will be developed in the future. There is evidence that some old assumptions are being challenged, and there is emerging a new theory focused on social control. It seems probable there will be less interest in attempts to explain crime as a personal "sickness" or as a result of broad social environmental conditions. The new theories will probably resemble closely the administrative and legislative theories described in this chapter, but they will also contain significant ideas from the other theories reviewed, especially the theories dealing with the social control of legitimate means of attaining social objectives.

Student Checklist

1. Can you explain the administrative and legislative theory for crime causation?
2. Can you identify three historical authors involved in the study of causal theories?
3. Are you able to explain the biophysical theory of crime causation?
4. Can you explain socioeconomic determinism as it relates to crime causal theory?
5. Are you able to explain at least two of the contemporary theories of crime causation?

Topics for Discussion

1. Discuss a comparison between the classical theories of crime causation with contemporary concepts.
2. Discuss the sociological viewpoint of crime.
3. Discuss a comparison between contemporary concepts of causal theories.

ANNOTATED BIBLIOGRAPHY

Mannheim, Hermann, ed. *Pioneers in Criminology*. Chicago: Quadrangle Books, Inc. 1960. A review of the contributions and theories of 17 European criminologists from the eighteenth through the nineteenth century.

Manheim, Hermann. *Comparative Criminology*. Boston: Houghton Mifflin Co., 1965. A comparative survey of criminalized theory in the Western World. An excellent source book covering all major theoretical approaches.

Schafer, Stephen. *Theories in Criminology: Past and Present Philosophies of the Crime Problem*. New York: Random House, 1969. Intended as a textbook, this work is a retrospective exposition of man's struggle for an insight into the problem of crime and a hint of its perspectives and prospects. All major theoretical approaches are covered in rather brief form.

Vold, George B. *Theoretical Criminology*. New York: Oxford University Press, 1958. An excellent review of criminological theory over the last two centuries.

Part Two

Evolution of the Justice System

The study of this chapter will enable you to:

1. Cite the contributions made by Sir Robert Peel.
2. Outline the origin of the word police.
3. Outline the origin of the police system in the United States.
4. Explain the historical contributions of the police departments of Boston, Philadelphia, and New York.
5. Cite examples of federal law enforcement agencies.
6. Describe some critical periods in the development of American policing.

4
The Police

The development of a police system in the United States has evolved over a long period of time, more as the result of external pressure for change than pressure from within. Today there are more than 40,000 police agencies in the United States, the majority consisting of ten men or less. This large number of individual police departments is the result of local citizens' fears of a centralized police bureaucracy and the desire for local control. The rapid proliferation of police agencies during the early 1900s, without adequate planning and coordination, has contributed to the problems facing many departments today. Only in the last twenty years have realistic efforts been made to develop minimum standards and a professional approach to police work. And because the worthwhile goals that many police departments are striving for today have not been adopted by law enforcement as a whole, the enlightened minority of police must continue to press for change if true professionalization is to come.

Historical Significance of the Police System

In attempting to understand the development of American policing we must go back to early times in Europe, where the first formal police departments began. One of the earliest police units, known as the Bow Street Runners or "Thief Takers," was formed by Henry Fielding, a London magistrate, who saw the need for such a group as early as 1725. It was not until 1750, however, that this small group of men were formed to fight crime in London.¹ Although the Bow Street Runners had some successes, their reputation was often marred by a willingness to cooperate with criminals to collect the rewards offered by citizens for the recovery of property; a practice that led to frequent instances of corruption.

Around the turn of the nineteenth century, largely as a result of the Industrial Revolution, many people began to move to the cities of Europe. During this period unemployment was high, housing was virtually impossible to find, and slums became a common sight. Crime began to rise. Riots and demonstrations became almost a daily occurrence. Policing was generally viewed as a community effort; citizens were required to take turns serving as watchmen. This system, known as the watch and ward, had been effective in the towns and villages but was inefficient in the cities. Merchants hired guards, and various types of private groups designed to meet specific crime situations were formed. Bands of thieves roamed the streets virtually at will, robbing the unprotected. When the people lost faith in the government and spoke out, greater restrictions on free expression were imposed by the government and they only worsened the problem.

Despite increasing public concern it was not until 1829 that Sir Robert Peel, the Home Secretary, after revising the criminal code to meet the needs of a reformed police service, introduced into Parliament, "An Act for Improving the Police In and Near the Metropolis." Known as The Metropolitan Police Act, this is seen by many as the beginning of modern law enforcement. The Act provided for a carefully selected police force, and was formed despite public opposition. The first 1000 policemen were selected from a list of 12,000, and during the first three years of operation there were 5000 dismissals and 6000 forced resignations; a tribute to the standards set for the fledgling department.² In less than a decade the London police force had become an accepted and admired department, and Robert Peel's name was immortalized. Even today the London policemen are referred to as Bobbies, in honor of Peel.

---

[1] Gilbert Armitage, *The History of the Bow Street Runners* (London: Wishart Books, 1932).
[2] A. C. Germann, Frank D. Day, and Robert R. J. Gallati, *Introduction to Law Enforcement and Criminal Justice* (Springfield, Ill.: Charles C. Thomas, 1972).

The term police was used by Peel in The Metropolitan Police Act, although there is some disagreement as to its actual origin. The most widely accepted view is that it comes from the Greek word *polis*, which means city, "... and it is defined as a judicial and executive system such as an organized civil force in a town or city for the preservation of the life, property, and health of the community, and for the enforcement of laws."[3]

Origins of Police in the United States

The development of a police system in the United States has been similar to that of England and other European countries in many ways, although the size of the United States and its division into sovereign states have resulted in some marked regional differences. As the settlers arrived in the United States each group brought many of the traditions of their homeland, with England having the most significant impact on American policing. The night watch, constable, and sheriff forms of policing were all English contributions to our system.

On the East coast the night-watch system, which required male citizens over the age of sixteen to serve without pay, was the most prevalent form of policing until the early 1800s. The families migrating inland and to the South and the West generally adopted the sheriff form of policing, in which an individual was either hired or elected to perform police functions, frequently in addition to another job.

These early systems provided adequate safety for citizens: people usually knew each other personally and this common bond, existing in each community, provided strong social control. Survival frequently meant depending upon one's neighbor. However, as the cities began to grow and fill with strangers, more crime problems began to develop. The night watch ultimately proved ineffective; as time went on people who were unable or unwilling to perform their watch were permitted to hire persons to take their place. Those who hired out as substitutes were frequently unfit for any work, much less as watchmen; inefficiency, laziness,

---

[3] John L. Sullivan, *Introduction to Police Science*, 2nd ed. (New York: McGraw-Hill, 1971), pp. 1, 2.

and corruption became more common. Where other forms of policing, such as the sheriff and constable systems, had been adopted, abuses of power became so frequent that by the turn of the nineteenth century there was growing unrest in virtually every American city.

The growth of police problems brought a move for reform in many cities that heralded the beginning of the modern American police system.

Development of Police Systems in the United States

The growth of American cities resulted in an increasing crime rate, and it was soon realized that a night watch was not only inefficient, but outdated. The rapid growth of American cities came as the result of immigrants arriving daily in great numbers, many without adequate funds or a job to sustain them. The growth of slums was inevitable and, in them, crime was rampant. In attempting to control the masses of the slums, those in power frequently passed laws designed to suppress the minorities—most of them recently arrived from Ireland, England, and other European countries—to "keep them in their place."

To cope with a growing crime rate, Philadelphia established a paid day and night watch in 1833 with a grant of money from Stephen Girard. The day watch consisted of 24 men and the night watch employed 120, all under the command of a captain. Promotion within the department was based on merit: this is believed to be the first police promotion system based upon capability rather than political favor.

Five years after Philadelphia established its force, Boston established a day watch that was separate from the night watch. The lack of coordination between the day and night watches created numerous problems; it was not until 1850 that they were combined.

In 1844 New York City established a police department of 800 men, headed by a chief of police. The New York department closely resembled the London department and became the model for other emerging police agencies throughout the United States.

By the middle of the nineteenth century all of the larger cities had established some form of paid police department. In the West, San Francisco founded a small police force in 1850 that grew to some 400 men by

Figure 4-1. A mounted squad of the early 1900s.

the police 77

1878. In 1851 Los Angeles formed a voluntary force of 100 men, and Chicago established a police force patterned on the New York department.

Despite the growth of formal police departments in American cities, counties and many towns continued to use a sheriff as the chief law enforcement officer. During these early years sheriffs were usually politicians and political hacks, many of whom had little interest in law enforcement. Today most states still have elected county sheriffs, although the quality of candidates has improved greatly, and most sheriff's departments are staffed by professional law enforcement officers. Unlike municipal departments, the sheriff is elected (in a few areas, appointed) to serve a county, and is responsible to a board of governors or supervisors. In many jurisdictions, especially in rural areas, the sheriff's department is the largest law enforcement agency and may be called in to assist small towns during disorders or to aid in the investigation of a major crime. Usually, the sheriff provides basic police services to unincorporated areas of the county and incorporated cities that contract for these services.

State-Level Policing
Policing on the state level came about either as a result of labor disputes or through the efforts of state legislatures to cope with corruption in the cities. The first state police agency was the Texas Rangers, formed in 1833, to deal primarily with cattle rustling. In subsequent years the Rangers broadened their powers, and today they represent a small force vested with general law enforcement powers.

The two most common assignments of state police agencies are highway patrol and assistance to small local departments in the investigation of crime, usually through the formation of state identification and investigation or intelligence units. Where state police jurisdiction is limited to highways, they usually handle crimes committed on highways as well as general traffic enforcement. Where a state agency has broad police powers, it may be responsible for the policing of towns and operate somewhat like the more traditional department, although on a broader scale, as is the case in Connecticut.

The growth of state police agencies has resulted in the greater use of technology in policing. Computerized records systems and the use of helicopters on patrol are but two examples.

Federal-Level Policing
On the federal level, the growth of law enforcement is directly related to specific national crime problems that emerged during the country's development. The authority for establishing a federal police agency rests with the Congress, and its first act in this area occurred in 1789 when the post of United States Marshal was established. Later that same year Congress created the Revenue Cutter Service to prevent smuggling.

In 1829 the Postal Act was passed, and this included a provision to employ special agents, who were redesignated Postal Inspectors in 1954. The primary role of the postal inspectors was to prevent mail fraud and, since its early beginning, the Postal Inspection Service has broadened its scope of responsibility to include any violations involving the mails. As one example of their activity, the Postal Inspectors made over 15,000 arrests in 1969.

The problem of counterfeiting brought the U.S. Secret Service into being in 1865, and since that time it has established itself as one of the more effective investigative agencies in the United States. In 1901, after the assassination of President McKinley, the Secret Service was assigned responsibility for protecting the Chief Executive and his family. This protective responsibility now extends to the Vice-President, presidential candidates, former presidents, their families, and embassies.

Twenty-five agents were hired by the Internal Revenue Service in 1868 to enforce income tax laws, and in 1870 the Department of Justice was formed, largely as a result of problems arising from the Civil War. But it was not until 1908 that President Theodore Roosevelt, recognizing the need for a federal investigative unit in the Department of Justice, authorized formation of the Bureau of Investigation. In 1924 J. Edgar Hoover, a 29-year-old lawyer, was appointed director of the Bureau. Hoover's contributions to American law enforcement are now legend, and during his tenure he did more than change the name of the agency to the Federal Bureau of Investigation. Today the FBI is viewed as one of the most effective law enforcement agencies in the United States, and it has jurisdiction over almost 200 federal crimes. The Bureau continues to be the largest and most prestigious law enforcement agency, employing over 7000 enforcement personnel.

Today there are over 50 federal agencies with some kind of law enforcement responsibility. The U.S. Department of Justice, headed by the Attorney General, incorporates the Federal Bureau of Investigation, the Drug Enforcement Administration, replacing the Bureau of Narcotics and Dangerous Drugs, the Immigration and Naturalization Service, and the Law Enforcement Assistance Administration (LEAA) which, while it does not have enforcement powers, is vested with the responsibility for assisting state and local law enforcement agencies in research, planning, and development.

The Department of the Treasury, in addition to having responsibility for the Secret Service, houses the Customs Department, the Internal Revenue Service, and the Alcohol, Tobacco, and Firearms Division of the IRS.

Every federal agency has some form of investigative arm or relies upon another agency to carry out its routine investigations. In most cases this involves background investigations on prospective employees and other similar assignments. Most of the criminal work accomplished by federal agencies falls within the domain of the Justice or the Treasury Departments. The work carried out by these agencies is frequently different than that of local police departments and, in large measure, their tasks are not related. For this reason there is little comparison between local, state, and federal law enforcement agencies, at least in terms of their functions. During the past 200 years the development of American policing has been rife with problems, many of them related to the country's history, and many of them unique to policing.

Critical Periods of Development in American Policing

Perhaps the most crucial factor prohibiting the development of professional policing in the United States has been a lack of adequate concern by the people, which might have led to better planning and support. Throughout the nation's history police have played a major role, yet in most cities they are not held in high esteem, despite the lip service that is paid to professionalization. No doubt, much of the fault lies with the police service itself, which until recently has not attempted to achieve the high standards and qualifications of those professions they wish to emulate.

The Early Years

The concept of organized policing in the United States did not really take shape until the turn of the nineteenth century, when most of the larger cities in the United States saw the need for some form of organized force to handle the growing crime problems. James Richardson believes that,

> ... The children of the foreign born suspended between two cultures and often learning the ways of the city more quickly than their parents, provided the raw material for the "dangerous classes."[4]

The rapid growth of slums and high unemployment contributed to the crime problem. In Chicago the great fire of 1871 not only leveled the city, but it brought new criminals in its aftermath, thereby adding to the problems of the Chicago police.[5] In the West law enforcement was more often than not carried out by Vigilantes, whose system of justice left much to be desired. Nathaniel Pitt Langford in *Vigilante Days and Ways: The Pioneers of the Rockies* describes the activities of Vigilantes in bringing law and order to the West.[6] His accounts of the tracking and hanging of robbers and thieves are in sharp contrast to present standards. The law was tempered with little mercy in those days.

During the early years corruption in policing was not uncommon, and it ranged from paying a city official to obtain a job, to the acceptance of bribes by policemen. Frequently, a new political administration meant an entirely new police department because police jobs were political appointments. As Richardson points out, "Many local and subsequently state political leaders looked upon the police department primarily as a source of patronage and a tool for swaying elections."[7]

In 1894 the New York State legislature formed the Lexow Commission to investigate the New York City Police Department. The Commission produced a report that highlighted many of the problems facing municipal police departments at that time. Unfortunately, its impact was relatively small, and few changes were made to improve the New York City department. During those years, gross lack of discipline,

---

[4] James F. Richardson, *The New York Police: Colonial Times to 1901* (New York: Oxford University Press, 1970), p. 51.
[5] John J. Flinn, *History of the Chicago Police* (New York: AMS Press, reprint, 1973), p. 137.
[6] Nathaniel Pitt Langford, *Vigilante Days and Ways: The Pioneers of the Rockies* (New York: AMS Press, reprint, 1973).
[7] Richardson, *The New York Police*, p. 54.

dishonesty, drunkenness, and extortion were the rule rather than the exception on city police departments, and during the latter part of the nineteenth century—frequently called the Spoils Era—American police morality was at its lowest.

By the turn of the century the spotlight of reform was on the police, and many departments began to change. Probably the most significant innovation in municipal policing was the adoption of the civil service concept.

Civil service was designed to remove politics from policing, by requiring police appointees to pass objective tests—the theory being that a written examination would reduce favoritism and insure impartiality. Most major police departments today have adopted the civil service system, although its requirements vary from area to area. Some departments require only a written examination, while others require a combination written-oral examination. The use of psychological examinations has also become popular in recent years.

While the civil service system did have beneficial effects on police selection, little was done to change the nature and working conditions of police during the early years, and little or no emphasis was placed upon education and training. Indeed, the best policeman was often viewed as the one who was the toughest, and brawn took precedence over brains.

The Turn of the Century

By 1900 the police had become a generally accepted part of the community, and departments were beginning to place greater emphasis upon selection by merit. Political influence, although still present, was lessening. In 1919, however, Congress ratified the Eighteenth Amendment (Prohibition) to curb the sale of liquor in the United States. Between 1920 and 1933 (when the Amendment was repealed), the police were burdened with the responsibility of enforcing a law that was almost universally unpopular. The police reaction generally was to ignore violations of Prohibition or to become involved themselves in the bootlegging activities brought about by the laws. Graft and corruption were common during this period, and many believe that Prohibition served more to hurt policing than it did to help the public.

The National Commission on Law Observance and Enforcement, known as the Wickersham Commission, was charged with investigating police abuses and procedures. Its 1931 report raised serious questions about law enforcement in the United States. Unfortunately, few of the Commission's recommendations were followed in the years following the report's publication.

Curiously, the depression years (1932–40), which hurt the public, had a beneficial effect on the police occupation. The large number of unemployed persons created a vast pool of manpower from which police agencies could draw. A different type of individual entered police service, some of whom were college graduates who could not find other jobs. This influx raised the general educational level of law enforcement agencies, and is viewed by many as the beginning of a new era in law enforcement.

In some measure, the beneficial changes brought about by the depression were slowed with the outbreak of World War II, which caused a manpower shortage. During the war years policing was generally stagnant, and few changes were made that improved the quality of police work. However, as the war drew to a close, and veterans began to return, many of whom had been policemen, the public once again began to focus upon the law-and-order issue. Organized crime came under greater scrutiny, and pressure was placed upon the police to control a rising crime rate.

An Era of Change

Returning veterans of World War II brought with them many new ideas; perhaps the most significant being the need for training in police work. Prior to 1945 training was sparse and haphazard, and it generally involved an in-service approach. The Federal Bureau of Investigation provided some training for middle-management personnel, but this was limited. By 1950 all of the large police departments had begun to examine their training needs to establish more relevant training programs. The emphasis during these years was on the legal, physical, and procedural—the rule book aspects of law enforcement. The move toward training based upon human relations was to come later. Nevertheless, it was a beginning; police departments had taken the first step toward providing a professional police service.

During this period the nation was beginning to change. A period of prosperity created new optimism; business began to boom, and each person set out to realize his own dream. But for the minorities, who inhabited the slums of our cities, swelled in numbers by a huge influx of blacks from rural areas, the American dream was hollow.

In the short period between 1950 and 1960 policing began to change once again. Law enforcement now included traffic enforcement. The foot patrolman was rapidly becoming a thing of the past; a new concept of policing removed patrolmen from the intimacy of the neighborhood, enclosing him in the metal and glass of a patrol car. The white middle class had begun their exodus to the suburbs, leaving the inner city to the minorities and the poor. The public's perception of the police, especially in the slums of the cities, was usually limited by seeing them only in a crisis or emergency situation or in a traffic incident. The personal aspect of police work, which was more common in the smaller towns and villages, virtually disappeared in the larger cities. And with the mass production of television, the public was introduced to a new image of law enforcement, through the eyes of the script writers.

The Korean war had little noticeable impact on policing, at least from an economic standpoint. New veterans returned, many of them entering law enforcement. The military model within police work was firmly established, and selection and training were geared toward the military concept. Most police departments had begin to think about professionalization and, in California, efforts were being made to stress the importance of education in law enforcement.

By 1960 the civil-rights movement had begun to pick up strength throughout the South, and efforts were being made in the northeastern and midwestern cities to inform the populace of the discrimination against black minorities. Soon police departments became objects of racial criticism, both for harshness in their daily contacts with blacks and for their "lily-white" employment policies. The urban disorders of the 1960s brought the hostility into the open, and police departments were faced with a new challenge—riots. The initial police reaction was frequently ineffectual. The establishment of community relations units and the addition of a few hours of riot control training did little to relieve the tensions between the police and minorities. The report of the National Advisory Commission on Civil Disorders pointed up a significant failure on the part of both the police and the community to deal with the problems of minorities.

Aware of their inadequacies in the field of race relations, the police responded by developing training programs that invited community participation, and they began placing a greater emphasis on the human relations aspects of police work. These efforts continue today, and their overall impact still is questionable.

Since the mid-1950s the nation has faced an increasingly severe drug problem. The use of narcotics and dangerous drugs by young people has continued to grow, and this phenomenon has added greatly to the police burden. Since the beginning of the 1970s the problem has reached epidemic proportions. The police have responded by making more and more arrests of users and only infrequently do they reach the sources of distribution. The results have been disastrous for thousands of young people caught up in the criminal justice system.

The narcotics and dangerous drug problem has continued to proliferate. Only in recent years have attempts been made to try new approaches, by affording treatment to addicts and concentrating law enforcement efforts on the pushers and traffickers. The police once again—as they did during Prohibition—have fallen victim to a nationwide problem created by law. In some cities the results have been disastrous, fostering corruption, illegal arrests, and the misuse of police resources.

Demonstrations resulting from the protest against the Vietnam war also contributed to a growing hostility between the police and young people. The tendency of the police to meet this tide of violence that swept the country with violence has strained the youthful public's trust in law enforcement.

More and more public concern resulted in the appointment of the President's Commission on Law Enforcement and the Administration of Justice in 1965. In 1967 the Commission submitted a report that called for sweeping changes in policing. Six years later few of the recommendations have been carried out, although there are significant signs of a willingness on the part of many police administrators to adopt the recommendations.

In recent years many departments have begun to stress higher education, and a new breed of policeman is now entering the ranks. Most departments have stressed the recruiting of minorities into policing, and, while slow, some gains are being made. The use of new technology in policing—especially computerized information systems and criminalistics—has also brought change, and the establishment of the Law Enforcement Assistance Administration on a national level has served as a catalyst for introducing these new educational and scientific innovations into police work. Many police departments have begun to move toward professionalization and, in doing so, they have begun to place greater

Figure 4-2. The early tendency of the police to meet violence with violence during demonstrations against the Vietnam war created great strains between the youth of our country and the police.

emphasis upon a college education for entrance. This posture is more likely to result in the recruitment of individuals who are prepared to make more complex decisions.

From the public's standpoint, the patrolman of today has come a long way; he is better educated, better trained, and is more aware of society's problems. Despite this, policing is only now on the threshhold of a new generation. In many ways the police are at the crossroads, and only the future holds the outcome.

Summary

The evolution of police systems in the United States has been a long, drawn-out process, with relatively little change in the basic concepts and philosophy of law enforcement. In more recent years police departments have begun to place greater stress on education, training, and technology, and today we are beginning to witness a new era in police service.

Figure 4-3. The policeman of today is better educated, better trained: he is moving toward professionalization.

With roots in the European model of policing, law enforcement in the United States closely resembles that of England, where Robert Peel pioneered the Metropolitan Police Act in 1829. The rapid growth of our cities combined with the Industrial Revolution resulted in a recognition of the need for organized police departments. By the mid-nineteenth century every major American city had its own police force. During those early years, corruption and political favoritism were the rule rather than the exception, and it was not until the turn of the twentieth century that Civil Service became widely accepted.

The onset of Prohibition contributed to the deterioration and disrespect of law enforcement by the public and, during this period, graft and corruption were not uncommon. Although the depression years had a negative impact on the country, they are generally viewed as having had a positive impact on policing, because many well-qualified individ-

the police **87**

uals, who could not find employment elsewhere, chose to enter law enforcement.

By the end of World War II the police service was beginning to question its progress and development and, with the manpower pool created by returning veterans, new ideas and a greater recognition of the need for training took hold. Training programs became a common aspect of most major police departments, and many of the smaller departments created regional training programs, or worked in cooperation with the larger cities. As America entered a period of unequalled growth in the 1950s, police departments began to share in the progress. However, for the minorities, law enforcement was frequently viewed with skepticism and outright hostility. As automobiles became commonplace, the police developed new patrol strategies, which often had the effect of removing them from the streets. By 1960 the civil-rights movement had begun to spread across the land; and the urban riots of the sixties further alienated the police and a large segment of the population. This, combined with an increasing drug problem, taxed even the most progressive departments.

The report of the President's Commission on Law Enforcement and the Administration of Justice in 1968 resulted in a recognition of the need for greater change. Sparked by federal assistance, police departments began to develop new and innovative programs, many of which are still in the embryonic stages. The concept of professionalization has begun to take hold dramatically, and throughout the nation a greater emphasis on training and education, combined with technological advances, are apt to leave a distinct impression on the police of the future.

Student Checklist

1. Can you cite two contributions made by Sir Robert Peel to the modern police system?
2. Can you outline the origin of the word police?
3. Can you outline the origin of the police system in the United States?
4. Are you able to explain the historical contributions made by the police agencies of Boston, Philadelphia, and New York?
5. Can you cite three examples of federal law enforcement agencies?

6. Are you able to list two examples of critical periods in the development of American policing?

Topics for Discussion

1. Discuss how the American police system came into being.
2. Discuss the difference between city, county, state, and federal law enforcement responsibilities.
3. Discuss the philosophy of policing in contemporary times.

ANNOTATED BIBLIOGRAPHY

Coffey, A.; E. Eldefonso; and W. Hartinger. *Human Relations: Law Enforcement in a Changing Community*. Englewood Cliffs, N.J.: Prentice-Hall, 1971. Covers the relationship of the police to the community, racial and community tension, community relations, and police approaches to dealing with human relations problems.

Germann, A. C.; F. Day; and R. J. Gallati. *Introduction to Law Enforcement and Criminal Justice*. Springfield, Ill.: Charles C. Thomas, 1970. Covers philosophical, historical, and constitutional aspects of law enforcement and criminal justice. Describes the processes of criminal justice and the various agencies of the system.

Hahn, Harlan. *Police in Urban Society*. Beverly Hills: Sage, 1970. Develops the growth of police problems, public perceptions of the police, police perceptions of public issues, and the emergence of police professionalism. Covers a wide range of material of interest to the student of policing.

More, Harry W., Jr. *Critical Issues in Law Enforcement*. Cincinnati: W. H. Anderson, 1972. A book of readings that have been integrated into the general text, providing an in-depth analysis of the police and their problems. Includes sections on the police in a free society, ethnic tensions and the police, the police and enforcement of law, civil disobedience and disorder, police conduct and unionization, civil disturbances and riots, and police professionalization.

Niederhoffer, A., and A. Blumberg. *The Ambivalent Force: Perspectives on the Police*. Xerox College Publishing: Mass., 1970. A comprehensive book of readings relating to all aspects of policing, including the social and historical setting, the police role, organization and control, values and culture, police discretion, the police and society, police and the legal system, and critiques of the police.

Skolnick, J. *Justice Without Trial: Law Enforcement in Democratic Society*. New York: Wiley, 1966. A comprehensive analysis of policing in two communities, this work provides the reader with an in-depth analysis of police work in two diverse cities.

The President's Commission on Law Enforcement and Administration of Justice. *Task Force Report: The Police*. Washington, D.C.:

U.S. Government Printing Office, 1967. The most comprehensive study of policing ever undertaken. This report covers an analysis of various aspects of policing, including patrol, specialization, supervision, technology, and police management.

Wilson, J. Q. *Varieties of Police Behavior: The Management of Law and Order in Eight Communities.* Cambridge, Mass.: Harvard University Press, 1968. This work covers an analysis of various "styles" of policing in the United States, and it identifies varying philosophies in different departments. A good description of the police role, administration, police discretion, and the impact of politics on policing.

The study of this chapter will enable you to:

1. Cite the constitutional authority for the development of inferior courts in America.
2. Give examples of social inequities that appear to be built into the judicial system.
3. Define the job responsibilities of paraprofessionals in judicial functions.
4. Define common law and trace its historical significance.
5. Outline the reasons justifying punishment under our current system of justice.
6. Trace the origin and development of the court systems of justice in America.

5

The Courts

No one can put his finger on a certain date in history and say, "This is when courts of law came into existence." Courts did not spring forth fully developed at any specific point in time, they evolved over a long period from primitive institutions and procedures. Courts could not have existed before there were written laws, although in the dim past the headman of a tribe dividing an animal (slain for food) among his people performed some of the functions of a judge. About 2000 B.C. the Code of Hammurabi (King of Babylon, 1947 B.C.–1905 B.C.), was engraved in 4000 lines of writing on a pillar of stone. This code of law covered crimes of adultery, personal violence, sorcery, and many others, and set forth the penalty for each violation. The Code had three essential features: individual responsibility for personal acts; belief in the sanctity of oaths sworn before God; and the necessity of producing written evidence in all charges made alleging violations of the Code. These features survive today in our court system.

Since the law was written and unquestionably enforced, some form of tribunals (courts) must have existed—perhaps in the form of a king or governor sitting as the sole judge and jury to decide guilt or innocence from the evidence presented.

Nineveh, the ancient capital of the Assyrian world, had tribunals that, according to ancient writings, meted out sentences to murderers, thieves, and adulterers. Egypt, one of the most ancient of civilizations, had a system of courts as early as 1500 B.C., punishing bribery and corruption. Enforcement of tax collection was one of the earliest forms of crimes referred to royal tribunals. Amenhotep, King of Egypt, in

1400 B.C. set up custom houses on his seacoast and punished tax evaders in special courts.

Since our original court systems in the United States were established under the influence of our British colonial heritage, the ancient origins of English courts are of interest to us. Courts in early Anglo-Saxon times, such as the courts of *pied poudre* ("dusty feet"), were set up in the county markets to handle minor matters with local officials appointed by the king sitting as judges. Certain practices that are in use today originated in these courts. The practice of suspending sentence, or withholding penalty on condition that the offender make restitution or reform his habits, developed in these courts as well as the practice of release on personal recognizance, whereby people who had sworn not to flee were given freedom until the date of their trial. Generally speaking, the sentences handed down by these courts were retaliatory—blinding, maiming, and execution were common forms of punishment.

Our system is based on the British common law that originated in decisions rendered by the English royal courts that were established by Henry II in the twelfth century. The basis of this law is legal precedent. In other words, the court looks backward to former court decisions in order to determine what the law is.

In the strict sense we do not have an American court system. We have 50 individual state court systems and one federal court system. These systems differ among themselves in some ways that may confuse the student, but they are similar in many other ways because they developed from a common British heritage and therefore show a strong family resemblance to each other. We shall concern ourselves mainly with criminal courts (as opposed to civil courts) that are the heart of justice administration in the United States. In general, we shall concentrate on the similarities of these courts, rather than on their dissimilarities, because it would be far beyond the scope of this book to attempt to describe each of the 50 systems in detail.

In the United States, courts originate from three sources; that is, they are created by three authorities: (1) the U.S. Constitution, (2) the state constitutions, and (3) legislative enactments. Therefore, there are two general types of courts in the United States, as far as their creation is concerned—constitutional courts and legislative courts. Remember that when we use the term constitutional court we mean a court created either by the U.S. Constitution or the constitution of a sovereign state.

When we use the term legislative court, we mean one created by the U.S. Congress or the legislature of a sovereign state.

Historical Perspective: The Federal Experience

Article III, Sections 1 and 2 of the U.S. Constitution, under the heading "The Judicial Division," provides for a federal court system.

Article III

Section 1. The judicial power of the United States, shall be vested in one supreme court, and in such inferior courts as the Congress may from time to time ordain and establish. The judges, both of the supreme and inferior courts, shall hold their offices during good behaviour, and shall, at stated times, receive for their services, a compensation, which shall not be diminished during their continuance in office.

Section 2. The judicial power shall extend to all cases, in law and equity, arising under this constitution, the laws of the United States, and treaties made, or which shall be made, under their authority; to all cases affecting ambassadors, other public ministers and consuls; to all cases of admiralty and maritime jurisdiction; to controversies to which the United States shall be a party; to controversies between two or more States; between a State and citizens of another State; between citizens of different States; between citizens of the same state claiming lands under grants of different States, and between a State, or the Citizens thereof, and foreign States, citizens, or subjects.

In all cases affecting ambassadors, other public ministers and consuls, and those in which a state shall be part, the supreme court shall have original jurisdiction. In all the other cases before mentioned, the supreme court shall have appellate jurisdiction, both as to law and fact, with such exceptions, and under such regulations as the Congress shall make.

The trial of all crimes, except in cases of impeachment, shall be by jury; and such trial shall be held in the state where the said crimes shall have been committed; but when not committed within any state, the trial shall be at such place or places as the Congress may by Law have directed.

Note to students: The number of Supreme Court judges is not specified in the Constitution. The original number was six; it is now nine. The number has varied from four to nine over the years. Congress has the power to change the number.

As can be noted above, Article III of the Constitution provides for a Supreme Court and allows Congress to establish inferior courts as they deem necessary. The Constitutional Convention of 1787 could not agree upon a specific framework for the federal court system and thus, Article III, by giving the power to Congress, represents a compromise. The first Congress, by passing the Judiciary Act of 1789, did establish an inferior court system that lasted, with some exceptions in its basic form, for over a century. The Judiciary Act of 1789 provided for a federal court district in each of the states. Congress also divided the country into three federal circuit court districts with two Supreme Court justices assigned to ride the circuit. Together with one district court judge, they would hold two sessions annually and hear appeals from district courts. Additionally, they had original jurisdiction to try some types of cases.

In 1801 the Federalists attempted to modify the system in two ways. First, they eliminated the circuit riding of the judges; second, they enlarged the jurisdiction of the inferior courts. When the Jeffersonian Republicans took office in 1802, the Judiciary Act was repealed. Congress, at that time, divided the country into six circuits. They also reinstituted the circuit riding by the justices of the Supreme Court.

In 1869 the basic structure was modified. The Act of 1869 provided for one circuit court judge for each of the circuits. Supreme Court justices were required to sit with the circuit court only once every two years.

Congress made major modifications in the federal judicial system again in 1891 when they removed the appellate jurisdiction from the circuit courts and created a Circuit Court of Appeal from each circuit. The Act of 1891 itself was changed in 1911 when the circuit courts were abolished and their jurisdiction was assumed by the district courts. The name of the Circuit Court of Appeal was changed in 1958 to Courts of Appeal.

Historical Perspective: California Experience

Each of the states has a judicial system that reflects its history and socio-economic needs. As our society has changed from rural/agricultural to urbanized/industrial, the judicial system has also changed. The change in the court system has not been as rapid as in some other areas of government, however.

The California Constitution of 1849, like the U.S. Constitution, provided for a judicial branch of state government. Unlike its federal counterpart, the California Constitution was specific in spelling out the judicial framework. The courts that were provided were:
1. Supreme court, with a chief justice and two associate justices with terms of office of six years.
2. District courts, to be held in each district as established by the legislature. The judges would hold office for six years.
3. County courts, one in each county and the judges to hold office for four years.
4. Courts of sessions, held by a county judge and two justices of the peace.
5. Municipal courts, established by the legislature.
6. Justice courts, elected in each county, city, or town.

When the California Constitution convention delegates were considering the judicial article, they studied constitutions of other states. The Constitutions of Texas, Iowa, and New York were to some degree copied.

The California Legislature exercised its authority to modify the judicial structure on several occasions between the years 1849 and 1879, when a new constitution was adopted. The new constitution created three courts of appeal and abolished the district courts. This change in the judicial structure reflected the increasing importance of the counties. County courts were changed in name to superior courts, and they assumed the jurisdiction of the abolished district courts.

The state's increasing population was reflected in the appellate overload facing the Supreme Court. The new courts of appeal were intended to meet this need.

The judicial section of the California Constitution has been amended on several occasions since 1879, always with the purpose of restructuring the system to meet contemporary needs. In 1925, municipal courts were added to the structure to reduce the workload of the Superior Court. The Court Reorganization Amendment, passed in 1950, was another attempt at court modernization.

Nelson has stated that:
"The objectives of the 1950 reorganization plan were to reduce the number and types of courts, to have a court structure adaptable to urban and rural areas, to have a court reasonably accessible to the

inhabitants of each community, and to have a uniform system throughout the state responsive to changing conditions. . . . The 1950 reorganization of the lower courts was the most important reform to take place in the California judicial system in the past 100 years.[1]

Since 1950 there have been other efforts at streamlining the California courts. One proposal was the establishment of a single trial court. Under this proposal the municipal, justice, and superior courts would be merged into a countywide court.

In 1970 a bill was introduced into the California Legislature that would, in effect, create a separate judicial department under the control of the State Judicial Council. The trial courts would be consolidated as mentioned above. One difference is that in some instances counties would be combined to form a district court. Also, several courts would be grouped together under a chief judge and court administrator.

Court reform and reorganization appears to be taking a series of steps forward in California and elsewhere. First, there is an effort to simplify the structure by structuring it into a two-tier or three-tier level. The two-tier structure would consist of (1) the appellate level and (2) a unified trial court. In the three-tier system there would be an added court of limited jurisdiction below the unified trial court.

Strong state control by a supreme court is also a goal. Using this concept all budgets, personnel matters, and even physical facilities would come under this court. There would be a strong court administrator to manage this system. Alaska and Hawaii currently are organized in this manner.

Justice Inequities

Certain social inequities were, of past necessity, built into the judicial system. These have led to contemporary demands for judicial reform. One of these is the bail-bond system.

Traditionally, in order for a defendant to obtain pretrial release from custody after being charged with a crime, he had to post bail in the form of cash or property in an amount set by the judge. If he failed

---

[1] Dorothy W. Nelson, "Should Los Angeles County Adopt a Single-trial-court Plan?," *Southern California Law Review, 33* (1960), pp. 117, 119.

to appear for trial, this bail was forfeited by the court.

This system discriminated against the poor who had to remain in jail because they did not have money to post the bond or pay a fee to a professional bondsman. As a result, the defendant suffered in several ways. First, he could not maintain his employment. This generally placed his family on some form of public support. Thus, the taxpayer not only had to pay for the maintenance of the man while he was in custody, but also had to support his family.

Second, since the defendant was confined to jail, he could not participate fully in the preparation of his defense. Counsel (if he had one) was hampered in not having easy access to his client in preparing his case for trial. Finally, the system of justice suffered if the defendant was found not guilty. The injustice of confinement to jail for a long period of time and later being acquitted could cause a bitter and extreme reaction against the system.

Studies today question the legality of using economic motivation as the principal support of the bail system. The pretrial release of those judged to be good risks without cash bail, commonly known as "own recognizance release," has proven generally successful. Statistics indicate that as many defendants released on their own recognizance have responded for trial as those who posted cash bail. The criteria of release is usually based upon community stability, employment patterns, and other values derived from middle-class concepts.

Another systems defect is the matter of counsel for those accused of a crime. Historically, people charged with a crime have had to provide their own counsel or attempt to defend themselves as best they could. Congress specified early in our history that in federal capital cases counsel must be provided at no expense to the defendant if he had no money. Generally, this provision was not required in the states.

As the issue developed, more and more states adopted the federal concept of providing counsel for the indigent. In *Powell* v. *Alabama*, 287 U.S. 45 (1932), the Supreme Court held that the denial of effective counsel to an indigent defendant was a failure to provide due process of law. With this decision, the Court extended the right to counsel to those charged with state *capital* offenses. (Capital offenses are those punishable with death.)

In *Betts* v. *Brady*, 316 U.S. 455 (1942), the Supreme Court held that states were not required to furnish counsel at trial to every defendant unable to pay for counsel. From the decision one can infer that the

Court was apprehensive of the logical lengths to which this extension would or could go.

However, in 1963, in *Gideon* v. *Wainwright*, 372 U.S. 335 (1963), the Court did extend the right to counsel to those charged with noncapital felony offenses in state courts. The Court ruled that the right to counsel at the time of trial was essential and further found that if a defendant is unable to employ counsel, one must be provided.

The question unanswered in this case was—did the right to counsel extend to misdemeanor cases? The "petty offense" standard was not ruled upon. Consideration was not given at that time as to what was expressed as "effective assistance." To a great degree these questions have been resolved by later decisions providing for counsel at all states of the proceedings. The Court has also adopted a standard that has as its criteria the possible loss of liberty for the defendant.

The old axiom, "justice delayed is justice denied" was never more pertinent. The civil litigant and the criminal defendant are entitled to a speedy trial, yet, in most parts of the country this does not occur. When a case is not heard promptly by a court, what are the resultant consequences? If the lawsuit is concerned with damages for personal injury, an indigent victim may be pressured by delay into accepting a reduced settlement. Undue delays cause problems with witnesses; they disappear or their memories fade.

In criminal cases, delays tend to be shorter, but the results may be more damaging. The indigent suspect may have to spend considerable time in custody, or to be released, he may be forced to engage in plea bargaining and perhaps even plead guilty to an offense he did not commit, in order to expedite release from custody.

What has been done to reduce court delay? The first approach has been normally to increase the number of judges available to try cases. This works, but with limitations, because of the high costs involved. It has been estimated that annual expenses run over $100,000, exclusive of salaries, to maintain one courtroom operational.

Plea bargaining is another activity used to reduce court congestion. The district attorney and the defendant's counsel engage in prehearing bargaining sessions with the prosecutor trying to get defense counsel to plead his client guilty to the highest category of crime, while the defense counsel tries to make a deal to plead to a lesser offense. This activity is necessary at this time, because without plea bargaining, the courts would collapse under their caseloads. Chief Justice Warren Burger has been quoted as stating that the judicial system can operate only because 90 percent of those charged with offenses plead guilty.

What effect does this process have on the values of society? Consider the victim who observes the offender charged with armed robbery pleading guilty to a lesser charge. Does he understand the caseload pressures exerted on the district attorney and the courts that force them to channel as many cases as possible through the system in the shortest time? In all probability he does not—and he loses his respect for the system. In some instances we find defendants who plead guilty to lesser offenses when they have reasonable defenses. The uncertainties of a jury trial are stressed by their attorneys to obtain consent to a quick guilty plea in exchange for a fine or short sentence. Here, the defendant will lose his respect for the system.

There are two solutions to the trial delay problem that have been used effectively. Some states have legally defined what constitutes a speedy trial. In California, for example, if the party charged is in custody on a misdemeanor charge, he must be brought to trial within 30 days. In instances where a misdemeanor citation has been issued, his trial must be held within 45 days. If the defendant does not waive his right to a speedy trial and his case is not heard within this period of time, it must be dismissed.

Another solution has been to utilize paraprofessionals to handle minor judicial functions so that the judges can concentrate on more important cases. In some states "referees" and "commissioners" are appointed to hear traffic violations and divorce matters.

The jury process itself has come under attack as creating court delay due to the time spent in jury selection and deliberation. To shorten selection and deliberation time, it has been suggested that the size of the jury be reduced from the traditional 12 members to 6, or that a majority only be necessary to reach a verdict of guilty or innocent, rather than a unanimous vote. Some states, such as Florida and Washington, have adopted the six-member jury to expedite the legal processes.

Foreign Judicial Systems

We have already discussed the concept of law on which the Anglo-American judicial systems are based with roots in the British common law. Common law, based on traditional customs and practices, was developed between the fifteenth and nineteenth centuries; the word "common" was used to denote its acceptance throughout England instead of local laws.

In contrast, most of the Western European countries base their concept of law upon "civil law." Civil law is, in turn, based upon a blend of church (canon) law, medieval law, and Roman law. These laws were consolidated and written (codified) into the Code Napoleon from 1800–1810. During the period of Napoleonic domination of Western Europe the Code was imposed in all conquered territories. After Napoleon's defeat at Waterloo and his subsequent exile, most European countries retained his code of law.

A primary difference between the two concepts (common and civil law) is the guidance provided judges in adjudicating cases. In "code" countries, judges theoretically base their findings strictly on the written code and are not allowed to consider past court decisions. In contrast, the Anglo-American common law system theoretically requires the judges to rely upon past court decisions (*stare decisis*). The legislatures played a minor role in the development of common law, but have since written most common laws into the state codes.

The differences, either historical or philosophical, are less significant today than they were one hundred years ago. Modern society is gradually forcing the British and American lawmakers to pass laws with a far greater amount of detail than in the past. The Western European judge is finding that he must occasionally make some laws rather than rely solely on the codes.

Contrasts with Other Systems

The judicial system of the United States is described in some length in Chapter 10, but we should consider a general contrast of our system with the systems of several other countries at this point.

The British System. The British judicial system is considered by most to be more complex than our system. At the lower levels there are two separate court systems; one for criminal matters and the other for civil (noncriminal) matters. The states of Texas and Oklahoma have similar structures except that the division extends to the courts of last resort (supreme courts), although in England criminal and noncriminal use the same appellate system.

The English criminal court system has three levels. In rural areas there are justices of the peace and, in cities, magistrates try misdemeanor cases. At the next higher level, the Quarter Session courts try less important felony cases. At the top is the Assize Court, which hears the most important felony cases.

The American judicial system relies upon a grand jury to function as a review body to pass judgment upon whether or not a crime has occurred and whether there is reasonable belief that the defendant committed it. This process is based upon English common law practice. The English discarded this practice in 1933 and have used the preliminary examination exclusively in felony cases.

The French System. The French judicial structure is more complicated than either the English or American because the French provide more specialized courts. Some of these are juvenile courts, labor relations courts, farm problems courts, social security courts, and commercial law courts.

This degree of specialization is followed in the United States to some degree, with some specialized courts and administrative bodies that hear judicial matters. Similar courts do not exist in England.

In France the lowest court is the Court of Instance that hears misdemeanor cases. At the next higher level is the Court of Major Instance with two divisions: the correctional tribunal and the civil section. This court hears low-grade felonies and civil litigation. They also hear appeals from Courts of Instance. As in England, at the top of the trial court structure is the Assize Court that hears the serious felonies.

The highest French court is the Court of Cossation. Its rulings have somewhat the same effect as those of the United States Supreme Court, except that they rarely deal with public policy.

The U.S.S.R. System. The legal system of the U.S.S.R. has had no effect on the Western world, but it is interesting in its evolution. When the Russian Revolution occurred in 1918, one of the first acts of the Soviet authorities was to abolish all courts, retaining only those whose laws were not specifically annulled by the new government.

The Soviet court system has been restructured several times, the last occurring in 1960. The present organization is three-tiered: People's Court, Regional Court, and Supreme Court.

The People's Courts are the courts at the lowest level located in rural districts and towns. Their jurisdictions cover all matters not specifically assigned to a higher court. The crime categories are not comparable to those in the Western countries. People's Court jurisdiction covers:

1. State crimes.
2. Crimes against state property.
3. Crimes against the political and working rights of citizens.
4. Crimes against private property of citizens.
5. Crimes against the administrative order.

Regional courts have jurisdiction over felony-type cases and crimes such as anti-Soviet propaganda and disclosure of state secrets. The Supreme Court of each Republic has broad jurisdiction over all cases of special interest.

Some Significant Differences

The judicial selection processes in philosophy and procedures vary widely among different countries. In the United States, popular control and political considerations are the dominant concerns. The British do not consider these factors important, but they do show some consideration for them.

The French consider neither popular control nor political considerations of importance; they are concerned with the level of training of judges. But judges in the U.S.S.R. must have the political support of the Communist party. Nominations of office are made by party organizations only.

The primary selection process is popular election in the United States. The Soviet judges—within the confines of the Communist party—are also chosen by an elective process, similar to any other election. It has been stated that in the 1965 Soviet elections candidates for judge received 99.56 percent of the total votes cast.[2]

---

[2] Robert Conquest, ed., *Justice and the Legal System in the U.S.S.R.* (New York: Praeger, 1968).

All British judges are appointed by the Lord Chancellor or by the Prime Minister. Although judges of the lowest criminal and civil courts are not required to have legal training, judges appointed to the high courts must have been barristers (trial lawyers) for a minimum of 10 years. This is similar to the rules of various states requiring that to qualify as a judge, a lawyer should have practiced a specified number of years.

In France, the practice used in judicial appointments is different in that the potential judge follows a different curriculum in law school than that prescribed for attorneys. After completion of law school, he must take a series of competitive examinations for admission to the National Center for Judicial Studies. Upon completion of a four-year course, the graduate is appointed to the Court of Instance.

There are no constitutional requirements for the candidate to have any legal training or experience in the U.S.S.R. It is estimated that in 1965 only 80.9 percent of the People's judges had received a higher education.[3]

In the United States, appointments or elections may be to any level of court in either the federal or state systems, if the candidate possesses the minimum requirements. A judge must run for election or obtain an appointment to advance to a higher court. Merit is not necessarily the basis for advancement.

The British judge is appointed initially to a higher level of court than his American counterpart, thus his chances for advancement occur more infrequently. When he is advanced to a higher court, it is through the same appointive process based upon merit.

The French jurist is promoted depending upon his performance evaluation. The actual advancement is supervised by the Supreme Judicial Council composed of officials from the Ministry of Justice and senior judges.

Soviet judges, prior to the latest reorganization, had to rely for promotions upon evaluation by the Ministries of Justice. This practice has been abolished; today, promotions are based upon evaluation by other members of the judiciary.

[3] Ibid., p. 27.

Sentencing

The judicial process ends with the completion of the trial if the defendant is found not guilty, and with the sentencing if he is found guilty. The sentencing is the thorniest problem of the process. The President's Commission has stated:

The difficulty of the sentencing decision is due in part to the fact that criminal law enforcement has a number of varied and often conflicting goals: the rehabilitation of offenders, the isolation of offenders who pose a threat to community safety, the discouragement of potential offenders, the expression of the community's condemnation of the offender's conduct, and the reinforcement of the values of law-abiding citizens.[4]

The unanswered question confronting the justice systems "Is the function of the courts penal or preventive?" is today's dilemma in the sentencing process. The traditional answer has been that the courts must punish the wicked and not be concerned with matters of rehabilitation. These questions will be examined in Chapter 6.

Summary

In a strict sense we do not have an American court system. We have 50 individual state systems and one federal court system. The courts in America are generally patterned after the British system. The courts are created by three authorities: (1) the U.S. Constitution, (2) state constitutions, and (3) legislative enactments; creating two general types of courts—constitutional and legislative. Article III of the Constitution provides for a court system.

The court systems undergo periodic changes at the hands of state legislatures or the Congress of the United States. The present trend is toward consolidation of the lower court functions.

Historically, certain social inequities were built into the judicial system that have led to contemporary demands for judicial reform. One

---

[4] The President's Commission on Law Enforcement and Administration of Justice, *Task Force Report: The Courts* (Washington, D.C.: U. S. Government Printing Office, 1967), p. 14.

of these is the bail bond system, which tends to discriminate against the poor. The matter of counsel for the defendant is another defect in the system.

Unlike the British legal system, the legal system of the U.S.S.R. has had no effect on the Western world. Judges in the U.S.S.R. must have the political support of the Communist party, nor are there constitutional requirements that the judges have legal training or experience. In fact, only 80.9 percent of the People's judges received a higher education.

The judicial function ends with the completion of the trial if the defendant is found not guilty and with sentencing if found guilty. The question confronting the justice system today is, "Is the function of the Courts penal or preventive?" It is this unanswered question that is today's dilemma in the sentencing process.

Student Checklist

1. Can you cite the constitutional authority for the development of inferior courts in America?
2. Can you give three examples of social inequities that are built into the judicial system?
3. Can you define paraprofessional and outline assigned job responsibilities in judicial functions?
4. Can you define common law, and are you able to trace its historical significance?
5. Can you cite three reasons justifying punishment under our current system of justice?
6. Are you able to outline the origin and the development of the court system in America?

Topics for Discussion

1. Discuss the early systems of justice in America.

2. Draw a comparison between American justice and justice systems found in foreign countries.
3. Discuss the legal authority supporting the existence of American courts.
4. Describe the effects of present-day justice inequities on the poor.
5. Discuss the elements of the California restructuring of the court system that seem applicable to other states.

ANNOTATED BIBLIOGRAPHY

Abraham, Henry J. *Freedom and the Courts*. London: Oxford University Press, 1967. Analyzes and evaluates the basic problem of drawing lines between individual rights and community rights and draws some conclusions and suggestions in those spheres that constitute the basic rights and liberties.

Abraham, Henry J. *The Judicial Process*. London: Oxford University Press, 1968. A selective comparative introduction to the judicial process, which seeks to analyze and evaluate the main institutions and considerations affecting the administration of justice.

Conquest, Robert, ed. *Justice and the Legal System in the U.S.S.R.* New York: Praeger, 1968. Covers the limitations and difficulties surrounding the legal profession in the Soviet Union. It is documented and based upon Soviet sources. It provides a clear theoretical and practical account of the machinery and principles of Soviet law.

Frank, Jerome. *Courts on Trial*. New York: Atheneum, 1969. Relates the need for judicial reform. Discusses the jury system, appellate procedures, legal education, and the role of the judge in the system.

Karlin, Delmar. *Anglo-American Criminal Justice*. London: Oxford University Press, 1967. Identifies common problems in the British and American criminal justice system and describes how each country has attempted to solve them.

The study of this chapter will enable you to:

1. Cite examples of how society dealt with criminals during the seventeenth and eighteenth centuries.
2. Cite the major influence on treatment of criminals that was felt during the nineteenth century.
3. Explain the philosophy behind modern penology.
4. Define and outline the basic responsibilities of parole.
5. Define recidivism.
6. Define rehabilitation and outline two examples of its effectiveness.

6
Corrections

Historical Background

The ways in which society has dealt with lawbreakers have evolved from the primitive people's simple revenge or retaliation to today's concepts of rehabilitation and return to society. As governments developed, they took over the protection of persons and property and the punishment of offenders in the name of peace and order. But the basis of the government's intervention remained retribution. In England alone, toward the end of the sixteenth century, there were 600 executions in one year—a high rate for a comparatively small population. The death penalty was the most common response to common crime. In Europe during the sixteenth and seventeenth centuries, there were some 30 ways of administering death penalties, from drawing and quartering to burning at the stake or breaking on the rack. Public floggings were administered for relatively minor offenses. Imprisonment was looked upon not as a means of punishment but rather as a form of safekeeping to insure the presence of the offender at his trial. Imprisonment as a form of corrections is an idea of rather recent origin.

The Pilgrim Fathers in 1620 brought the stern criminal codes from Europe nearly intact. It was not until well into the eighteenth century that William Penn and the Quakers introduced a more humane element: the substitution of imprisonment for capital and corporal punishment.

In 1794 Pennsylvania adopted a new code that reduced the list of capital crimes to first degree murder and prescribed fines or imprisonment for other crimes.

The Walnut Street jail, the first American penitentiary (1790) located in Philadelphia, stressed two features: (1) solitary confinement without labor for more serious offenders, and (2) labor together in small groups at approximately the prevailing wage for less serious offenders.

Incarceration for felons had been initiated in England by the reformer, John Howard (1726–1790) as a worthy substitute for the death penalty, the most frequently used penalty at the time. It was Howard who coined the word *penitentiary*, and the philosophy of penitence or expiation gradually became the prevailing hope or "wave of the future." But it was Pennsylvania and later New York that were destined to implement and develop Howard's ideas, first in the Walnut Street Jail in Philadelphia and later in the Western Penitentiary in Pittsburgh, Cherry Hill (Eastern Penitentiary), and Auburn.

The degree of optimism about the effectiveness of the penitentiary approach is seen in the following report:

> *From the experiments already made, we have reason to congratulate our fellow citizens on the happy reformation of the penal system. The prison is no longer a scene of debauchery, idleness, and profanity; an epitome of human wretchedness; a seminary of crimes destructive to society; but a school of reformation and a place of public labor.*[1]

The Quakers in this period campaigned for moral regeneration through solitary confinement without labor. By 1827, the Western Penitentiary in Pittsburgh was in operation; it had tiny solitary cells—cells that were miniature prisons too small for labor. It was thought that isolation would prevent criminal contagion, and that solitary reflection would be a means of achieving moral regeneration.

In this period there was much controversy about types and kinds of facilities and, eventually, a range of architecture and a series of approachs were developed. Naturally, architecture alone solved no problem except, perhaps, that of "security," because in this period all approaches sought to break the spirit by using isolation coupled with work. Prison discipline was as unique as its architecture. For example, where prisoners worked together, silence was maintained. Other harsh punitive measures prevailed. Prisoners were treated as less than human. The failure to rehabilitate was inevitable because of the very same problems that beset us today: idleness, monotony, crowding, and poor custodial personnel.

---

[1] Francis C. Gray, *Prison Discipline in America* (London: John Murray, 1848), p. 22.

Figure 6-1. Types of prison structure.

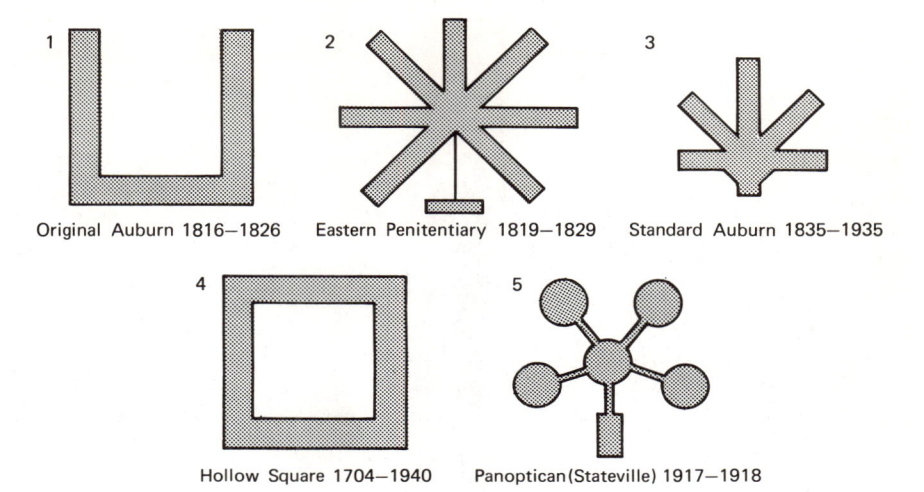

1 Original Auburn 1816–1826
2 Eastern Penitentiary 1819–1829
3 Standard Auburn 1835–1935
4 Hollow Square 1704–1940
5 Panoptican (Stateville) 1917–1918

Cherry Hill, the notoriously famous model of the system of separate confinement, still stands today in Philadelphia. This Bastille-like structure of stone and iron cell block warrens is considered by some to be the most famous prison in the world—certainly not for its enlightened approach, but as a monument to social futility. In its 141 years of existence (1829–1970), 75,000 men and 1900 females were entombed for many years of their lives. Negley K. Teeters, sociologist and chronicler of this special prison and penology generally, provides the opportunity to live in its history by a moving account of that institution.

> *Actually, this old structure has been not so much a prison as it has been the epitome of one of the most unique concepts of penal treatment ever conceived. Its founders, citizens primarily of the city of Philadelphia, created it on the principle of separate, but not solitary confinement (however, this subtle distinction might be regarded by some as merely a bit of casuistry), by which a prisoner could be separated from all others. This was accomplished by providing an individual cell for each inmate in which he worked, slept, and ate alone. He was provided an exercise yard attached to his cell where he was permitted to enjoy the outside for a few short intervals each day. His only contacts were his keepers, the chaplain, and a few interested citizens, members of the Philadelphia Prison Society, who by law were not only permitted to visit him, but admonished to do so. When it became necessary for a*

corrections

Figure 6-2. When it became necessary for a prisoner to leave his cell, his masked face prevented recognition, even for short exercise periods.

prisoner to leave his cell he was obliged to wear a mask or hood drawn over his face in order to prevent recognition. He carried a number and was known by name only to the warden and keepers.

The first prisoner to enter Cherry Hill was an eighteen-year-old black youth from Delaware County, named Charles Williams. He was sentenced on October 22, 1829 to serve two years for larceny of "one silver watch, value $20; one gold seal, value $3; one gold key, value $2" from the home of Nathan Lukens, known as Dowling House in Upper Darby. He entered the prison three days after sentence was passed and as there were no cells yet completed, he was temporarily housed in a room fitted up as an apothecary shop in the massive central tower. He was removed to his individual cell on the following November 10th.[2]

Like the optimism that prevailed at the time of the Walnut Street Jail

---

[2] Negley K. Teeters, "The Passing of Cherry Hill," *The Prison Journal,* L, No. 1, The Pennsylvania Prison Society (Spring-Summer, 1970).

reflected in Francis Gray's report, the eminent Frenchman, De Tocqueville (statesman and author) in 1831 similarly was to be deceived. He wrote:

> *The man works with ardor. His mind seems tranquil; his disposition excellent. He considers his being brought to the Penitentiary as a signal benefit of Providence. His thoughts are in general religious. He read to us in the Gospel the parable of the Good Shepherd, the meaning of which touched him deeply; one who was born of a degraded and depressed race, and had never experienced anything but indifference and harshness. The young man was set to making shoes and the French visitors reported that he made as many as ten pair per week. While all prisons are the receptables of heartache, despair, rascality, gloom, and vitriolic hostility mixed with a slight modicum of hope and compassion, Cherry Hill, at least in its inception, was dedicated in the name of reform and rehabilitation. It was believed that this worthy objective could be consummated by means of expiation.*[3]

In this period, the Auburn System, a bold new experiment, was begun. While subscribing to the essential elements indicated above, the Auburn prison in New York began to look seriously at the prisoner as an individual.

Auburn incorporated the one important principle that was excluded from other experiments—the classification of prisoners. A three-grade system was used:

1. Solitary cells for incorrigibles without labor.
2. Tractable persons in solitary cells with labor as recreation. Not incredibly, labor was accepted readily and considered a privilege.
3. The best candidates for reformation were offered group work dur- the day and held in isolation during the night.[4]

Nevertheless, the Auburn system failed also, especially with the incorrigibles held in solitary idleness. Many went insane; some attempted suicide. The health of many was impaired and the experiment did not lead to moral regeneration. Auburn was a failure in these terms, but it did provide an economic advantage over the other systems because of the cheap contract labor it offered.

---

[3] Gustave de Beaumont and Alexis De Toqueville, *On the Penitentiary System in the United States and its Application to France*, translated by Francis Leiber (Philadelphia: Carey, Lea and Blanchard, 1933).

[4] Orlando F. Lewis, *The Development of American Prisons and Prison Customs, 1776-1845* (Albany Prison Association of New York, 1922), pp. 11-12.

> It is a paradox that practically every prison system abroad adopted the system, but it was rather universally shunned by the several states. This is largely due to the fact that the Auburn System appealed more to the capitalist economy because of its use of power machinery which was beginning to be utilized at the time and hence made possible a maximum exploitation of convict labor. Reformers persisted in taking the policy of redemption or reformation of prisoners seriously. Handcraft labor pursued in the prisoners' cells, it was believed, would hasten reformation.
> The cornerstone of penology, reformation in isolation, had many critics. Keeping men locked up in solitary cells 24 hours each day with few human contacts is hardly a respectable criterion of reformation. As the late Harry Elmer Barnes, noted authority of corrections, put it some years ago: "No system can be successfully tested by its ability to turn out Robinson Crusoes or broken down unoffending hermits." Thomas Mott Osborne wrote that the system "showed a touching faith in human nature although a precious little knowledge of it." These remarks are reminiscent of the classic statement made by the British prison expert, Alexander Paterson, when he likened a prison to a "monastery inhabited by men who do not choose to be monks."[5]

In the nineteenth century, a heavy religious influence was felt. In fact, most prison administrators considered their Christianity, common sense, and practical experience sufficient qualification for their task. The strongly religious Zebulon Brockway, for example, surpassed the average reformer of the time. He incorporated some important measures in the reformatory at Elmira, New York, in 1877. Included was the grading of prisoners (the forerunner of modern classification), work for wages, and the mark system with the indeterminate sentence providing an opportunity for a prisoner to make his way out.

> Probably the first steps toward the indeterminate sentence were taken by Maconchie, who in 1840 used the mark system to allow a man to work his way out of prison. . . . This system utilized the prisoner's desire for freedom as an incentive for reformation. Maconchie said of the mark system, "When a man keeps the key of his own prison he is soon persuaded to fit it into the lock."[6]

---

[5] The Pennsylvania Prison Society, *The Prison Journal,* L, No. 1 (Spring–Summer, 1970), pp. 6-9.
[6] Barner and Teeters, *New Horizons in Criminology,* 2nd ed. (Englewood Cliffs, N.J.: Prentice-Hall, 1951), p. 520.

The reformatory idea ripened in the early 1900s, but declined in a decade or so. The reformatories had basic characteristics that made them junior prisons; their punitive philosophy overcame their major improvements: the indeterminate sentence and treatment of the prisoner as an individual.

Nevertheless, a modern penal philosophy was emerging. In 1916, when Thomas Mott Osborne at Elmira insisted on inmate participation in the operation of the prison, a major breakthrough was made in viewing the prisoner as a person. The old idea that all prisoners should be treated alike now gave way to classification of individuals to be treated as individuals.

Modern Penology

The prison of yesterday, based on retribution, is dying fast. Neither punitive measures, "moral regeneration," nor solitary confinement are viable today, but punitive prisons, like other social institutions, die slowly. Today's prisons, which have rehabilitation as their strategy, must subsist on an inheritance of outmoded facilities, erroneous beliefs, and inadequate personnel.

The trend from a punitive to a therapeutic ideology is based on the simple fact that the punitive approach has never been effective. Imprisonment today as a form of punishment is used widely with one explicit purpose—to "deprive one of liberty." The courts, when they resort to imprisonment, simply deprive a person of liberty. A court's jurisdiction ends upon execution of a sentence, and the convicted offender then becomes the responsibility of keepers whose statutory and administrative demands will determine the actual treatment of the offender in the correctional institution. Prisons, reformatories, penitentiaries, and jails are all classified as *correctional* institutions.

In the U.S. today, only Delaware, which allows whipping, resorts to punitive measures. Although there are no drastic measures of punishment, such as torture, mutilation, or banishment, there is heavy use of fines and reparations, which are permitted by legislatures and used by the courts. The ultimate form of punishment, however, still exists today. It is capital punishment—always a topic of interest and deep controversy.

All the states allowed capital punishment until the 1940s, by

Figure 6-3. "If only you had some compassion."

118 *introduction to the administration of justice*

which time half a dozen states had abolished it. Some abolished capital punishment and then reinstated it—a pattern that is being repeated in the 1970s—although the U.S. Supreme Court has ruled that the states must create new statutes to conform to Supreme Court guidelines so that capital punishment will not be of a discriminatory nature. Within a year of the Court's decision, nearly every state had considered reestablishing the death penalty, and the efforts of abolitionists do not yet seem able to stem this reversal. The general increase in lawlessness including assassinations, bombings, and skyjackings has strengthened the trend to reinstate capital punishment for specific crimes.

Treatment: The Modern Approach to Offenders

Any response to criminality less harsh than imprisonment is usually considered leniency. Amnesty and pardon are two forms, among others. The two that primarily concern corrections are *probation* and *parole*.

Probation

Probation is the conditional release of the offender into the community; the imposition or execution of sentence is withheld on the condition that the offender show good behavior. All who have been convicted of a crime are theoretically entitled to probation in some form; although in practice we find, ironically, that probation is more frequent in cases involving serious crimes (felonies) than in cases involving minor offenses (misdemeanors). Although this appears patently unfair, it is necessary to note that judges in minor courts can easily use variations of probation —for example, simple suspension of sentence without investigation or the use of fines. The convicted felon has by law the right of consideration for probation in most states. Some exceptions are stated in the laws, usually for certain crimes, primarily murder, and a range of other offenses that vary from state to state. Noteworthy here is that persons convicted of more than one felony in many states are not eligible for probation.

Historical Background. The history of probation began in 1841 with an unpaid volunteer, John Augustus, a Boston shoemaker, who asked the

Figure 6-4. A cell block still in use after 107 years, which houses about 500 inmates.

court to release a convicted offender to his care instead of sending him to jail. This successful experiment showed that a person could be restored to useful life and work, and that the community could be protected at the same time. From this modest beginning, the use of probation spread rapidly and its use now is the foremost community treatment model. There is no state that does not use probation. Its effectiveness is constantly being questioned; attacks on probation are frequent. Some of the criticism is justifiable—much is not. As a method of dealing with the offender, it is at least as effective as other methods and, unlike imprisonment, it is considerably cheaper.

The occasion on which probation comes under severe attack is when a serious crime is committed in the community by a probationer. When the crime is one against a person and that person is a law enforcement officer, the hue and cry is heard in all quarters. And justifiably so. For many years, the late J. Edgar Hoover, head of the Federal Bureau of Investigation, served as a strong and vociferous spokesman for the police and the community in attacking the use of probation (and parole). The message was clear. Soft judges who dispensed leniency instead of substantial prison sentences, and parole boards who released men from prison before their full sentences were served, were contributing to the crime problem. They were aiding and abetting the very problem that they were in operation to fight.

The issue, however, is much more complex. All agree that up to 80 percent or more prisoners would not be dangerous to the public outside of prison. This, coupled with the fact that 98 percent of all prisoners will return to life in the community, clearly point to the flaws in this argument. It is not that judges or others are any less concerned about the crimes committed by convicted offenders, but rather that the repeat crime rate could be affected only minimally by "tough" judges and sentences without parole. The problem is to use our limited knowledge to make better decisions about who remains in the community. With such a humanely perplexing task, one can only marvel that we do as well as we do.

Parole

Parole differs from probation in that a portion of the sentence is served in a correctional institution, and release into the community before the completion of the sentence is provided for with conditions similar to probation—namely, good behavior. In both probation and parole, if the behavior of the individual violates any of the conditions, the person may be committed or recommitted to prison.

In practice, the statutes of the 50 states governing both probation and parole make for a wide variety of operational conditions. It is because of this, that injustices within the system are so widespread. In urban areas, passing of a bad check is usually treated as a probation case, whereas in small towns, this offense may be considered more harshly. Similarly, use of drugs is dealt with in different ways in different sections of the country.

Parole, too, is subject to many variations—the type of offense, the nature of the paroling organization, the confidence in parole practices, and (a factor not to be overlooked), how a community feels about an individual returning to that community. A good deal of community pressure against release, for example, would develop in the case of a rapist/murderer returning to a small town, the scene of the offense.

In the past 50 years, parole has become an indispensable part of the justice system. Parole as we know it today is closely identified with the American reformatory movement. The development of institutional classification emphasized the importance of individualizing the treatment of the offender in terms of the causes of his criminal behavior and his potentials for treatment and training. Some time later the indeterminate sentence laws and the appointment of parole boards to administer parole statutes were instituted.

Indeterminate sentences differ from definite sentences in which a judge makes a determination of sentence within a maximum penalty. The judge will fix the number of days, months, and years up to that maximum that he feels the crime and the circumstances warrant. The prisoner has to serve that sentence, less whatever time off he earned for good behavior. Modern innovations in sentencing have broadened and yet restricted the discretion of the court in determining sentencing. First, courts have the power to suspend sentence and place the offender on probation. If the offender is to be sent to jail, a considerable degree of flexibility is provided for the judge. Under some state laws, he may fix the maximum; under others, the minimum; under still others, the minimum and maximum. Where a minimum and maximum sentence is levied, a considerable amount of discretion is within the prerogative of the parole board although the board may not keep a man beyond his maximum. Sometimes a judge may fix the minimum and maximum so close together that little discretion is left to the parole board.

There is a school of thought that would like to see the entire sentencing function moved out of the court and the responsibility for sentencing placed with sentencing boards. Numerous studies show wide disparity in sentencing practices. The effect on the system in terms of commitment levels and on the offender in terms of injustices is a serious issue.

There is not yet a standardized method for releasing an offender on parole, but one board can and will make much more consistent decisions in individual cases than the courts and their many judges could ever accomplish. Boards seek to selectively release a prisoner at the psychologically opportune time when, in the board's estimation, he has received the maximum benefit from his institutional experience.

In recent years, there has been a sharp movement to bring to the parole hearing, especially the revocation hearing, all of the procedural safeguards of a court of law. This is in contrast to the long-prevailing attitude that due process should not be a requirement of parole hearings, and that the basic purpose of parole will be thwarted by converting the hearings to quasi-judicial hearings. It has been stated as early as 1956 by the National Conference on Parole that:

> *The parolee is still serving a sentence imposed by a court. Many existing statutes refer to such parolees as being in the legal custody of the institution even though, by an act of grace of the parole board, they may be serving the sentence beyond the confines of the institution. Therefore, no unnecessary obstacles or handicaps should be placed in the way of a prompt return to the institution whenever such return is in the interest of the public or the parolee. The decision to return a violator is administrative rather than judicial, and only such checks or limitations should be set up as are necessary to prevent hasty or ill-considered action.*[7]

This opinion, it appears, is giving way to the legalistic approach. The legalistic trend is apparent not only in parole but in probation and in juvenile law. Court decisions are building a solid base upon which offenders' rights to due process in parole hearings are certain to be insured.

[7] National Conference on Parole (1956), pp. 32-33.

Correctional Effectiveness

If corrections could return all or most of the people in its charge to a law-abiding life in the community, America's crime rate would drop significantly. Today, however, a substantial percentage of the correctional population become repeaters—they go on to commit more crimes. Estimates vary, but rates of recidivism (falling back into previous criminal habits, especially after punishment) range between 65 and 68 percent.

Of the over 2 million prisoners each year in prisons, juvenile institutions, and jails, 99 percent are released within a year. As for the 250,000 serious offenders in our prisons, the following information constitutes a serious indictment of the ineffectiveness of the system of corrections: 90 percent have a juvenile delinquency record or other criminal record; and 50 percent have served at least one previous prison sentence.

Of the approximately 115,000 serious offenders released from prison each year, most are released on parole. The only sound way to find out how many of those are imprisoned again is to follow all the people released in a given period for a number of years and determine what percentage commit new crimes and are returned to prison. This task is an enormous one. One simple way of doing this would be to examine every released offender's FBI fingerprint file a few years after release. Many in the field of corrections believe this should be done because society can no longer afford to speculate about the effectiveness of parole.

There is a substantial foundation for the belief that prison and parole (and probation) do not begin to satisfy the cost benefits expected from our investments in these systems. There is equal doubt about the effectiveness of the many new approaches in corrections. The latest of these approaches, group counseling, has been devastated by one of the truly honest efforts to assess effectiveness in corrections. This is the Kassebaum, Ward, and Wilner study that found group counseling to be unrelated to prisoner success as were most of the other enlightened approaches.[8]

---

[8] Gene Kassebaum, David A. Ward, and Daniel M. Wilner, *Prison Treatment and Parole Survival* (New York: Wiley, 1971).

Parole, which was seen to be a vital tool in offender rehabilitation, has not achieved its promise. As an intermediate step between the institution and the free community, it was meant to be instrumental in helping to reestablish the offender in the community while protecting society by means of a surveillance of the released offender. Today, most prisoners are released on parole. Their release is usually to a parole plan, which, at a minimum, includes a place to live and employment. Certain conditions are imposed, many of which if strictly enforced, would ensnare most free citizens, let alone former offenders. When it is realized that violations of these conditions is cause for revocation of parole and return to prison, some idea may be had of the pressure that is on the parolee. The parolee must obtain approval before leaving the town or county or changing residence, must submit regular reports, and must not drink to excess. The parolee must not associate with "disreputable persons," must obtain approval to drive, and must get permission to marry. If any condition is violated, that is theoretically the basis for return to prison. In practice, return depends on the judgment of the parole officer.

Survival on parole following prison treatment, it has been determined, is not significantly different than from the rate of those who received no treatment.[9] This startling conclusion is reported on in the aforementioned Kassebaum, Ward, and Wilner study in which the following conclusions are also cited:

1. There is no evidence to support claims that one correctional program has more rehabilitation effectiveness than another.
2. Statistics on recidivism exaggerate the extent to which convicted offenders return to serious crime.
3. The likelihood of a citizen being subjected to personal injury or property loss can be only infinitesimally lessened by the field of corrections.
4. The increase in public protection gained by imprisonment of large numbers of offenders, of whom few are dangerous, is outweighed by the public cost involved.

---

[9] As long ago as 1940, Lewis Diana of the University of Pittsburgh made a follow-up study of 280 delinquents in 1950-51 in which one group received treatment and another group received no treatment. There was no difference in success rates.

Figure 6-5. In many cases, the ineffectiveness of imprisonment has created a strong consideration of community-based treatment.

The study makes a strong case that various correctional treatments are ineffective and that imprisonment is the most inffective and uneconomic course. This provides some sound basis for the trend to divert the offender from institutionalization into community-based programs. Whether these programs are more or less effective than those of the institutions and corrections generally is not yet known; but they are surely more economical. If only for economic reasons, the trend to community treatment is on the rise.

Summary

This chapter gives a brief historical view of corrections. The Pilgrims brought the stern European penal code with them that provided the base for our penal code today. The Quakers sought confinement without labor to replace harsh criminal penalties. This action brought about the Western Penitentiary in Pittsburgh.

The Auburn system, developed in New York, began to consider the prisoner as an individual; classification of prisoners began here. Auburn failed in that many of the inmates became insane or attempted suicide, although it did succeed in providing cheap contract labor.

Religious influence was strong in the nineteenth century. This brought about many reforms in prisons, particularly at Elmira, New York.

The prison of yesterday, based on retribution and the punitive approach, is dying fast. Today's prisons have rehabilitation as their strategy, with probation and parole as the two major programs used. The usefulness of such programs is constantly being questioned. However, they have proved to be just as effective as prisons and less expensive.

Hearings to grant parole or revoke parole have come under fire lately because they may violate the constitutional rights of offenders. However, court decisions are building a solid base upon which offenders' rights to due process in parole hearings are certain to be insured.

Community-based programs are increasing. Whether those programs are more or less effective than institutions of corrections is not yet known. Economic considerations may give rapid rise to these programs.

corrections

Student Checklist

1. Can you cite three examples of how society dealt with criminals during the seventeenth and eighteenth centuries?
2. Are you able to cite the major influence on treatment of criminals during the nineteenth century?
3. Can you explain the philosophy behind modern penology?
4. Can you define parole? Can you outline the basic responsibilities of parole?
5. Are you able to discuss recidivism?
6. Can you define rehabilitation? Can you outline examples of its effectiveness?

Topics for Discussion

1. Discuss the early philosophy of punishment versus treatment.
2. Discuss the historical significance in the development of the American correctional system.
3. Outline the various types of prison structures and discuss their respective strengths and weaknesses.

ANNOTATED BIBLIOGRAPHY

Annals, "The Future of Corrections," January 1969. A compilation of writings of some of the most astute practitioners and scholars. Deals with the past, present, and future of corrections with an emphasis on special problems, research, and programs.

Glaser, Daniel. *The Effectiveness of a Prison and Parole System.* New York: Bobbs-Merrill, 1964. This is a study of federal correctional practice using the analytic techniques of social science to determine the effectiveness of prison and parole on recidivism.

Johnson, Elmer Hubert. *Crime, Corrections, and Society.* Homewood, Ill.: Dorsey, 1964. A basic text that is lucidly written, thorough, and broad in scope, covering the range of standard topic areas of criminology.

Kassebaum, Gene; Ward, David A.; and Wilner, Daniel M. *Prison Treatment and Parole Survival.* New York: Wiley, 1971. One of the finest studies of the effectiveness of correctional treatments, especially group counseling. It is a well-documented, definitive book written by practitioner scholars.

President's Commission on Law Enforcement and Administration of Justice. *Task Force Report: Corrections.* Washington, D.C.: U.S. Government Printing Office, 1967. This is the result of a national survey of corrections in the United States with analyses and recommendations.

Part Three

Roles of Components of the Justice System

The study of this chapter will enable you to:

1. Cite the four traditionally accepted functions of the police.
2. Outline at least two activities of each one of the accepted functions of the police.
3. Give three examples of future functions of the police in the United States.
4. Outline the various responsibilities of city, county, state, and federal police.
5. Outline the organizational structure of a medium-size police department.
6. Understand the levels of private security and the processes basic to all security endeavors.

7
Primary Functions of the Police

Introduction

The purpose of this chapter is to provide a listing and analysis of the primary functions and specific purposes of the various agencies and levels of law enforcement agencies. Traditionally these functions and purposes have been categorically listed in various textbooks, in speeches by politicians, and in police training manuals. In recent years, however, Jerome Skolnick, O. W. Wilson, Norval Morris, and several others have provided the criminal justice system with an array of information that indicates that these traditionally accepted functions and purposes do not actually exist in modern democratic America. Perhaps one of the most tragic ramifications of this dilemma is that police may see their function and purpose differently from the way present-day society does.

In order to satisfy the purpose of this chapter, both the traditional and recently suggested functions and purposes of the various law enforcement agencies will be examined. This will be accomplished by providing a survey or listing of the various levels of law enforcement agencies throughout the nation and the specific functions they may have. To highlight this, a brief explanation of the administrative organization of a typical law enforcement agency will be offered. Finally, the rapidly growing world of private security and its impact on the present system of law enforcement will be discussed.

Administration of Justice in a Democratic Society

Police in America are one part of a vast governmental bureaucracy most recently named the administration of justice system. Three basic elements: police, courts, and corrections make up this system, and they influence and interact with each other. Society relies heavily on the mutual cooperation of all three to provide the type of service that it demands.

The administration of justice system operates within our democratic society, hence, the difficulties involved in running a democratic society often reach the criminal justice system and present it with problems that are difficult to solve. The police, as part of the vast justice bureaucracy, operate as an arm of the government at all levels. Their function then must be, as all governmental agencies in a democratic society, to serve the people in the way the people wish to be served.

Traditional Functions of Police in America

The primary functions of the police in America have traditionally been:
1. Prevention of crime.
2. Preservation of order (maintenance of peace).
3. Protection of person and property.
4. Protection of personal liberty.

Prevention of Crime

To prevent crime, police engage in patrol activities (visible evidence of police readiness and availability), work with youth, educate the public, and cooperate with other criminal justice agencies. Police authorities have worked to prevent crime in these ways for many years and believe that these activities prevent crime. Research, in the form of saturation, proves that more policemen on the street will reduce some crime in a particular area that is saturated. However, some observers have suggested that even saturation tactics do not actually prevent crime but "move" it to a different area of the city—one that is not saturated with police. But each police rookie soon realizes that most crime is not visible and he will rarely ever actually "see" any crime. Crime is social behavior and criminals do not commit crime—people do. The only real crime prevention is a social climate where the group and each individual decide to respect the dignity of each other to the point that crime is despicable. Until that utopian point is reached and until scientific technology finds a better way, police will continue to patrol the streets in the hope of preventing crime.

Police have been working with youth for many years in many different ways. In recent years, a separate division of the police department or specially designated juvenile officers have been common. Usually a separate youth bureau or juvenile division is established in larger agencies that work exclusively with juveniles and youth. In spite of these ambitious programs, one out of every four male youths in the United States comes to the attention of a juvenile court before his eighteenth birthday. Needless to say, more work must be done in the area of juvenile and youth crime and delinquency.

Police agencies use various means and media to educate the public toward crime prevention. It is impossible to estimate the effectiveness of these programs, but a better informed citizenry is always positive. Some critics of police insist that police crime prevention programs tend to frighten the public, which results in people locking themselves in their homes each night. The idea that a street crowded with people is a safe street becomes inoperable when people remain locked in their homes. Police education programs that result in fewer people on the street enhance the chances of crime occurrence. However, the question arises whether police public education programs or television sets are responsible for keeping people in their homes at night.

Police agencies cooperate with the prosecutor, the courts, and the correctional agencies in many ways. They provide the prosecution with the information concerning crimes and incidences, provide testimony concerning crimes and carry out instructions from the court concerning defendants, and provide correctional agencies with much information concerning offenders.

In general, police agencies attempt to prevent crime in the ways they know best: patrol, working with youth, educating the public, and cooperating with other criminal justice agencies. Other police activities that may assist in preventing crime include computerized systems that "predict" where and when crime will take place in some cities. Although the evidence is still not conclusive on the effectiveness of these computerized systems in preventing crime, it is becoming apparent that computers have a place in police work. More research and development are needed to place the computer in its proper function in preventing crime.

Preservation of Order
Police attempt to preserve order and promote community tranquility using various methods but primarily through the use of crowd control, the handling of family and other domestic disputes, and traffic regulation and control. In general, the police are very successful in accomplishing this task.

Public events with large numbers of people involved are controlled by police almost routinely with what often appears to the public to be ease. Actually, good crowd control can only be accomplished by detailed and deliberate planning. New York City police sometimes control 105,000 people entering Central Park from various entrances, seat them on the grass, observe them during a three-hour concert, and supervise their exit with no injuries at all on a hot summer evening. To the trained police observer, who is aware of the difficulties and possible serious ramifications involved in handling a crowd of that magnitude, it is truly a thing of beauty. Granted, a certain amount of consent on the part of the public is necessary to accomplish such a task, but professional police work by experienced men is the key to control. Other similar situations involving large numbers of people are handled every day by police with excellent results.

In answering noise complaints or family or other domestic disputes, the police are arbitrators and frequently settlers. These potentially volatile situations take up a large share of police time and are often very difficult to handle from a police perspective.

The area of preservation of order that is most demanding of police time and effort is the handling of traffic. Included in the handling of traffic are not only vehicles, pedestrians, and parking, but also traffic accident investigations, accident prevention, school safety programs, crossing guards, bicycle licensing and regulations, and various other traffic-related agencies and programs. Imagine the number of traffic and parking signs that must be created, designed, painted, and hung in a city like New York or Chicago.

The migration of city residents to suburbia has resulted in a particular problem. Most of the occupations take place within the cities, and each weekday hundreds of thousands of people must be moved into

Figure 7-1. Good crowd control can be accomplished by detailed and deliberate planning. Although a certain amount of consent by the public is necessary to achieve this, professional police work by experienced men is the key.

primary functions of the police 137

and out of these cities. The entrance into a city comes usually between 7:00–9:00 A.M. and the exit from 4:00–6:00 P.M. In a city like Detroit nearly 300,000 people are moved in and out five days a week. In cities like New York and Chicago, subways carry large numbers of people, and transit police are hired to police these modes of transportation.

Traffic control is perhaps the largest single and most expensive function of most police agencies. To handle the problem most large metropolitan police departments formed traffic divisions or bureaus to work exclusively with traffic. Smaller local police units, who cannot afford a separate traffic section, include it with daily duties of all uniform police.

Many large police agencies use meter maids and traffic wardens who work only in traffic situations and earn less than does a patrolman. Several European countries have utilized traffic wardens for a number of years with apparent success. London police officials insist that female traffic wardens find much less antagonism from motorists in giving tickets for traffic violations. Some American police officials argue that only trained policemen should handle traffic because many criminals and potential criminals are apprehended during routine traffic duties. But their critics insist that general police training and patrolmen's salaries are not needed. It is probable that future traffic and its auxiliary functions will be handled by quasi-police agencies, and the personnel involved will be limited in function and will receive lower salaries. A possible future influence on this decision will be the necessary environmental control of petroleum use. Since automobiles cause a large part of the pollution in cities like Los Angeles and New York, it is possible that automobiles will be limited or banned from sections of these cities in the near future. Shortages of gasoline may also restrict individual use of automobiles. It may be centuries before the effects of the automobile on the environment is fully realized. At any rate, traffic in the form of automobiles and trucks has consumed vast amounts of police time and public money in America in the past few decades.

Protection of Person and Property
Many policemen see the protection of person and property as their primary function during both on- and off-duty time. Traditionally both the

public and the police have agreed that this function is their most important reason for existence. Most police feel that they accomplish this by the following activities:
1. Enforcing the law.
2. Apprehending violators.
3. Recovering stolen property.
4. Investigating crime.
5. Assisting in the prosecution and conviction of those who violate the law.

Protection of Personal Liberty
Police are designated as the protector of America's personal liberties, and both the public and the police feel that they serve this function. Police supposedly provide this service by instructing the citizenry as to their rights and privileges in reference to law and by protecting the individual citizens against unwarranted interference by the state.

The New Concept of Functions of Police in America

The new concept of police functions in America, as opposed to their traditional functions, is threefold and of a simple nature. The difficulty involved, generally speaking, is that neither the police nor the public recognize these functions. A massive training and educational program is necessary to point them out to both the police and the public. Once this has been done, police can gain levels of expertise in these areas.
These functions are:
1. Response to citizen complaints.
2. Provision of services to the community.
3. Arrest of suspected criminals.

Response to Citizen Complaints. Police must respond to citizen complaints. According to Ahern:
> ... the policeman finds that his essential role is never to initiate investigation but to respond to complaints. He does not seek incidents out; they confront him.... More often than not, he must deal with people who demand that something be done but who are unwilling to resort to criminal sanctions; in other cases an arrest may be totally inappropriate.

In these situations, the patrolman has to deal not with crime but with people. That is his stock-in-trade.[1]

Provision of Services to the Community. Traditionally, police have resented being placed in a nonlaw-enforcement role. In spite of the evidence that indicates that "8 out of 10 calls a patrolman answers will be of a 'social service' variety,"[2] many patrolmen insist they are "cops" and not "social workers." The public call police when they are in great need of help. When a child is struck by a car, when a child is lost or runs away, when a person needs legal advice, and in many other situations where crime is not a concern, the public seek help from the police. Many parents call the police for help when their sons and daughters are found with drugs. They are not asking the police to enforce the law but to provide aid in a family problem. Most police cooperate by answering questions, providing suggestions, giving directions, and rendering a variety of services.

Arrest of Suspected Criminals. A third primary function of the police is the apprehension of suspected criminals. This can be accomplished by the use of warrants that result from complaints and investigations, and in cases where police actually see crime occur.

Police Agencies in America

Crime, or the violation of law, is regarded as a local problem; this attitude has persisted for centuries. If crime is a local problem, a violation of local laws, then the enforcement of these laws must be accomplished at the local level.

Modifications of the local enforcement concept, however, became necessary when certain types of crimes began to flow across community, county, state, and even international boundaries. The result has been the creation of approximately 40,000 separate and distinct policing agencies in the United States. Private police agencies, though they exist in large numbers, are not included in the above figure. The villages, towns, cities,

[1] James F. Ahern, Police in Trouble: *Our Frightening Crisis in Law Enforcement* (New York: Hawthorne Books, 1972), pp. 167-168.
[2] Ibid., p. 168.

counties, and states all require agencies to enforce their laws. Some law enforcement bodies are also in existence at the federal level. It should be stated that most of these agencies consist of 10 or fewer men, and that the size of one agency may be as high as 30,000.

> Among the over 40,000 United States law enforcement agencies, there are only 50 . . . on the federal level . . . 200 on the state level. The remaining 39,750 agencies are dispersed throughout the many counties, cities, towns, and villages that form our local governments . . . Only 3050 agencies are located in counties and 3700 in cities. The great majority of the police forces—33,000—are distributed throughout boroughs, towns, and villages.[3]

In order to gain a clear picture of the many levels, they must be examined separately. All of these agencies are involved in the enforcement of laws that prohibit certain types of behavior that each unit has deemed socially unacceptable. The examination will point out that certain of these agencies also have certain specific purposes.

County Police Agencies
The counties in America, over 3000 in number, range from those that are entirely rural to those whose entire boundaries are part of a large city. It follows, then, that policing in counties will vary depending upon population density and other characteristics. However, there are certain similarities throughout nearly all county police agencies.

The County Sheriff. The county sheriff is generally recognized as the highest police officer of the county. However, the qualifications for sheriff in most counties are usually only that he be a citizen, a registered voter, over 21 years of age, and be able to win an election. Experience, education, and special knowledge of law enforcement or a related field are not formal qualifications. Fortunately, most men who hold this office in large agencies are qualified police officials, but the burden of having to run for office every few years cannot help but distract incumbents from many law enforcement duties.

The duties of the county sheriff vary greatly in different areas.

---

[3] President's Commission on Law Enforcement and Administration of Justice, *Task Force Report: The Police* (Washington, D.C.: U.S. Government Printing Office, 1967), pp. 7, 8, 9.

primary functions of the police

In some counties he may be sheriff, coroner, tax collector, supervisor of roads and highways, process server, and play a host of other roles. In most counties the sheriff operates the county jail and, in highly populated areas, this is his major responsibility. As sheriff he also heads the county police, and he is responsible for enforcing the orders of county level courts—a major task in itself. In most cases he serves as supervisor of a staff of deputies who are usually appointed. In more and more cases these deputies may fall under civil service or merit system regulations and are required to pass qualifying examinations.

In some areas the county sheriff derives his income from many sources, usually in the form of a salary plus fees. Other county sheriffs' salaries are fixed by the county board of supervisors and cannot be adjusted during the term of office. Special fees in some counties may be gained from the service of court orders and writs, and from the stipulated amounts he receives for each meal served a prisoner in the county jail. In a few rural counties the sheriff and his family live in the same building that houses the county jail; his wife may serve as jail matron.

In all cases, the county sheriff provides law enforcement services to the unincorporated portion of the county. In the rural counties he will generally provide patrol and general police services to unincorporated territories and sometimes maintain a suboffice on a contract basis in the smaller villages that want a resident police officer. In some counties, generally in the West, an incorporated city that does not wish to establish its own police force may contract with the county sheriff for policing services. In highly populated county areas the police service that the sheriff provides may be extensive, consisting of traffic, patrol, service for juveniles, vice, narcotics, investigative, and other general police activities.

The Constable. The constable, like the sheriff, is usually elected and serves for a short period of time, usually one to four years. The office of constable is recognized in approximately 20 states, primarily in New England, the South, and the West. Qualifications for the position are minimal—21 years of age, a citizen, and a registered voter or on the tax rolls. The constable may be a minor law enforcement officer, poundkeeper, issuer of election notices, prisoner escort, court bailiff, and tax collector. In some jurisdictions the constable serves under the sheriff and like some sheriffs gains his salary, or part of it, from the collection of fees. In most jurisdictions he serves civil papers issued by justices of the peace.

The Marshal. The role of the marshal is similar to that of the sheriff, but is comparatively limited in scope. The marshal is usually an officer of the local municipal court who serves subpoenas and civil papers, warrants of arrest, and sometimes acts as bailiff in lower courts of record and as an escort for prisoners to and from court. He is elected depending on the local jurisdiction. In a few restricted local jurisdictions the marshal's office is incorporated to include the duties of the chief of police as part of his role as town marshal.

Policing the Cities
The very center of American policing is in the cities—about 4000 cities that employ and enjoy the highest levels of police service in the country. Policing the large metropolitan urban areas has become a highly complex task and neither the advances of technology nor any advances in the behavioral sciences have had meaningful impact on the difficulty of this task. The vast intricacies and complexities of city life have posed a monumental challenge to urban police agencies. As families and industries migrate to the suburban areas and massive shopping centers are built, the city tax base declines—yet the demands on city police agencies increase.

The largest metropolitan police agency is the New York City Police Department. This department is made up 305 separate commands and employs more than 34,000 people. One can only speculate on the problems of coordination and control. The annual budget for this agency is approximately $680 million, processes about six and one-half million calls for assistance, and effects nearly 250,000 arrests in the same time period. In the following major section of this chapter, the administrative organization of city police agencies, the "how" of the above data will be discussed.

State Law Enforcement Agencies
Of utmost importance to this analysis are the state police agencies that exist in varying forms in all states. Indeed, in some states the most pro-

fessional police units may be those of the state police. One reason for this reputation is the fact that many of these state police agencies were developed after the beginning of the twentieth century and have avoided the customs and traditions that have long plagued county and local agencies.

The development of state law enforcement agencies resulted from several factors, including the increased use of the automobile for long-distance transportation, the realization that local and county law enforcement agencies could not deal with crime that may span hundreds of miles across many jurisdictions, social mobility factors in the United States, and the strong need for specialized police units at a state level.

State Police

State police agencies are usually of two types. The first is often called the highway patrol, most of whose attention is directed to traffic functions. The second type is usually called state police and has all general police powers. Each state differs from the others in small degrees, probably because each state police unit developed on its own, within the confines of its own geographic borders, and was designed to serve the state's peculiar needs. In some states the state police serve as examiner for vehicle operators' licenses; court attendants on Indian reservations; fire, fish, and game wardens; and serve as guards in and around governors' offices and homes. The state police function is designed to best serve the needs of the particular state; their powers and duties relate to that need.

Investigative Agencies

State bureaus, divisions, and departments of investigation exist in nearly all states. The investigatory agencies found at state level conduct all types of investigation, both civil and criminal, for various state agencies and bureaus, and often for local law enforcement agencies. Many of these units in different states possess great powers and accomplish professional levels of investigation in a vast number of areas that benefit the populace. Examples of this type of agency are the state narcotics commissions.

Identification Agencies. Central identification agencies exist in most states. Their purpose is primarily to store criminal records and maintain fingerprint files. These state agencies are invaluable to local law enforcement agencies and provide a professional service. In some states these identification agencies are operated by state police, while in others separate state agencies are responsible for the operation.

Criminalistics Agencies. Criminalistics laboratories exist at state level in most states and serve local, county, and state police agencies in examination, identification, and comparison of physical evidence. These criminalistics units provide professional assistance in crime-scene search in serious cases and lend their equipment and technology in other cases.

Motor Vehicle Divisions. Motor vehicle divisions exist at a state level in all states and compile license, registration, traffic law and offense violations, and serve local agencies heavily in motor vehicle theft and unauthorized use cases. They house a record-keeping center for all types of traffic and motor vehicle information.

Liquor Control Boards and Commissions. All states have a board or commission to license sellers, regulate alcoholic beverage sales, and collect revenues from the sales. Their activities include investigation of potential license holders, enforcement of liquor laws, and detection of illegal production. These agencies work closely with the Alcohol and Tobacco Tax Division of the Internal Revenue Service.

Conservation Agencies. Every state has an agency to protect and help to conserve its natural resources. Many states use state park policemen, forest rangers, or conservation officers to protect their state parks, historic landmarks, and recreation areas. In some, fish and game wardens act to protect wildlife and illegal hunting and fishing activities.

Fire and Safety Agencies. Fire and safety officers and marshals at state levels are responsible for the elimination of fire and safety hazards, investigation of fires, enforcement of fire and safety regulations, and the development of safety and fire prevention programs. These agencies work closely with local fire and safety officials.

Public Health Regulatory Agencies. These agencies have the responsibility of enforcing state laws and regulations concerning communicable diseases, licensing of hospitals and nursing homes, food and drug adulteration, and public sanitation.

National Guard Units and State Militias. All states have national guard or state militia units, called into action by the chief executive of the state—

the governor, who may take this action only in emergency situations to preserve order and protect public safety. This exercise of power by the executive branch of state government is called martial law or martial rule and is invoked only when all other authority and power are ineffective in attempts to protect the state.

Miscellaneous State Law Enforcement Agencies. On a state level, in all states, there exists a myriad of law enforcement agencies. Authors Germann, Day, and Gallati explain the situation well:

> *Investigatory and enforcement units of state agricultural, finance, commerce, employment, insurance, investment, mental hygiene, motor vehicle, civil service, industrial relations, and marketing departments conduct a wide variety of enforcement functions of a civil and criminal nature.*
>
> *Many states have turf commissions or horse racing boards which control horse racing and wagering at major and fair race tracks, and which inspect, investigate, and enforce state laws pertaining thereto.*
>
> *All states have processes for the control, examination, licensing, inspection and investigation of members of various professions and occupations—such as accountants, architects, barbers, chiropractors, engineers, contractors, cosmetologists, dentists, detectives, doctors of medicine, nurses, optometrists, osteopaths, pharmacists, shorthand reporters, social workers, teachers, veterinarians—BUT, as yet, do NOT examine, license, and investigate law enforcement officers working for state, county, and local governments. . . . That is an interesting speculative matter for every thoughtful student of law enforcement and for every citizen.*[4]

Federal Law Enforcement Agencies

On the federal level there are a vast number of law enforcement agencies and smaller agencies within agencies that have a law enforcement function. These agencies vary not only in size but in function. Some are involved in security matters, others in criminal matters, and still others in civil or military matters. These agencies are located throughout the entire federal government and vary in importance. Most are located in

---

[4] A. C. Germann, Frank D. Day, and Robert R. J. Gallati, *Introduction to Law Enforcement and Criminal Justice* (Springfield, Ill.: Charles C. Thomas, 1969), pp. 166-167.

the executive branch of the federal government. For the purposes of this chapter only the more important law enforcement agencies will be listed. Governmental reorganization is continuously taking place, and some of these agencies have found themselves in different sections of the federal government at different times. The following listing will place them in their traditional positions in the federal government structure. The titles of some of these agencies encompass their functions, which need not be explained. In the agencies where the functions are not self-explanatory, they will be described.

Executive Office of the President. The National Security Council was established in 1947, and its function is to advise the president with respect to the integration of domestic, foreign, and military policies relating to the national security. Under the direction of the Council is the Central Intelligence Agency (CIA), which has an intelligence-gathering function that is both domestic and foreign. It has come under much public scrutiny in the past five years as the public is questioning the unstated functions of this agency.

Department of the Treasury. The Bureau of Customs was created in 1927. Its principal functions are to collect and assess duties and taxes on imported goods, control carriers and merchandise into and out of the United States, and to prevent smuggling and frauds on the revenue process. With the upsurge of the illegal sale and use of narcotics internationally, the Bureau of Customs has become an important and busy law enforcement agency.

    The Internal Revenue Service has had, since 1862, tax law enforcement functions and other duties. The two major units of the IRS, Intelligence Division and the Alcohol and Tobacco and Firearms Division, perform the bulk of the investigative work of the Service.

    The United States Secret Service, which began in 1860, is charged with the responsibility of protecting the person of the president and vice-president and members of their immediate families, the president-elect, the vice-president-elect, and the enforcement of laws relating to counterfeiting or forging of United States government notes, securities, bills, and coins. Operating under the Secret Service is the White House Police Force that protects the Executive Mansion and grounds, and the Treasury Guard Force that protects the main Treasury buildings and the cash, bonds, and other securities in the Treasury vaults.

Department of Defense. The Army, Navy, Marine Corps, and Air Force operate within the Department of Defense as do the police agencies of these armed services. Also within the Department of Defense are such intelligence and security agencies as the National Security Agency, the Defense Intelligence Agency, and the Assistant to the Secretary of Defense (Special Operations).

Department of Justice. The United States Attorney General is head of the Justice Department, and under his command are the Federal Bureau of Investigation, the Immigration and Naturalization Service, the Bureau of Narcotics and Dangerous Drugs, the United States Marshals, and the Law Enforcement Assistance Administration.

The FBI is responsible for the investigation of all federal laws that have not been assigned to other federal agencies.

The FBI has jurisdiction over violations of espionage, sabotage, treason, and other matters pertaining to the internal security of the United States. Contrary to popular belief, the jurisdiction of the Bureau, particularly relative to criminal matters, is limited by law. Included among approximately 170 investigative matters defined in specific federal laws as being within the jurisdiction of the FBI are the following: Kidnapping; extortion; bank robbery, burglary, and larceny; crimes on government or Indian reservations; thefts of government property; the Fugitive Felon Act; interstate transportation of stolen motor vehicles; aircraft, cattle, or property; interstate transmission or transportation of wagering information, gambling devices, or paraphernalia; interstate travel in aid of racketeering; fraud against the government; election law violations; civil rights matters; and assaulting or killing the president or a federal officer.[5]

The Immigration and Naturalization Service began in 1891 and has been a member of the Justice Department since 1940. Through its Border Patrol it searches out aliens who have entered the United States illegally and investigates violations of immigration and naturalization laws. The Bureau of Narcotics and Dangerous Drugs was created in 1968, and it functions to prevent, detect, and investigate violations of federal narcotic and marijuana laws. The United States Marshals, founded in 1789, in general perform many of the same services for the federal government that a sheriff performs for a county. The Marshals

---

[5] Germann, *Introduction to Law Enforcement*, p. 171.

handle prisoners of the federal district courts, serve orders of the courts, and assist the courts in other matters.

In 1968 the Office of Law Enforcement Assistance (OLEA), later changed to the Law Enforcement Assistance Administration (LEAA), was created to offer federal assistance to state and local governments and to private nonprofit agencies to improve the administration of criminal justice in America. This agency accomplishes its task through financial and technical assistance to state and local law enforcement agencies. The Law Enforcement Education Program (LEEP) is a division of LEAA, which disburses funds in the form of loans and grants to college students presently employed in the criminal justice system and to some other students.

Department of the Interior. The Department of the Interior has jurisdiction over 750 million acres of land, including the conservation and development of mineral resources, mine safety, fish and wildlife resources, arid land development through irrigation, and the management of hydroelectric power systems. It is also responsible for the welfare of persons in the territories and island possessions of the United States, plus the nation's scenic and historic areas. Its Bureau of Indian Affairs has guardianship over nearly one-half million native Americans. To perform its duties, the Department of the Interior has established the Division of Inspection, Division of Security, United States Fish and Wildlife Service, Bureau of Commercial Fisheries, and The Bureau of Sports Fisheries and Wildlife. Its National Park Service is well known to all Americans who have visited the many historic sights and national parks.

Department of Agriculture. The Department of Agriculture enforces regulatory laws designed to protect the farmer and the consuming public, and it also administers the national forests. The Department concerns itself with animal disease eradication, animal quarantine, meat inspection, and the importation of harmful insects. Its Forest Service administers 150 national forests located in 40 states and Puerto Rico. The Commodity Exchange Authority works to prevent false information concerning crops, markets, and prices, and to protect users of the commodity futures markets.

Department of Health, Education, and Welfare. The Department of Health, Education, and Welfare has the responsibility of promoting the general welfare in the fields of health, education, and social security. The

Food and Drug Administration, which was created in 1930, has recently been strengthened by Supreme Court decisions, and it works toward promoting purity, standard potency, and truthful labeling in food and drug sales and consumption.

Department of Transportation. The Department of Transportation has jurisdiction over the Coast Guard when the country is not at war (in wartime it becomes part of the Navy). The Coast Guard is responsible for the security of seaports and enforces federal laws on the high seas or waters subject to the jurisdiction of the United States. The Federal Aviation Administration enforces safety regulations relating to the manufacture, registration, safety, and operation of private and commercial aircraft. It also inspects air crashes. The Federal Highway Administration supervises a program designed to reduce deaths, injuries, and accidents on U.S. highways.

Independent Agencies. In the vast number of minor bureaucracies within the federal government, many minor types of law enforcement agencies exist. Most of them are investigative and security branches of larger, regulatory-type agencies such as the Federal Communications Commission or the Federal Trade Commission.

Characteristics of Police Organization

A distinguishing feature of police organizations is their quasi-military structure. The typical military symbols—uniforms, rank hierarchy, insignia, weapons, and equipment—are visible in nearly all police organizations. This quasi-military organization creates a tighter organization but may detract somewhat from flexibility.

Nature of Police Organizations

Police agencies usually organize their personnel, equipment, and materials into line, staff, and line and staff functions. The line function is the primary operating function and is accomplished by the patrolmen and detectives. The line function is performed by investigation; traffic; and patrol, vice, and juvenile activities. The staff function is a supervisory and supportive activity and is usually accomplished by a person holding the rank of lieutenant or higher or provides line personnel with needed services. Other personnel in staff positions are training officers, planners and researchers, fiscal officers, public relations workers, and other ancillary personnel. All departmental inspectional services, intelligence activities, and criminalistics specialties are also staff positions.

Line and staff functions merge when collaboration is required on particular cases, as when persons in supervisory positions supervise investigations or raids.

Four basic organizational principles are used by many police agencies in their attempt to deliver police service to the public. They include:

1. Chain of command.
2. Unity of command.
3. Span of control.
4. Definition of authority.

Chain of Command. Chain of command represents the authority by which one gives and another receives orders, and it is the path along which this authority flows. For example, the police chief will tell the deputy chief of a particular method of enforcement procedure he wants carried out on the street. Written orders from the deputy chief will then flow to the commanders who will, in turn, instruct the precinct captains. The precinct captains will see that the chief's wishes are implemented on the street—through the lieutenants to the sergeants to the patrolmen. The chain of command thus allows the chief's orders to be relayed downward quickly. The same process, although in reverse order, is followed when information from patrolmen is relayed to the chief.

Unity of Command. This concept assures that no patrolman or any other person in the department will have more than one supervisor. This eliminates confusion and insures clarity and coordination. Because police shifts rotate through 24 hours each day, and because time off for personnel is insured by labor laws, police often find themselves with a different person as immediate supervisor on different days.

Span of Control. This comprises the number of persons a supervisor can effectively manage, with the determinants of people, distance, and time. The number of people supervised depends on the type of work involved: routine, varied, technical, or complicated. A larger number of people can be effectively supervised doing routine tasks than doing complicated work.

Distance also affects a supervisor's span of control. If a supervisor's subordinates work within close range of supervision, it is easier than when they are scattered at some distance from him.

The time factor is the third aspect of span of control. Because police departments are open 24 hours a day, the equivalent of 1095 working days a year must be considered. Personnel must be deployed to three different shifts depending on each shift's criminal activity. Some agencies use special task forces during high crime times, often between 6:00 P.M. and 2:00 A.M. A few police agencies are experimenting with 40-hour, four-day weeks for increased effectiveness. Supervisors find it much more difficult to supervise large numbers of personnel during peak periods than during slow periods.

Definition of Authority. Charts, manuals, and rules and regulations generally define the authority in a step-by-step fashion from the chief to the patrolman and vice versa. These organizational charts are usually posted on personnel bulletin boards and in police locker rooms. The departmental rules and regulations and manuals of procedure outline exactly which positions report to which, and the responsibilities of each position.

Organization of a Typical Police Agency

Organization is the bringing together of people to perform specific tasks and dividing the total workload into individual units for assignment to individual people. Organization by itself will not complete any task. A typical organizational chart for a community of 23,000 is shown in Figure 7-2, and a chart for a large police agency is offered in Figure 7-3.

Most police agencies organize around functions that they must perform in their communities. A complaint comes into the police agency or pressure is applied through various channels, and the police organization initiates an order at the top of the structure that filters down through to operations, verbally or in memorandum form. Depending upon the content of the order, it will be channeled to administration, operations, or services. If the order applies only to one shift, the supervisor of that shift will receive it. He will instruct has shift members on how he wants the order carried out. His men will perform these particular tasks and report the results back to him. The process is then reversed and the results are channeled upward to the originator of the order. Standing

Figure 7-2. Typical organization chart for a community of 23,000 people.

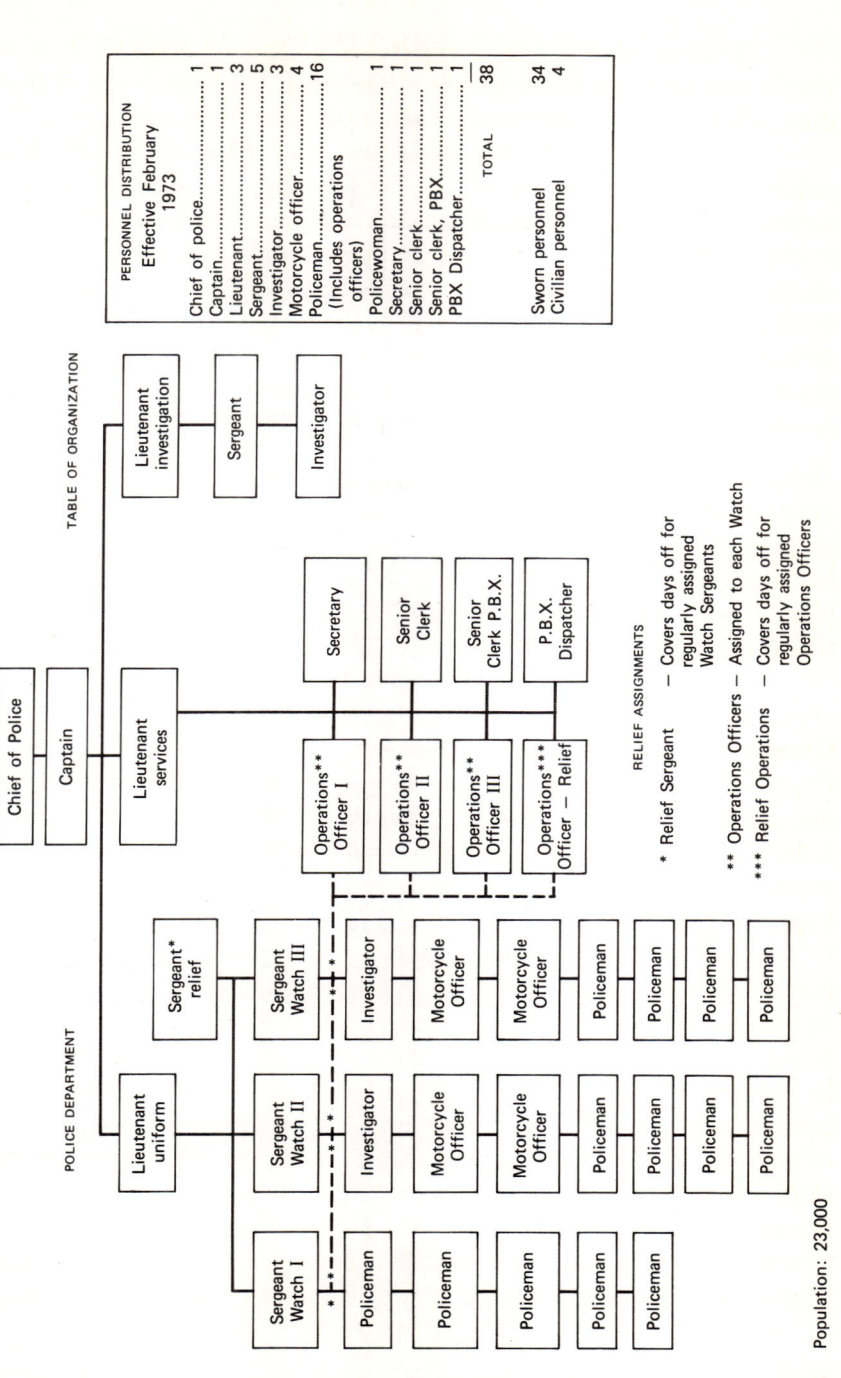

POLICE DEPARTMENT

TABLE OF ORGANIZATION

PERSONNEL DISTRIBUTION Effective February 1973	
Chief of police	1
Captain	1
Lieutenant	3
Sergeant	5
Investigator	3
Motorcycle officer	4
Policeman (Includes operations officers)	16
Policewoman	1
Secretary	1
Senior clerk	1
Senior clerk, PBX	1
PBX Dispatcher	1
TOTAL	38
Sworn personnel	34
Civilian personnel	4

RELIEF ASSIGNMENTS

* Relief Sergeant — Covers days off for regularly assigned Watch Sergeants

** Operations Officers — Assigned to each Watch

*** Relief Operations — Covers days off for regularly assigned Operations Officers

Population: 23,000

primary functions of the police   **153**

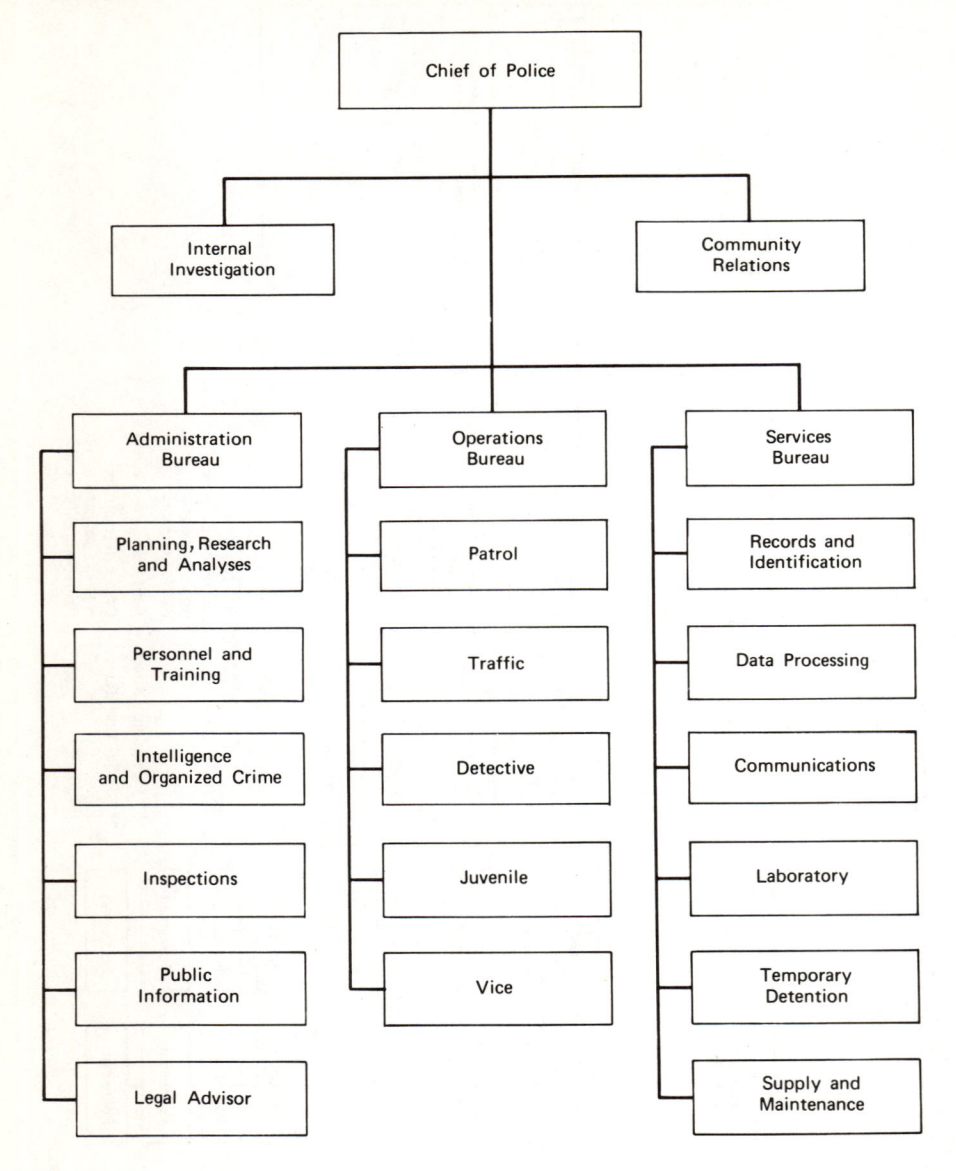

Figure 7-3. One form of a well-organized municipal police department.

```
                        ┌─────────────────┐
                        │ Chief of Police │
                        └─────────────────┘
                                 │
                ┌────────────────┴────────────────┐
      ┌─────────────────┐              ┌─────────────────┐
      │    Internal     │              │    Community    │
      │  Investigation  │              │    Relations    │
      └─────────────────┘              └─────────────────┘

   ┌──────────────────┐      ┌──────────────────┐      ┌──────────────────┐
   │  Administration  │      │    Operations    │      │     Services     │
   │      Bureau      │      │      Bureau      │      │      Bureau      │
   └──────────────────┘      └──────────────────┘      └──────────────────┘

   ┌──────────────────┐      ┌──────────────────┐      ┌──────────────────┐
   │ Planning, Research│     │      Patrol      │      │   Records and    │
   │   and Analyses   │      │                  │      │  Identification  │
   └──────────────────┘      └──────────────────┘      └──────────────────┘

   ┌──────────────────┐      ┌──────────────────┐      ┌──────────────────┐
   │   Personnel and  │      │      Traffic     │      │ Data Processing  │
   │     Training     │      │                  │      │                  │
   └──────────────────┘      └──────────────────┘      └──────────────────┘

   ┌──────────────────┐      ┌──────────────────┐      ┌──────────────────┐
   │   Intelligence   │      │     Detective    │      │  Communications  │
   │and Organized Crime│     │                  │      │                  │
   └──────────────────┘      └──────────────────┘      └──────────────────┘

   ┌──────────────────┐      ┌──────────────────┐      ┌──────────────────┐
   │    Inspections   │      │     Juvenile     │      │    Laboratory    │
   └──────────────────┘      └──────────────────┘      └──────────────────┘

   ┌──────────────────┐      ┌──────────────────┐      ┌──────────────────┐
   │      Public      │      │       Vice       │      │    Temporary     │
   │    Information   │      │                  │      │     Detention    │
   └──────────────────┘      └──────────────────┘      └──────────────────┘

   ┌──────────────────┐                                ┌──────────────────┐
   │   Legal Advisor  │                                │    Supply and    │
   │                  │                                │    Maintenance   │
   └──────────────────┘                                └──────────────────┘
```

orders or policy statements are permanent and are maintained permanently by those concerned to be used as regular guidelines and procedures.

Weston and Wells provide an excellent description of police organization in America:

> The total task of achieving an organization's objectives is differentiated so that particular persons or groups are responsible for the performance of specialized activities. Differentiation is segmenting an organizational system into subsystems, each of which tends to develop particular attributes in relation to the work that has to be done to achieve the objectives of an organization. In differentiation, there is a vertical dispersion of the work to be done and the responsibility for its completion among operating personnel.
>
> The executive is responsible for organizing and controlling all activity in achieving the ultimate objectives of an organization. However, in a vertical differentiation, he may establish program objectives for supervisors in charge of segments of the organization and delegate related duties to them. In turn, these officers in charge may set objectives for subordinates and delegate related duties. This is a pyramidal management structure. The various levels of management between the executive at the top and the operations personnel who turn out the product are primarily dependent upon the size of the organization. There must be sufficient levels in the vertical differential of an organization to provide adequate communication and control.
>
> The three primary bases of horizontal differentiation are: (1) location, (2) function, and (3) product. Universally, police forces in America use location as a primary organizational base. The municipal, town or village police department, the sheriff's office, and the state police are all responsible for certain geographical areas. This territorical jurisdiction is broken down into posts and sectors to secure a basic unit for the assignment of personnel. Concurrently, because police must provide services on a 24-hour and 7-day basis, there is also a universal division of work and responsibility by time. Not all posts and sectors are manned by police officers every hour of the day, but within the total territorial jurisdictional area of a police force there are one or more police officers on duty or available when required.[6]

---

[6] Reprinted by permission from P. B. Weston and K. M. Wells, *Law Enforcement and Criminal Justice: An Introduction* (Pacific Palisades, California: Goodyear, 1972), pp. 47-48.

Criticisms of Police Organization

American police agency organization has been criticized severely on occasions by people within and outside the police community. Most of the criticisms center around those areas pointed out in the President's Commission Report of 1967. Some of the criticisms are the following: the agencies' lack qualified leadership; chiefs and middle management personnel lack sufficient education and training; many departments are not organized in accordance with well-established principles of modern business management and resist change; many departments lack trained personnel in specialized fields, such as research and planning, law, business administration, and computer analysis; many departments fail to deploy and utilize personnel efficiently; and many departments have not adequately applied technological advances that would benefit law enforcement.

However, it should be said that more and more police agencies, with financial and technical aid from LEAA and other federal and state sources, have instituted long-range programs of organizational development and change from within and are well on the road to overcoming these organizational weaknesses. They are seeking the advice of non-police organizational and management specialists. Good organization has become the goal of practically all large police agencies.

Security as an Integral Part of the Administration of Justice

Loss prevention, campus security, plant protection, bank security, and retail security are related terms covering a broad range of activities in the security field. There are approximately 800,000 people in security services with some 400,000 of these in government law enforcement. In 1969, over $8 billion was devoted to security services and equipment (0.85 percent of the gross national product). One in every 100 persons in the civilian labor force, or one in every 250 persons in the entire population, was employed in security work, and over $40 per capita was spent on security.[7]

---

[7] U. S. Department of Justice, Law Enforcement Assistance Administration, National Institute of Law Enforcement and Criminal Justice, *Private Police in the U.S.: Findings & Recommendations, 1*, R-869/DOJ.

The student of the administration of justice should have a basic understanding of the field of security since many of the concepts and basic functions are interrelated. For example, the municipal police in the United States are presently developing and adopting a concept known as crime prevention. The basic theoretical and functional concepts in crime prevention have been the basis of many private and cooperative security loss prevention programs for some years.

The British definition of crime prevention as developed by the Home Office Crime Prevention Center in Stafford, England, is that "Crime prevention is the anticipation, recognition, and appraisal of a crime risk (physical opportunity for crime) and the initiation of action to remove or reduce it." It is significant to note that the components of this definition are being accepted as a model for the United States crime prevention programs.

The description of security and protection systems can best be considered by establishing a historical reference between security and the administration of justice. Chronologically, the development of security techniques (physical barriers, manmade, natural, and related concepts) were originated and instituted many years before most police techniques of today.

Initially, security was the responsibility of the person, and only when individuals came together in groups did the responsibility of public safety become somewhat organized. In effect, a police force as we know it today, is really no more than a formalized and structured group within the total concept of security and loss prevention. Many of the present-day policing organizations have as one of their goals the prevention of crime.

Historically, the quasi-military or police force with security emphasis has developed in countries that have a highly centralized form of government. Likewise, private security services of the world have developed in countries with an Anglo-Saxon history. One deterrent to the development of security is that only a small number of terms used in security are translatable into foreign languages. Conversely, most of the terminology used in the police field may be translated into other languages with very little connotational differences. This has restricted communications and, to some degree, the exchange of ideas and theories.

The average person often tends to have a distorted image of the individual employed in the field of security; that is, that all security personnel are elderly and in some cases not very competent. On the contrary, the major portion of individuals in the security field are capable

primary functions of the police

and, at the senior management level, the individuals in many cases equal or exceed their counterparts in other fields in terms of academic degrees and training. Another example of misunderstanding is the usage of terms that are incorrect. This refers to "industrial security," which, in reality, as defined by the U.S. Government is "that portion of internal security which is concerned with the protection of classified information in the hands of U.S. industry." This term is often used as a catchall for all activities and organizations involved in security services. To further understand the field of security, a definition is necessary that encompasses all facets of this large group and categorizes the functions of security.

Defining Security

In defining security, the context in which the term is used depends upon the type and level of application.

> *The term security is often used quite loosely and in many different contexts. For example, such things as national security, international security, private security, retail security, physical security, and industrial security are all enumerated and used in daily conversations. The definitions of these terms are not often clear and are often used interchangeably. In reality, there are two major levels of security: governmental and proprietary. Within each of these levels various types of security do exist.*
>
> *In governmental security such things as international security, national security, and state security are all present. In the broadest sense, the governmental level of security deals with those problems and issues which protect the interests of the government and its dealings with other nations. In its dealings with subnational units of government, or maintenance of power, or the administration of government services, demands are made that its operations be free from interruption and that an environment is established which provides citizens with an opportunity to go about their business in relative safety and freedom from inconvenience.*
>
> *Proprietary security is the other level of security. This includes all measures to be taken by individuals, partnerships, or corporations to protect their private property or interests. In providing security for specific applications, the purpose of security may be described as providing protection of materials, equipment, information, personnel,*

physical facilities, and preventing influences which are undesirable, unauthorized, or detrimental to the goals of the particular organization being secured.

Obviously, then, there are different levels of security which may be discussed. One can discuss the total security of the society, the security of the vast industrial complex, or the security of the small privately owned supermarket. The problems and issues involved are quite similar, the variables being the scope of the problem and the specific security goals. The moral and legal issues are, however, identical.[8]

Public and Private Sectors

In conjunction with a definition of security, the classifications of private and public security forces and organizations are outlined in Table 7-1, pp. 162–163.

Security Field Job Titles

The individual seeking career opportunity information in the security field will find that a number of choices exist. The following selected list depicts a series of job titles in the security field.

Security Director
Security Manager
Security Representative
Classification Management Advisor
Executive Security Advisor
Security Supervisor
Loss Prevention Director
Investigations Manager
Classification Specialist
Fire Protection Administrator
Retail Store Security Representative
Transportation Security Specialist

Airline Security Specialist
Security Training Specialist
Document Control Manager
Emergency Planning Coordinator
Special Staff Assistant
Protective Services Captain
Police Sergeant
Government Security Representative
Credit Investigations Manager
Alarm Technician
Maritime Security Specialist
Petroleum Refinery Protective Services Specialist
Hotel Security Manager

---

[8] Arthur A. Kingsbury and Richard S. Post, *Security Administration: An Introduction* (Springfield, Ill.: C. C. Thomas, 1973), p. 4. Reprinted by permission.

primary functions of the police

Intelligence Representative	Security Education
Prison Security Officer	Representative
Hospital Security Manager	Park Security Representative
Insurance Investigator	Campus Security Chief
Security Management Analyst	Security Consultant
Classified Security	Special Agent
Representative	General Security Supervisor
Proprietary Security Specialist	Special Investigator
Chief of Plant Protection	Security Specialist
Chief of Fire Protection	Security Department Head
Fire Engineer	Chief Special Agent
Manager, Physical Security	Internal Audit Manager

Generally, the administration of justice field has a clear distinction of titles based on difference in function and emphasis, but the security field tends to be grouped by occupational terms. A person working in the retail area with the responsibility of loss prevention or total store protection would normally be referred to as being employed in the "retail security field."

One of the most difficult concepts to grasp in the study of private security is that at the present time there is no one agreed-upon definition of terms. This is vividly demonstrated in the different titles and categories that exist within the security field. Yet in most cases, the function or techniques used are quite similar. The process used to prevent crime and loss within a retail establishment may be very similar to the one used in industry to alleviate or deter crime. The publication, *The Private Police Industry: Its Nature and Extent, II* (R-870/DOJ), published by the U.S. Department of Justice, LEAA, lists over 400 occupational titles of security officers.

Functional Aspect

There are three processes basic to all security endeavors. They are by classification as follows:
1. *Physical security.* The tangible aspects of security, locks, alarms, manmade and natural barriers, and related security equipment.
2. *Personnel security.* The measures taken through a careful selection process of personnel for employment.
3. *Information security.* The concept of safeguarding all information, ideas, correspondence, and the like.

These three processes should be considered inseparable and included in any security-oriented program. Furthermore, the techniques utilized in security tend to be similar in nature and scope.

It is important to understand that most security organizations have a common element and purpose within their corporate and/or individual goals and objectives. This is described as loss prevention. The major purpose or rationale for the existence of all proprietary security is the denial or prevention of loss—either man-made or environmental. Eventually the public policing organizations will assume a larger role in the prevention area, such as the crime prevention units. This will undoubtedly affect the private security sector. This is not to imply a philosophical change, but rather a need or functional modification within the field of private security or protection.

Finally, it is emphasized that security is a philosophy of self-defense for both individuals and organizations and must be kept in its proper perspective at all times.

Recommendations

At present, the security field is growing and developing at a significant rate. With this rapid development and renewed attention there are three areas that need immediate attention. Three recommendations for improvement of the security field are as follows:
1. The development of certification or licensing programs for private security organizations and individuals.
2. The development and modification of legal ramifications pertaining to the private security sector. In effect, the private security sector does not generally operate under the strict codes and legal precedents that the public law enforcement sector does.
3. The immediate need for basic research in the total area of security and loss prevention.

An interesting phenomenon in regard to security is that it is so large an industry, yet so little is known or written about it.

The public tends to be more cognizant of public law enforcement and its growth and problems. Yet the public law enforcement agencies seem to be assimilating those crime and loss prevention concepts that have been initiated by the security industry. Therefore, this broad area of security should be understood by all individuals who are interested in the administration of justice field.

TABLE 7-1. **Public and Private Security Forces**

THE PUBLIC SECTOR	THE PRIVATE SECTOR

LAW ENFORCEMENT AGENCIES
Local Government
  Regular local police (municipalities, counties, townships, special districts)
  Reserve local police
  Special local law-enforcement agencies
    Park police (municipal, county)
    Transit police
    Public-housing police
    Building-department police
    Sanitation-department police
    Airport police
State Government
  State police and/or state highway patrol
  Special state law-enforcement agencies
    State park police or forest rangers
    Narcotics agents and other investigators in state bureaus
    Fish and game wardens
    Police in state universities or colleges, Etc.
Federal Government
  Department of Justice
    Federal Bureau of Investigation
    Immigration and Naturalization Service
    United States marshals
    Border patrol
    Drug Enforcement Administration
	PURCHASED OR CONTRACT PRIVATE SECURITY SERVICES[a]
	  Guards employed by detective agencies and protective-service establishments
	  Detectives, investigators, and undercover agents employed by detective agencies and protective-service establishments
	  Patrolmen employed in private patrol establishments
	  Guards employed in armored-car-service establishments
	  Guard respondents employed in central station alarm services establishments
	IN-HOUSE OR PROPRIETARY PRIVATE SECURITY SERVICES
	  Guards and watchmen employed by industries, business, institutions, and individuals
	  Detectives, investigators, and undercover agents employed by industries, business, institutions, and individuals

THE PUBLIC SECTOR

Treasury Department
    Secret Service
    White House police
    Customs Bureau (ports investigators, customs agents)
    Internal Revenue Service
        Alcohol, tobacco, and firearms special investigators
        Intelligence special agents
        Internal security inspectors
Department of the Interior
    United States Park rangers
    United States Park police
    Bureau of Indian Affairs investigators
    Sports fisheries and wildlife game management agents
Post Office Department
    Postal inspectors
Department of State
    Security agents
Zoo police, Smithsonian, Etc.
GUARDS
    Local government
    State government
    Federal government
    General Services Administration guards, Etc.

[a] Each class of private security service can be subcategorized by type of client or user, e.g., by broad industry, business, and institutional categories.

Summary

The criminal justice system in the United States is composed of three basic elements: police, courts, and corrections. These three components are often plagued by problems that face society as a whole. However, as a part of the government, their function must be to serve the people in the manner in which the people wish to be served.

Traditionally, the police have four primary functions. They are: (1) prevention of crime, (2) preservation of order, (3) protection of person and property, and (4) protection of personal liberty. Many of the policemen see the protection of person and property as their primary function.

The protection of person and property is accomplished by the following activities: (1) enforcing the law, (2) apprehending violators, (3) recovering stolen property, (4) investigation of crime, and (5) assisting in the prosecution and conviction of those who violate the law. Although the police feel that the protection of person and property is their primary function, the preservation of order is the most time-consuming.

The new concepts of police functions in America are threefold. A massive training and educational program is necessary to bring these new concepts to the recognition of the police and the public. These functions are: (1) response to citizen complaint, (2) provision of services to the community, and (3) arrest of suspected criminals.

Crime in the United States has generally been considered a local problem. This attitude has resulted in the creation of over 40,000 separate police agencies in the United States. These agencies have assumed many different faces under many different names, such as sheriff, marshal, and constable; their primary functions and jurisdictions vary from state to state. Many specialized agencies, such as motor vehicles divisions, liquor control boards, and conservation agencies are also in operation. The federal government has added to the numerous agencies with many specialized police agencies.

Whatever the function of the police agency, a distinguishing feature that is found in most of them is their quasi-military structure. Four basic organizational principles are used by many police agencies. They are: (1) chain of command, (2) unity of command, (3) span of control, and (4) definition of authority.

Criticism of police organizations tend to center around areas pointed out in the President's Commission Report of 1967. However, with the financial and technical assistance of LEAA (Law Enforcement Assistance Administration) and other federal and state agencies, change is occurring in police organizations.

Security is gaining importance in the administration of justice. There are three processes basic to all security endeavors: (1) physical security, (2) personnel security, and (3) informational security. One of the most difficult concepts to grasp in the study of private security is that at the present time, there is no agreed-upon definition of terms.

Student Checklist

1. Do you know the four traditionally accepted functions of the police?
2. Can you outline at least two activities of each of the accepted functions of the police?
3. Can you cite three examples of future functions of the police in America?
4. Can you outline the various responsibilities of city, county, state, and federal law enforcement agencies?
5. Do you know the organizational structure of a medium-size police department?
6. What are the processes basic to all security endeavors?

Topics for Discussion

1. Discuss the primary purposes of law enforcement agencies.
2. Draw a comparison of organizational structure between small, medium, and large police agencies.
3. Explain the primary differences between the responsibilities of city, county, state, and federal law enforcement agencies.

ANNOTATED BIBLIOGRAPHY

Adams, T. F., ed. *Criminal Justice: Readings*. Goodyear, Palisades, Calif.: Pacific, 1972. A very large collection of essays written about police work from the street level. Nearly all concern police work, in spite of the title. A good sourcebook for the beginning student, although many articles are dated.

Ahern, J. F. *Police in Trouble: Our Frightening Crisis in Law Enforcement*. New York: Hawthorn Books, 1972. The first of its kind, this work by a former police chief of a metropolitan area concerns itself with the real issues of police work. This book, both widely praised and criticized, is an enlightened view of everyday realisms in police service. It deals with highly volatile issues and the mythology that holds police science from scientific progression.

Bayley, David H., and Harold Mendelsohn. *Minorities and the Police*. New York: Free Press, 1969. A survey of the relationships between the police and minority groups in Denver, Colorado. The analysis of the police as an occupational group and the discussion of police attitudes toward Mexican-Americans and blacks are the important areas of concern.

Clark, R. *Crime in America: Observations on its Nature, Causes, Prevention and Control*. New York: Simon and Schuster, 1970. A must reading for all citizens concerned with the future of America. This widely read work by the former United States Attorney General deals with the issues of criminal justice and destroys many of the most popular myths of the American system. Not only does Clark criticize the American current criminal justice system, but he offers sound alternatives that must be seriously considered.

Cressey, D. R., ed. *Crime and Criminal Justice*. Chicago: Quadrangle Books, 1971. An excellent book of readings by one of foremost authors in the field of criminal justice. The total work concerns itself with "what is wrong" type issues. The chosen selections represent many articles that rarely made this type publication in the past. A good exploration into the impact of human judgment on the system.

Douglas, J. D., ed. *Crime and Justice in American Society*. Indianapolis: Bobbs-Merrill, 1971. A good exploration from drugs to systems analysis, this book of eight readings covers a fair section of the American criminal justice system. It is a little too restrictive to be considered as a sourcebook.

Germann, A. C.; F. D. Day; and R. R. J. Gallati. *Introduction to Law Enforcement and Criminal Justice.* 10th Printing. Springfield: Charles C. Thomas, 1969. Considered by many to be the "bible" of introductory texts in criminal justice, this work is now in its tenth printing. The material is put forth in a package encased in an atmosphere of the basic freedoms of all Americans. Many of the book's recommendations have become standards of police service.

Healy, Richard J. *Design for Security.* New York: Wiley, 1968. This volume defines the hazards that each organization or business may face and describes in detail how defenses can be planned. This book shows how businesses and organizations can save in their security operations.

Morris, N., and G. Hawkins. *The Honest Politician's Guide to Crime Control.* Chicago: University of Chicago, 1969. The intent of this work is to unclutter the American criminal justice system. In spite of the possible misinterpretation of the title, this is a very serious exploration of the problems of the system. Its recommendations are clear and concise and represent the strongest reasons for change of any recent work.

Office of Programs and Policies. *Overview, 1,* No. 1. New York City Police Department, April, 1973. This is the first issue of an innovative journal from a metropolitan police department. Most of the articles are put forth by young creative people in management positions. Real issues in the administration of a large urban police force are explored.

Office of the Federal Register, National Archives and Records Service. *United States Government Organization Manual,* 1968–69, revised June 1, 1968. Washington, D.C.: General Services Administration, 1968. This manual is periodically revised and is considered the "bible" for governmental agency listings.

Oliver, Eric, and John Wilson. *Practical Security in Commerce and Industry.* Epping, Essex: Gower Press Limited, 1972. This book gives you up-to-date security practices. Contents cover new legislation under the Criminal Damage Act, the Industrial Relations Act, and the Fire Precautions Act. Measures against industrial espionage have been developed. Planning for emergencies, including bomb threats and on risks to security arising from drug addiction have also been included. This is a comprehensive and practical reference work.

Post, Richard S., and Arthur A. Kingsbury. *Security Administration: An Introduction.* Springfield, Ill.: C. C. Thomas Publisher, 2nd Ed., 1973. This is a basic introduction to security administration, and a historical and legal framework for security operations, specific security processes, and programs currently and historically utilized in providing security. This book views and analyzes governmental and proprietary security activities to insure that both the student and those engaged in security and law enforcement activities will have a better understanding of its total security field.

President's Commission on Law Enforcement and Administration of Justice. *Task Force Report: The Police.* Washington, D.C.: U.S. Government Printing Office, 1967. This work represents the most thorough survey of police work ever accomplished. It contains truly a wealth of material and is probably the most quoted book concerning police service. So many of the recommendations of this exhaustive study were adopted that many feel it is already dated.

Skolnick, J. H. *Justice Without Trial: Law Enforcement in Democratic Society.* New York: Wiley, 1966. This work was considered the best in its field when published in 1966, and its impact was significant and lasting. The book explores the core of an American city's police department. The article concerning the policeman's working personality is truly a classic in the field of criminal justice literature.

Weston, P. B., and K. M. Wells. *Law Enforcement and Criminal Justice: An Introduction.* Pacific Palisades, Calif.: Goodyear, 1972. This recent work represents one of the better introductory texts in print. Unlike so many other works of this kind, an in-depth study of the offender is offered. This book also contains explorations into causative factors in criminality and a sound listing of the rights of the accused.

Wilson, James Q. *Varieties of Police Behavior*. Cambridge: Harvard University Press, 1968. This is a sociopolitical analysis of the management of eight municipal police agencies in the United States. The development of different styles of policing is discussed and a threefold typology is developed; the types are the legalistic, watchman, and service style.

The study of this chapter will enable you to:

1. Define police role conflict.
2. Cite three examples of police role conflict.
3. Cite examples of how the police adjust to role conflict.
4. Define the term police discretion.
5. Give three examples of discretion used by police officers in the community.
6. Cite J. Q. Wilson's three basic policing styles.
7. Explain the model approach to community policing styles.

8
Styles of Policing

In this chapter we shall examine how the police go about their daily business in communities. We shall demonstrate that as organizations and as individuals they differ among themselves in philosophies of policing. By philosophies of policing we mean their viewpoints and opinions about how they should enforce the laws and preserve the peace. For example, some police departments spend a lot of time on juvenile delinquency programs; others concentrate on patrol and the investigation of crimes, and they deal with juveniles only when they arrest them for specific offenses. Some departments have large, separate traffic divisions; others let the patrol division handle traffic along with its other duties. These differences in emphases indicate differences in policing philosophy. The distinctive pattern of such emphases displayed by a department is that department's policing style.

We shall also look at the individual police officer. Just as departments have styles, so do police officers. For example, in answering a disturbance call involving a fighting husband and wife, one officer may walk in, stop the fight, and ask if either party wishes to file a legal complaint against the other. If neither wishes to do this, as is generally the case, the officer will drop the matter and leave after warning them not to make any further disturbance. Another officer of the same department, however, may sit down and spend considerable time with the couple, listening to their grievances, and trying to help them work things out. Still another officer may help them fill out the forms requesting marriage counseling assistance from a community service organization. He may even fill out the forms himself if they cannot read or write. Each officer handles problems according to his own style, and each style illustrates how that officer makes on-the-spot decisions and how he exercises—note the following phrase, you will see it often in this chapter—*his power of discretion.*

Keep in mind that policing styles and police discretion are complex and controversial subjects. Some veteran police officers and administrators will not even admit that they exist. They are wrong; style and discretion do exist and police display them every day. We shall not attempt to make any rigid rules about whether or not they should be applied. Our purpose is to show that they may benefit or harm a community, depending upon how they are applied.

We shall limit our discussion to community police agencies—generally speaking, these are municipal and county departments—whose broad general jurisdictions put them in close daily contact with the public. Because of their wide range of activities, and the broad discretion they give their members in performing these activities, they develop the most diversified and distinctive organizational and individual policing styles.

Conflict in the Police Role

One of the basic reasons for the American Revolution was that people wanted freedom from an oppressive government. A fear of the potential power of the government to abuse its citizens has long prevailed in the United States. This places the police officer in a difficult role because he represents governmental authority, and he happens to be the representative of government with whom most citizens have the most frequent contact. Furthermore, he is the only governmental official authorized to use force to carry out assignments. This threat of force, although often needed, is frequently resented by citizens. Historically, the police response to this public resentment has been a tendency to isolate themselves from the community and develop a strong feeling of group solidarity.

What do we mean by role? Role can be generally defined as the expectations held by individuals and groups about *what* an organization or individual employee of that organization is supposed to do and *how* they are supposed to do it. Keep in mind that both organizations and individuals have roles. The police organization has a role in the community, and the police officer has a role in the community and in his organization. Expectations aimed at defining the police organization's

172 *introduction to the administration of justice*

role come from the law, the community, and the police organization itself. Expectations aimed at the individual police officer's role come from all of the same sources and also from his fellow employees. These expectations may not be communicated clearly, or they may contradict each other. In both instances, role conflict results.

Most expectations concerning the police role, both as organizations and as individuals, come from the criminal law. Criminal law is both substantive and procedural. Substantive law defines or describes the acts that are prohibited or required. Robbery, murder, and larceny, for example, are prohibited acts; having a driver's license, or obtaining a license to go hunting or sell liquor are required acts. Procedural criminal law describes the correct way to apply the substantive criminal law. Particularly, it describes the procedures that the police must use to enforce the substantive law in a legal fashion, such as warning a suspect of his constitutional rights prior to an interview, bringing him before a magistrate without delay after arrest, and affording him the opportunity to consult with legal counsel.

Conflict Caused by Substantive Criminal Law
Two factors create the conflict in the case of substantive criminal law. The first is the shortage of police officers available to enforce laws. Because of this lack, in most communities the police must be selective in the laws they enforce. This is not always a source of conflict, however, because a second source of police role expectations—the community—*does not* want some laws rigidly enforced. But a conflict always arises when there is a difference of opinion between the police and the community over which laws should be selectively enforced. A case in point might be gambling for charitable purposes. A raid on a church bingo game might set off a violent community uproar against the police. The second sensitive area concerns traffic laws. Citizens normally expect a certain tolerance in speeding cases; they expect "warnings," rather than tickets, in such nonmoving violations as faulty headlights and tail-lights. If the police suddenly began to rigidly enforce traffic laws, the community, through its political leaders, may demand a return to the old level of tolerance.

In communities where there is a police-community consensus on what laws are to be selectively enforced and what laws are to be enforced tolerantly, the conflict is minimized. Such a consensus is most likely to occur in rural and suburban communities where a substantial majority of the population have the same socioeconomic and racial/ethnic backgrounds. In these communities the expected standards of community conduct are generally agreed upon and are clearly communicated to the police. The community-police relationship in this type of community tends to become a personal one because the police and citizens know each other rather well.

This close personal relationship between citizens and police rarely exists in large cities. Large cities usually have diverse populations composed of a wide variety of socioeconomic and racial/ethnic groups. Each neighborhood in the city has different expectations concerning the manner in which the police should handle such law violations as gambling, liquor violations, traffic violations, peace disturbances, and juvenile delinquency.

Conflict Caused by Procedural Criminal Law
Another source of role conflict for police, as we have said, is procedural criminal law. Ideally, the police should always enforce substantive criminal laws in the manner prescribed by procedural law. Ideally, police should never make illegal arrests, illegal searches of persons and property, or coerce confessions. However, they occasionally do violate procedural laws. The reason for this may arise from community expectations concerning the police role. The community expects the police to deal efficiently with the crime problem and may exert pressure, often through political leaders or the news media, to reduce the crime rate. Occasionally, this pressure has led the police to be more concerned with solving crimes and making arrests (enforcing substantive laws) than with doing so in the proper manner (observing procedural criminal law). Here again the legal expectations of the police role and community expectations conflict, and the police organization must adjust to the conflict. The adjustment contributes to the development of a policing style.

Another important source of role conflict is the expectations derived from the police organization itself. Historically, community police agencies have had a tendency to assume that the most important part of their job is dealing with major crimes like murder, rape, robbery, burglary, larceny, and others. This view is given support by the public concern shown to these crimes. At times, however, the policemen's desire to deal efficiently with crime is hampered, in their opinion, by the procedures they must use to solve these criminal cases. Many police officers criticize court decisions that they believe limit their ability to fight crime. Many police departments, especially in the urban areas, have developed a strong orientation toward crime-fighting, and they disregard procedural laws in some cases.

A training officer for an urban police agency once stated that it was important to distinguish between "good" police work and "legal" police work. "Good" police work, according to him, was the fulfillment of a combination of community and organizational expectations of police performance. He gave as an example of "good" police work a case in which an individual was suspected of selling drugs, but the police had insufficient evidence to arrest him. The training officer said a "good" policeman would stop the individual's car, search it, remove and destroy any drugs found, and then release the individual because of the illegal arrest and search. This is clearly a case in which the policeman would violate procedural criminal laws to do what he perceived his organization and community expected him to do. "Legal" police work would not have allowed stopping the suspect at all.

Adjustment to Role Conflict: The Development of Policing Styles

Role conflict requires that some degree of adjustment be made in role performance. How do the police respond to these diverse expectations? Numerous individuals have contributed their thoughts on the police role adjustment conflict. Some of the more important attitudes will be discussed in this section. In the discussion, the word police will be used mainly to apply to organizations, and only in a lesser degree, to individuals.

Varying Theories

In 1931, Hopkins[1] described what he called the police "war theory" of crime control. According to him, considerable public pressure is exerted on police to control crime. This creates a police attitude that favors

[1] E. Jerome Hopkins, *Our Lawless Police* (New York: Viking Press, 1931).

settling matters with criminals in the streets by the use of excessive physical force if necessary. Hopkins found a belief widespread among police that crime was controlled by punishment and that the police job was to administer that punishment. Any police illegalities involving excessive force and violation of procedural rights of suspects were considered acceptable.

From these observations, Hopkins developed his war theory of crime control. His theory was that police believed they were waging a war on crime and that any methods were justified in winning that war. The basic role conflict discussed by Hopkins is essentially that between the conflicting demands of the substantive and procedural criminal law. The public and the police organization desire that crime be controlled by application of the punitive measures in the substantive law. The police organization and, in some cases, the police officer, desire to punish the offender by legal arrest and confinement in jail. But if procedural criminal law will not permit this because of a lack of evidence, the police may take matters into their own hands and deal out street justice by beating up a suspect with a nightstick or running him out of town.

Westley,[2] in his 1951 research of a Midwestern city, makes observations similar to the observations of Hopkins. Westley found that some police officers believed it permissible to use violence to gain respect from citizens. Westley also noted that the public regarded the policemen as corrupt and inefficient and that the policemen tended to view the citizens as their enemies. The police believed strongly that the manner in which they wanted to perform their job was in conflict with what was desired by the community.

This is a basic role conflict and the adjustments made by the police were as follows:

1. The police tended to withdraw from the community and isolate themselves by associating only with each other.
2. They disagreed with community desires because of the negative attitude displayed by the public toward the police.
3. They developed the belief that the use of violence to gain respect from citizens was acceptable (e.g., a person who "talks back" should get slapped or punched).

---

[2] William A. Westley, "The Police: A Sociological Study of Law, Custom, and Morality" (Ph.D. diss., University of Chicago Press, 1951). Published by M.I.T. Press, Cambridge, 1970.

4. They sought to lessen public criticism of police by apprehending as many criminals as possible. In addition, the police organization rewarded its members for catching criminals with citations for bravery and promotions.
5. They accepted the use of violence, and the violation of the procedural rights of suspects in cases where information was required to apprehend criminals, and as punishment for sexual criminals when reluctant witnesses would not testify against them in court.

Banton[3] refers to Westley in his comparative study of American and Scottish Police Departments. In the three American cities studied, two Southern and one Northeastern, Banton also found that, because of his job, the officer tended to become separated from the community. This separation created some problems in how police officers made decisions; that is, how they exercised discretion. According to Banton, the exercise of discretion is important to an officer on patrol because much of the time he is a peace officer (peace-keeper), rather than a law officer (law enforcer). The peace-officer role is important in the discussion of policing styles because it illustrates what laws the department or the community desire to be selectively enforced and how the officer acts when he is faced with violations of a law not on the list to be enforced. The role of peace officer forces the policeman to make his own decisions as to how he will handle violations that come to his attention, without leaning on the exact letter of the law as a guideline. This is an especially important role, according to Banton, because ordinarily the patrolman spends much more of his time as a peace-keeper than as a law enforcer.

Another important contributor to understanding how police adjust to role conflict is Skolnick.[4] The adjustment that he describes concerns that between substantive and procedural criminal law. In a 1966 study of two urban police departments, Skolnick found a tendency on the part of police to emphasize a social-order role more than a legal-actor role. The police seemed more concerned with using substantive laws to main-

---

[3] Michael Banton, *The Policeman in the Community* (New York: Basic Books, 1964).

[4] Jerome H. Skolnick, *Justice Without Trial* (New York: Wiley, 1967). Skolnick's distinction concerning the order-maintenance and legal-actor role of police is similar to Herbert Packard's crime control and due process models. The former emphasizes social control and factual guilt instead of legal guilt and individual justice. Herbert C. Packard, "Two Models on the Criminal Process," *University of Pennsylvania Law Review 113* (November 1964), pp. 1-68.

tain order than in following the guidelines of procedural laws. Above all, says Skolnick, the policeman sees his job as ferreting out crime by being alert and ready to respond vigorously to it, and only later to be concerned with justifications for the arrest or search made.

Skolnick also believes that the emphasis on police managerial efficiency in the United States encourages police to adopt the social-order role, and he believes that this managerial efficiency is often construed as "professionalism." The managerially efficient police administrator advocates statistical production in the form of arrests, traffic tickets issued, and the like.

The more arrests and tickets produced, the more efficient the individual officer and his organization appear on paper, and the more "professional" they seem. Police emphasis on social order through apprehending suspects is given support by this idea of professionalism. Skolnick believes that policemen are too concerned with controlling crime by any means necessary, and not enough with the legal expectations of their role. The police organizations' expectations of the social-order role (which have some community support) are to be efficient in making arrests and to be concerned about how the arrests were made only afterward, when the statistics are in.

Wilson[5] has also made an important contribution in understanding the role adjustment of police agencies. In a study of eight community police organizations, Wilson identified three basic policing styles: (1) watchman, (2) legalistic, and (3) service. He said that the differences in styles could be noted when observing how each police organization handled two basic types of situations confronting police: order-maintenance and law-enforcement situations.

Order-maintenance situations are those related to disturbances of the peace or minor conflict between two or more people. Handling these situations is similar to the peace-keeping activities identified by Banton. Examples of peace disturbances might be a noisy drunk, a panhandler, or an apartment dweller's loud radio; examples of minor conflict might be a tavern fight, a family disturbance, or a landlord-tenant dispute. In these situations it is not simply a matter of applying the law; the law must also be interpreted and an attempt made to determine who is wrong

---

[5] James Q. Wilson, *Varieties of Police Behavior* (Cambridge, Mass.: Harvard University Press, 1968).

and what to do about it. The power of arrest can be used, but frequently it is not. The police officer has broad discretion in handling these situations.

Law-enforcement situations demand a predetermined pattern of police response and much less discretion on the part of the patrolman. In cases of robbery, burglary, or serious assaults, the officer will always make an arrest if possible. Such situations require little interpretation of the law. Although traffic violations are not as serious as robbery and burglary, some of them are serious enough to warrant a predetermined pattern of response. For example, reckless speeding in a school zone will almost automatically result in the issuance of a ticket.

Wilson found more degrees of emphasis given to order-maintenance than to law-enforcement situations. The *watchman* style was frequently used by police involved in order-maintenance functions. This style, he said, tended to overlook, tolerate, or ignore many minor violations of the law, or at most, handle them short of arrest. The organization encouraged the patrolman to follow the path of least resistance. However, while many crimes were ignored as a matter of general practice, the police would occasionally adopt a "get tough" approach when they thought that certain activities were getting out of hand, such as when juvenile fights began developing into large-scale gang fights.

The second style Wilson identified was *legalistic*. The police department using this style encouraged the patrolman to take a law-enforcement view of as many of the situations he encountered as possible. He was encouraged to view every situation in terms of legal alternatives. The legalistic department desired a single standard of conduct—the law—for the whole community, and generally only one appropriate solution—a legal one—for each situation.

Wilson's third style, *the service*, takes seriously all situations encountered. However, the service style does not formally apply the law as frequently as the legalistic. Order-maintenance situations are taken seriously, but alternatives other than arrest are often used. Some common alternatives are referral to a social service agency, or the development of special police programs (e.g., traffic education, drug education, and others) to cope with order-maintenance problems.

A useful way to compare Wilson's three policing styles would be to contrast their respective responses to an order-maintenance situation involving juveniles drinking beer. The watchman-style police department would ignore the situation, or perhaps confiscate the beer, pour it out,

styles of policing **179**

and tell the juveniles to go home. The legalistic-style police department would arrest the juveniles and confiscate the beer for evidence. The service-style police department would probably confiscate the beer for evidence, take the juveniles home to their parents, and then suggest attendance in an educational program on the problems of alcohol, as an alternative to filing juvenile charges.

In a law-enforcement situation such as a "robbery in progress" call, all three organizations would undoubtedly respond in the same way; that is, attempt to arrest the suspect, since there would be little difference among the three styles in police role expectations.

A Policing Styles Model

To help the reader understand more about community policing styles, we shall describe a model that can be used to analyze them. The model is a general one and should not be considered definitive or absolute, but rather as a useful method of examining the distinctive characteristics that represent an organization's adjustments to role conflict.

A basic assumption of this model is that a primary goal of police is to reduce crime and maintain order, in a manner designed to establish a trusting relationship between them and the great majority of citizens. Trust insures community support. The desire for community support reflects a desire to fulfill community expectations of the police role. The concern for reducing crime and maintaining order involves both the law-enforcement and order-maintenance situations described by Wilson, and the law officer and the peace officer roles of Banton. How these activities are carried out determines the style of the police organization.

Police Methods

Generally speaking, police methods of reducing crime and maintaining order are directed at two broad causes of crime: (1) the opportunity to engage in crime and (2) the motive for engaging in crime. The word motive will be applied to both the desire and the reasons for the desire to engage in criminal or disorderly behavior.

From the standpoint of the general community, the police methods can be generally classified as either positive or negative in nature. Positive methods are those the general community tends to see as helping to solve crime and disorder problems; negative methods are those the general community tends to see as mere devices used by the police to punish citizens for lapses of behavior. A positive method of response to a rash of juvenile traffic violations would be a police-sponsored training course; a negative method would be to issue more traffic tickets to juveniles.

Some typical methods employed by police organizations to cope with crime and disorder are described in the following pages.

Education. The education of the community to protect their own lives and property and keeping the community informed about such matters as drug problems, the law, and driving problems are standard projects. The contemporary concept of crime prevention often involves educational programs encouraging the citizen to engage in "target hardening" (i.e., increasing protection for home or business). Education can be directed toward both opportunity and motive. Educational programs designed to "harden targets" primarily concern opportunity; programs designed to educate about drugs concern motive. Education is essentially a positive police method.

Apprehension. This is essentially a "punishment" method. It implies the "catching" role of the police and includes such activities as criminal investigations (in which the intent is to arrest), undercover work, stakeouts, raids, and the like. It also involves the issuance of traffic tickets, which usually constitutes the most frequent police contact with citizens. Generally, this method is negative as far as the general community is concerned because of its "punishment" connotations.

Deterrence. This method generally consists of making the police visible to the public in uniform or marked mobile units. Commonly called patrolling, it is designed to limit both the opportunity and desire to engage in inappropriate behavior. The uniformed, walking beat officer, the marked police car, and the helicopter are the primary means of deterrence. This is both a positive and a negative method because police presence reassures some citizens but frightens or creates anxiety for others.

Saturation. This is an extreme form of deterrence that is carried out by "flooding" an area with police officers, usually troublesome areas. It is directed at both opportunity and motive. The saturation method generally includes aggressive patrolling and interrogation practices by police. The aggressiveness of these tactics and their frequent emphasis upon arrests make saturation a negative method.

styles of policing

Figure 8-1. A community program in "target hardening." In this case, a neighborhood has been educated to rely on itself as well as on the police.

Mediation. This is also called conflict management, crisis intervention, and violence prevention. Essentially, it relies on the ability of specially trained police officers to act as mediators in interpersonal and intergroup conflicts. An example is a family disturbance in which an officer tries to act as mediator between a fighting husband and wife by reducing tensions and identifying some of the reasons for the conflict in order to lessen the likelihood of a recurring fight. Since the police are placed in a helping relationship with the citizen, this is a positive method.

Referral or Diversion. This consists of referring or diverting individual problems to community agencies outside of the criminal justice system. Referral of a fighting husband and wife to a family counseling center may be an alternative after mediation has taken place. Diversion is most common in juvenile and drug cases. Referral and diversion are designed to deal with the motive for inappropriate behavior rather than the opportunity. These are positive methods because their purpose is to help, not punish, people.

Community Perceptions of Police

Figure 8-2 illustrates police methods concerning opportunity and motive, and their general positive and negative impact on community perceptions of police.

Figure 8-2. Categories of police methods: general community reaction.

	Positive	Negative
Opportunity	Education Deterrence	Deterrence Saturation
Motive	Education Mediation Referral–Diversion	Apprehension Deterrence Saturation

Causative factors

styles of policing **183**

The combination of emphases given these methods constitutes the style of the police organization. To assist in developing a model of policing styles, the term *counselor method* will be applied to a positive method used by police, and the term *enforcer method* will be used to apply to a negative method. Then, generally speaking, the police can be placed in counselor or enforcer roles in the community. Figure 8-3 uses these two basic police roles to create a matrix that identifies styles of community police organizations.

Figure 8-3. The counselor–enforcer model of policing styles.

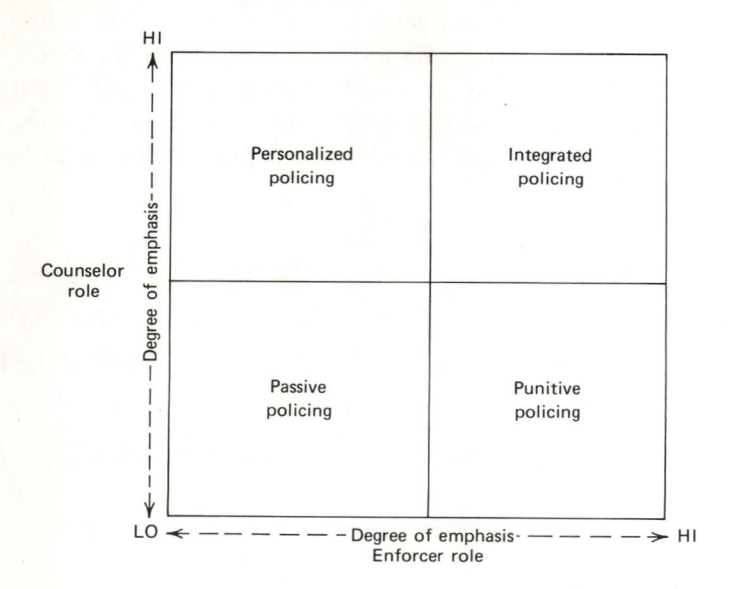

	Low Enforcer	High Enforcer
High Counselor	Personalized policing	Integrated policing
Low Counselor	Passive policing	Punitive policing

Depending on the degree of emphasis given to the enforcer and counselor roles of police, several styles of community policing can be identified. Emphasis is defined as the tendency and willingness to use certain methods.

Degree of Emphasis	Policing Style
Low counselor and enforcer	Passive
Low counselor, high enforcer	Punitive
High counselor, low enforcer	Personalized
High counselor and enforcer	Integrated

introduction to the administration of justice

There is a tendency in discussing styles to think of only one style for each police organization. This is not the case because one organization can have several styles. These styles can follow shift lines (e.g., days, evenings), specialty (e.g., traffic, investigations), or neighborhoods in the community. This is the result of different expectations of performance within the police organization itself; and different expectations create role conflict for which adjustments are necessary.

Passive policing is similar to Wilson's watchman style. Generally, the police ignore many violations and avoid initiating any active programs to deal with crime problems. Passive policing usually occurs because of excessive political influence exerted on the police department to curb formerly aggressive activities. The other extreme, *punitive policing,* occurs when political pressure is put on the police to do something drastic about crime. An urban community that has had a passive police suddenly faced with a rising crime rate may pressure the police to "control" crime. The police response will probably be to engage in aggressive saturation tactics and increase arrests. In practice, punitive policing usually does not last long. The more aggressive the police become, the more the community resists and forces them back into a passive role. The passive-punitive cycle occurs frequently in many cities in which considerable political influence is exerted on the police department.

Personalized policing usually prevails in small communities where police officers and citizens know each other very well. This familiarity results in police decisions based on both the person and the problem, rather than merely on the problem itself. For example, in personalized policing, juvenile delinquents are much more likely to be taken home to their parents for punishment rather than be arrested.

Personalized policing can also exist in large cities that have precinct or neighborhood police stations because the people and the police get to know each other as individuals. This results in police decisions similar to those made in small communities.

The main problem with personalized police decisions is that they often reflect a "helping" role that may not be at all objective. It is one thing for a police officer to refer a person to a family counseling center to help solve a problem; it is another matter for an officer to let a person get away with a law violation because of friendship.

Another problem in personalized policing is that "favorite" groups

Figure 8-4. Personalized policing can, and does, exist in large cities that have neighborhood police stations. These two photographs, with at least a 70-year span between them, illustrate a continuity of efforts toward good community relationships. The two contemporary officers are not in uniform.

may develop. In communities with diverse racial populations, middle-class whites may be treated favorably by the police, while the racial minority may be subjected to strict enforcer action. In such instances, personalized policing restricts the helping relationships to selected groups, usually the groups who "run" the community.

Integrated policing represents a balance between the enforcer and counselor roles of police. This balance usually occurs when a community, of whatever size, decides it wants objective, impartial, and effective policing, after the community becomes "fed up" with the other three styles and demands a change. The integrated style uses the enforcer and counselor roles in the combination that is found most effective in achieving the twin goals of controlling crime and maintaining community support. The leadership in an integrated department is likely to use all the police methods described above as community problems call for them. Success will lie in maintaining the correct balance.

Many police organizations are now attempting to change from personalized, passive, or punitive policing to something else by "professionalizing." Two types of professionalism that are now emerging are related to the integrated style. One is the service model of Wilson and the other is the model characterized by Skolnick as "efficiency-oriented."

At present, Wilson's service model appears to be prevalent in suburban communities that have no internal social strife. These communities generally have no serious crime problems and are wealthy enough to demand a professional police force.

Skolnick's efficiency-oriented professionalism is prevalent in many large, urban area police departments. This professionalism supports punitive policing by rewarding arrests, the issuance of tickets, and other negatively aggressive tactics. The efficiency-oriented department has not yet rewarded the police officer for success in the counseling role. Until these departments recognize that the enforcer and the counselor roles must be balanced, and both rewarded, the integrated style will not develop, and efficient professionalism will not become effective professionalism.

The integrated police style is aimed only at effectiveness. It recognizes the following rules:

1. To be successful in crime control an organization must develop community trust and support. The police will never be effective without the active support of the community.
2. There are many offenses of the law that can best be handled by positive counseling methods.
3. The legal expectations of the police role demand a strong commitment to a strict observance of the procedural rights of citizens.
4. The police role in controlling crime and disorder should not be overly militant. Citizens of the community should be encouraged by the police to accept a large part of this responsibility.
5. Historically, the more punitive the police have become in doing their job, the more restrictions have been placed upon them. Alternative roles to that of the enforcer must be found.
6. The individual police officer must have a strong personal commitment to professional growth and must constantly educate and train himself to insure this growth.

Police Officer Discretion

As we have said before, discretionary decisions make up the style of the individual police officer. Several forces mold his discretionary decisions.

Some of these are the law, organizational policy, opinions of the other officers he works with (peer group), his personal orientation, the facts of the situation in which he has to make a discretionary decision, and the actions of the other parties involved in the situation. Many police organizations have attempted to formulate departmental policies to provide guidelines for the exercise of discretion, but the police officer faces such a wide variety of tasks and situations that it is probably impossible to formulate policies to cover them all.

Another vital force exerted on the officer that greatly affects the manner in which he makes decisions is what Skolnick calls the danger-authority conflict. Police authority brings some unavoidable danger that creates anxiety for the officers. They become acutely sensitive to threatening situations and threatening people, and they act aggressively to protect themselves in situations in which they suspect danger is likely. The problem is that the police officer may stereotype certain people and situations as threatening when they are really not, and then make faulty decisions as a result. Some of these faulty decisions have precipitated riots and bloodshed in the past.

Another factor that influences discretionary decisions is the fixed idea that, in encounters with citizens, most police expect to be treated with respect and to have their wishes obeyed. When they do not get this response they may exercise their discretion to punish the lack of it. Citizens who "talk back" to police officers may receive traffic tickets for violations that would earn a "polite" citizen only a verbal or written warning.

Many police officers make decisions in peace-keeping, order-maintenance, and law-enforcement situations based on the status of the person involved. Some police treat young people, minority groups, and poor people differently than they do older people, nonminority group members, and people of higher socioeconomic status.

Police officers make decisions daily that do not reflect the expectations of the law or what their organization desires. Police tend to under-enforce the law far more frequently than they overenforce it. They are much more likely to make discretionary decisions that are less restrictive than the law than they are to make decisions that interpret the law strictly or abuse the legal rights of citizens.

However used, discretion must be kept in mind by each police officer and police organization. To insure fair decisions by officers, organizations must develop policies insuring a reasonably objective approach to each encounter. Education and training will help in this endeavor. These policies should give police officers guidance as to the performance expected when dealing with specific community groups. As police organizations branch out into counseling activities, it is especially important to create alternatives to arrest that will assist in solving community problems rather than avoiding the problems or punishing the participants.

The importance of guiding the discretion of police officers cannot be overemphasized. The day-to-day behavior of officers is the practice of justice in society. If this behavior is objective and equitable, justice is more likely to become a reality to the citizens of the United States.

Conclusions

During the twentieth century the role of the police has been changing, seeking a definition acceptable to the expectations of the law, the community, and the police themselves. The likelihood is that the role assumed by community police will continue to vary from locality to locality as it always has. The direction is unquestionably toward professionalism, but community expectations will undoubtedly shape the form that this professionalism will take.

Certainly, professionalism is needed. The problems confronting police are complex and must be dealt with by well-educated, dedicated individuals. However, one of the unintended consequences of professionalism is that of developing the attitude that the professional is always right. Just as the police have isolated themselves in the past from the community by a negative attitude toward the public, they could also isolate themselves in the future by retreating into a narrow concept of "efficiency-oriented" professionalism.

This isolation must not be allowed to develop. A community–police partnership is essential if problems of crime and disorder are to be solved. To create this partnership, it will be necessary for the community to trust its police organization and police officers. This trust will come only after police officers begin making consistently equitable decisions in the treatment of citizens and after police organizations balance their counselor and enforcer roles in the best interests of the community.

Summary

One of the major influences on policing is role concept: the role concept of the police organization, the role concept of the individual officer, and the role expectations of the community. If role expectations are not clearly communicated and, sometimes even if they are, role conflict may occur. Criminal law, substantive and procedural, may also cause role conflict. This role conflict requires that adjustments be made in role performance.

Generally speaking, police methods of reducing crime and maintaining order are directed at two broad causes of crime: opportunity and motive. The methods used are generally classified by the community as either positive (crime-solving) or negative (punishment). Typical methods employed by police agencies include: (1) education, (2) apprehension, (3) deterrence, (4) saturation, (5) mediation, and (6) referral/diversion. These methods are not inclusive, but they are the most common ones used at this time.

Depending on the degree of emphasis given to enforcer and counselor roles of police, several styles of community policing can be identified. They are: (1) passive policing, (2) punitive policing, (3) personalized policing, and (4) integrated policing.

The individual police officer uses discretion in decision making. Several forces effect his discretion: laws, opinions of other officers, personal orientation, and the facts of the case all play an important role.

Student Checklist

1. Can you define police role conflict?
2. Are you able to cite three examples of police role conflict?
3. Do you know how the police adjust to role conflict?
4. Can you define the term police discretion?
5. Can you cite three examples of discretion used by police officers in a community situation?
6. Are you able to list J. Q. Wilson's three basic policing styles?
7. Can you develop a model approach to community policing styles?

Topics for Discussion

1. Discuss the distinction between the various philosophies of police service.
2. Discuss the need for the development of various styles of policing.
3. Discuss the need for professional thinkers as members in a contemporary justice system.

ANNOTATED BIBLIOGRAPHY

American Bar Association. *The Urban Police Function*. Project on Standards for Criminal Justice, Chicago, 1972. This report is a tentative draft of the work of a special project of the American Bar Association. It establishes general principles for the operation of the urban police department. Areas covered include law enforcement policy-making, public support, police unions, and police objectives and priorities.

Banton, Michael. *The Policeman in the Community*. New York: Basic Books, 1964. A sociological study of the role of police in the United States and in Scotland. Significant areas covered are control of interpersonal relations, conflict between police and private roles, and a discussion of the comparative isolation of the police from the community.

Bayley, David H., and Harold Mendelsohn. *Minorities and the Police*. New York: Free Press, 1969. This is a survey of the relationships between the police and minority groups in Denver, Colorado. The analysis of the police as an occupational group and the discussion of police attitudes toward Mexican-Americans and blacks are the important areas of concern.

Berkeley, George. *The Democratic Policeman*. Boston: Beacon Press, 1969. This is a comparative sociological study of police in the United States and selected Western European countries. The discussion of the apparent conflict between the idea of police and democracy is most interesting. The book includes a discussion of recruitment and education, the policeman at work, policing the police, and police and society.

Bittner, Egon. *The Functions of the Police in Modern Society*. Chevy Chase, Maryland: National Institute of Mental Health, Center for Studies of Crime and Delinquency, 1970. This is a sociological analysis of the role of the police in the United States. Significant discussions are given to the relationship between police and the courts, the use of force, and the importance of professional education for police officers.

Davis, Kenneth. *Discretionary Justice: A Preliminary Inquiry*. Baton Rouge: Louisiana State University Press, 1969. A legalistic and administrative analysis of discretionary justice. The author suggests concrete ideas for dealing with the abuses of discretion. His emphasis is in the area of administrative role-making for dealing with discretionary abuse.

Hahn, Harlan, ed. *Police in Urban Society*. Beverly Hills, Calif.: Sage Publications, 1971. This is a book of readings covering a broad area in the relationship between police and community in the urban setting. Significant areas of discussion include public perceptions of police problems, police perceptions of public issues, and the emergence of police professionalism.

La Fave, Wayne R. *Arrest: The Decision to Take a Suspect into Custody*. Chicago: Little, Brown, 1965. A legalistic study of the implications of the arrest of suspects. A significant portion of the book concerns the legal implications of the use of discretion by police officers and the impact of that discretion.

Niederhoffer, Arthur, and Abraham S. Blumberg, eds. *The Ambivalent Force: Perspectives on the Police*. Waltham, Mass.: Ginn, 1970. This is a book of readings concerning a wide variety of problems regarding the role of police and police relationships. The most interesting sections concern police values and culture, discretion, and a discussion of police and the legal system.

More, Harry Jr., ed. *Critical Issues in Law Enforcement*. Cincinnati, Ohio: Anderson Press, 1972. A book of readings covering several important contemporary issues in policing. Areas of most significance include a discussion of the police role, police professionalism, civil disorder, ethnic tensions, control of police conduct, and policy formulation.

Reasons, Charles, and Jack L. Kuykendall, eds. *Race, Crime, and Justice*. Pacific Palisades: Goodyear Press, 1972. A book of readings covering the relationship between the judicial system and minority groups. The section on police and minority groups is most valuable in understanding the dynamics of police-minority group encounters and the exercise of police discretion in minority communities.

Reiss, Albert J. *The Police and the Public*. New Haven: Yale University Press, 1971. A sociological study of three municipal police agencies. The purpose of the study is to analyze police-citizen encounters. Results indicate the importance of social support for police in encounters, the need for officer and citizen civility in encounters, and the importance of proactive and reactive police intervention with citizens.

The study of this chapter will enable you to:

1. Cite the various functions assigned to line type activities.
2. Define staff functions.
3. State five examples of police patrol responsibilities.
4. Cite the primary functions of the investigative services unit.
5. Outline the primary responsibilities of supportive services.
6. Define two styles of contemporary police communications systems.
7. Cite the steps of the generally accepted selection process for a police officer.

9
Overview of Police Services

Line Functions

Patrol

The patrol function is the hub of the law enforcement wheel around which all other functions revolve. While most authorities, academic and professional, would readily agree with such a statement, the public has the general impression that the patrol officer's duties are the least important of a police department's responsibilities. Novels, movies, and television programs have elevated the significance of the detective out of proportion at the expense of the uniformed patrol officer. Ironically, the majority of the patrol officers are the most inexperienced members of a police department, yet their function is considered the most important.

A review of the responsibilities of the patrol officer may help to bring the picture back into its proper prospective. At the outset, however, it should be made clear that in the majority of all cases investigated, it is the patrol officer who sets into motion the activities of all other police officers, including the detective.

Under general supervision, more theoretical than real, the patrol officer is responsible for the maintenance of order, the enforcement of laws and ordinances, the prevention and suppression of crime, and the protection of life and property. These goals are achieved by the following activities:

1. Patrolling an assigned area of the community by vehicle, foot, or as otherwise assigned.
2. Responding to emergencies, assigned or observed.
3. Investigating unusual or suspicious conditions.
4. Making arrests, serving subpoenas and warrants, and guarding prisoners.

5. Investigating traffic accidents and directing traffic.
6. Issuing citations to traffic violators.
7. Administering first aid and giving assistance to the injured.
8. Noting and reporting unsafe conditions.
9. Preparing evidence for criminalistics examination or court presentation.
10. Searching for stolen and lost property and lost or missing persons.
11. Providing general information to the public.
12. Writing reports relating to investigations or potential investigations of crime.
13. Analyzing facts, clues, and evidence in the investigation of crime.
14. Operating radio and other communications equipment.
15. Maintaining effective relationships with other law enforcement agencies, employees, and the public.

At some point, each of these responsibilities can become a specialty itself. As the patrol officer develops information, the scope of his investigation may require more detailed inquiry than he has the time or the training for. This is where the remainder of the line, staff, supportive, and investigative service functions come into play. It is here that they lend their particular skills to the patrol officer's investigation in an effort to maintain order, enforce laws and ordinances, prevent and suppress crime, and protect life and property.

Traffic

The traffic officer performs a secondary line function specifically designed to diminish losses from accidents. He accomplishes this by:

1. Determining facts related to accidents as a basis for accident prevention, and service to involved parties requiring impartial and objective evidence in order to seek civil justice in the settlement of accident losses.
2. Aiding accident victims by administering first aid, seeing to the transportation of those requiring further medical attention, and protecting property inside vehicles.
3. Obtaining the most expedient flow of vehicular and pedestrian traffic consistent with safety.
4. Obtaining compliance with traffic laws and ordinances from motorists and pedestrians.
5. Assisting traffic engineers and traffic safety educational agencies by providing pertinent information relevant to their function.
6. Serving as an inspection, investigation, and reporting force for

municipal government in detecting problems and proposing corrective measures.
7. Planning for traffic routing during predictable emergencies and catastrophes.
8. Providing assistance and information to motorists and pedestrians.[1]

The traffic officer may work alone or with another traffic car or motorcycle and may utilize sophisticated radar equipment.

Juvenile
Much of the violence of the early 1960s involved youths and students. Numerous studies, surveys, and commissions have reflected a need for increased police involvement in dealing with young people. The juvenile officer is in perhaps the best position to work the most effectively with teen and preteen youngsters. It is his responsibility to strive toward the reduction and prevention of delinquency as well as investigate cases involving juveniles.

In most police departments today, one or more officers are assigned to this secondary line function. These officers generally review all reports involving police contact with young people. Follow-up investigations are initiated in cases where charges are to be presented before the juvenile court, or when further contact with the youngster and his parents may seem to be beneficial to that youngster. It is the purpose of juvenile court laws to secure for each youngster the care and guidance necessary for his spiritual, emotional, and physical welfare, preferably in his own home.

Working with that premise, farsighted law enforcement agencies, through the juvenile officer, attempt to cope with a youngster's problems within the community rather than sending him to a juvenile detention center where he may receive little if any meaningful help. It is believed that far better results are reached when a youngster's problems are dealt with locally. A juvenile officer may involve himself with family counseling or make referrals to any number of local social service agencies, one of which may be specifically equipped to deal with a particular need.

Alternatives to the juvenile justice system were suggested in 1967

---

[1] George D. Eastman, ed., *Municipal Police Administration*, 6th ed. (Washington, D.C.: International City Managers Association, 1969), p. 106.

by the Task Force Reports.[2] And in 1968, federal funds were authorized under the auspices of the California Youth Authority to finance four pilot projects called the Youth Service Bureau (YSB). Since then, their numbers have increased and spread to states other than California. These agencies were designed as an alternative to the juvenile justice system. Counseling and other activities can be arranged for the youngster and his parents. Referrals come from other agencies, the schools and, of course, the police. The service provided by YSB is not mandatory, but it does assist the juvenile officer in the social work aspect of the job. This aspect removes the stigma attached to most "establishment" agencies that deal with the problems of young people. The police are obviously in the best position to provide referrals in need of the greatest help. The wise juvenile officer will work closely with the Youth Service Bureau where it is available to him.

Vice/Narcotics

Major law enforcement agencies have separated the vice and narcotics functions from the general investigative services because of the uniqueness of the problems involved in their investigation. Medium and small police departments, however, must often continue to include these functions as part of general investigative services due to a lack of manpower.

Vice includes prostitution, illegal gambling, use and sale of illegal alcoholic beverages, and the distribution and sale of obscene or pornographic material, and it is almost always tied in some way to organized crime. The investigation of narcotics and vice is best facilitated by a single unit. And since organized crime knows no boundaries, the Omnibus Crime Control and Safe Streets Act of 1968 and the Organized Crime Control Act of 1970 were passed to coordinate investigations at all levels of government: federal, state, and local. The effects of such legislation and cooperation between agencies have yet to be felt, but they will undoubtedly prove beneficial to society.

Officers involved in such activities often take on the appearance and dress of those involved in vice and narcotics. These so-called under-

---

[2] The President's Commission on Law Enforcement and Administration of Justice, *Task Force Report: Juvenile Delinquency and Youth Crime* (Washington, D.C.: U.S. Govt. Printing Office, 1967), pp. 19-21.

cover operations are extremely dangerous. It is not uncommon for an undercover officer to mingle alone and unarmed with extremely dangerous criminals. Because there is no regular pattern to the comings and goings of such criminals, a great deal of time is required for an unknown to become accepted by a group of criminals. This acceptance enables the undercover agent to gather the evidence necessary for a successful prosecution.

Plainclothes
The last of the secondary line functions to be discussed will be that of the plainclothes, or general investigative services. Their responsibilities may be basically the same as those of the patrol officer when they operate in civilian clothing and in unmarked cars. At other times they are used in the investigation of such crimes as commercial and residential burglaries, auto thefts, thefts from autos, and grand theft from persons. They usually work in teams; occasionally with marked patrol units and frequently with vice and narcotics officers. Where a uniformed officer feels that his presence may hamper the apprehension of someone in the act of committing a crime, he can ask that plainclothes units continue the surveillance or investigation.

Officers assigned to the plainclothes and general investigation unit are usually seasoned officers who have demonstrated an ability and a desire to perform in such a capacity. The value of using such tactics is related to the kind of illegal activity involved and is within the capabilities of even the smallest police departments; even if only on a part-time basis.

Information discovered as a result of the arrests made in the Watergate case can be directly attributed to plainclothes officers of the Metropolitan Police Department of Washington, D.C. The Ervin Committee Senate Hearings have disclosed that a lookout equipped with a walkie-talkie had been positioned across the street from the Watergate complex. He most assuredly would have alerted his confederates inside the Democratic National Convention Headquarters had he seen uniformed officers in marked patrol cars.

Staff and Supportive Functions

Investigative

The investigator or detective's responsibility lies in following up and supporting the patrol officer. Investigations are usually classified in two categories: crime against persons (simple and aggravated assault, murder, rape, and robbery) and crimes against property (burglary, auto theft, grand and petty larceny, and fraud).

The patrol officer generally does not have the time necessary to conduct extensive or drawn-out interviews, laborious file searches, tedious and extensive crime report reviews, or contacts with other law enforcement agencies for assistance. The detective is able to perform these functions. Generally, officers assigned to an investigation unit have had many years of experience and have developed expertise in a particular type of crime, such as murder or robbery, but this is not always the case.

The uniformed patrol officer who is unable to apprehend the perpetrator of a crime at the scene becomes the preliminary investigator. In some departments he simply protects the evidence at the scene until the arrival of other investigators whose sole responsibility is to take charge of the case. Since most law enforcement agencies are small, the investigator may be the uniformed officer who responds to the call.[3] It is his job to protect, preserve, and search for evidence that will determine the nature of the crime. From the evidence and the questioning of witnesses, the officer attempts to identify the offender and arrest him.

When it appears that the case is complex or time-consuming, and the necessary personnel are available, the patrolman will turn over the case to an investigator. From the evidence and identifications developed by the patrolman, the investigator follows up by developing other evidence and identification necessary to lead to arrest and eventual conviction. The rate of clearing cases if the offender is not apprehended at the crime scene or shortly after is very low. Despite the image of investigators in the media, a police agency at any governmental level would be highly efficient if cases cleared by its investigators were greater than 12 to 15 percent. The patrolman's response time in relation to the actual time of occurrence is the key for apprehending offenders.

---

[3] Gordon P. Whitaker, "Urban Police Forces: The Effect of Scale on Neighborhood Services" (Ph.D. diss., Political Science, Indiana University, 1971), p. 42.

Records

Great strides in the record-keeping function have been made in the last decade, such as adding, automated, and electronic data processing; retrieval and storage capabilities, and computer printout and visual scanning systems. Furthermore, they are updated almost on a daily basis because of the advances in technology.

Record keeping is important in crime rate determination, uniform classification of crimes, identification, property, persons, and methods of criminal operation. Manpower studies and planning are conducted on the basis of recorded information. Control of property and evidence is also a function of the records unit. Records provide cross-indexing, master name index, traffic and other citations, warrants, and personnel identification information for the entire department. Because of the tremendous cost involved in maintaining modern systems, some agencies have consolidated both records and communication systems in much the same way as private business utilizes computer time sharing.

A police department's efficiency and effectiveness can often be measured by simply examining its record-keeping system. If it is in a state of disarray and confusion, it is likely that the rest of the department is operating at the same level of inefficiency.

More and more agencies are turning over this key function to civilian personnel trained in administrative duties. The advantage is in terms of reduced operating and wage cost as well as increased manpower utilization when police officers are reassigned to duties where their training can be put to more effective use.

Communication

To be effective, a police department needs an adequate communication system, particularly important in agencies providing emergency services. For the police there are essentially four areas of communication: the first and most important is between the citizens and their police departments; the second is among the personnel within the department; the third is between the department and other police agencies; and last, since law enforcement does not function alone, but is merely a subsystem within the criminal justice system, communication is necessary between the police and the various other components of the system. To this last area we might add communications with other units of government and the private sector.

Communication takes a variety of forms; doing nothing or leaving a task uncompleted can be kinds of messages, as are body movements and gestures. However, written reports, memorandums, and other paperwork are the bulk of police communication; and, of course, there are the countless spoken words.

The necessity for being precise, concise, and conveying the message quickly in law enforcement communications is primary. Whatever is said must have an exact meaning because dubious or double meanings can reduce effectiveness and unnecessarily jeopardize the lives and property of others. Any message must be brief or concise, since long and tedious messages consume the important minutes of others and delay the delivery of services to the public. The need for speed of message transmission and reception in police work is well known; codes like the 10-code are designed specifically to reduce the amount of time consumed.

One of the primary communication links between the public and the police is the request for service. Generally, it is done by telephone, but the public will also walk into the station, hail a passing patrol unit, or go to an officer's residence. The public has a wide variety of needs and problems; some are criminal, some are emergencies, and some involve people who do not know where else to turn. Since the police are often the only 24-hour representatives of government, the public turns to them for almost everything. In 1968 the Detroit Police Department received 1,027,000 telephone calls, of which 370,000 (36 percent) did not require the dispatch of a patrol unit. Of the number not requiring a responding unit, 9.6 percent were referred to another agency of government, 2.2 percent were referred to a private agency, 52.6 percent were resolved over the phone without having to refer the call, and 35.5 percent did not require a response by the uniformed bureau but were referred to another bureau in the police department.[4]

An interesting observation by a citizen volunteer rider in a patrol car regarding the 30-minute break for a meal by a police officer showed that the officer spent 13 minutes of his break answering inquiries as to when the phone company opened in the morning for paying bills, how one went about shutting off water service, where the good fishing was

---

[4] Thomas E. Bercal, "Calls for Police Assistance: Consumer Demands for Governmental Service," Harlan Hahn, ed., *Police in Urban Society* (Beverly Hills: Sage, 1970, 1971), pp. 268-269.

(from a tourist), and how did one report a neighbor for letting his dog run loose without the neighbor discovering the source of the complaint.

The calls that involve a crime in progress or suspicious circumstances are emergency business in the police department. A large part of the new officer's career is spent learning how to report by radio or to write up his responses to these emergencies. He learns during academy training the radio codes and the proper method of report writing that will lead to the determination of just what crime occurred, who did it, and all the other details that will lead to a successful prosecution. From these oral and written communications comes the information needed to function. Many of the calls are for services, and these are also important, requiring the same skill and expertise as investigating and reporting crimes.

Because of the mobility of criminals, it is a requisite of today's law enforcement that police agencies contact each other and place information at the other's disposal. Many local agencies are within easy phoning distance or are part of statewide leased line systems. Some share the same radio frequencies. Because of the increased demands on airwaves, agencies are forced to seek alternative means of transmitting and receiving information. Telecommunications have provided the vehicle. A variety of national, regional, state, and local information and message networks have been developed. In Atlanta, Georgia, METROPOL serves the needs of fourteen agencies; in the District of Columbia, WALES serves the Capital and five adjoining counties; SPIN and PIN service the two large metropolitan areas of California respectively. State systems exist almost everywhere: CLETS (California), LETS (Idaho), LIEN (Michigan), FCIC (Florida), as well as many others. Regionally, NESPAC (New England State Police Administrators' Conference), a cooperative network in the six New England states, provides the much needed information for local law enforcement.

The exact information capabilities of these and other telecommunication systems vary from system to system. The PIN network in California deals with outstanding criminal and traffic warrants. The system is being expanded to handle parole/probation violators and the names of those who have a propensity to resist arrest.[5] The most com-

---

[5] George T. Payton, *Patrol Procedure* (Los Angeles: Legal Book Corp., 1971), p. 166.

Figure 9-1. It is a requisite of today's law enforcement that police agencies place information at each other's disposal. Telecommunications have provided the vehicle. In the foreground, a dispatcher requests information from the CJIC computer; in the background an officer receives information from a CLETS terminal.

plete is New York's NYSIIS. It provides information on vehicle registration, operator's licenses, firearms, criminal histories, fraudulent checks, personal appearance, names, voice prints, fingerprints, warrants, wants, stolen vehicles and parts, and missing persons among others. Information needed "on the street" has always been a critical problem, and what is available varies from jurisdiction to jurisdiction, depending upon the available technology and funds.

National systems are also available. The National Crime Information Center (NCIC), begun in 1967, provides the working officer with information about stolen vehicles, stolen license plates, wanted persons, stolen firearms, stolen property, criminal profiles and histories, and stolen securities. A national telecommunication service, LETS, headquartered in Phoenix, Arizona, allows agencies to send messages to one another. A new project called SEARCH will allow agencies to exchange criminal histories on a national basis.

Despite these technological advances in information transmittal, many of America's smaller departments find these communication services beyond their reach. Many of the departments in the Toledo, Ohio area cannot afford the $100 per month hookup charge for Ohio's LEADS (Law Enforcement Automated Data System). The smaller depend upon the larger to take care of their communication needs.[6] The national NCIC terminal in Atlanta, Georgia, alone, costs the Department of Public Safety $365.50 per month (1968 figure).[7] Unless the systems are paid for by the agencies having the resources, many local departments cannot participate.

Communications, in the administrative sense, between members of the same agency is an important aspect for the direction and control of that agency. Paperwork and the spoken word provide the data necessary for decision-making, policy, allocation, budgets, and other tasks. The paperwork of the uniformed patrol officer alone is staggering and a major portion of his working hours is spent in filling out reports.[8] Communication is upward, downward, and horizontal.

Communications outward from the law enforcement subsystem to the rest of the system and private agencies are equally important. Diversion programs and community-based corrections require that the needs and capabilities of each be known. The quality of police work and the way it is communicated, orally and written, determine matters of prosecution and defense and influence the sentencing process. Poor communications make a sham of justice. It takes little imagination to visualize the necessity for precise, concise, and prompt communication in the criminal justice system.

---

[6] Julius A. Gylys, "Allocative Problems of Sheriff's Police Services in a Metropolitan Setting" (Ph.D. diss., Economics, Wayne State University, 1969), p. 105.
[7] Governor's Commission on Crime and Justice, *Report* (Atlanta: State of Georgia, 1968), p. 63.
[8] Of 21,380 minutes observed, some 23.25 percent of a patrolman's time is spent in filling out forms and writing reports. Observations were made during Spring 1973 with the following police departments: Campbell, Menlo Park, Larkspur, Milpitas, Monterey, San Jose, and Palo Alto, California.

Crime Laboratory

Criminalistics, the application of biological and physical sciences to the investigation of crime, is conducted in the crime lab. Here, the scientist uses his knowledge to evaluate, measure, compare, and test pieces of evidence collected from the scene of a crime by a police officer or trained criminalist.

The first thing the average person thinks about when a crime lab is mentioned is ballistics (the evaluation of the motion of projectiles shot from firearms, or fingerprints). Actually the range of the crime lab's capabilities are far greater than one might suspect. Gas chromatography—separating components of complex mixtures; paper chromatography—separating components of complex organic matter; neutron activation analysis—measuring concentrations of trace elements; electrophoresis—studying and separating protein molecules; X-ray crystallography—X-ray analysis of electron distribution and atomic structure; polygraph examination—(lie detection); and voice printing—classifying speech characteristics in much the same way as fingerprints are classified, are some of the capabilities of the crime lab.

Recently, there have been studies that may lead to the identification of microorganisms as being as unique to a particular individual as fingerprints, and that can be collected at the scene of a crime within hours after its commission. This new technique is called germ-typing. When available to patrol officers and investigators, it has been used only in cases that invoke emotions or have the public's attention.

Special Considerations

Field Interviews

This preventive patrol tactic has come under considerable criticism and scrutiny by the community at large, but it is most pronounced among the minority faction of the community. The temporary detaining of a person on the street to determine his identity and the reason for his presence at a particular location and time has been challenged as being violative of Constitutional guarantees. Thus far, the U.S. Supreme Court has ruled otherwise, most notably in their rendering of the decision in the case of *Terry* v. *Ohio* (392 U.S. 1 (1968)). The *Terry* decision defined a "stop" as opposed to an arrest and a "frisk" as opposed to a search. Furthermore, the Court specified that a "protective search" for weapons was a lawful police technique.

Critics contend that the majority of the reasons for stopping people, particularly minority group members, are for other than legitimate and lawful purposes. The police contend that their right to stop and question people is fundamental, particularly as it applies to individuals observed in an area where a crime has been committed. Both arguments bear further examination.

In a climate where law enforcement officers may arbitrarily detain a person, it is almost inconceivable that police administrators would not have long ago recognized the potential for indiscretion. Yet relatively few agencies across the country have developed guidelines for their officers in an effort to ensure that such "interviews" are limited and employed under conditions justifying their use. Preventive patrols, of which field interviews are an important element, are effective in the reduction of crime, but just how effective they are has yet to be substantiated.[9] Perhaps such a study would provide valuable insight for police administrators who could then weigh the benefits obtained against the resulting animosity on the community's part.

Beyond the establishment of guidelines of *when* and *where*, police administrators should also concern themselves with *how*. A mature patrol officer will soon learn that the manner in which he conducts himself makes a great difference. It is often the young, inexperienced rookie who, out of eagerness to cure the world of its ills, develops a "badge-heavy" syndrome that results in great animosity on the part of the people stopped on the street. A courteous, professionally conducted field interview can achieve better results in obtaining valuable information than can an arrogant and rude mannerism. Arrogance and rudeness on the part of an officer act as a catalyst to alienate and incite the person being questioned. Law enforcement must come to grips with those critical issues with which an officer comes into contact almost on a daily basis; the field interview would be a good place to begin. Communities concerned with rising crime must also be aware that their demands for more preventive patrol has a cost.

[9] Harry W. More, *Critical Issues in Law Enforcement* (Cincinnati: W. H. Anderson, 1962), p. 180.

Figure 9-2. Preventive patrols, of which field interrogations are an important element, are effective in the reduction of crime, but the extent of their effectiveness is not substantiated.

Citations (Traffic)
Ironically, the only aspect of law enforcement with which the majority of the public ever comes into contact draws almost as much negative criticism as does the field interview. Traffic citations are generally a means of undeserved harassment—or so the recipient of a citation would have one believe. The difficulty is that many people honestly believe that such is the rule rather than the exception.

Again, the lack of appropriate discretion and professional tact on the part of the issuing officer lends itself to the kind of resentment depicted in the cartoon of the sneering, cynical motorcycle officer, who hides behind a billboard waiting for the unsuspecting motorist.

When warnings are issued instead of citations, authorities generally agree that they lose their effectiveness when issued indiscriminately where a citation was warranted, when officers are allowed the freedom of "excusing" violations because of a driver's good intentions, when accepting frivolous excuses, or when the officer does not wish to be perceived as a "tough cop."

No matter how distasteful a traffic citation may be, there is a direct correlation between the amount of enforcement and the accident rate at any given location. This alone would justify a policy of firm but fair traffic enforcement. If an officer conducts himself professionally, unwarranted criticism will be greatly reduced. Perhaps the cited motorist will examine his driving habits rather than characterize the police officer as rude.

Women's Role in Law Enforcement
The date of appointment of the first policewoman appears to be lost or is in dispute. Some say the first policewoman was Mrs. Lola Baldwin, appointed in 1905 to work at the Lewis and Clark Centennial Exposition in Portland, Oregon.[10] Others say it was Alice Stebbins Wells or Mrs. Marie Owens of the Los Angeles Police Department who received their appointments in about 1910.[11] Regardless of who and when, police-

---

[10] Edward Eldefonso, Alan Coffey, and Richard C. Grace, *Principles of Law Enforcement* (New York: Wiley, 1968), p. 121.
[11] Lois L. Higgins, *Policewoman's Manual* (Springfield, Ill.: Charles C. Thomas, 1961), p. xiii.

Figure 9-3. No matter how distasteful a traffic citation may be, there is a direct correlation between the amount of enforcement and the accident rate at any given location.

introduction to the administration of justice

women are a twentieth century addition to law enforcement in the United States.

Prior to the 1970s, the primary duties of women were those special assignments best achieved by a woman as protective/preventive agents in the social sense—dealing with the welfare of women and children. They looked for lost children and runaways; investigated and protected women and children in sex offense matters; worked in stores where shoplifting was prevalent; and carried out general duties in the juvenile division. Occasionally, they investigated bad check cases or fraud of the elderly. But the full range of peace officer assignments were generally not available to them.

The years since World War II have seen a rapid dedomestication of American women and an ever-increasing entrance into the ranks of the work force. For law enforcement, the 1970s have been the period in which the American female has demanded full police status and is being placed in the formerly "forbidden" areas—particularly the uniformed patrol division. There has been no doubt about their capability to function effectively as administrators, investigators, or staff aides. The issue now before law enforcement is whether a woman can function as well as the male peace officer in the patrol function.

Policewomen have patrol functions in many jurisdictions: the Pennsylvania State Police, the San Francisco Police Department, the Army's Military Police, Washington D.C. Metropolitan P.D., and the Los Angeles County Sheriff's Department, to name but a few. To date, the women selected, trained, and operating in the field have been reported as being as capable as their male counterparts in performing most police functions and more capable in some. For instance, policewomen handled domestic disturbances far better. The question of how effective overall they will prove to be can only be answered when sufficient numbers are deployed "on the streets" and sufficient data is collected and evaluated.

The largest question marks concerning policewomen in the uniformed patrol division are the ones where the likelihood of violence is present; suppression of tavern disturbances, and the apprehension and subduing of criminals, to name a few. Can they handle the situations? Will they react well if they have children at home? Although the occurrences of violent incidents do not take up the major share of a policeman's time, the environment can be hostile and sometimes the clients have a propensity to violence. The majority of the other tasks within the patrol function are well within the capabilities of the policewomen. Should the violent and distasteful aspects of police tasks prove beyond their physical capabilities, they can still be used in the less hazardous aspects of patrol work.

Special Investigative Functions

The general investigation of cases in law enforcement is aimed at a specific criminal event committed usually by a single offender or a loosely organized group of offenders. The majority of cases investigated fit this pattern. However, cases of a very special nature occasionally arise in which the criminal activity is not confined to one event or violation; they may be a continuing series of various crimes perpetrated by an organized group. Faced with situations of this nature, agencies have begun to experiment with new investigative techniques and procedures to meet these conditions.

An example of some of the attempts to deal with complex problems, extended investigations, and organized criminal elements is the intraagency task forces. In the Kansas City area a metro squad, composed of personnel from seven sheriffs' departments and twenty municipal departments combined with two state police agencies, attacks problems common to all jurisdictions on a priority basis. Special narcotics units like Lane County, Oregon, operate on a permanent basis investigating complex narcotics cases that are prevalent in the area. Other similar organizations, such as the fugitive squad, METROPOL, in the Atlanta, Georgia area, and the Major Case Squad of the greater St. Louis area perform the complex, extended investigations that sometimes involve organized crime.

Presently, most American law enforcement agencies are not structured to handle criminal activities that cross jurisdictional lines and that are multiviolational and interconnected. An addict buys drugs from pushers at a local level. The same addict supports his drug habit as a burglar, car thief, or panderer for prostitutes. The drug pushers may be associated with the people who fence the stolen goods and vehicles or operate prostitution rings. Although each criminal act is isolated, it is interconnected with others and may be directed from above in a loose or formal fashion. The police, however, make initial contacts through isolated or separate incidents: a stolen car, a business burglary, or a complaint from a tourist who lost a wallet in an encounter with a prostitute. Until some pattern emerges, an informer explains the connection, or an investigator discovers a connecting thread between the crimes, the follow-up investigation is ineffectual except, perhaps, in solving the individual cases.[12] The criminal organization may be unnoticed and therefore left untouched.

A particular problem area is in the so-called nonvictim crimes—prostitution, gambling, narcotics, payoff to police, and loansharking. Instead of a crime scene in the traditional sense and a complaining party who brings the criminal activity to law enforcement's attention, the police must go out and seek the occurrences and proceed differently. The nonvictim crime is often profitable; enforcement is carried out in an apathetic environment; and prevention is developed only by the police pretending to be the victim. But from these investigations, the interconnected crimes and organized activity can often be discovered because the money from loansharking, narcotics, prostitution, and gambling attracts and often fosters other criminal activities.

Law enforcement agencies require two other functions in the confrontation with organized and interconnected crime. These are intelligence and internal affairs units. The objective of the intelligence unit in an agency is to collect data, collate and store the data, and evaluate and attempt to "read" it, so that information can be made available to the line operations. Other than the broadest outline, little is actually known about intelligence in a police department.[13] Occasionally, the intelligence collection about individuals and their beliefs becomes news and proves embarrassing, but that is about all one knows about the inner workings of a unit. Intelligence officers are selective in choosing those who receive their estimates, facts, and opinions.

Interest in internal affairs, or the police investigation of police, has been renewed as a result of the Knapp Commission Report on the New

---

[12] B. Greenberg, et. al., *Enhancement of the Investigative Function,* Vol. III (Menlo Park, Calif.: Stanford Research Institute, 1972), pp. 27-28.
[13] E. D. Godfrey and D. R. Harris, *Basic Elements of Intelligence* (Washington, D.C.: LEAA, Department of Justice, 1971).

York City Police Department. Police investigators are assigned the responsibility of investigating allegations of wrongdoing by the police. The types of alleged wrongdoings range from insulting behavior to brutality to the public; and from accepting a free cup of coffee to accepting bribes for allowing crimes to occur. Like all "crimes without victims," the victim in police payoffs is actually the public, general morality, or other unmeasurable aspects. The fact that policemen sometimes have to investigate policemen does not inspire confidence in the public. But if internal affairs are conducted correctly, it helps to keep officers from succumbing to temptation and from becoming a law unto themselves.

Police Personnel

Who Will Be a Peace Officer?
The most important requirement for assuring honest, dependable, and competent police services is not only the efficiency of internal affairs but the recruiting, selecting, training, and educating of the right people. The public expects quality personnel enforcing their laws. But these qualities are a subject of controversy today. Sheriff's departments are being sued over height requirements; IQ tests are being questioned; and waivers are even being demanded for applicants with criminal records.

In deciding what type of man or woman makes a good police officer, there are some unchallenged qualities. First, there is honesty. The public will accept an uneducated policeman before it ever accepts a dishonest one. Honesty, of course, is difficult to establish. A law enforcement agency attempts to do this by background investigations showing a lack of criminal records and the opinions of associates.

The police officer must also be intelligent. A variety of measures are available to test intelligence, although cultural disadvantages occasionally affect test results. Despite the seeming unfairness of excluding a person for cultural shortcomings, the justice system is built on reports and records that require skills in reading and writing. The courts will have to decide just what measurements for intelligence or educational level are valid for the entire system.

Psychologically and physically, the peace officer must be adaptable to a variety of situations; in an emergency he must be capable of dealing effectively with violence. Some measurements of psychological stability and physical fitness are available but not often used, although a background check can indicate some of these qualities.

The question of height is open to question. Only when a sufficient number of people of varying heights are allowed to become peace officers and some measure of their capability and effectiveness is analyzed will the question of height requirement be resolved.

The basic recruitment minimum must include honesty, intelligence, and good physical and psychological health. Only by recruiting the best can the public be assured that the personnel delivering the police services are the best.

Recruitment of Police

The objective of recruitment for the law enforcement agency is finding men and women who have the following characteristics:

> ... the wisdom of Solomon, the courage of David, the strength of Samson, the patience of Job, the leadership of Moses, the kindness of the Good Samaritan, the strategical training of Alexander, the faith of Daniel, the diplomacy of Lincoln, the tolerance of the Carpenter of Nazareth, and finally an intimate knowledge of the natural, biological, and social sciences . . .[14]

and then encouraging them to apply. The law enforcement administrator will find little guidance in police literature on how to proceed.

Joseph Kimble, in one of the few books available on the topic of recruitment and selection, pays scant attention to this segment of a personnel program.[15] Recruitment generally includes the placement of an ad in a local newspaper, maintaining a quality police image with the news media, and searching local police science programs for likely prospects. The objective of any recruitment program should be to create interest in the department and to demonstrate that a police career will lead to personal satisfaction.

The recruitment material that many departments use gives a description of the department, the duties of an officer, and a brief description of the type of person sought. The media, posters, and news-

---

[14] August Vollmer, *Police and Modern Society* (Berkeley: University of California Press, 1936), p. 222.

[15] Joseph Kimble, "Recruitment," Richard H. Blum, ed., *Police Selection* (Springfield, Ill.: Charles C. Thomas, 1964), pp. 71-84.

paper releases should be and often are used. Many departments have an individual assigned specifically to the task of seeking the qualified and familiarizing them with the opportunities of working for the department. Files are maintained on past applicants and are kept current. The search for the potential peace officers continues all the time.

Junior or community colleges have proven to be excellent recruiting grounds. Most of these colleges have criminal justice courses and the people completing their courses of study usually have reached the minimum age and have an interest in a law enforcement career. Many officers attend college classes and keep the preservice students advised of openings. Departments throughout the service area send their notices of openings to the colleges in order to attract the students upon completion of their studies. In many regions, the community college is probably the best investment of the recruiting dollar.

The Selection Process

There are several steps involved in selecting peace officers. The steps vary from agency to agency. Generally, these steps are (1) a set of minimum qualifications, (2) a comprehensive application, (3) a test for aptitude, interest, or intelligence, (4) a medical examination, (5) a test of physical agility, (6) an oral interview, (7) a thorough background investigation, and sometimes (8) a psychiatric evaluation. The actual employment of all of these steps or a combination of them often depend upon a variety of factors. Idealistically, all of these steps and more, such as a polygraph examination, should be included in order to select the best qualified.

A set of minimum standards is the first step of the process. Often these minimum standards are state law. By publicizing the minimum standards the agency is spared the expense of testing those who obviously cannot meet the standards. An example of minimum standards is as follows:

1. Citizen of the United States.
2. Minimum age generally 18 through 21.
3. Absence of a criminal record; conviction that could have involved imprisonment.
4. Good moral character.
5. Graduation from high school or GED equivalent.
6. Free from a physical, emotional, or mental condition.
7. Appearance and ability to communicate (ascertained by an oral board.

Since these are minimum standards, each individual department can raise the standards, for instance, and require two years of college instead of graduation from a high school.

The fundamental objective of a comprehensive application form is for the applicant to provide information that will assist the agency in determining the applicant's suitability. It asks for information that is relevant to the objectives of selection; data that can be used in evaluating the success potential of the applicant, such as education, employment, interests, and special skills. All of the information assists the investigators conducting the background and character investigation. Many states, such as Idaho,[16] Texas, and California, through their Peace Officer Standards and Training Advisory Council, have standardized applications for the agencies in their states. Standardized applications provide sufficient verifiable information of proven value for the selection process.

Most departments employ a written test that requires mental dexterity or measures interest. Some use the Army General Classification, the revised Army Alpha test, the achievement tests, or the College Ability Test. Some departments also require tests of interest such as the Kuder Preference Record or the Strong Vocational Interest Test. Since a great deal of time and money must be invested in a new police officer before he goes to work, departments want to know if the applicant has the suitable potential for the job.

Most police recruiting materials emphasize that the applicant must be physically fit. The term physically fit—in addition to assuming good health—also requires that the applicant be physically adept at performing the tasks demanded of a police officer. The physical agility test is usually designed to measure the natural physical characteristics or abilities capable of being developed more fully to complete strenuous police tasks. The parts of the test often include a test of muscular strength, muscular endurance, circulatory endurance, muscular power, and speed and body balance. Some even require a swimming test. Since work in the uniformed patrol division often requires physical exertions, some departments require that the test be taken annually.

The applicant must also be in excellent physical health. The juris-

---

[16]Peace Officer Standards and Training Advisory Council, *Policies and Procedure Manual* (Boise: Law Enforcement Planning Commission, 1969), pp. 19-26.

diction generally requires that the applicant submit to an examination by an appointed medical doctor. Although there are no universal physical standards, many departments follow the lines laid down by the Professional Standards Division of the International Association of Chiefs of Police.[17] Periodic medical exams are required by the more progressive departments.

The oral interview or oral board is a fairly common step in the selection process and probably the most controversial. The composition of the oral board varies from agency to agency. As a rule there are from three to six members, and they are chosen by a variety of means. Usually board members are peace officers, personnel administrators, or council members. (For further discussion of the interview, see Chapter 14.)

The character of the peace officer should be above reproach. No department should ever accept an applicant until his background has been comprehensively and thoroughly explored, and the investigator can assure his department that the applicant's habits, emotional stability, and the many other characteristics investigated are such that he can perform the duties with credit to the profession. Anything less is unacceptable. The recent Rand Corporation research into the New York City Police Department bears out the importance of the background investigation.[18]

Occasionally, a psychiatric evaluation of the applicant is made. The President's Commission on Law Enforcement and Administration of Justice was deeply concerned with the emotional stability of prospective peace officers. In its *Task Force Report*, it stated:

The emotional stability to withstand the stresses of police work must, of necessity, be a primary requisite of police personnel. Officers must rationally cope with violence, verbal abuse, resentment, and emergencies. The emotionally unfit cannot meet these stresses. Although a comprehensive character investigation will eliminate many socially maladjusted applicants, personality defects in some of the applicants will be latent and not easily discernible.[19]

---

[17] Professional Standards Division, *Model Police Standards Council Program* (Washington, D.C.: I.A.C.P., 1968), Section G-2.
[18] Rand Institute, *Police Background Characteristics and Performance* (New York: Rand Institute, 1972), p. 18.
[19] President's Commission on Law Enforcement and Administration of Justice, *Task Force Report: The Police* (Washington, D.C.: U.S. Govt. Printing Office, 1967), p. 129.

Whatever the reason, certain personality types do not make good peace officers, and personality and temperament testing should be a standard part of the peace officer's selection process. The Kansas Highway Patrol found that it saved money as well.[20]

Some departments use the polygraph in verifying the information provided by an applicant. Candidates often give misleading data in the application, psychological tests, and the oral interview. A polygraphic evaluation may substantiate the results of the other screening devices so that a decision of acceptance or rejection can be made with a higher degree of assurance.

Recruit Training and Probation as Part of the Selection Process
Regardless of how sound the selection process may be, a few malcontents and misfits will, in all probability, be appointed. In the best interests of a public service profession, they should be eliminated as soon as their inadequacies become apparent. Close supervision during the academy and probationary periods is crucial in discovering shortcomings and determining whether corrective action will be effective in salvaging borderline employees. All too often an individual has no idea of the nature of police work nor of his own strengths and weaknesses. Just as some employees in other lines of work become malcontents and misfits, so do police officers. Only by exposure to the real world of police work can the individual and the professional know whether or not they are suited to each other. The academy and probation periods are the most important parts of the mutual selection process, according to the Rand study previously referred to.

Training
Almost all states have a series of training programs designed to provide the skills necessary for the tasks performed by policemen. From the time of his entry on duty with an agency as a patrolman through promotion to any rank he might attain, the policeman will have a variety of training

---

[20] Allen C. Rush, "Better Police Personnel Selection," *The Police Chief XXX*, No. 9 (September 1963), p. 20.

courses, formal and in-service, available to him. In many cases, he will be required to attend and satisfactorily complete the training.

The first training program encountered by the newly hired recruit is an academy designed to develop the skills necessary to function as a patrolman. The length of the academy training varies with different departments, but the content of each has similar characteristics in terms of the subjects taught. All academy courses include law, evidence, penal code, communications, report writing, patrol, accident investigation, first aid, and gunnery, to name a few. After completing the academy, the new officer usually serves under a more experienced officer to obtain practical police experience.

The skills and subjects learned at an academy are continually updated and refreshed by in-service training and occasional specialized courses such as burglary investigation. Some states utilize television (South Carolina and California) to keep their officers up-to-date. Other states provide films. Some professional groups provide training pamphlets on a regular basis to aid in maintaining a high level of skills.

Specialty training is generally available. Courses from agencies, the private sector, and associations often assist the officer who is sharpening an expertise or just developing one. As one advances in rank, supervisory, management, and executive courses prepare the officer for his new responsibilities. When an agency institutes changes, the whole department often receives training, such as in organization development, management-by-objectives, and the like. The rapid expansion of training programs and instructional delivery systems equips the officer for each new step taken.

Education
The applicant for police work generally is a high school graduate. In the drive for professionalism of law enforcement, policemen seek out continuing and higher education where and when it is available. Police are fortunate in that most courses of study have some value to their work. Obviously, some courses have more value than others. For instance, social science taught by a former peace officer, or someone familiar with the lawman's needs, would be of greater value than an art appreciation course. In an investigation of art thefts or forgeries, the art appreciation takes on new values. Generally, related courses are

somewhat more valuable than general ones when thinking of the benefits to the delivery of services to the public.

A variety of degree programs are available to the officer. The most common and the most crucial program is the associate degree offered by the community colleges. The police science courses give him skills, develop attitudes, and provide familiarity with his role as a police officer in the criminal justice system. Four-year programs have expanded in a manner that can only be termed phenomenal. Until recently, the number of bachelor degree programs were sparse; today few campuses lack programs. Advanced degrees are being developed in an accelerated fashion, both at the master and doctoral levels. The demand is present, and the colleges and universities are expanding or instituting programs to meet that demand.

It is hoped that the increased emphasis on education will lead to an even better quality delivery of police services. At present, however, the ideal level of education for a patrolman, as well as for other ranks in policework, has not yet been identified. The rapid expansion and the desire for education will help meet the desires of the President's Commission.

> *Due to the nature of the police task and its effect on our society, there is need to elevate educational requirements at entry to the level of a college degree from an accredited institution for all future personnel selected to perform the functions of a police agent.*[21]

The Direction of Law Enforcement

It is always difficult to forecast with accuracy the trends and directions of any public service when it is in a period of radical change. Several prominent occurrences of the late 1960s and early 1970s give some indication of trends and directions. These are civilian involvement; the increasing education, training and knowledge desires of the rank and file; the alternative means of service delivery; and the increasing demands by rank and file to have some say in the direction and control of their chosen profession.

---

[21] *Task Force Report: The Police*, p. 127.

A growing phenomenon is citizen involvement in law enforcement. Two major trends are occurring and are likely to continue and expand with the coming years. First, police departments are utilizing the reserves in greater numbers, and they are increasing the roles they are performing. The fact that Texas, California, and other states are developing standards and training for reserves attests to the growing importance and usage. The task of policing is simply too great, and the demands on the peace officer are too many. With proper training and selection, reserve programs can and are becoming a vital part of American law enforcement. Second, crime prevention programs are being developed that enlist the eyes and ears of the public. The police cannot do the job alone, and they need information. For instance, a good neighborhood antiburglary program not only marks valuables but trains neighbors to watch each other's homes, observe and record descriptions of people who are strange to the area, copy license numbers of suspicious vehicles, record make and model, and generally observe what goes on around them. By advising the public to observe and record significant information, the task of the police is greatly aided. Public involvement, either as a reserve or as being an observant neighbor, is likely to increase.

Alternative methods for the delivery of police services will continue to be developed and sought. Consolidation of agencies, contractual services, and agency coordination will continue. The success of such consolidations as Jacksonville, Duval County and Miami, Dade County in Florida; Knoxville, Davidson County in Tennessee; and Indianapolis, Marion County in Indiana will be imitated where feasible. Contractual services, such as those in Los Angeles County, will be developed elsewhere. The joint task forces used to handle area problems such as narcotics will probably be extended to other forms and functions as needs arise. Some jurisdictions, like Spokane and Spokane County, are experimenting with joint usage of a public safety building. These are just a few of the interagency attempts to deliver better services. Within departments, new ways are also sought. In hardware, some police departments are experimenting with the use of small import cars, and the South San Francisco Police—located in a high smog area—use propane for cleaner emissions. Departments are using more cadets and civilian personnel in the stations in order to put more sworn personnel "on the streets." Community service officers in some areas are being employed to deliver services not requiring a uniformed officer. All of these are attempts to find new ways. This search will continue.

The years ahead will undoubtedly see a more militant stand by rank-and-file police. For years police have been poorly paid, criticized, and generally held in low esteem. Today they are organizing into collective bargaining units. Whether the organizations representing policemen are desirable or not from a public service standpoint, and whether what they demand is right or not, one thing is certain—policemen have ceased to be quiet and will in the future make their desires known.[22]

Summary

This chapter has discussed police services, which generally fall into one of two categories: line function or staff and supportive functions. Line functions are led by the patrol unit. Patrol is the center of the law enforcement wheel around which all other functions revolve. Also included in line functions are traffic, juvenile, vice and narcotics, and plainclothes. The staff and supportive functions are investigative, records, crime laboratories, and communications. Communications is of vital importance to the entire criminal justice system. Advances are being made in the area and many experimental programs are underway.

The preventive patrol tactic of field interviews has come under considerable criticism from the community. However, the Supreme Court has ruled in *Terry* v. *Ohio* in favor of this police procedure.

In recent years the role of the policewoman has expanded to include police functions that had been previously closed to them, particularly in the area of uniformed patrol. Another change is the increased citizen involvement in law enforcement. Two major trends are occurring and are likely to expand with the coming years. They are the utilization of reserves and the development of neighborhood crime prevention programs.

Police are working more in the area of special investigations. Cases that cross jurisdictional lines and are multiviolational require special investigation units. Many agencies across the country are trying new programs so as to better deal with this problem.

---

[22] See William J. Bopp, ed., *The Police Rebellion: A Quest for Blue Power* (Springfield, Ill.: Charles C. Thomas, 1971).

Another major aspect discussed in this chapter is the selection of new officers. Many departments use a combination of tests that often include a test of muscular strength, muscular endurance, circulatory endurance, muscular power, speed, and body balance. Oral interviews are fairly common in the selection process. In most states, training programs exist to provide the skills necessary for task performance by policemen. The length and type of training vary depending upon the requirements of the agency and state laws. As officers advance in rank, special training is necessary.

Generally, a high school education is all that is required for law enforcement. However, a growing demand is being placed on colleges to provide graduate and undergraduate programs in this area. The demand is being met at an ever-increasing rate, and the growing number of four-year programs is phenomenal. It is believed that the increased emphasis on education will lead to better quality police service.

Student Checklist

1. Can you cite the various functions assigned to line type activities?
2. Are you able to define staff functions?
3. Can you cite at least five examples of police patrol responsibilities?
4. Are you able to cite the primary functions of the investigative services unit?
5. Can you outline the primary responsibilities of supportive services?
6. Do you know at least two different styles of police communications systems?
7. Do you know the different steps of the selection process for a police officer?

Topics for Discussion

1. Discuss police discretionary decision-making in the contemporary community.

2. Explain the current and future role of women in the police service.
3. Discuss the selection of police officers.
4. Outline the future direction of the law enforcement service as you view it.

ANNOTATED BIBLIOGRAPHY

Eastman, George D., ed. *Municipal Police Administration.* 6th ed. Washington, D.C. International City Managers Assoc., 1969. A broad view of all aspects of law enforcement. Sets forth the traditional management of the police mission. Describes the standard models of service and their delivery.

Godfrey, E. Drexel, and Don R. Harris. *Basic Elements of Intelligence.* Washington, D.C.: LEAA, Dept. of Justice, 1971. A basic manual that explains the theory and operations of the police intelligence function. Covers general aspects of organized crime and complex criminal or conspiracy activities.

O'Hara, Charles E. *Fundamentals of Criminal Investigation.* Springfield, Ill.: Charles C. Thomas, 1969. Explains the application and significance of the investigator's basic tools—investigation, interrogation, information, and instrumentation. Relates the importance of the crime scene as critical to the investigation.

President's Commission on Law Enforcement and Administration of Justice. *Task Force Report: The Police.* Washington, D.C.: U.S. Govt. Printing Office, 1967. One of the most recent evaluations of the police with a series of recommendations for public consideration. Many agencies have used the *Report* as a gauge by which to measure their organization or activities and to plan for the future.

Wilson, James Q. *Varieties of Police Behavior.* New York: Atheneum, 1968. A study by students of how law enforcement is practiced in eight communities, primarily in the Eastern United States. Author describes styles of enforcement and the politics of each.

The study of this chapter will enable you to:

1. Define the levels of the state judicial system.
2. Define the responsibilities of the state appellate courts.
3. Cite three examples of inferior courts.
4. Cite at least two responsibilities of the U.S. Supreme Court.
5. Define the responsibilities of the counsel for the indigent.
6. Outline the duties of the marshal or the bailiff in the court system.
7. Understand the concepts underlying the adoption of the Missouri Plan.

10
Primary Functions of the Court

The structure of the judicial system at the local, state, and federal levels reflects the influence of social and political growth. An examination of the historical development of the courts, which we discussed briefly in Chapter 5, reveals that social and economic forces have greatly influenced our laws and judicial operations. The court system, like other branches of our government, has, for better or worse, been molded by its environment.

As an example, the California Court Act of 1851 reflected contemporary issues when it provided for the trial of lawsuits concerning mining claims. Justice of the peace courts, the lowest courts in the land, were given the right to conduct jury trials in these matters. Why? This was the era of the Gold Rush and hundreds of people were filing mining claims; naturally, many of these resulted in legal disputes over ownership, many of which led to bloodshed. The Act of 1851, allowing these cases to be tried in the lowest courts, reflected the economic and social needs of California at that time. The resulting court decisions had a significant impact upon the historical development of American mining and water law.

As new social, economic, and political needs develop, modifications will be made in the court system to meet them. We cannot look into the future and say with any great accuracy what these modifications will be. We can say, judging from history, that the changes will not be made uniformly or without opposition.

The 50 states entered the Union at different times over a period of 170 years from 1789 to 1959. The origins of the courts in the older states go back to Colonial times. The courts in the newer states are not as burdened with tradition and, generally speaking, they are more amenable to change. Historical, geographical, social, and political differences caused the state court systems to vary from state to state. Even the names of courts are not uniform among the states, or within some states, nor are their jurisdictions. Naturally, this is a source of great confusion.

General Characteristics

To avoid some of the confusion resulting from conflicting and duplicated court names, we shall attempt to classify courts by function and jurisdiction, regardless of their names. The three basic court functions, characteristic to all states, are (1) hearing appeals from lower courts (appellate jurisdiction); (2) conducting trials in cases arising from a broad array of crimes and civil matters (general jurisdiction); and (3) conducting trials in cases of specified or specialized crimes (limited jurisdiction). But we must also be aware that some courts perform a combination of these functions.

Using the three-jurisdiction model, we will find it somewhat less complicated to compare the various state judicial systems. The model gives us a three-tier plan. The tiers, from top to bottom, are (1) state appellate courts, (2) trial courts of general jurisdiction, and (3) inferior courts (courts with limited jurisdictions). This description, although essentially correct, fails to consider combination functions. For example, a state appellate court may have trial jurisdiction over some cases in addition to appellate duties, or a trial court of general jurisdiction may have appellate jurisdiction over an inferior court and hear appeals from the court in addition to conducting trials.

Another type of judicial system is beginning to emerge, which may signal a new direction in court reorganization and reform. Some states are eliminating the bottom tier—the inferior courts. In 1969, Idaho eliminated this level of trial court by consolidating its jurisdiction into the next court above. Several other states, including California, have introduced legislation to establish two-tier systems consisting of only appellate and trial courts.

State Appellate Courts

All 50 states have provided a system of appeal from the decisions of trial courts. Most states call their court of last resort the supreme court.

(In the state of New York, however, it is called the Court of Appeals; the New York Supreme Court is a court of general jurisdiction.) The supreme courts of most states hear both civil and criminal appeals. In Oklahoma and Texas there are two separate courts of last resort, one for civil and one for criminal cases. (For example, the Supreme Court of Texas handles only civil appeals, and the Court of Criminal Appeals does just what its name implies. Both are courts of last resort.)

The term courts of last resort is misleading. Its proper meaning is: "the court that provides the last possible appeal of a judgment or finding within the state judicial structure." If there are federal questions involved, the interested party may appeal for relief to the federal court system in either criminal or civil cases.

Originally, the state supreme courts could easily accommodate all cases that the system produced. Most state supreme courts had a chief justice and two associate justices. As the number of cases appealed increased, the state usually added additional justices to share the workload. This practice succeeded up to a point, then it became apparent that there was a limit to the number of justices to be used in a single court.

In the 1960s New Mexico decided to create an intermediate appellate court to filter out some of the cases and thus limit the number of appeals reaching the docket of their supreme court. Other states have followed New Mexico's example. The intermediate appellate courts are organized on a regional basis. In large states, such as California, they may be further subdivided into divisions. This regionalization creates a new problem—a lack of uniformity, since district court of appeal decisions may differ between districts.

In California, as in many other states, the courts of general trial jurisdiction may exercise appellate jurisdiction over inferior courts within their geographical areas. The appellate procedure in these courts can be of two types: a trial *de novo* (the retrial of a case as though it had never been tried before), or a formal appeal with briefs and all records.

Courts of record are those whose acts and judgments are recorded. A court may be a court of record for some purposes and not others. For instance, California municipal and justice courts are courts of record except for small claims court cases.

Judicial delay results when there is a wide range of cases that may be appealed in this manner. In some states, all cases from inferior courts may be appealed to the court of general jurisdiction, which hears them *de novo*. In these states defense attorneys customarily use the lower court as a hearing session to obtain all the evidence, and then they appeal all guilty verdicts to the higher court for retrial.

State Courts of General Jurisdiction

The state courts of general jurisdiction have broad authority to hear in both civil and criminal cases. Some of the court titles used are superior courts, chancery courts, circuit courts, district courts, criminal courts, and courts of common pleas. The states of Arkansas, Delaware, Indiana, Maryland, Mississippi, New Jersey, Oklahoma, and Texas have more than one court of general jurisdiction. They have courts of general jurisdiction for criminal matters and others for civil matters.

The California Superior Court is an example of a court of general jurisdiction with a full range of judicial functions performed. The Superior Court will try all cases not specifically assigned to a lower court.

Court Organization

The California Court of General Jurisdiction (the Superior Court) is organized upon a geographical basis with each county in the state having a superior court. A sparsely populated rural county may have a judge who does not have a large enough caseload to keep him busy. In contrast, a county with a large population may have a number of judges assigned to its superior court. A large number of judges in a county with a large caseload causes specialization. In courts with five or more judges the judges will generally specialize in criminal, civil, probate, family law, and juvenile cases. If there are not enough cases to warrant a full-time judge being assigned to each of these categories, the judges may decide to schedule certain types of cases on certain days of the week, which results in a form of specialization.

Criminal Cases

In California the Superior Court has constitutional authority in all criminal cases that are felonies and in those misdemeanor cases not otherwise provided for by the legislature. The legislature has given jurisdiction over all misdemeanors to California inferior courts (municipal and justice). Thus, as the result of legislative enactment, the California Superior Court has no misdemeanor criminal jurisdiction.

Some states provide for concurrent jurisdiction in a court of general jurisdiction and inferior courts for state misdemeanor offenses. In these states the law enforcement officer decides in which court he will file the case. Many times his decision is based upon the amount of bail the defendant will have to post. If he wants to be hard on the defendant, he will file on him in a "high bail" court, and vice versa.

The major criminal workload of the courts of general jurisdiction are felony trials. This type of case originates in the court by the filing of either an indictment (hearing held by a grand jury) or information (based upon a preliminary examination conducted by a magistrate).[1] There are some states that require a grand jury hearing even though a preliminary hearing has been conducted.

Juvenile Matters

Some states have established separate juvenile courts. There has been an increasing use of the California practice to give jurisdiction over juveniles to the Superior Court. In California, the Juvenile Court exists as a separate department of the Superior Court. One judge is assigned to hear this type of case under special rules specified by the legislature.

The types of cases generally handled are criminal acts, delinquency, child abandonment, and other miscellaneous provisions of the law. The Juvenile Court is given the authority to determine whether the juvenile is a fit subject for action by that court or should be remanded to another court department for trial as an adult.

Civil Matters

Civil (noncriminal) actions constitute the largest single category of filings for superior courts. Civil filings in California Superior Courts for

---

[1] The use of the preliminary hearing conducted by a magistrate has been used in California since 1879. California was challenged in Hurtado v. California 11OUS 516 (1884) on Fourteenth Amendment grounds that it did not provide the defendant with due process under the law. The states are not required to follow the federal practice of using a grand jury.

the year 1969–70 amounted to 88,087, while criminal filings for the same period were 72,048.[2] This is generally the ratio in all states.

Filings for civil actions heard by the court are for return of money, breach of contract, to determine title to personal or real property, to declare laws unconstitutional, and other actions. Civil actions are limited only by the imagination of the litigant.

All types of civil cases may be filed in the California Superior Court. If inferior courts have not been given specific legislative authority to hear a case, jurisdiction is retained in the Superior Court.

Probate Matters

Probate cases deal primarily with the estates of deceased persons. Wills are administered and the assets are distributed. The California Superior Court has jurisdiction over probate hearings. However, in Michigan and other states, probate jurisdiction is vested in independent courts.

Mental Incompetency

California superior courts conduct hearings into the mental competency of individuals. At the conclusion of the hearing the judge, upon ruling the person incompetent, may commit him to a mental institution for safekeeping and treatment.

Inferior Courts

The inferior courts, or lower courts as they are also known, are extremely difficult to place in classes throughout the various states. In contrast to courts of general jurisdiction, where matters heard are fairly uniform, the inferior courts in most states are completely fragmented. For example, prior to their 1972 constitutional change, Florida had 10 different types of inferior court. Courts with the same names had different jurisdictions depending upon the county in which they were located.

Early in our history each county, ward, city, town, village, or township had to have a court to hear cases involving violations of the

---

[2] Annual Report of the Administration Office of the California Court (January 4, 1971), pp. 159, 160, 161.

law. Many were in remote, isolated areas. Due to transportation difficulties, these small courts, completely out of contact with each other, developed in individual ways. They were given individual names that they maintained over the years. In Table 10-1 you may examine the titles of inferior courts throughout the country; the lack of uniformity will become apparent. If you were to compare a particular court in one state or area with one of the same name somewhere else, you would find yourself in a quandary. The name of an inferior court in one state may be the title of a court of general jurisdiction in another state.

What common characteristics do inferior courts share? In rural areas they are usually small in size and workload, with a single part-time judge. In metropolitan areas they may have several full-time judges. California requires that municipal court judges be practicing attorneys for a period of five years prior to sitting on the bench, but justice court judges are not required to be admitted to the practice of law. All that is required of the justice court judge is that he pass a written qualifying test administered by the California Judicial Council.

California inferior courts recently have served as the model for other states reorganizing into a three-tier system. On January 1, 1952, California consolidated its inferior courts into municipal and justice courts. Prior to that time a fragmented judicial system had existed that was composed of city, police, justice of the peace class A and B courts. As a result of the 1952 reorganization, the entire state was divided into judicial districts with two restrictions: (1) a district has to be wholly within a single county, and (2) the municipal court may hear cases that

TABLE 10-1. **United States Inferior Court Titles**

Courts of probate	Municipal courts
County courts	Courts of common pleas
Justice courts	Police courts
Recorders courts	Superior courts
Magistrate courts	Juvenile courts
City and town magistrates courts	Probate courts
Civil courts of record	Courts of ordinary
Courts of claims	Small claims court
City courts	Mayor courts
Family courts	Traffic courts
Court of criminal corrections	District courts
Surrogates courts	Land courts

occurred in its own district or in any justice court's district in the county.

In California, since there are uniform penal and traffic codes that take precedence over local codes, there is no advantage to be gained by filing a case in one court instead of another. In some states the decision to file under a municipal code violation rather than a state section is made because the local jurisdiction receives more money from a local code violation than from a state violation.

Federal Judicial System

The Constitution of the United States insures that two judicial systems, one state and the other federal, operate within the nation. Article III of the Constitution outlines the specific jurisdiction of the federal courts, the Fifth Amendment relegates all other cases to be heard in the state courts.

Supreme Court

The U.S. Supreme Court is the highest court in the land. Currently, its membership consists of a chief justice and eight associate justices. The number of associate justices has varied from four to nine during the history of the country. The current membership size of the court was established in 1869.

Article III, Section 2 gives the Supreme Court both original and appellate jurisdiction. For practical purposes the majority of the Court's work is appellate in nature.

The appeal procedure is established by Congress. There are currently three principal ways in which a case reaches the Supreme Court. They are (1) by appeal, (2) by *writ of certiorari* (review), and (3) by certification.

When considering appeals from state courts, the Supreme Court must accept cases that fall into two categories. First, if the validity of a treaty or statute of the United States has been questioned and it has been held invoked by a state court. Second, the Court must accept cases where a state law has been questioned on the grounds that it violates the Constitution, the laws of the United States, or treaties made by the United States with a foreign power, and the state court has upheld the law.

The Supreme Court also considers appeals from the courts of appeal. In certain instances the Court will also consider direct appeals from district courts. The right to appeal to the Court is extremely limited. Congress has given the Court almost unlimited power to decide which cases it will hear.

The Court may approve a *writ of certiorari* to require a lower court to send the record of the case to it for review. This is only done when four justices believe the issues important enough to warrant consideration.

The certification is a little-used device that the lower courts use. In this process an appellate court asks the Supreme Court to answer a question of law. Currently, only courts of appeal and courts of claims may use this process.

Courts of Appeal

The courts of appeal exist for much the same reason that the state district courts of appeal exist: to relieve the Supreme Court of some of its workload. They were created in 1891 as circuit courts of appeal and were given their current title in 1948. They hear appeals from U.S. district courts and independent regulatory agencies.

District Courts

The district courts are courts of original jurisdiction. They hear, with some exceptions, all cases and controversies involving federal questions. They consider both criminal and civil litigations. The district court is the only federal court that has jury trials.

Judicial System Personnel

The judicial system is similar to any other system in which people have roles and interact. In some instances the individual has a single role, yet as a part of a larger group he participates as a part of a larger organization. It is this concept that we want to consider at this time.

Justices and Judges

In general usage the justice or judge is a person who sits as part of an appellate court. There is usually a chief justice or presiding justice and two or more associate justices. In the federal system they are appointed by the president and confirmed by the Senate for life terms.

At the state level a justice or judge may be elected, appointed by the governor, or appointed from a list supplied by a nonpartisan commission composed of lawyers, judges, and laymen. There have been major criticisms of the elective and appointive processes for the judiciary. The major objection to these processes is that they fail to procure men qualified to become judges. Either system tempts candidates to "play politics" to obtain a judicial post.

Missouri Plan
During the past century there has been an effort to avoid the defects of both the appointive and the elective system for the selection of judges. The Missouri Plan, which has been adopted either partially or totally by several states, provides for selection based upon merit. This plan calls for the following:
1. A nonpartisan nominating committee or commission composed of members of the bar association and laymen appointed by the governor, chaired by a judge.
2. A specified number of candidates nominated by the commission for each judicial vacancy.
3. The judicial vacancy will be filled by the governor from the list.
4. Judges will run for reelection solely on the question of whether they should be retained in office or not.

The Missouri Plan is based upon the concept that nonpolitical judges are more apt to be impartial than political judges. The plan attempts to eliminate the political process, elective or appointive, in the selection of judges by substituting the selection process, in the hope of procuring better qualified judges. The person appointed under this system theoretically will shed whatever political and social bias he might otherwise have when he assumes his role on the bench.

Retirement, Discipline, and Removal of Judges
Until the 1960s the only methods of removal of judges were by impeachment by the legislature or defeat at the polls when they came up for election. Since both methods are inadequate for most situations, the feeling developed that traditional processes needed to be supplemented.

In 1960 California was the first state to pass a constitutional amendment providing for the retirement, discipline, and removal of judges. The amendment provides for the establishment of a Commission on Judicial Qualifications consisting of nine members: two judges of the courts of appeal, two judges of the superior court, one judge of the municipal court, two members of the bar, and two nonlawyers. The judge numbers are selected by the state supreme court, the two lawyers by the board of governors of the state bar association, and the two non-lawyers by the governor and approved by the state senate. The terms of office are for four years.

Any judge is subject to action of the Commission. Any person may complain about a judge to the Commission. The procedure is for the staff to conduct an informal confidential investigation. If the facts warrant, the Commission may hold formal hearings or order hearings before three special masters appointed by the state supreme court.

The Commission can recommend to the state supreme court the removal, retirement, or censure of the judge. The supreme court will review the matter and make the final decision.

Attorney General

The attorney general is elected in 42 states, appointed by the governor in six states, appointed by the legislature in one state, and appointed by the supreme court in one state. Historically, this office has been an appointive rather than an elective post. In contemporary times the attorney general is one of the most active officials in state government.[3] His duties require him in some instances to represent the state in civil matters. He sues and defends in the name of the state on all litigation. He is usually required to give written advisory opinions on any ques-

---

[3] *National Association of Attorneys General,* "Report on the Office of Attorney General" (February 1971), p. 62. Nine states provide a two-year term for the attorney general; 38, a four-year term; one, a five-year term; one, an eight-year term; and one, an indefinite term. The trend is from a two-year term toward a longer one. The main justification for the increase is the rapid turnover of personnel and the lack of continuity. Although admission to the bar is a practical necessity for holding office, it is not required in all states; 20 states do not require admission to the bar as a prerequisite.

tions of law to the governor, heads of state agencies, and the legislators.

Among his other duties he supervises the department of justice. In some states the attorney general has the constitutional duty to supervise district attorneys, sheriffs, and local police. He can direct the sheriff to perform investigations or, if he deems it necessary, he can appoint someone else to perform the duties of the sheriff in conducting the investigation. He can also prosecute criminal actions if the district attorney is disqualified and can supersede the district attorney where he feels the laws are not being adequately enforced.

District Attorneys and County Prosecutors

The district attorney or county prosecutor is usually an elected county officer. He is required to have been an attorney for a period of time, the length varying from state to state. If his office is a large one, he may appoint assistant district attornies or deputies to assist him in his work. For example, the Los Angeles district attorney employs 430 deputies in 24 major locations.

The district attorney has a fairly wide range of discretionary power as to whether to file a criminal complaint or not. In *Taleaferro* v. *Locke* 182 CA 2nd 755 (1960), the California Court of Appeal stated:

As concerns the enforcement of the criminal law the office of the district attorney is charged with grave responsibilities to the public. These responsibilities demand integrity, zeal, and conscientious effort in the administration of justice under the criminal law. However, both as to investigation and prosecution that effort is subject to the budgetary control of boards of supervisors, or other legislative bodies controlling the numbers of deputies, investigators, and other employees. Nothing could be more demoralizing to that effort or to efficient administration of justice than requiring a district attorney's office to dissipate its efforts on personal grievance, fanciful charges and idle prosecution.

Although district attorneys have the power to decide which cases to prosecute, they do not always have the power to terminate a case once it has commenced. Generally, a judge must rule on all dismissals.

There are two other areas where district attorneys exercise discretion subject to some controls by the court. The first is in plea bargaining; the second is in granting immunity in order to obtain testimony.

Criminal Defense Counsel (General)

The theory that a defendant has the *right* to counsel to aid in his defense has slowly evolved since the beginning of common law practices. The Sixth Amendment of the Constitution states that the accused is ". . . to have the assistance of counsel for his defense."

Early usage considered that this was a privilege that the defendant could avail himself of, but that it was not mandatory.

That the defendant could not afford counsel in noncapital federal cases was not considered to be important until *Johnson* v. *Zerbst* (1938). Earlier the Supreme Court, in *Powell* v. *Alabama* (1932), had ruled that a state had to provide defense counsel to defendants in capital cases if they were unable to afford one on their own.

This principle has been expanded until the landmark case of *Gideon* v. *Wainwright* (1963), which states that:

> . . . any person hailed into court, who is too poor to hire a lawyer, cannot be assured a fair trial unless counsel is provided him.

Although this case did not answer all of the questions concerning the right to counsel, it did formally establish the responsibility to provide counsel for the poor.

Currently, those who can afford to pay legal fees must engage their own attorney, with complete freedom of choice. The fee charged is theoretically in direct ratio to the chosen attorney's skill in criminal law.

Criminal Defense Counsel (Indigent Defendant)

States provide defense counsel for indigent defendants in two ways. Some assign counsel and pay his fee. The names of attorneys willing to perform this service are usually obtained in rotation from a volunteer panel. However, there are several drawbacks to this procedure. Those who volunteer may be newly admitted to the bar and inexperienced. In addition, since the state has to pay the volunteer's expenses and overhead, the costs may be higher than anticipated.

The second approach is to create an office of public defender, which generally costs less than the assigned-counsel method. The principal complaint against this system is that the public defender's office may be understaffed and subject to political pressure, perhaps resulting in a lowered quality of defense.

Marshal or Bailiff

Ohio and Iowa use the title of bailiff, which is comparable to the title of marshal used in California. Both are charged with carrying out orders of the court; for example, serving warrants of arrest, writs, other civil processes, and maintaining order of the court while in session. They are also charged with taking custody of prisoners while awaiting court action and, if necessary, transporting prisoners to other detention facilities after sentence.

During jury trials, they are sworn to closet the jurors, maintain seclusion, and tend to their requirements during deliberation. It is their duty to escort jurors to and from the court room during this time and be alert for any attempts to tamper with the jury.

Court Administrators

The position of court administrator is relatively new. The first court administrator was appointed in 1950 for the Media, Pennsylvania Court of Common Pleas. This concept did not flourish until the years 1964 to 1966.

There are no uniform educational or experience standards established for this critical position. Several degree programs to train personnel in this field have been established; however, most job descriptions are similar to that of the court clerk.

Some of the more important duties of the court administrator are:

1. Personnel management services.
2. Financial management service including preparation of the budget.
3. Management of physical facilities.
4. Information services with law enforcement and public agencies.
5. Intergovernmental relations assistance.
6. Jury administrative services.
7. Statistical recordings.
8. Systems analysis.
9. Calendar management.
10. Training seminars, and providing of manuals for day-to-day operations for deputies.

Court Clerk

Traditionally most of the duties of the court administrator have been performed by the clerk of the court. In addition to these, the clerk is responsible for all ministerial duties of the court. All papers and processes except warrants of arrest are issued in the clerk's name.

Again, there have been no uniform educational or experience criteria developed for this position. It may be filled either by election, appointment, or through a competitive Civil Service examination.

Supporting Court Personnel

As with other departments associated with the courts, the number of deputies depends upon the business of that particular jurisdiction.

In large courts it is normally the practice to have three divisions consisting of civil (including small claim filings), criminal, and traffic. Each division specializes in that segment.

However, in smaller courts, the above mentioned divisions may be handled by one or two deputies, and this requires them to be adept at all phases of the handling of the processes of the court.

Summary

In this chapter we have discussed the growth of the judicial system as a reflection of historical, geographical, social, and political influences. Differences among the states have caused their court systems to vary considerably. Although the names and jurisdictions of the courts differ among states, or within a state, the basic court functions are the same. They are (1) hearing appeals from lower courts, (2) conducting trials in cases arising from civil or criminal matters (general jurisdiction), and (3) conducting trials in specified or special crimes (limited jurisdiction). This three-jurisdictional model gives us a three-tier plan. The tiers from top to bottom are (1) state appellate courts, (2) trial courts of general jurisdiction, and (3) inferior courts (limited jurisdiction). Some states are presently eliminating the inferior courts.

The Constitution insures a two-judicial system, one state and the other federal. The Supreme Court is the highest court in the land, with both original and appellate jurisdiction. However, for practical purposes, the majority of the Court's work is appellate in nature. Appeal cases may reach the Court in three ways. They are (1) by appeal, (2) by *writ of certiorari,* and (3) by certification. The courts of appeal and district courts are also maintained in the federal court system.

Justices, or judges, preside over the courts. Federal judges are appointed by the President and confirmed by the Senate; judges at the state level may be elected or appointed. Several states have adopted the Missouri Plan that provides for selection based on merit.

In most states an attorney general is elected, whose duties are to (1) represent the state in civil matters, (2) give written advisory opinions, and (3) sue or defend in the name of the state on all litigation. He also must supervise the department of justice.

The district attorney, or county prosecutor, represents the county in court. He has a wide range of discretionary power involving what charges to file, which cases to prosecute, when to engage in plea bargaining, and the granting of immunity in order to obtain testimony.

In theory, the defendant has a right to counsel. Supreme Court cases, such as *Gideon* v. *Wright* (1963), have generally established the right to counsel. The defendant who cannot afford counsel may be represented by a public defender or a court-appointed attorney.

Court administrators, court clerks, and other supportive personnel are extremely valuable to the everyday functions of the court. However, there has been no uniform educational or experience criteria developed for them.

Student Checklist

1. Can you define the levels of the state judicial system?
2. Can you define the responsibilities of the state appellate courts?
3. Can you cite at least three examples of an inferior court?
4. Do you know at least two responsibilities of the Supreme Court?
5. Can you define the job requirements of the counsel for the indigent?
6. Are you able to outline the duties of the marshal or the bailiff in the court system?
7. Can you discuss the concepts underlying the adoption of the Missiouri Plan?

Topics for Discussion

1. Briefly discuss the philosophy underlying the development of our court system.
2. Outline the social and political situations that affected the judicial process objectives.
3. Discuss the process for disciplining or removing magistrates from the bench.

ANNOTATED BIBLIOGRAPHY

Abraham, Henry J. *The Judicial Process*, 2nd ed. New York: Oxford University Press, 1968. It is a selective comparative introduction to the judicial process, and it seeks to analyze and evaluate the main institutions and considerations affecting the administration of justice. Included are discussions of staffing of the courts, courts of the United States, and courts of England and Wales.

Cardoza, Benjamin, N. *The Nature of the Judicial Process*. New Haven: Yale University Press, 1921. This work is a discussion by one of the most famous justices of the United States Supreme Court about the conscious and unconscious processes by which he decides cases. Major segments deal with history, tradition, and sociology.

Frank, Jerome. *Courts on Trial*. New York: Atheneum, 1969. Deals with the function of the courts. It analyzes procedural reforms, the jury system, the role of the judge, judicial training, and precedents.

Jacob, Herbert. *Justice in America: Courts, Lawyers, and the Judicial Process,* 2nd ed. Boston: Little, Brown, 1972. The three major sections of this book deal with the functions of the courts, the participants in the judicial process, and the structure and rules of the judicial system.

James, Howard. *Crisis in the Courts,* rev. ed. New York: McKay, 1972. Deals with failures in the judicial system. Discusses such issues as trial delay, bail juries, sentencing, and requirements for judicial education.

Karlen, Delmar. *Anglo-American Criminal Justice*. New York: Oxford University Press, 1967. Examines the similarities and differences between the British and American criminal justice system. This includes an analysis of the institutions such as the police, prosecution, defense, and courts, as well as the systems procedures.

Roche, John P. *Courts and Rights: The American Judiciary In Action,* 2nd ed. New York: Random House, 1966. Covers the judicial process, the structure of the federal judiciary, legislative courts, common law, the Bill of Rights, and citizens' rights. The first section provides a good insight into the federal system.

Watson, Richard A., and Randal A. Downing. *The Politics of the Bench and the Bar*. New York: Wiley, 1969. This book is an empirical examination of the nonpartisan court plan. It covers the recruitment and selection process of judges, the Missouri Selection Plan, and judicial performance.

The study of this chapter will enable you to:

1. Explain the degree to which unreported crime exists.
2. Outline the number of people arrested for crime and the number sentenced to prison.
3. Define presentence investigation report.
4. Understand the two reasons for classification in prison.
5. Cite at least two objectives for probation.
6. Discuss two of the four treatment strategies.

11
Primary Functions of Corrections

Introduction

Corrections is the least visible and least understood segment of the criminal justice system in America. Its prisons, jails, juvenile training schools, and probation and parole machinery deal with the most troubling and troublesome members of society—the unrespectable and irresponsible. The institutions in which about one-third of the "corrections" population lives are out of view of most citizens, often in rural areas remote from the population centers. The two-thirds of the population on probation and parole are dispersed in the community and nearly invisible to all. Society seldom looks at corrections, except when there is a riot, jailbreak, or sensational scandal. Society has been content to keep corrections out of sight.

The invisibility of corrections belies its size, complexity, and importance in the control of crime. Corrections consists of scores of different kinds of institutions and programs of the utmost diversity in approach, facilities, and qualities. On any given day it is responsible for approximately 1.5 million offenders; in the course of a year it will handle 2.5 million "new" cases at a cost of over a billion dollars a year, with costs rising each year.[1]

Of these 1.5 million offenders, one-third are in institutions and two-thirds are in the community under the supervision of probation or

---

[1] The President's Commission on Law Enforcement and the Administration of Justice, *The Challenge of Crime in a Free Society* (Washington, D.C.: U.S. Govt. Printing Office, 1967).

parole agencies. It is estimated that two percent of all males over the age of 12 are under correctional jurisdiction at any one time.

The Offender in the System

There is a selection process that takes place in the criminal justice system, one which results in a disproportionately small number of offenders officially handled, who "represent" crime in the United States. Those who come into the correctional system are a small percentage of the offenders in the society. The fallout is greatest between the point where an offense is committed and the point where charges are filed. Arrests reflect one-fourth of known serious crimes. Charges filed will be reduced as much as one-third and, of those charged, there can be another one-third fallout. Again, we can expect the screening out of a large number, as much as 20 percent who are not found guilty. Figure 11-1 depicts this fallout for one jurisdiction.

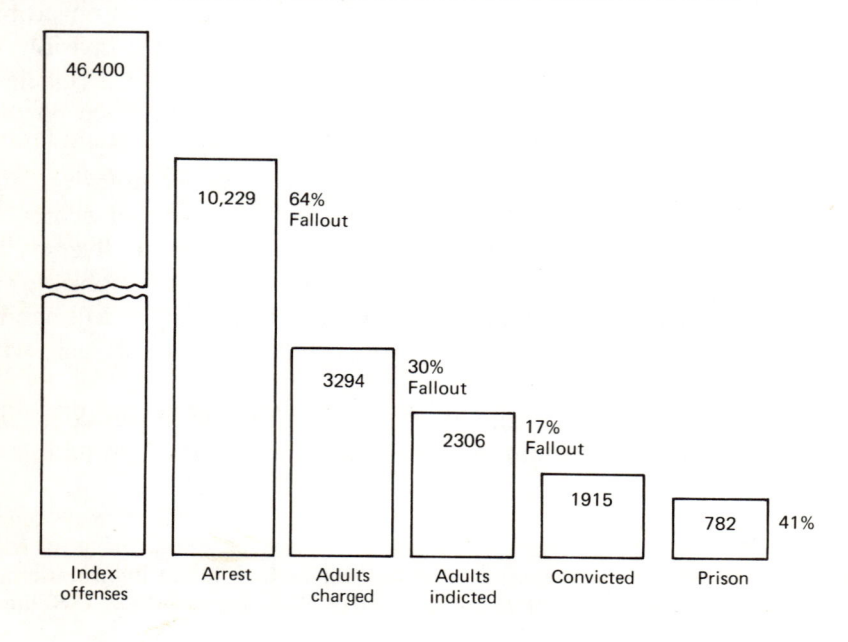

Figure 11-1. Criminal justice fallout, 1971. Source: Dallas Police, 1972.

Stage	Number	Fallout
Index offenses	46,400	
Arrest	10,229	64%
Adults charged	3294	30%
Adults indicted	2306	17%
Convicted	1915	
Prison	782	41%

250 introduction to the administration of justice

The data shown are not unusual. They are similar for most jurisdictions. It is important, therefore, to realize that the numbers in prison do not truly represent the numbers of criminals in the United States.

Corrections follows last in the sequence of activities after police arrest, prosecution, and court disposition. It is the court disposition that sets corrections in motion. Corrections follows two broad paths: institutionalization or community treatment (most commonly probation or parole).

Institutionalization

Following a determination of guilt in court, all offenders are generally subject to a presentence investigation.[2] This is a written report to the court setting forth a systematic, thorough inquiry into the offender's life and background, the details of the immediate offense and any prior criminal history. This report is used to analyze and interpret the offender's personality for the purposes of determining if he or she should be sentenced to prison and for how long, or if he or she can be released into society on probation and with what degree of risk to the community. The personal history of the defendant set forth in the report includes developmental data, health, education, employment habits, character, behavioral patterns, associates, marital history, and mental and physical condition. This basic information assists the court in making its determination. Although in the past presentence investigations have been kept confidential, the present trend has been against this. Many judges share the information at least with the defense attorneys at the time of sentencing. Sentencing takes place at a special hearing set at a date in the future by the judge at the time the defendant is found guilty. This usually entails a two-week to four-week waiting period.

It is estimated that in the United States about one-half of the convicted offenders in the criminal courts are imprisoned and the other

---

[2] The Standard Probation and Parole Act of 1955 provides that "No defendant convicted of a crime, the punishment for which may include imprisonment for more than one year, shall be sentenced or otherwise disposed of before a written report of investigation by a probation officer is presented to and considered by the court."

half are released to the community under supervision. Statutory limitations in many states preclude anything but imprisonment for certain offenses. In fact, some states quite narrowly limit the use of probation as an alternative. The presentence investigation is used for more than merely an aid to the judge in passing sentence. It is also used as a basis upon which a program of individual treatment and classification is begun in prison. If the person is granted probation and remains in the community, the report is used by the probation department in its treatment program.

There is a wide range and variety in the more than 400 institutions for adult offenders in this country. Some are grossly deficient; conditions are such that racial, ethnic, and religious tensions build up to the breaking point. A rash of riots in the late 1960s and early 1970s repeated a pattern of disturbances of less than a generation earlier. The mid-1950s had witnessed a similar explosion of riots in prisons across the country. The earlier riots were attributable in large measure to changes that were occurring in the field of corrections. Today's riots are more closely linked to changes taking place in the society.

Figure 11-2. The aftermath: Attica.

Prisons have a long history of the twin scourges, idleness and monotony. When these two factors are mixed with racial and ethnic tensions, riots are almost inevitable.

Prisons designed of stone, steel, and concrete for custody purposes have little humanizing atmosphere. Sixty-one prisons opened before 1900 are still in use. The American Correctional Association (ACA), the professional organization of wardens and other allied correctional groups, reports an average population of over 2000 inmates in each of the 21 larger prisons. Four have over 4000 inmates each. The ACA studies indicate that the prison system itself causes the riots and demonstrations; they recommend strongly that a prison house fewer than 500 inmates and that it be located near the urban center from which the majority of inmates come.

A correctional institution, whether maximum security prison, reformatory, or minimum security farm or ranch, is an inmate community; a society with its own culture, its own set of values and attitudes. This inmate "culture" is the all-important focus of the individual offender, and often it is in strong opposition to the objectives of prison programs. Prisonization, which means the adopting of the values of prisoners and prison life as normal by the inmates, is an important way of enabling the inmate to avoid devastating psychological effects.

> *The welfare of the individual inmate, to say nothing of his psychological well-being and dignity, does not importantly depend on how much education, recreation, and consultation he receives but rather depends on how he manages to live and relate with other inmates who constitute his crucial and only meaningful world.*[3]

The social gap between the staff and the inmates is such that it reinforces the need of inmates to conform to the inmate subculture. The mass handling of prisoners contributes mightily to maintaining this social distance. Furthermore, security concerns dominate all staff activity. High walls, fences, and gun towers seek to insure security and custody. Censorship of mail, monitoring of visits, lack of privacy, and identification by number all lead to insuring an increasing social distance between staff and inmates.

---

[3] Lloyd W. McCorckle, "Social Structure in a Prison," *The Welfare Reporter, 8* (December 1956), p. 6.

Classification and Treatment in Prison

Classification of the prisoner is an extension of the presentence investigation. Classification, a basic tool of modern penology, serves two purposes. Its first and most basic purpose is to determine security or custody considerations for each inmate, where he is to be housed, and what his (or her) assignment will be while serving the sentence. Its second basic purpose is to determine the type of treatment to be afforded the inmate.

During the initial period of confinement, the offender is studied and diagnosed by the various specialists who make up the classification committee. Psychiatric, medical, and psychological studies are made, and written reports providing information on the inmate's background and conduct are given to the classification committee, whose judgments and analysis will be the basis of the inmate's assignment and treatment plan. The inmate is interviewed and the information obtained becomes a part of the classification committee's data bank. Within the institution's scope of resources for employment and treatment, the inmate is given

Figure 11-3. An inmate is interviewed by a classification committee, whose judgments and analysis will be the basis of his assignment and treatment plan.

an assignment. Table 11-1 provides an idea of the variety of classification schemes.

Treatment
Today's correctional institutions have as their stated purpose the rehabilitation of the offender. In reality, however, correctional institutions are sorely lacking in trained personnel with the treatment skills needed for rehabilitation. In the 24-hour-a-day total institution, "treatment" as a separate facet of a person's life is not possible—every detail of living is ultimately intertwined with all others. Therapy, with its permissiveness or its exposure of hidden emotions, carries over to the inmate's life beyond therapy sessions. Emotions loosed in therapy spill over into the life of the prison community. Often this means fights with inmates, attacks on guards, or anger turned inward toward the self.

The traditional institutional approach to rehabilitation has been the individual treatment approach, that is, the "sick person" model. The offender is regarded as one suffering from a defect of personality that has led to crime. The medical approach of organizing treatment based on diagnosis, prescription, and application of therapy is the fundamental current approach to treatment in corrections. Psychotherapy (or variations of psychotherapy) coupled with casework have been the basic treatment approach. It is practiced by psychologists, psychiatrists, and social workers. Others at lesser levels of training practice unique innovations upon this treatment—these include institutional parole officers, institution counselors, and even correctional guards. The psychological form of treatment relies on the healer's ability to mobilize healing forces within the sufferer by psychological means.[4] "Talking" is the basic tool of the therapist. There are three ingredients in this treatment mode—a trained healer accepted by the sufferer; a sufferer seeking relief; and a circumscribed, somewhat formal series of conversations between healer and sufferer intended to help the sufferer solve his problems.

This approach to the offender was held out hopefully as an important rehabilitation method. Its practice has dominated the field since World War II. Yet, there are many indications that it has not achieved

[4] James D. Frank, *Persuasion and Healing* (Baltimore: Johns Hopkins Press, 1961).

TABLE 11-1. **Cross-Classification of Offender Typologies**

Subtypes	Jesness	Hunt	Hurwitz	Mac-Gregor	Makkay	Quay	Reiss	Warren
1. Asocial		Sub I	Type II	Schizophrenic				I_2
Aggressive	Immature, aggressive				Antisocial Character Disorder-Primitive Aggressive	Unsocialized-psychopath		Asocial, aggressive
Passive	Immature, passive				Passive-aggressive			Asocial, passive
2. Conformist		Stage I						I_3
Nondelinquently-oriented	Immature, passive				Antisocial Character Disorder-Organized Passive-aggressive	Inadequate-immature		Conformist, Immature
Delinquently-oriented	Socialized conformist					/?Subcultural/	/?Relatively integrated/	Conformist, Cultural
3. Antisocial-manipulator	Manipulator			Autocrat	Antisocial Character Disorder-Organized Aggressive		Defective superego	I_3 Manipulator
4. Neurotic		Stage II	Type III		Neurotic		Relatively weak ego	I_4 Neurotic
Acting-out	Neurotic, acting-out							Neurotic, acting-out
Anxious	Neurotic, anxious Neurotic, depressed			Intimidated		Neurotic-disturbed		Neurotic, anxious
5. Subcultural-identifier	Cultural delinquent	Stage II	Type I	Rebel	Subcultural	Subcultural	Relatively integrated	I_4 Cultural identifier
6. Situational		Stage II						I_4 Situational, emotional reaction
Types not cross classified					Mental retardate psychotic			

256   introduction to the administration of justice

Subtypes	A P A	Argyle	Gibbons	Jenkins and Hewitt	McCord	Reckless	Schrag	Studt
1. Asocial	Passive-aggressive personality	Lack of sympathy					Asocial	Isolate
Aggressive	Aggressive		Overly aggressive	Unsocialized aggressive				
Passive	Passive-aggressive							
2. Conformist	Passive-aggressive personality	Inadequate superego			Conformist			
Nondelinquently-oriented	Passive-dependent		Gang offenders	/?Socialized/			Antisocial	Receiver
Delinquently-oriented								
3. Antisocial-manipulator	Antisocial personality	Inadequate superego			Aggressive (psychopathic)	Psychopath	Pseudosocial	Manipulator
4. Neurotic	Sociopathic personality disturbance	Weak ego control				Neurotic Personality	Prosocial	
Acting-out			Joyrider					
Anxious			Behavior problems	Overinhibited	Neurotic-withdrawn			Love-seeker
5. Subcultural-identifier	Dyssocial reaction	Deviant identification	Gang offenders	Socialized			Antisocial	Learner
6. Situational	Adjustment reaction of adolescence		Casual delinquent			Offenders of the moment		
Types not cross classified			Heroin user Delinquent			Eruptive Behavior		

Source: Northwestern University School of Law, *The Journal of Criminal Law, Criminology, and Police Science*, 62, No. 2 (June, 1971).

primary functions of corrections   257

the degree of success expected, so it has been supplemented with a group approach.

Group Treatment. In addition to the offender's own personality structure, his or her group affiliations are often cited as causes for the persistence of criminality. Human personality is acquired and shaped through social relationships. Therefore, groups are employed in rehabilitation programs, as both the instrument of change and the targets of change.

This approach sprang from attempts to restore delinquent soldiers to duty at army rehabilitation centers through group methods. The use of group therapy reached a peak of popularity in American corrections by the mid-1950s and early 1960s.

Guided group interaction is one term used to describe the approach in which offenders freely discuss their problems in a supportive group atmosphere under a leader. The object is to create a group climate without threat. A marked give-and-take discussion is encouraged, in which members are free and equal and the leader adopts a permissive but noncondoning role. Successful interaction is heavily dependent on the leader's skill in developing a pattern of meaning for the participants. The leader's primary technique is to turn questions and issues back to the group for discussion rather than addressing them directly.

Group therapy is intended to have several benefits—participants should gain new insights into their problems and themselves, attitudes should change, and a reevaluation of the participants' place in the environment should begin.

Other Programs of Rehabilitation in Prison. Both individual and group therapies have been supported in prisons by a series of other programs that were aimed at the goal of rehabilitation.

Since the establishment of the Elmira Reformatory in 1876, correctional education has been a standard rehabilitation program in prison. The great value that we Americans place on education, in terms of its potential for providing the good things in life—position, money, and social acceptance, is reflected in the expenditure it represents in our personal lives. Our faith in education to do as much for the offender is based on our own experience with it. However, we cannot expect education alone to achieve correction and rehabilitation goals, but it can offer a greater likelihood of this achievement. As many studies have shown, prison populations are considerably behind the norms in academic achievement. Providing basic education to inmates may return them to

Figure 11-4. A prison group therapy approach toward treatment.

society with social and vocational assets that they lacked before. It also aids in their treatment programs. In both individual and group therapy programs, the enhanced ability to use language in communication makes for a more effective patient-therapist relationship.

The importance of education in prison has been stressed in the past decade, and more resources are now placed at the disposal of educational efforts than ever before. Correspondence courses, adult basic education, and programmed learning are quite common today in most institutions. The recent increase in college-level course work is a great step toward the education of offenders in correctional institutions.

The important role of academic education in career vocations is the main reason for the flourishing of academic education within institutions. This factor, more than any other, has provided the impetus to develop the widespread upper-level education programs.

Career Training. Career preparation in prison to better fit the inmate for employment upon release has long been part of the prison rehabilitation concept. Almost all institutions have fairly sophisticated vocational training programs. These are usually tied into the institution's maintenance and industrial program where possible. In the more sophisticated programs, academic courses and vocational training are closely linked together. In the United States today, about 3.5 percent of all institutional staff are teachers. Although this is not an optimum figure, it is a significant increase over the past decade and points to a heavier involvement in the future.

Other Programs. Religious and psychiatric counseling and recreational programs are fairly standard in nearly all institutions. All are geared toward encouraging the inmate to adopt a life of responsibility after release.

Today the use of prison, whatever its programs, is being seriously questioned. Of the $1.5 billion spent annually for corrections, three-fourths goes to maintain institutions that hold only one-fourth of the total number of convicted offenders. The remaining three-fourths of the offenders remain in the communities at a fraction of the total cost. The data available show that treatment of offenders in the community is at least as successful as institutional treatment. In fact, it is generally agreed that institutional experience is more damaging. One state, Massachusetts, closed all of its juvenile correctional institutions in 1971 and

Figure 11-5. Training in a federal correctional institution frequently involves the use of sophisticated teaching tools.

1972, and other states are moving in this direction. Most states have placed a moratorium on building prisons. The present trend is definitely toward community-based treatment, the most common being probation and parole. These traditional corrections programs are beginning to play a much larger role in the treatment of the offender.

Probation

The most frequently used community-based alternative to incarceration is probation. It began in 1841 when a Boston shoemaker named John Augustus urged the court to release certain offenders to his custody rather than send them to prison. The use of probation is widespread in America and abroad, especially in the United Kingdom. After a finding of guilt, the court decides to place the defendant on probation with the understanding that he will live up to certain conditions and submit to the supervision and assistance of court probation officers. If the probationer violates any of the conditions of his probation, the court may impose sentence to imprisonment. In some situations, sentence is *imposed* at the time of granting of probation and its *execution* withheld on the condition that the individual live up to the conditions. Whether it is the imposition or execution that is withheld matters little to the probationer. If he abides by the conditions of probation, he has the opportunity to remain out of prison, serving his sentence in the community.

In addition to requiring acceptable modes of personal conduct, the court may order a wide variety of other conditions, such as restitution to the victims of the crime, payment of support to dependents, or fines to be paid on the installment plan. In most jurisdictions in which probation is used, approximately one-half of the adult offenders and considerably more than one-half of the juveniles are placed on probation as an alternative to incarceration.

The essential weakness of probation has been the lack of qualified probation officers. Case loads that vary widely in terms of numbers and types of offenders make supervision difficult. Probation officers are essentially case workers who also have peace-keeping functions. These two roles frequently conflict. Interest in "helping" versus "keeping the peace" is a continuing dilemma.

As the use of probation has grown, it has been recognized that the task of the probation officer has become more specialized, requiring highly developed skills and special training. For a time, the preferred training was social work. Since three-fourths of those on probation are male, it was generally accepted that they should be supervised by male officers. But most trained social workers are women. Recruitment of a sufficient number of trained men to work in probation was not successful, resulting in the recruitment of many persons with considerably less than the needed skills.

Today, people with a startling mix of educational backgrounds work in the field. Disciplines from anthropology to zoology are represented. A large number of teachers, especially those with religious backgrounds, work in juvenile probation. In the adult field, many workers have military and law enforcement backgrounds. Training in social work as a requirement is giving way to the broader behavioral science requirements (college work in sociology, anthropology, and psychology) in recruiting specifications.

The probation officer's task falls into three roles: the punitive officer who is the guardian of middle-class morality and who protects society through the exercise of controls; the "protective agent" who vacillates between helping the offender and protecting the community; and the welfare worker whose primary goal is the offender's well-being.[5] But the probation officer has many other roles—employment agent, vocational counselor, marital counselor, school counselor, junior-grade psychoanalyst, father confessor, and law enforcement officer. He is the one who helps the offender comply with the order of the court; he has the option of playing many roles.

As the use of probation increased, studies of its effectiveness were made. An early one was the Saginaw Project, conducted in Michigan between 1957 and 1962. The study demonstrated that most of those placed on probation succeeded, that no appreciable risk to the community was incurred, and that it was an economical venture saving money by reducing construction and maintenance costs of institutional facilities. Many other studies supported these findings.

Probation is the prerogative of various branches of government: the executive and judicial branches in some states, and welfare authorities in others. The different formats have produced confusion for those studying the process and its effectiveness. The question of where jurisdiction over probation should lie becomes critical as its use and staff size are expanded. A primary question now is whether probation should be granted and administered by the judiciary or by the executive branch.

The best argument against court-based probation is that courts, particularly criminal courts, are adjudicatory and regulatory rather than service-oriented. As long as probation remains a part of the judicial branch, it will remain an extension of the courts and have no identity of its own.

A strong argument for having probation within the purview of the executive branch is that most service-oriented agencies are already located there. It would increase the interaction between corrections and other allied human services and increase the prospects for using the full resources of the community.

Probation takes place in the community. Probation officers are

---

[5] Lloyd E. Ohlin, Herman Piven, and Donnel M. Pappenfort, "Major Dilemmas of the Social Worker in Probation and Parole," *National Probation and Parole Association Journal* (July 1956), p. 215.

responsible for assisting the convicted offender to adjust to the community. The probation process has overwhelmingly been one closely identified with casework; that is, the probation officer diagnoses the client's problem and develops a treatment plan, in a one-to-one relationship. Probation officers have been concerned with developing interviewing skills, creating therapeutic relationships with their clients, counseling, providing insight, and modifying behavior. The typical case load is heavy, often totaling more than 100 clients.

Some authorities believe that probation is beginning to move away from this medical model, which relies heavily on the therapist-client relationship. They see probation officers taking on the advocacy role, assisting their clients in overcoming the social, legal, educational, and political barriers to their full and responsible participation in the community.

Probation means surveillance for many. Requirements or conditions are imposed by the court for the probationer to follow, and the probation officer is responsible for seeing that they are followed. In many cases, this regulatory function becomes the sole or overriding concern of the officer, demanding extensive surveillance and supervision. This function often conflicts with treatment. Probationers often must obtain permission to buy a car, change jobs, get married, change residence, and so on. These restrictions interfere mightily with the individual probationer's freedom of choice. Technical violations of probation conditions can result in revocation and commitment to an institution. Probation officers have great authority, and the way they use it determines, in large part, the nature of their relationship with the probationer.

Often probationers are assumed to be similar to one another. This assumption is wrong. Adults differ from juveniles; girls and women differ from boys and men and, as individuals, they all differ from each other. The range of individuality demands a like range of individual treatment.

Casework is the most frequently used model, but probation staffs also utilize several others. These include specialized supervision programs, guided group interaction, delinquent peer-group programs, and out-of-home placement, as well as residential treatment. These are essentially treatment-oriented programs. Increasingly, correctional staffs urge a move away from concentration on "changing" the offender to changing the conditions in society that cause crime and produce offenders.

President Nixon's National Advisory Commission on Standards

and Goals for the Criminal Justice System in 1973 proposed a new direction for the delivery of probation service. To implement an effective system for delivering services to all probationers, it will be necessary to:
1. Develop a goal-oriented service delivery system.
2. Identify service needs of probationers systematically and periodically, and specify measurable objectives based on priorities and needs assessment.
3. Differentiate between these services that the probation system should provide and the services that should be provided by other resources.
4. Organize the system to deliver services, including the purchase of services for probationers, and organize the staff around workloads.
5. Move probation staff from courthouses to residential areas and develop service centers for probationers.
6. Redefine the role of the probation officer from caseworker to community resource manager.
7. Provide services to misdemeanants (those charged with lesser offenses than felonies).

The most important goal of probation must be to maintain in the community all offenders who can function acceptably with probation support and to select for confinement only those who, on the basis of evidence, are a danger to themselves or to others and cannot complete probation status successfully, even with optimal probation support.

Parole

Parole is the second most frequently used form of corrections in the community. Over 95 percent of the offenders committed to a correctional institution will eventually be released, and most of these will be under some form of parole. Parole has been defined in the Attorney General's Survey of Release Procedures in 1939 as "the release of an offender from a penal or correctional institution, after he has served a portion of his sentence, under continued custody of the state and under conditions that permit his reincarceration in the event of misbehavior."

Parole is similar to probation in many ways. Data about offenders are gathered and presented to an authority with power to release the person to community supervision under specific conditions. If the person violates the conditions, he is usually sent to prison. Probation and parole differ in one major way: probation is granted by a judge instead of any kind of incarceration, while parole means release from confinement after a period of time in a penal institution. Probation is a court function; parole is almost always an administrative decision.

Parole in this country began at the Elmira Reformatory in New York which opened in 1876. Under the Elmira system, sentences were indeterminate, dependent on "marks" earned by good behavior. Release was for a six-month parole term, during which the parolee reported to a volunteer. This practice spread and, by 1945, parole laws had been passed in all the states.

Parole and the Sentencing Structure
All parole systems are part of a larger process involving trial courts and legislative mandates. Sources of sentencing authority and limits on sentencing alternatives affect the parole systems of the different states. Uniform sentencing does not exist in this country in spite of the long-standing efforts of professional organizations, such as the National Council on Crime and Delinquency, the American Correctional Association, and the American Bar Association.

The National Advisory Commission on Standards and Goals for the Criminal Justice System states that the sentencing system that seems most consistent with parole objectives has the following characteristics: (1) sentencing limits set legislatively with the sentencing judge having discretion to fix the maximum sentence up to legislative limits; (2) no minimum sentences, either by mandate or by judicial sentencing authority; (3) comparatively short sentences for ordinary offenses with a legislation maximum not to exceed five years for most offenders; (4) a system of mandatory release with supervision for offenders ineligible for parole, yet not held in an institution until their absolute discharge date; (5) all parole conditions set by the paroling authority, but with the opportunity for a sentencing judge to suggest special conditions if he so desires; (6) legislative prohibition against the accommodation of consecutive sentences if it interferes with minimum parole eligibility; (7) legislative provisions for alternatives to reimprisonment upon parole revocation; and (8) no offense for which parole is denied by legislation.

Parole Board Decisions
Parole board members decide on parole primarily on the basis of risk to the community and the offender's potential for further crime. Other

factors are also important: fairness and procedural regularity; supporting appropriate and equitable sanctions (equalizing penalties); and the need to support other criminal justice operations, such as aiding in the solution of institutional problems of population control or the like within the facility.

The parole function has gone through three periods in which it has been directed by an overriding philosophy. In the beginning it was assumed that its purpose was to reform the offender—to make him a contributing member of the society in every way. In the 1930s, parole came under the influence of the medical model, with its diagnostic methods and stress on individual treatment as the means of rehabilitating the offender. Today, the emphasis appears to be on reintegration, changing the conditions causing crime, and creating in the offender's world realistic alternatives through which he can find a satisfying lifestyle that is tolerable to the larger community.

Parole board personnel have long been in the center of controversy because of several conditions—their means of appointment, the range of their responsibilities, and the part-time status of some members. Most experts agree that parole board members should have knowledge in three basic fields: law, the behavioral sciences, and corrections. They should have full-time positions with appropriate training. Most appointments of board members today are subject to criticism. Ideal standards for appointment that would eliminate the most common criticisms would include:

1. Full-time status.
2. Appointment for six-year terms by an advisory group that is broadly representative of the community.
3. Understanding of legal issues and behavioral and decision-making processes.
4. Opportunity to receive training periodically.
5. Maximum number set at five members.

Representation at the Hearings

No other issue has unsettled the parole process more than that of the offender's right to have legal representation at parole-granting hearings and revocations. The trend is clearly toward provision of legal representation at hearings on parole or revocation. In addition, the parolee must be able to be present at the hearing and also have access to a review of the information on the basis of which the decisions are made. Parole effectiveness and fairness depend upon these two rights.

The rights of the prisoner to representation, to access and disclosure of information, to witnesses, and cross-examination are being granted more and more in a continuing reversal of the procedures existing before the late 1960s. This increased emphasis and insistence on prisoner rights has been achieved as the result of numerous court decisions.

The Community as Site and Source of Corrections
Community-based corrections—probation and parole—have three aspects: humanitarian, restorative, and managerial. Custodial coercion places the offender in personal physical jeopardy, reduces access to sources of personal satisfaction, and reduces self-esteem. To the extent that an offender can be relieved of the burden of custody, a humanitarian objective is realized. The restorative aspect involves taking measures expected to achieve for the offender a position in the community in which he or she does not violate the laws. Efforts are made to reintegrate the offender into the community. Finally, the managerial aspect involves keeping the offender in the community at reduced fiscal costs while providing protection to the public. The emphasis must be on insuring public safety as programs are developed to bring about effective rehabilitation.

The greatest significance of the move toward community corrections is the implication that communities must assume responsibility for the problems they generate. Problems and people, crime and the criminal, are imbedded in community life and must be dealt with there.

Community programs have two operating objectives: to use and coordinate existing community service agencies offering resources in areas such as family planning, counseling, general social services, medical treatment, legal representation, and employment; and to involve public spirited volunteers in the mission of corrections.

Community Alternatives to Corrections
Nonresidential Treatment. Structured correctional programs that supervise a substantial part of an offender's day but do not include "live-in" requirements are one form of community corrections. The clients need more intensive services than probation usually offers, and yet they are

not in need of 24-hour-a-day confinement. School and counseling programs, day treatment centers with vocational training, and guided group interaction are among the strategies used, along with many related services to families.

Foster and group homes are used. The group homes appear to have the greater success because they give a semiindependence from the family while still providing a supportive environment and rewarding experiences with adults.

Work and training release began to be used extensively in the 1950s. The practice permits selected inmates to work for pay outside the institution, returning at night. Variations include weekend sentences, furloughs, and release for vocational and academic training. Each helps reestablish links to the community.

The federal prison system pioneered in the development of prerelease programs in the early 1960s. In several cities it organized small living units, usually in rented quarters, to which inmates could be transferred for the final months of a sentence as part of a preparation for release. Halfway houses, both halfway in and halfway out, have been used by corrections in the continuing move to use the community as the site and source of rehabilitation.

Treatment Strategies

Throughout correctional history several strategies of treatment have been created and applied. They can be grouped under four major headings:
1. Clinical models.
2. Group interaction models.
3. Therapeutic community models.
4. Social action models.

The assumptions underlying each strategy should be discussed.

Clinical Models. The basic assumption underlying the clinical model is that the clients are disturbed in their emotional and mental development and are in need of assistance to work out their problems. Correcting disorders comes through a one-to-one relationship in which a skilled therapist works with the client, helping him or her to gain insight and emotional support to resolve the troubling emotional and mental disorders. The clinical model has been referred to as a medical model because it is built on the doctor-patient role in medicine.

The clinical process usually takes place in an office, is a verbal exchange that is heavily dependent upon an understanding of emotional reactions, is intensely interpersonal, intellectual in nature, and is clearly a dominant-submissive relationship between the helper and the one to be helped.

This model has been widely applied to the probation, parole, and institutional treatment function because of its adaptability to a casework approach.

Group Interaction Models. The assumptions underlying this model are similar in many ways to those of the clinical model. The major difference is that the treatment mode changes from the one-to-one to the one-to-many. Intellectual and emotional experiences are shared by members of the group as well as the therapist. The concentration is mainly upon correcting faulty thought processes, disorders of the mind, and behavior that hurts or offends the self or others. The clinical dimension is expanded by adding more to the relationship and by increasing the size of the group. Troubled persons can test out their thoughts, feelings, and behavior on other troubled persons in a therapeutic setting.

Therapeutic Community Model. This model is deeply influenced by the assumptions underlying the clinical and group interaction models. But it differs in the belief that a concentration on the person's total social and personal environment will help the treatment process. Escaping from the narrow confines of the office and the therapeutic hour, this model rests on the belief that the total life experience is therapeutic and, if all the actors in the setting are guided by this belief, the individual will be able to overcome the troubling malady and emerge as a well person. The programs following this model are residential in nature, with strong controls applying to almost all behavior. Successful treatment is usually measured by movement from a totally controlled environment toward freedom. An assumption is made that the person has intense trouble in personal and social relations and can only overcome these in a 24-hour-a-day, residential, treatment-controlled environment. Some adult and juvenile correctional programs have adopted similar programs in halfway houses, residential treatment facilities, and specialized institutions.

Social Action Models. This model differs considerably from the others. Its basic assumption is that the problems lie in the structure and function of the social order and, in order to reduce crime and assist the offender, the conditions responsible for the trouble with society must be changed.

The focus is away from treating the offender and toward changing the social world wherever it operates to the detriment of many. Some people see corrections moving toward this role, particularly as advocacy replaces therapy and community-based corrections become less like correctional centers placed in the community, and more like a link to social action.

The proponents of this model emerged in the 1960s and are associated with the civil-rights and poverty-workers' movements; they have been joined by student activists and reform-minded political and legal activists. The major goals of this group are the elimination of racism, removal of ghettolike conditions in urban areas, establishment of justice and equity throughout the criminal justice system, eradication of poverty, provision for access to equal opportunity for all citizens, renewal of social institutions to make them responsive to needs of the citizenry, and the provision for relevance in education, employment, and government. The people who foster this model are often at odds with the proponents of the three other models. The emerging debate and conflict will have an impact on the criminal justice system as well as on society in general.

Specific Treatment Modifications
Two treatment techniques that have gained currency in the early 1970s and are being used quite widely are behavior modification and transactional analysis.

Behavior Modification. Behavior may be defined as anything a person does, says, or thinks that can be observed directly or indirectly. Shaping or changing of behavior by contingent reinforcement (giving approval or disapproval) is a simple and direct manner of influencing behavior. It is useful in learning and can be used for control. The latter purpose, control, may be one reason why this approach has been heartily endorsed by many people in corrections, especially in institutions, where control of groups is basic. Behavior modification in prison has also been applied to learning through *programmed* instruction. Courses are programmed in such a way that the learner is reinforced (rewarded) by getting the right answer at each step. Much progress has been made in education through this method, especially in basic arithmetic, English, and other related coursework.

Transactional Analysis. Psychiatrist Eric Berne's experience in therapy led him to believe that there are three ego states, popularly called parent, adult, and child. These states are present in everyone, and one or another of them is operative at any one time. In various situations a person may act as a child, an adult, or a parent. This may be reflected in facial expressions, positions, gestures, vocabulary, and the like. A parent may stiffen when being defied by his or her child, may turn pale and tremble on hearing the police siren, or may exclaim with childlike excitement when hitting the jackpot. Changes from adult to child or parent to child, for example, can be observed in the same person. Thomas Horns, a disciple of Berne, depicts transactions as units of social intercourse in which two persons are involved. One speaks or gestures, and this transactional stimulus leads to a transactional response. Transactional analysis is the determination of what part of the parent, adult, or child is providing the stimulus or giving the response. And it systematizes these transactions in words that mean the same thing to each person that uses them. This agreement on the meanings of the words is an important element of the therapy's effectiveness.

The concepts of transactional analysis have been used in a range of institutions, generally in group sessions. A therapist leader participates and in the first stages uses a blackboard for diagramming explanations and studying transaction. Although transactional analysis does not have all the answers, remarkable improvements in offenders have taken place. The process seeks to inspire each individual to improve and to become responsible for his or her behavior and, in the terminology of the transactional analysis school, to "feel O.K."

There are many specific techniques used in corrections to help the offender. Most have some degree of effectiveness and can assist the individual. That some persons are not helped does not mean the treatment is bad; it is simply ineffective for that person. There is, it appears, a growing mandate to match the treatment with the person to be treated. Efforts to do so have been sparse, but significant progress has been made in some quarters and it appears that the need to do so has been accepted. Soon now we might expect a person to take some sort of standardized test that will determine the type of treatment needed. Some progress has been made also in matching the person to be treated with the treater. For example, the offender and parole officer can be assigned to each other on the basis of certain personality characteristics that are found in both and that will better support the development of their relationship.

Personnel in Corrections

Correctional personnel work today takes place in widely differing settings and under a variety of auspices. The American public has never quite made up its mind which is more important: to punish offenders, to protect society by locking them up or keeping them under close supervision, or to try to change them into useful citizens. There is little argument against keeping the dangerous offender under control, both as an immediate protection to society and as a deterrent to future crime. But since almost all offenders must legally be released to the community someday, the public is coming to see the need for rehabilitating and equipping them to become productive members of the community. Otherwise (as is far too often the case today) they are likely to return to crime and eventually into the correctional system. Reintegration of the offender into society, therefore, is seen by correctional personnel as one of the major objectives.[6]

Correctional programs are carried on in institutions and in the community through probation and parole. Although states have the major responsibility for corrections, local jurisdictions are involved (primarily in providing probation services), and the federal government is heavily involved in a parallel system of courts, probation, institutions, and parole. There is wide variation among the public agencies that have responsibility for corrections at any given level and, often, several agencies at the same level of government may operate different facets of corrections. This illustrates the complexity of the corrections system today—and how seriously it is fragmented. This has contributed to inadequate funding, scattershot programming, and a lack of public support.

Staff training programs in corrections were literally nonexistent until the early 1970s. An impetus to provide staff development programs was provided in the creation of the Law Enforcement Assistance Administration by Congress in 1968. LEAA has created a remarkable surge of staff programs in the nation's agencies and institutions of corrections. Furthermore, it has provided funds to 80,000 students in 962 schools to attend college courses for either preservice training or continuing education.

Nevertheless, there are far too many employees in corrections who

---

[6] Joint Commission on Correctional Manpower and Training, *A Time to Act* (1969), p. 6.

are there not because they are educated and trained for their jobs, but because they are political appointees, and there are too many trained corrections workers who leave the field and seek employment elsewhere because they cannot earn a decent living in corrections.

Educational Preparation
The educational level of correctional employees ranges from high school dropouts to Ph.Ds. Generally, those working with juveniles have a higher level of education than those working with adults.

Field personnel (people in probation and parole) are better educated on the average than employees in institutions, a fact that may be explained by the large number of institutional guard personnel with only a high school education. Nowhere is the published preferred standard for probation and parole officers—a master's degree from an accredited school of social work or comparable study in psychology, sociology, or a related field of social science—being met. Over three-fourths of correctional employees, *excluding line workers*, are college graduates. However, only 13 percent of those in adult institutions, 21 percent in adult probation and parole, 27 percent in juvenile institutions, and 30 percent in juvenile probation and parole have graduate degrees.

There is no consistent education pattern. College graduates working in corrections represent an extremely broad array of major areas of study. Although just over half have B.A. degrees in sociology, education, or psychology, the remainder have degrees in a wide range of other subjects. Undergraduates in social work and criminology or corrections programs represent a very small minority of college graduates in the field.

There is little connection, in current practice, between educational background and the performance of particular functions. Corrections has no well-defined link to any level or discipline of the educational system. A college graduate with a B.A. in history who somehow has managed to get into correctional work is as likely to be an institutional counselor as is a person holding a master's degree in social work.

The Future of Corrections

The field of corrections has many plans, procedures, policies, and laws that have failed to achieve their purposes, but that have survived regardless of their limited usefulness or obsolescence. Corrections has emphasized the banishment of offenders to isolated, large-scale, dehumanizing institutions.

The present shift in emphasis is clearly toward using the community as the site and source for rehabilitation rather than relying on the institution. Because most recognize the failures of institutions, solutions are being sought that are closer to the seat of the problem—the offender's community. Where confinement is needed, it should be within a community rather than in a remote and isolated cage, detached from the vital resources of the environment to which the ex-offender will return. The trend toward community-based corrections is one of the most promising developments in corrections today, being based on the recognition that much delinquency and crime is a symptom of failure of the community, as well as of the offender, and that a successful reduction of crime requires changes in both.

Institutionalization costs are soaring. Because of their limited effectiveness, they are being criticized because of these expenditures. Community-based corrections are more economically advantageous, because they use all of the existing community resources and human service agencies that are, or can be, related to crime prevention and control.

Toward a Consistent System of Corrections

The American system of criminal justice is complex, and the interrelationships among its components are so varied that few people understand it. Some call it a nonsystem.

The National Advisory Commission reports that this nonsystem includes:
1. Thousands of probation departments, some adult, some juvenile, some large, and some small.
2. Competing state agencies that are attempting to establish and supervise probation and parole standards, frequently without power of enforcement.
3. Thousands of county jails and hundreds of prisons ranging in size up to an average daily population of more than 3000.
4. Departments or bureaus of corrections operating many institutions, ranging from small halfway houses and facilities for juveniles to large maximum-security penitentiaries.

5. Hundreds of unrelated and unsupervised juvenile detention centers servicing some parts of states while the majority of youngsters in other parts are left to the uncertain mercies of the county jails.
6. Departments of social services and public welfare operating hundreds of youth development centers and forestry camps.
7. State planning agencies attempting to use the power of the federal dollar to bring order and change, and working against political pressures to maintain the status quo.

The result is confusion. To overcome this, effective systems planning must be instituted from top to bottom. Uniform state planning is an attainable goal that must be pursued.

Finally, the thrust is toward increased public involvement—a move long overdue. The correctional system is one of the few public services left today that is characterized by almost total isolation from the public. This condition must be reversed; meaningful roles must be given to an involved and concerned citizenry.

Summary

Corrections is the least visible and least understood segment of the criminal justice system in America. The invisibility of corrections belies its size, complexity, and importance in the control of crime. Corrections consists of scores of institutions and programs of the utmost diversity in approach, facilities, and qualities. Some of these institutions are grossly deficient with conditions that produce racial, ethnic, and religion tensions that build up to breaking points.

A correctional institution, whether maximum or minimum security, is an inmate community; a society with its own culture, its own set of values and attitudes. The social gap between the staff and the inmates frequently reinforces the need for inmates to conform to the inmate subculture.

Correctional institutions have as their stated purpose the rehabilitation of the offender. However, most institutions lack trained personnel needed for rehabilitation. The traditional approach has been the "individual treatment," that is, the "sick person" model. Psychotherapy coupled with casework has been the basic treatment approach. The group therapy approach has been used to supplement individual treatment. Group therapy is intended to help participants gain new insights into their problems and themselves, so that negative attitudes can be changed, and a reevaluation of the participant's place in the environment can emerge. Both individual and group therapies have been supported in prisons by a series of other programs.

The most frequently used community-based alternative to incarceration is probation. After a finding of guilt, the court may place a defendant on probation. It does so with the understanding that the probationer will live up to certain conditions and submit to the supervision and assistance of court probation officers. The essential weakness of probation has been the lack of qualified probation officers. The most important goal of probation must be to maintain in the community all offenders who can function acceptably with probation support and to select for confinement only those who are a danger to themselves or to others, and who cannot complete probation status successfully even with optimal probation support.

Parole is the second most frequently used form of corrections in the community. Parole is defined as the release of an offender from a penal or correctional institution, after he has served a portion of his sentence, under continued custody of the state and under conditions that permit his reincarceration in the event of misbehavior. Parole is granted by a parole board. They have been criticized because of their means of appointment, range of responsibilities, and the part-time status of some members. At present, the trend is toward allowing the parolee to attend hearings with legal representation on granting and revocation of parole.

Throughout correctional history four major treatments have been created: (1) clinical models, (2) group interaction models, (3) therapeutic community models, and (4) social action models. In the 1970s two treatment techniques being used are behavior modification and transactional analysis.

The educational level of correctional employees ranges from high school dropouts to Ph.Ds. There is little connection in current practice between educational background and the performance of particular functions.

Student Checklist

1. Can you explain the degree to which unreported crime exists?
2. Are you able to outline the number of people arrested for crime and the number sentenced to prison?
3. Can you cite two examples justifying the presentence investigation report?
4. Are you able to cite the two reasons for classification in prison?
5. Can you cite at least two objectives for probation?
6. Can you discuss two of the four treatment strategies?

Topics for Discussion

1. The general characteristics of personnel in corrections.
2. Contemporary treatment philosophies currently used by correctional institutions.
3. Various treatment models applied by the correctional system.

ANNOTATED BIBLIOGRAPHY

FBI, *Crime in the United States, Uniform Crime Reports*. Washington, D.C.: U.S. Govt. Printing Office, 1972. Statistical tabulation of crime information from law enforcement agencies in the United States.

Johnson, Elmer Hubert. *Crime, Corrections, and Society. Federal Probation*. A monthly publication of the Administration Office of the U.S. Courts that covers the breadth of the corrections system in terms of methods, programs, lectures, and legal developments.

Joint Commission on Correctional Manpower and Training. *A Time To Act*. 1969. A comprehensive look at correctional manpower and its use in the United States. Recommendations based on the analysis of data obtained from as many sources as possible.

The Journal of Criminal Law, Criminology, and Police Science. A publication of Northwestern University School of Law that provides in-depth scholarly articles on criminal law, criminology, and police science. It includes abstracts of recent cases, police technical abstracts, book reviews, and reader comments.

President's Commission on Law Enforcement and Administration of Justice. *The Challenge of Crime in a Free Society.* Washington, D.C.: U.S. Govt. Printing Office, 1967. A comprehensive view of the criminal justice system and recommendations for its improvement.

President's Commission on Law Enforcement and Administration of Justice. *Task Force Report on Corrections.* Washington, D.C.: U.S. Govt. Printing Office, 1967. The most up-to-date and comprehensive report of its kind for corrections. Covers each facet of the system and provides incisive analysis and recommendations.

The National Council on Crime and Delinquency. *Crime and Delinquency.* Published quarterly. A professional journal with current articles of interest, book reviews, and personal items of interest.

Tappan, Paul W. *Crime, Justice and Corrections.* New York: McGraw-Hill, 1960. A sound basic text written by a proponent of returning legal safeguards to correctional clients in a time of administrative decision-making based on a social rather than a legal basis.

Part Four

Professionalism within the Justice System

The study of this chapter will enable you to:

1. Define a profession.
2. Outline at least three essential elements required of a profession.
3. Outline the development of the law enforcement code of ethics.
4. Cite three canons of judicial ethics.
5. Cite three principles of belief as developed by the American Correctional Association.

12
Canons of Ethical Conduct

Members of the police, courts, corrections, and the subsystems are today being freely referred to as professionals. When we examine the definition of a profession, and the requisites (essential elements) attached, we find that some people employed in the criminal justice system have reached professional status and some have not.

The dictionary definition of a profession is: "A calling requiring specialized knowledge and often long and intensive academic preparation: a principal calling, vocation, or employment." A more detailed and in-depth definition might be: "A vocation whose practice is founded upon an understanding of the theoretical structure of some department of learning or science, and upon the abilities accompanying such understanding. This understanding and these abilities are applied to the vital affairs of man. The practices of the profession are modified by knowledge of a generalized nature and by the accumulated wisdom and experience of mankind, which serve to correct the errors of specialism. The profession, serving the vital needs of man, considers its first ethical imperative to be altruistic (unselfish) service to the client."[1]

The Elements of a Profession

The many views expressed concerning the essential elements or requisites of a profession are all contained within the following paragraphs.

---

[1] Morris L. Cogan, "Toward a Definition of a Profession," *Harvard Educational Review, XXIII* (Winter 1953), pp. 33-50.

1. A basis of systematic theory or a discrete (individually distinct) body of knowledge. It has often been stated that the very basic difference between professional and nonprofessional vocations lies in the element of greater skill. But great skill at a complicated task is not, by any means, restricted to recognized professions. Vocations such as engraving or cabinetmaking, require a greater degree of skill and intricacy than do many recognized professions. The real distinction lies not in the lengthy training to perfect an intricate skill, but in gaining the knowledge of the basic theory supporting the profession, and by applying this theory to concrete situations. This requires long, sometimes arduous academic training, lengthened by periods of internship, or on-the-job training, wherein the candidate gains experience in concrete application of his academic training.
2. Authority recognized by the clientele of the professional group. Customers seeking ordinary goods and services can comparison shop for the best price and quality, presumably knowing what is best for them. But, in the case of professional service, the assumption is that the professional knows what is best for the client because of his specialized knowledge and ability to apply this in judging what is good or bad for his client.
3. Broader community sanction and approval of this authority. The profession has persuaded the community to confer certain powers on it. Some of those powers are the right to say who can enter the profession, who can use the titles pertaining to the profession, and what the training and academic course content will be.
4. A code of ethics regulating relations of professional people with clients and with colleagues. Without a code of ethics, the professional could charge exorbitant fees, restrict entry into the profession to such a degree as to create a shortage of practitioners, and cause all sorts of other abuses against the public interest. Without binding codes of ethics, biased or prejudicial practices within the profession could become rampant due to a lack of control. Maximum quality professional service would be endangered, since the codes generally insure the sharing of new knowledge within the profession, thereby assuring the clientele of the benefit of up-to-date service. We will discuss codes of ethics later in the chapter.
5. A professional culture sustained by formal professional association. Besides establishing norms and values, these associations have the informal power to ostracize these members who may display undesirable qualities, such as a lack of dedication to the profession and their clientele.
6. A formal licensing authority or agency. This implies that the profes-

sion has persuaded the community to grant it the legal power to say who may practice the profession and who may be excluded. This may include administering a standard examination approved by a board, and the enforcement of criminal penalties against those who practice the profession without obtaining licenses.[2]

In most countries of the world the practice of law is a recognized profession. When one of the prerequisites to becoming a member of the judiciary is that the candidate be an attorney, the judiciary, too, becomes a recognized profession. This condition exists in all but the lowest courts in the United States. Therefore, we have professionals conducting our courts (the judges) and acting as officers of the court (the attorneys).

Professionalism throughout the System

There is an increasingly widespread belief that all members of the other criminal justice subsystems—the police, probation, corrections and parole—should attain a professional status equal to that of the members of the courts. In weighing this belief, the individual citizen should consider some questions. Would any person, regardless of race, ethnic origin, or socioeconomic position, want an amateur to deliver his wife of a baby or tend a seriously ill member of his family? Faced with a serious lawsuit, either criminal or civil, how many would want to enter court and be represented by someone not thoroughly trained in the law? Who, among knowledgeable citizens, would permit their children to be tutored by an illiterate? Each of these instances calls for a professional: a physician, an attorney, and a teacher.

Why then, in view of the above, should the people trust their personal safety, the protection of their property, and the safeguarding of their constitutional rights and civil liberties to other than professionals?

It has been previously stated that all components of the criminal justice system had not reached the status of a true profession. However, if we apply Cogan's definition of a profession (discussed at the beginning of this chapter) to each subsystem of the criminal justice system, it is our contention that the practitioners in the subsystems; the police, courts,

---

[2] Ernest Greenwood, "Attributes of a Profession," *Social Work*, 2, No. 3 (July 1957), pp. 44-45.

probation, parole, and corrections are professionals. They do fall within the definition in the following ways: their practices are founded upon an understanding of law and the social sciences; these understandings and abilities are daily applied to the most vital affairs of man, modified by generalized knowledge and accumulated experience; and for the most part, the practitioners have an altruistic dedication to the service they render to their communities and to their fellow man.

The education and training requirements in police, probation, parole, and corrections are steadily increasing, and the bulk of relevant case law that must be absorbed by judges, defense attorneys, and prosecuting attorneys is growing at a tremendous rate.

In view of this, the professional must reconcile two things: the ideal for which he enters a profession and the remuneration or fee that he receives. Although a professional should not render service for the fee alone, ideals do not provide for physical sustenance. There must be adequate remuneration so that financial worries do not plague the professional, distract him from his work, and even tempt him to take bribes to support his family and educate his children. The members of the criminal justice system should be recognized as professionals and be assured of an income commensurate with the services performed and the risks taken.

Shortcomings
When we begin to apply the requisites of a profession to each of the components of our criminal justice system, some shortcomings can be perceived. Certainly, the members of the judiciary system; the judges, prosecutors, and defense attorneys are members of an established, universally recognized profession. It is in the police, probation, parole, and corrections that shortcomings are noted. The bodies of knowledge within these subsystems have not all been completely systematized, and there are areas of disagreement as to what should be taught, and how it should be taught.

The recognition of professional authority by the clientele has not been thoroughly gained; nor do police, probation, parole, and corrections yet have complete community sanction and approval as professionals.

Formal professional associations in police, probation, parole, and corrections are to be found in abundance. In fact, in some areas, these associations are so numerous that their numbers dilute their effectiveness. An answer might be a nationwide association for the members of each group (similar to the American Bar Association) with state and local chapters.

Formal licensing agencies or authorities for police, probation, parole, and corrections are becoming more common but are not universal. This requisite needs to be met.

The case for professionalism has been briefly stated and leaves the student wide latitude for more research on the subject. We have, however, left one requisite of a profession to be discussed more in depth: a code of ethics.

Codes of Ethics

The mere existence of a code of ethics does not satisfy the requisite. Unless the professional and his clientele apply the meaning and the intent of the words contained with the code, it has no value. This application must become routine in the day-to-day relationship between professional and client.

In 1957 the International Association of Chiefs of Police adopted a Law Enforcement Code of Ethics. This had been developed the previous year by the Peace Officers Research Association of California and the California Peace Officers Association. Many law enforcement accrediting agencies have since adopted this code.

Law Enforcement Code of Ethics

As a law enforcement officer, my fundamental duty is to serve mankind; to safeguard lives and property; to protect the innocent against deception, the weak against oppression or intimidation, and the peaceful against violence or disorder; and to respect the constitutional rights of all men to liberty, equality, and justice.

I will keep my private life unsullied as an example to all; maintain courageous calm in the face of danger, scorn, or ridicule; develop self-restraint; and be constantly mindful of the welfare of others. Honest in thought and deed in both my personal and official life, I will be exemplary in obeying the laws of the land and the regulations of my department. Whatever I see or hear of a confidential nature or that is confided to me in my official capacity will be kept ever secret unless revelation is necessary in the performance of my duty.

I will never act officiously or permit personal feelings, prejudices, animosities, or friendships to influence my decisions. With no compromise for crime and with relentless prosecution of criminals, I will enforce the law courteously and appropriately without fear or favor, malice or ill will, never employing unnecessary force or violence, and never accepting gratuities.

I recognize the badge of my office as a symbol of public faith, and I accept it as a public trust to be held so long as I am true to the ethics of the police service. I will constantly strive to achieve these objectives and ideals, dedicating myself before God to my chosen profession—law enforcement.

Parole Officers Code of Ethics

The Board of Pardons and Paroles of the State of Texas adopted the Parole Officers' Code of Ethics in 1961. Other states have similar codes. The Texas code of ethics is typical of the majority.

As a parole officer I shall:

Abide by and uphold the laws of my community, state, and nation, remembering always my duty to protect the community which I serve; and, share, within the limits of my office, in a general responsibility for making my community a better place in which to live;

Regard as my professional obligation, consistent with the public welfare, the interests of those assigned to my supervision; and respect both their legal and moral rights at all times;

Assure that professional responsibility and objectivity take precedence over my personal convenience or biases; and, when not inconsistent with my obligation to my agency or the welfare of society, to maintain in strict confidences any personal revelations which are given to me;

Support the policies of my agency; work to improve its standards and performance; and dedicate myself to improve my knowledge and understanding in order to better serve my community and those from whom I have responsibility;

Treat the accomplishments of my colleagues with respect and express critical judgement of them only through established agency channels; support them always in fulfilling their responsibilities; respect differences of opinion between myself and my colleagues and take positive steps to resolve them;

Work cooperatively with other agencies in matters affecting the welfare and protection of the community; protect the confidentiality of shared information; and respect the functions and limita.. agencies;

Conduct myself, both privately and publicly, in such a manner . enhance public confidence in my agency and its objectives; neithe. grant nor receive favors in the performance of the duties of my office; and treat all persons with whom I have contact with courtesy and respect;

Always recognize my office as a sacred trust which has been given to me to guard and sustain.

Probation and parole are closely linked in the criminal justice system. Since they perform similar functions, it is only natural that organizations of both probation and parole officers have adopted codes of ethics similar to the one set forth above.

The Legal Code of Ethics

The American Bar Association, in writing the Code of Professional Responsibility for lawyers, divided it in three separate, interrelated parts: canons, ethical considerations, and disciplinary rules. The canons express, in general terms, the standards of professional conduct for lawyers in their dealings with the public, the legal system, and the profession. They are as follows:

A lawyer should assist in maintaining the integrity and competence of the legal profession.

A lawyer should assist the legal profession in fulfilling its duty to make legal counsel available.

A lawyer should assist in preventing the unauthorized practice of law.

A lawyer should preserve the confidences and secrets of a client.

A lawyer should exercise independent professional judgement on behalf of a client.

A lawyer should represent a client competently.

A lawyer should represent a client zealously within the bounds of the law.

A lawyer should assist in improving the legal system.

A lawyer should avoid even the appearance of professional impropriety.[3]

It should be remembered by all, especially by those working within the criminal justice system, that the term lawyer as used in the canons of

---

[3] Henry Campbell Black, *Black's Law Dictionary*, 4th rev. ed. (St. Paul: West Publishing Company, 1968).

the American Bar Association is intended to include lawyers who are engaged in the prosecution of cases as well as the lawyers in private practice who represent their clients as lawyers for the defense.

The Judicial Code of Ethics

In addition to the canons for professional conduct of lawyers which it has formulated and adopted, the American Bar Association, mindful that the character and conduct of a judge should never be objects of indifference, and that declared ethical standards tend to become habits of life, deems it desirable to set forth its views respecting those principles which should govern the personal practice of members of the judiciary in the administration of their office. The Association accordingly adopts the following canons, the spirit of which it suggests as a proper guide and reminder for judges, and as indicating what the people have a right to expect from them.[4]

The Canons of Judicial Ethics, including the amendments of January 1, 1968, are summarized below. Students who want to read the complete version are directed to *Black's Law Dictionary*, 4th rev. ed., pp. 59–73, or to the American Bar Association.

Relations of the judiciary with the people whom he serves, the practitioners of law in his court, the witnesses, etc. should be duties recognized as incumbent on him when he assumes the office.

The judges should conduct their courts in the best interests of the public, assuring speedy and careful administration.

The judges are duty-bound to support the U.S. Constitution and that of the state whose laws they administer.

A judge's official conduct should be free from impropriety and the appearance of impropriety.

A judge should be temperate, attentive, patient, impartial.

A judge should exhibit an industry and application commensurate with the duties imposed upon him.

A judge should be prompt in the performance of his judicial duties.

A judge should be courteous and considerate of all in attendance upon the court.

The remainder of the canons deal with the specific areas of responsibility that are unique with the judiciary, such as appointments made by judges,

---

[4] Preamble to the Canons of Judicial Ethics, American Bar Association, adopted at its 47th annual meeting on July 9, 1924.

interference in conduct of trials, *ex-parte* (one-sided) communications, continuances, review, private law practice, and others. Canon 34 best summarizes the obligations of a member of the judiciary:

> *In every particular his conduct should be above reproach. He should be conscientious, studious, thorough, courteous, patient, punctual, just, impartial, fearless of public clamor, regardless of public praise and indifferent to private political or partisan influences; he should administer justice according to law, and deal with his appointments as a public trust; he should not allow other affairs or his private interests to interfere with the prompt and proper performance of his judicial duties, nor should he administer the office for the purpose of advancing his personal ambitions or increasing his popularity.*

The Correctional Code of Ethics

The American Correctional Association has issued a Declaration of Principles for its members. Although this document does not address itself directly to what is and what is not ethical conduct for the correctional community, the principles formally state the beliefs of this subsystem of the criminal justice system. In summary, 36 principles cover the feelings of the Association toward the following:

1. The application of the growing body of knowledge in the behavioral sciences against the problem of crime.
2. The strengthening and expansion of correctional methods.
3. The preparation and dissemination of objective information needed for public policy decisions at all jurisdictional levels.
4. The need for a direct relationship between the length or severity of the punitive sentence assessed and the seriousness of the offense perpetrated.
5. The need to assure that no law, procedure, or system of correction should deprive any offender of his ultimate return to full, responsible membership in society.
6. The aim of the correctional process to reintegrate the offender into society as a law-abiding citizen.
7. The integration of institutional and community-based programs into a system that is responsible for guiding, controlling, unifying, and vitalizing the correctional process.
8. The release of all offenders under parole supervision with parole being granted at the earliest date consistent with public safety and the needs of the individual.
9. The use of work and study furlough programs to provide a

smoother transition for the offender from institutional life to community life.

10. The assurance of the preservation of an offender's human dignity.

Although each of the principles espoused by the American Correctional Association is not paraphrased in the sampling above, some of the more obvious points have been noted. These Declarations of Principles may be found in their entirety in the *Manual of Correctional Standards*, 3rd ed., issued by the American Correctional Association.

Conclusions

The system of justice of our land has developed through the years with service to people as the main objective. Throughout this development, the members of the legal profession have been the only group belonging to one of the classic professions (military, medicine, law, and the ministry). The police, corrections, probation, and parole groups are attaining professionalism or are on the threshold of that status. They have specialized training and skills derived from a discrete body of knowledge which are, in many cases, systematically passed on to new members through both formal and informal training and education; they have professional organizations and codes of ethics; members of some of the groups must be licensed or certified after having met certain minimum requirements; and all demonstrate a spirit of public service.[5]

Cogan, whose definition of a profession was mentioned at the beginning of the chapter, draws the one thread from all of the codes of conduct that can best tie the American criminal justice system together: altruistic service to the client. No other profession deals more consistently with the problems of people's interactions with people than does the system of justice. People and their problems are the ingredients that justify the existence of the system of justice. Yet, in dealing with these problems, criminal justice practitioners must maintain their altruistic approach if they are to truly serve the justice needs of their clients.

[5] Hazel B. Kerper, *Introduction to the Criminal Justice System* (St. Paul: West Publishing Company, 1972), p. 416.

Summary

Professionalism requires six essential elements: (1) a basis of systematic theory or a discrete body of knowledge, (2) authority recognized by the clientele of the professional group, (3) broader community sanction and approval of this authority, (4) a code of ethics regulating relations of professional people with clients and with colleagues, (5) a professional culture sustained by formal professional associations, and (6) a formal licensing authority or agency. There is an increasing belief that all members of criminal justice system should attain a professional status. At this time only the members of the judiciary are considered professionals.

The requisite of a code of ethics is not met by the simple existence of such a code. If the code is not applied to its fullest it will be meaningless. Several law enforcement agencies and boards of pardon and parole have adopted such codes. The American Correctional Association has issued a Declaration of Principles for its members. Although this document does not directly address what is and what is not ethical conduct, it does formally state the beliefs of this subsystem of the criminal justice system.

Student Checklist

1. Can you define a profession?
2. Are you able to outline at least three essential elements that are required of a profession?
3. Can you outline the development of the law enforcement code of ethics?
4. Can you cite three canons of judicial ethics?
5. Can you cite three principles of belief developed by the American Correctional Association?

Topics for Discussion

1. What constitutes a profession.
2. Why it is desirable for the personnel in the justice system to attain professional status.
3. The segments of the justice system that are currently acknowledged as professions.

ANNOTATED BIBLIOGRAPHY

Black, Henry Campbell. *Black's Law Dictionary*. St. Paul: West Publishing Co., 1968. In addition to the usual legal definitions, this volume contains the Lawyer's Code of Professional Responsibility, Canons of Judicial Ethics, and a digest of the minimum requirements for admission to the practice of law in the United States.

Harriman, E. A. "The Need for Standards of Ethics for Judges," *The Annals of the American Academy of Political and Social Science, 101*, No. 90, May 1922. The author uses the case of Judge Kenesaw M. Landis to justify the need for a sovereign power to prescribe standards of judicial ethics.

Germann; Day; and Gallati. *Introduction to Law Enforcement and Criminal Justice*. Springfield: Charles C. Thomas, 1970. This text contains in the introduction 12 basic principles that can be applied to the law enforcement service. Chapter XIX contains the Law Enforcement Code of Ethics and Canons of Police Ethics, and Chapter XXI contains a code of ethics for all who control or participate in criminal justice data banks.

Kerper, Hazel B. *Introduction to the Criminal Justice System*. St. Paul: West Publishing Co., 1972. Part Three of this recent addition to the already extensive list of books on the subject is devoted to professionals in the system and their interrelationship. Codes of ethics for the various members of the system are included.

Kooken, Don L. *Ethics in Police Service*. Springfield: Charles C. Thomas, 1957. The author presents a code of ethics that he feels is acceptable to law enforcement. The remainder of the book is an analysis of the code and its major provisions.

MacIver, Robert. "The Social Significance of Professional Ethics," *The Annals of the American Academy of Political and Social Science, 297,* January 1955. The author discusses ethics of professions in general along such lines as the ideal of service, common standards and distinctive codes, responsibility to the community, professional interest and the general welfare, and danger of specific group bias.

The study of this chapter will enable you to:

1. Cite at least three reasons for establishing minimum standards for training and education for justice system personnel.
2. Cite the recommendation by the President's Commission on Law Enforcement and Administration of Justice in 1967 regarding the ultimate educational aim of all police agencies for their personnel.
3. Explain what the initials LEEP mean and what this agency's objectives are.
4. Cite two areas in the judicial section that require improved training.
5. Define the current status of training programs for correctional agencies.
6. Cite two examples of state standards councils for training and education of law enforcement officers.
7. Cite at least two different styles of regional training systems for criminal justice personnel.

13
Education and Training Concepts

Imagine for a moment a young high school graduate reporting for his first day of employment at a large, metropolitan hospital. "Congratulations, Mister Smith," his new supervisor tells him. "You are now Doctor Smith! Your initial assignment will be brain surgery. Of course, you'll have to be very careful at first, but Doctor Jones here will coach you until you learn the routine. Good luck in your new profession!"

Fortunately, neither the medical profession nor the public would tolerate such an absurd initiation into the practice of medicine. Yet, with some regional variations, thousands of new employees enter the criminal justice system each year with the same lack of academic preparation or training. There has been a growing awareness in recent years, however, that the power of the criminal justice system to deprive a person of his liberty, and even his life, can be as deadly as the surgeon's scalpel. Therefore, people charged with exercising that power must be well-educated, highly trained professionals.

The terms education and training are often used interchangeably and, indeed, their definitions are nearly synonymous. However, criminal justice educators differentiate between the two terms, especially when considering the roles of the colleges, universities, and in-service training academies, so we will note this difference.

Generally, education refers to a program of broad, academic study in a college or university that prepares the student to better understand and deal with the natural and social environment in which he lives and works. Education attempts to explain the "why" of things and teaches the student to think, evaluate, and analyze.

Training generally refers to the process of imparting specific knowledge and skills to perform a job or task. It tends to be more procedural and teaches the "how-to-do-it" of a particular function or role.

Many professors believe that colleges exist solely to educate the student, and that training courses such as police firearms and defensive tactics have no place in them. This probably is an oversimplification because most colleges and universities grant academic credit for physical education courses such as archery and wrestling, which are as training-oriented as defensive tactics and firearms. It is impossible to differentiate between education and training in all cases. But, for the purposes of this chapter, we shall use education to refer to the formal course of study that leads to an academic degree in a college or university, and training will refer to in-service instruction provided to an employee to equip him to perform a particular job.

Today's criminal justice practitioner needs both education and training to fulfill his important role in society. His intellectual armament can best be acquired through the study of the liberal arts and behavioral sciences, supplemented by formal training in the skills required of his profession.

Education and training programs in the criminal justice system are in an evolutionary stage. Academic degree programs for law enforcement, for example, once taught many of the same subjects as the basic recruit academies; now they concentrate on the administration of justice, leaving the procedural training—the "how-to-do-it" subjects—to the academies. Training was once considered primarily an entry-level experience for new employees only. Criminal justice administrators now realize that training is a process that must continue throughout an employee's career. As the knowledge and skills necessary to perform adequately in the criminal justice system change and expand, the practitioner must constantly train to keep up-to-date.

Police Education and Training

In 1967, the President's Commission on Law Enforcement and Administration of Justice published its recommendation that "the ultimate aim of all police departments should be that all personnel with general enforcement powers have baccalaureate degrees."[1] This recommendation

[1] President's Commission on Law Enforcement and Administration of Justice, *The Challenge of Crime in a Free Society* (Washington, D.C.: U.S. Govt. Printing Office, 1967), p. 109.

shocked many police administrators and renewed the controversy over how much formal education a police officer really needed. Unfortunately, the President's Commission did not offer much factual evidence to prove that a four-year college education was necessary for today's policeman, nor did it state in what major subject areas the potential police officer should concentrate his studies. Most police administrators have personal opinions as to the length and type of education they think necessary, but those opinions differ widely. Educational requirements for new policemen vary throughout the nation from no standard at all in some departments, to a baccalaureate degree requirement for all new patrolmen in two or three departments. A growing number of police agencies are requiring the equivalent of two years of college, but the average educational requirement throughout the nation still remains a high school diploma. The controversy will continue until research scientifically proves how much education, and in what subject matter, the police recruit should have. Meanwhile, criminal justice educators, researchers, and police administrators agree that formal education alone does not make a person a good police officer; however, they believe that higher education usually makes a good officer better.

There is no accepted definition of a "good police officer." The earmarks of success in police work vary with observer's concepts of the police role in society. Until that role is clearly defined and agreed upon, it will be impossible to establish exact educational standards for police recruits.

Although there is no agreement on an educational entrance standard, there is ample evidence that police officers and their departments are emphasizing postemployment and continuing education. Throughout the nation, law enforcement officers are enrolled in college and university degree programs, and the average educational level of the employed officer is steadily climbing. Many law enforcement agencies have adopted educational incentive programs, and it is not uncommon for departments to defray some or even all of the expenses of an officer who voluntarily continues his education. Many enlightened police administrators schedule an officer's working hours to accommodate his class schedule. There also is a growing trend to require higher education for promotion. And, where college education is not required as a formal standard for promotion, officers who have not continued their studies often find it difficult to compete with their better-educated colleagues. With the rapid growth of community colleges, four-year college, and university systems throughout the country, there are relatively few areas where a policeman cannot continue his education. New degree programs are established each year in police science, criminology, and criminal justice, and economic assistance programs such as the U.S. Department of Justice's Law Enforcement Education Program (LEEP) make it easier than ever before for the policeman to pursue a baccalaureate or graduate degree.

The number and types of in-service training programs are growing even faster than the college degree programs. Although a few police agencies still fail to provide their recruits with formal basic training, most department heads realize that the untrained policeman is a danger to himself and to others. Formal academy training in a wide variety of subjects is necessary before today's law enforcement officer can adequately fulfill his complex role.

The academy training received by most new policemen varies from a few weeks of indoctrination training to more than eight months of intensive instruction interspersed with supervised field training. The President's Commission on Law Enforcement and Administration of Justice in 1967 recommended:

> *Formal police training programs for recruits in all departments, large and small, should consist of an absolute minimum of 400 hours of classroom work spread over a four- to six-month period so that it can be combined with carefully selected and supervised field training.*[2]

Extensive research is being conducted to determine the ideal content and emphasis of basic recruit training, and all academy courses must be constantly evaluated to ensure that they are relevant, adequate, and practical. Most men and women entering law enforcement have misconceptions about police work. Many imagine they will be continually playing a dramatic and glamorous game of "cops and robbers," a misconception perpetuated by the entertainment media. Often they are surprised and disillusioned to find that only a small part of their work involves the detection and apprehension of criminals; that most of their activities are a round of dull-nonenforcement functions that they, as police, must perform to protect life and property. While the investigation of crimes and the apprehension of violators certainly are important parts of police work, recruit academy training should also prepare the officer for the many other functions he will perform in his community. The President's Commission recommended:

---

[2] Ibid., p. 112.

> *All training programs should provide instruction on subjects that prepare recruits to exercise discretion properly, and to understand the community, the role of the police, and what the criminal justice system can and cannot do. Professional educators and civilian experts should be used to teach specialized courses—law and psychology, for example. Recognized teaching techniques such as problem-solving seminars should be incorporated into training programs.*[3]

A police officer's training does not end with his graduation from the basic academy. Most departments assign the academy graduate to work with an experienced officer for a period of supervised field training. The older officer acts as a coach and should have special training as a field training officer.

Every police agency has a responsibility to continually assess its internal training needs and to provide adequate instruction to meet those needs. The day-to-day training within a department may consist of short, roll-call training sessions conducted by supervisors, individualized instruction received by an officer from his supervisor, and short courses presented to meet a special need. The Federal Bureau of Investigation provides an invaluable service to law enforcement by offering short, technical courses for local officers on a wide variety of police subjects.

In addition to the day-to-day training conducted within a department, officers should return to an academy periodically for refresher and continuation training. Changes in laws, court decisions, technology, techniques, and procedures occur constantly, and officers cannot be expected to keep abreast of these changes without periodic training. New knowledge simply cannot be absorbed "through the seat of the pants" while on patrol, and skills learned earlier must be practiced and sharpened through refresher training. Recognizing this need, the President's Commission on Law Enforcement and Administration of Justice recommended that "every general enforcement officer should have at least one week of in-service training a year."[4] As a first step toward carrying out this recommendation, the California Commission on Peace Officer Standards and Training (POST) requires that officers in that state complete an approved Advanced Officer Course at least once every four years and strongly encourages officers to attend annual in-service classes.

---

[3] Ibid.
[4] Ibid., p. 113.

POST

The knowledge and skills required of a police officer differ from those required of a police supervisor. With each step up the promotional ladder, an officer must master new subjects, techniques, and skills in order to perform his job adequately. POST has developed a statewide training program for all levels of peace officers, and that system is being adopted by many other states. It is described here as an example of a statewide training program aimed at increasing the competence of all ranks of officers. It is based on the premise that there are three broad groups of police supervisors and commanders: first-line supervisors, middle managers, and executives.

Supervisory Course. The supervisory course is required of each newly promoted first-line supervisor (most often to the rank of sergeant, in some departments termed corporal or police agent), and must be completed within the first 18 months of promotion. The course, consisting of a minimum of 80 classroom hours, must meet curriculum standards prescribed by POST. The subject matter is designed to develop the supervisor's leadership and, recognizing that training is an integral part of supervision, his training abilities. Practical problem-solving and leadership are taught through a variety of techniques including role playing and case studies.

Middle Management Course. The next level of training is the middle management course, an intensive 100 hours of instruction for the newly promoted lieutenant or captain. All of California's middle management courses are presented by four-year universities, and their faculties are made up of teachers from a wide variety of disciplines. The curriculum prescribed by POST concentrates on developing the officer's personal management and administrative skills and techniques. The wide variety of topics covered include subject matter from the fields of public administration, psychology, and communications.

Executive Development Course. The executive development course is designed to develop and enhance the knowledge, skills, and techniques of the department head (chief of police or sheriff) and his immediate assistant. Like the middle management course, it is at least 100 hours long and is offered at the university level.

Types of Courses

Regardless of its size, the modern police agency performs a wide variety of functions and services that demand special and technical skills and knowledge. Any change of assignment or function within a department requires some training. All too often, however, agencies expect their

Figure 13-1. An adequate training system must prepare personnel for a wide variety of technical and specialized tasks. Deputies of the Los Angeles County Sheriff's Department are shown participating in a helicopter rescue training exercise.

education and training concepts

officers to learn how to perform in new assignments by trial and error, asking questions, or simply observing other officers at work. This method is neither efficient nor cost-effective and often results in poor performance.

The types of courses needed should be aimed directly at the various jobs and tasks within the department. They might include special or technical courses on patrol, traffic enforcement, accident investigation, radar enforcement, special or tactical enforcement, juvenile procedures, investigations, riot control, emergency medical services, intelligence operations, jail operations, motorcycle utilization, record maintenance, communications, preservation of physical evidence, photography, fingerprint records, aircraft pilot (fixed wing or helicopter) training, rescue procedures, community relations, training, administrative services, court liaison, organized crime, applicant investigation, polygraph operation, crime lab techniques, and many others. Many of these categories include more than one technical function requiring special training. For example, the investigative function includes several areas of specialization, such as robbery, burglary (residential, commercial, safe), sex, checks, credit card fraud, auto theft, and so forth. Each law enforcement agency should identify all of its functional assignments or tasks and develop minimum training standards for each. Training standards should be developed for nonsworn civilian employees as well as for sworn officers.

Education and Training for Court Personnel

One of the most important segments of the criminal justice system is the courts. The activities of judges, criminal prosecutors, and defenders set the tone for the administration of justice. The efficient operation of the courts is also dependent upon day-to-day administration by nonlawyer administrative personnel such as court clerks. Unfortunately, there is an increasing indication that these vital employees in the criminal justice system are not adequately prepared for their important roles.

All criminal prosecuting and defense attorneys and most magistrates are, of course, lawyers and they are admitted to the bar to practice law. However, just because a person is an attorney does not necessarily mean that he is competent in criminal trial work. Law schools generally place little emphasis on teaching criminal law, and many general practitioners of the law find criminal practice distasteful. Few law schools permit students to specialize in criminal law, and many young lawyers seek employment in prosecuting agencies such as district attorney's offices solely to gain trial experience before moving on to more lucrative specialties. Commenting on this dilemma, the President's Commission on Law Enforcement and Administration of Justice noted:

> Until recent years most law schools offered only a basic course in criminal law, emphasizing the substantive law of crimes, with perhaps an advanced course in some aspects of criminal procedure. This lack of attention to criminal law, as compared to the emphasis on commercial law, may be partly explained by the bar's general disregard for the field and the lack of financial reward. Law schools feel obligated to provide training related to the work their graduates will do. But the subordination of criminal law in legal education has served to reinforce the attitudes which produced it.[5]

The gap in training left by the law schools is seldom filled by public agencies employing criminal prosecutors and defense attorneys; the newly employed lawyer usually is put to work immediately with little or no indoctrination. Research is needed to develop realistic basic training standards beyond what is now offered in law schools for new criminal prosecutors and public defenders. Lawyers employed by government agencies to defend or prosecute criminal defendants should be required to complete specific mandated courses in this important phase of criminal justice.

While most judges are lawyers, that alone does not necessarily qualify them to preside over criminal trials. Some training does exist, notably that offered by the National College of State Trial Judges established by the National Conference on State Trial Judges in affiliation with the American Bar Association. However, one observer commented:

> . . . a college whose stated original concept was that "it would be formed of judges, for judges, and by judges," in which "this idea is true today as it was in the beginning," and which reports that, "almost the entire faculty of the College are from the ranks of the judiciary"—the others being practicing attorneys or law professors—is not likely, however valuable its in-group contribution, to reduce judicial intellectual isolation and inbreeding nor to give judges the interdisciplinary contacts

---

[5] President's Commission on Law Enforcement and Administration of Justice, *Task Force Report: The Courts* (Washington, D.C.: U.S. Govt. Printing Office, 1967), p. 61.

that are becoming essential as a basis for well-rounded professional competency in the administration of criminal justice.[6]

Postgraduate training for judges does exist in some states, such as the seminars and institutes offered by the California Judicial Council. However, like the National College of State Trial Judges, these courses are neither mandatory nor universally attended by the judiciary.

As is the case with criminal prosecutors and public defenders, law schools should develop practical and realistic basic training and refresher courses for judges, and judicial standards should be developed to ensure that all judges attend.

Only in very recent years has the need for professional training for court administrative personnel, such as court clerks, been recognized. It is encouraging to note that a few community colleges have begun to develop and offer courses to meet that need. However, such programs still are widely scattered around the nation and are not yet readily available to most court personnel.

Corrections Education and Training

The field of corrections is similar to the police in the wide range of views on the amount and type of education necessary for employees. In actual practice, the preservice education of corrections personnel ranges from less than high school to doctorate degrees. There is a nationwide tendency for field workers (probation and parole officers) to have a higher level of education—most often a baccalaureate degree—than institutional personnel (prison guards, counselors, and correctional officers), and administrative personnel tend to have higher degrees than line or operational workers. However, there is no agreement on subject area requirements and, where college degrees are required, they often may be in any subject.

The 1967 report of the Task Force on Corrections of the President's Commission on Law Enforcement and Administration of Justice commented on the lack of educational programs for future correctional workers:

---

[6] Albert Morris, "What Is the Role of the Judge in the Correctional Process?" *Correction Research Bulletin 18* (November 1968), p. 15 (Boston: Massachusetts Correctional Association, 1968).

> *Like other areas of criminal justice, corrections has long been regarded by many colleges and universities as inappropriate for academic specialization. Courses in corrections have in many cases been vocationally oriented, and preparation in such relatively established fields as sociology and psychology has often been at least as valuable for imaginative correctional service. Indeed, the recruitment advantages that a discrete corrections curriculum no doubt offers may ultimately be offset by the danger that such an approach will intensify the intellectual isolation of corrections and perpetuate its status as a second-class occupation.*
>
> *But it is also true that courses in sociology, psychology, social work, and other fields relevant to corrections have tended to ignore the potential of corrections, both as a career for graduates and as a source of example for the enrichment of classroom discussion. The advantages of bringing a "community of skills" to bear on corrections have, in other words, seldom been fully realized.[7]*

Criminal justice educators recently have begun to develop and offer preservice academic degree programs designed specifically for potential corrections employees. However, it will take a number of years for these programs to increase nationally to a number sufficient to meet the needs of the profession. Meanwhile, college students planning a career in corrections should be encouraged to concentrate on behavioral science courses and subjects dealing with interviewing and counseling.

Unlike the police, most corrections agencies have woefully inadequate training programs—if any—and none have programs approaching the thorough police training system based upon rank and functional assignments described earlier. Where college degrees are required, they too often are considered sufficient preparation for correctional work. Realistic and practical training programs, including basic and continuation training courses, should be developed for all categories and functions of correctional personnel. And, of course, such training should be mandatory.

State Standards Councils

Although great strides have been made during the past two decades, the present state of criminal justice education and training nationwide is still

---

[7] President's Commission on Law Enforcement and Administration of Justice, *Task Force Report: Corrections* (Washington, D.C.: U.S. Govt. Printing Office, 1967), pp. 99 and 100.

inadequate. Better programs are urgently needed in all areas of criminal justice, and administrators must work hard to provide adequate training for all personnel. A partial solution to the training problem should come from the continued creation and expansion of state standards councils.

Most states now have some form of minimum standards for training law enforcement officers. Those standards usually are established by a state council or commission composed of police professionals and representatives of local governments. The California Commission on Peace Officer Standards and Training (POST) and the New York Municipal Police Training Council were established almost simultaneously in 1959, setting an example that was followed by 40 additional states in the ensuing decade. Although some state councils are responsible only for establishing and supervising minimum training standards for police, others also prescribe minimum personnel selection standards and provide police consulting services to local jurisdictions.

The future will see the creation of standards councils in all states, and some degree of uniformity in police training will result. The staffs of the various standards councils are cooperating and assisting one another through the National Association of State Directors of Law Enforcement Training (NASDLET). This organization has become a vehicle for the exchange of ideas, information, and materials. Among its goals are uniform training standards and reciprocal agreements among all states to foster professionalization and lateral mobility. As the professional law enforcement certificates awarded by state standards councils become interchangeable among states, they will become, in effect, nationwide "licenses to practice" the profession of law enforcement—a healthy step toward true professionalism.

As state standards councils have been highly successful in upgrading the competence of police, it follows that they should be equally successful in improving personnel working in other segments of the criminal justice system as well. Police standards councils could be expanded to become true criminal justice standards agencies, with subdivisions for police, courts, and corrections personnel. An alternative would be the establishment of a separate standards council in every state for each segment of the system. Maryland, for example, has separate standards councils for police and corrections, but the administration of the two programs is done by a single staff.

Providing good training and maintaining high standards is costly for local agencies, especially small jurisdictions. Some state standards councils provide financial assistance to local jurisdictions to assist them in complying with the state standards. For example, the California commission allocated more than $12 million in 1973 to local agencies to assist them in defraying the costs of training their officers. The need for state aid in financing training expenses increases as standards are raised and more training required.

Regionalization of Resources

The vast majority of criminal justice agencies in the United States are small. Most police departments, for example, employ less than 25 officers; the giant law enforcement agencies of New York, Chicago, and Los Angeles are the exception rather than the rule. Most courts and corrections agencies also are relatively small. Thus, few individual criminal justice agencies can afford to develop and staff sophisticated, well-equipped institutions. In too many cases this results in the employee receiving either no formal training for his job or inadequate training. He may be expected to learn his job only by trial and error, and by observing and working with more experienced employees. This, obviously, is a risky practice in a profession that deals with human lives and liberty.

Even where larger agencies do conduct training programs, they usually rely almost exclusively upon their own employees for instructors and rarely look outside their organization for faculty. The quality of instruction may suffer as a result because the practice tends to perpetuate an inbred, insulated set of practices and attitudes. Questionable and even harmful procedures and behavior patterns are passed on from one generation of employee to the next for no better reason than, "we've always done it that way." George W. O'Connor, director of the Professional Standards Division of the International Association of Chiefs of Police, commented on this unfortunate tendency:

> *Myths die hard. Perhaps it is because at one obscure moment in history there was an incident upon which the myth was based. Within the field of police education and training, there continue to be myths which, like all others, exhibit vitality greater than their validity. A myth which appears to be under severe attack and which shows hopeful signs of being placed to rest, holds that "it takes a policeman to teach a policeman." While the value of this doctrine may be worthwhile in terms of*

developing the how-to-do-it skills of the job, its worth is severely limited as it relates to the creation of a sound educational foundation for individuals entering the police service. . . . No longer can we clutch a dead myth to our breasts.[8]

Regional Training and Resource Systems

An encouraging trend that may solve the problem of insufficient and inadequate training for all agencies is the development of regional criminal justice training and resource systems. Although they are still few in number, their success undoubtedly will cause more centers to be developed throughout the nation.

Their basic purpose is to provide the best possible training to criminal justice personnel within a specific geographical area. In addition to the basic, continuation, supervisory, administrative, and technical courses described earlier, they also provide interdisciplinary training. Seminars designed to bring together judges, police officers, public defenders, probation officers, prosecutors, parole officers, and correctional officers enable the participants to understand better each other's role and how they interrelate in the total justice system.

Although they share common goals, several different kinds of regional training systems are evolving. One type consists of a single physical facility operated by a state agency, or a group of agencies, which provides training programs for all categories, ranks, and functions of criminal justice personnel.

Another type of system is the large, department-operated academy that serves all agencies within a region. While it is administered by a single criminal justice agency, it is closely affiliated with one or more academic institutions. Such alliances with colleges and universities have many advantages to the center and its students. Academic credit may be awarded for some courses. The center may draw upon the college or university for faculty, especially in nonjustice subjects such as public administration, behavioral sciences, communications, and language skills. Some centers have been successful in blending in-service, skill-oriented training with academic, noncriminal justice courses, such as English, psychology, and political science. Other resources of the college

---

[8] George W. O'Connor, the Foreword to Thompson S. Crockett, *Law Enforcement Education: 1968* (Washington D.C.: International Association of Chiefs of Police, Inc., 1968), p. iii.

or university are also available to the center, such as audiovisual aids and equipment, library facilities, student counseling, and health services. This model has been successful in several states, especially in providing high quality law enforcement training.

A third model is the college-operated regional system. In addition to offering academic, preservice degree programs, a college develops a regional training center to serve all criminal justice agencies within its service area. The college uses a blend of its own faculty and part-time instructors drawn from the criminal justice agencies themselves. Direction of the center is usually influenced by an advisory committee composed of representatives from the criminal justice agencies served. Such feedback from the user agencies is essential to insure that training is meeting the needs of the criminal justice system.

The first truly interdisciplinary center developed by a college was the Modesto, California, Regional Criminal Justice Training Center, established by the Yosemite Community College District in Modesto under a grant from the Law Enforcement Assistance Administration. Located on the spacious grounds of a former state hospital, the Modesto

Figure 13-2. The Modesto Regional Criminal Justice Training Center in California was the first true interdisciplinary center developed by a college. Peace officers from many local, state, and federal agencies join with courts and corrections personnel attending a wide variety of courses in the administration of justice.

center provides full live-in facilities for students attending a wide variety of courses in all areas of criminal justice. Among the many users are officers from city, county, state, and federal law enforcement agencies, including the U.S. National Park Service; the State Department of Corrections; the California Youth Authority; county probation departments; and courts within the region served by the center. Management courses for criminal justice personnel have been presented at the center by California State University, San Jose.

In its "Outreach Program," the center uses a mobile classroom to take training to criminal justice agencies in remote and isolated areas of the Sierra Nevada mountains. And the center provides training assistance to local criminal justice agencies by providing counseling and by developing materials and programs for internal training programs, such as roll-call training.

Still another model is a regional training delivery system. Instead of a single physical facility, this system is an alliance and affiliation of many existing institutions and agencies that provide criminal justice training. A central coordinating body assists in planning and scheduling the training programs for criminal justice personnel presented by a wide variety of agencies, such as law enforcement academies, corrections academies, colleges and universities, law schools, state and other governmental agencies that provide training, and in-service training programs within individual departments. The Northern California Criminal Justice Training and Education System is patterned after the regonal delivery system concept. NCCJTES consists of four training and education delivery centers that service the training needs of approximately 10,000 criminal justice personnel in the 26 northern counties.

The regional system concept has the advantage of maximum utilization of existing resources without duplication, which results in an economical and effective use of training funds. By pooling and coordinating resources, high quality training is available to all criminal justice personnel, regardless of their employing agency's size. Training aids (films and videotapes) and curriculum development are among the services which a single agency or college might not be able to afford. Regional pooling of faculty resources results in the best instructors being available for all training.

With the financial assistance, of LEAA and state standards councils, the ideal of high quality training for all ranks and functions is not only possible, but it is more and more becoming a reality.

Future Trends in Training

As criminal justice training programs increase in quantity, quality, and availability, the need continues to constantly reevaluate the training needs of the system and the programs developed to meet those needs. The very best training programs presented this year will not meet the needs of criminal justice personnel ten years from now. The disciplines that make up the administration of justice are continuously changing: constant adaptation is necessary. Trainers must never be content to "leave things the way they are."

Instructional technology will have a great impact upon criminal justice training in the future. Television, for example, can bring the best instructors on any subject into every criminal justice agency in the nation. Prerecorded television cassettes can be produced on an infinite variety of subjects, pooled regionally, and used whenever the need arises. Other media, such as tape-slide training programs, will replace many hours of less productive lectures and can be used whenever convenient. Regional systems will have sophisticated training equipment and resources which are beyond the economic reach of single agencies. Examples include programmed instruction packages on any subject, audio-tutorial learning centers, computer-assisted instruction, "live" televised training programs with audio-tutorial learning centers and student-instructor feedback, and other applications of media and instructional technology as they are developed, tested, and validated.

The future will see an increased emphasis upon realism in training, making the student apply the principles learned to real-life situations. The use of learning techniques such as role-playing, simulation, and gaming will increase with heavy emphasis on practical types of learning. The use of more supervised field training, internships, and student worker programs will enable the trainee to test his new knowledge and skills in the actual environment within which he will be working. And training standards will move from the basis of instructional hours earned to the basis of attainment of behavioral or terminal performance objectives—the trainee's ability to demonstrate that he has learned everything the training was supposed to impart. Classroom hours of instruction will cease to be the measure of training because they simply measure exposure and not results.

With the development of regional training systems and interdisciplinary training programs for all personnel, the several components of

Figure 13-3. Realism is the keynote in training techniques: (below) a plaster cast of a footprint is being prepared; (right) a model city is being used to study tactics.

314 introduction to the administration of justice

the criminal justice system will become less insulated from one another and will better understand and appreciate each other's role and problems. While training primarily upgrades the competence of the individual practitioner, it also can become the means of blending the police, courts, and corrections elements into a more integrated and effective team in the battle against crime.

Summary

Vast improvements have been made in recent years in both the quantity and quality of education and training programs for criminal justice personnel. This is especially true in the field of law enforcement, due to the efforts of enlightened administrators and, in many states, police standards councils or commissions. However, when viewed nationally, the education and training systems for criminal justice practitioners are still inadequate.

In many areas of the United States, mandatory training standards for law enforcement officers are nonexistent. Where minimum standards are established, they too often apply only to entry-level "threshold" training. Only a few states have adopted standards for supervisory, administrative and technical tasks performed by peace officers.

Little has been done to develop training programs for corrections personnel. Prison guards and correctional officers often are expected to learn their jobs from their colleagues, with no formal classroom training. Probation and parole officers, youth counselors, and other caseworkers usually are assumed to have learned all they need to know in their pre-service college courses. Where in-service training is provided, it usually is inadequate in duration, quality, and subject matter.

Despite the vital role of the courts in the administration of justice, trial lawyers and judges usually are expected to have received all the training necessary for criminal trial work while studying for their law degrees. There is very little training available for the newly appointed judge or the attorney who wishes to specialize in criminal law practice.

Every state should identify the many roles, functions, and tasks within the criminal justice system, and adopt minimum training standards for each position. Each state also should provide assistance to justice agencies in meeting those standards.

Good training programs are expensive. Most criminal justice agencies are small and cannot afford to provide much more than day-to-day informal training. The sophisticated and extensive training courses needed to support realistic training standards can best be provided by pooling and regionalizing training programs, using such existing resources as colleges, universities, law schools, and large academies. The best techniques of teaching and instructional technology, presented by competent, interdisciplinary faculties, must be made available to all criminal justice agencies. Until adequate professional training for all criminal justice personnel becomes a reality in every part of the nation, the individual practitioner cannot be considered a member of a true profession.

Student Checklist

1. Can you cite at least three reasons for establishing minimum standards for training and education for justice system personnel?
2. Can you cite the recommendation regarding the ultimate educational

goal of all police personnel as set forth by the 1967 President's Commission on Law Enforcement?
3. Can you explain what LEEP stands for and its objectives?
4. Can you cite two areas in the judicial section that require improved training?
5. Are you able to define the current status of training programs for correctional agencies?
6. Can you cite two examples of state standards councils for training and education for law enforcement officers?
7. Are you able to cite at least two different kinds of regional training centers for law enforcement officers?

Topics for Discussion

1. Discuss the distinction between education and training.
2. Draw a comparison between education and training required for members of the law enforcement, corrections, and judicial subsystems.
3. Discuss the regional training system concept.

ANNOTATED BIBLIOGRAPHY

Advisory Commission on Intergovernmental Relations. *State–Local Relations in the Criminal Justice System.* Washington, D.C.: U.S. Govt. Printing Office, 1971. The Advisory Commission on Intergovernmental Relations spent 18 months of intensive study of the criminal justice system. The report includes 44 specific recommendations for state–local action to improve all segments of the system.

American Bar Association Project on Standards for Criminal Justice. *Standards Relating to the Prosecution Function and the Defense Function.* New York: Office of the Criminal Justice Project. Approved Draft, March 1971. This volume of standards for the prosecution and defense function is one of 15 volumes containing standards for the improvement of the criminal justice process.

Eastman, George D., ed. *Municipal Police Administration,* 7th ed. Washington, D.C.: International City Management Association, 1971. Chapter X (Personnel Management) contains a basic overview of the training function within a municipal police agency.

Hartinger, Walter; Edward Eldefonso; and Alan Coffey. *Corrections: A Component of the Criminal Justice System.* Pacific Palisades: Goodyear, 1973. This introductory textbook describes the role and functions of the corrections component of the criminal justice system. Chapter IV discusses the increasing emphasis on education and training, and describes academic qualifications for correctional workers.

More, Harry W. *Critical Issues in Law Enforcement.* Cincinnati: W. H. Anderson, 1972. The problems facing police are discussed; solutions are objectively presented. The professionalization of police is perceptively presented.

President's Commission on Law Enforcement and Administration of Justice. *The Challenge of Crime in a Free Society.* Washington, D.C.: U.S. Govt. Printing Office, 1967. Chapter IV (The Police) and Chapter VI (Corrections) contain specific and significant recommendations by the Presidential Commission relating to education and training standards for criminal justice personnel.

President's Commission on Law Enforcement and Administration of Justice. *Task Force Report: The Police*. Washington, D.C.: U.S. Govt. Printing Office, 1967. This report deals more extensively with the Presidential Commission's far-reaching recommendations on educational requirements and training programs for law enforcement personnel. Chapter VIII of the report deals exclusively with the establishment of a state standards council.

President's Commission on Law Enforcement and Administration of Justice. *Task Force Report: Corrections*. Washington, D.C.: U.S. Govt. Printing Office, 1967. Chapter IX (Manpower and Training) of this report contains an excellent discussion of education and training of correctional workers, including recommendations for sub- or paraprofessionals.

Wilson, James Q. *Varieties of Police Behavior*. Cambridge: Harvard University Press, 1968. The development of three different styles of policing (legalistic, watchman, and service) is fully described.

The study of this chapter will enable you to:

1. Understand the job elements common to most criminal justice agencies.
2. Cite at least four areas to be researched during the background investigation.
3. Describe the four major stages of the interview process.
4. Cite at least five points of interest that the interviewer is looking for in an applicant.
5. Discuss the types of question asked.

14
Preparation for Employment

The employment process is a maze, but there are guidelines for the novice. He need not grope blindly. Although entrance standards, testing, and evaluation methods differ widely throughout the country, there are many similar elements in employment opportunities in criminal justice agencies. In this chapter we shall discuss the general employment system in these agencies, with particular emphasis on the interview.

Figure 14-1 illustrates some generalized procedures. Dependent upon the agency's requirements, some of the steps may be waived or eliminated. However, the process is found in varying degrees in most criminal justice agencies. The three alternatives—rejection, acceptance, or hold—are possible in any phase, but with the proviso that acceptance is derived only at the end of the process.

Common Job Elements

The elements common to all agencies consist of (1) a formal application seeking factual background and current information; (2) a background investigation (extensive or not); (3) a medical examination; and (4) the interview.

The applicant has little control or influence over the first three elements, since the characteristics sought in the three aspects have been determined by his past behavior and natural development. But he may be able to overcome some deficiencies by remedial actions: he might delay his application until he has finished some course preparation.

Figure 14-1. General employment system in the criminal justice system.

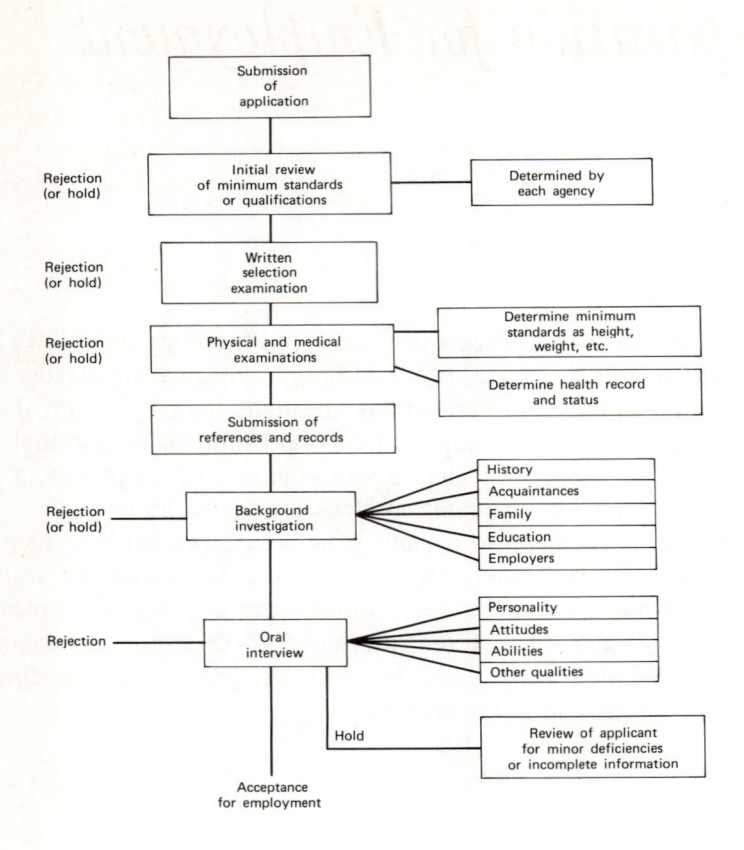

Examples of this might be radio operation courses for police dispatcher jobs, chemistry courses for crime laboratories, court reporting curricula for court stenographers, and sociology and psychology courses for juvenile work.

Other remedial actions are limited due to natural development

322   *introduction to the administration of justice*

limitations or are irreversible due to past occurrences that cannot be eradicated by any present actions or endeavors. But the applicant should avoid seeking employment with a particular agency when he knows that he will encounter physical requirements that he cannot meet. However, the applicant should not become discouraged since different agencies in his hoped-for field have physical requirements that vary considerably. The applicant should obtain data from recruiting agents, advertisements, counseling and placement centers, or the specific potential employer before he applies, so that he can determine his potential candidacy. It is often better to decide not to apply and thereby avoid rejection. A rejection might become a detriment in later applications to other agencies. That is, the candidate with no rejections from other agencies seems to have a clear and perhaps desirable background while the applicant who has been denied employment, often for minor reasons, might be considered less desirable by some personnel examiners. In other words, the interested person should first determine if he has the prerequisite qualities, skills, and experience that are stated for the employment position before application, to reduce the potential for rejection.

In the past, the applicant faced more problems in obtaining this type of information than in the present. Some attempts to collect and collate this data are found in documents published by the Government Printing Office entitled: *Criminal Justice Agencies in U.S. Department of Justice*; *Criminal Justice Agencies in LEAA*; *Criminal Justice Agencies in the National Institute of Law Enforcement and Criminal Justice*; and *Criminal Justice Agencies in the Statistics Division*. These documents and similar ones from state agencies are limited, but often crucial, sources of information. They can help an applicant who seeks specific knowledge of his anticipated employment or they can suggest other areas of potential employment. This information cannot overcome the almost universal inconsistencies of employment standards, but it can give the novice a form of guide through the maze of the criminal justice employment process.

The Interview

Regardless of the other variations in the process, one component, the employment interview, whether it be a few cursory questions or a comprehensive series of formalized interviews, has a definite impact upon the applicant's employment status. Even the agencies that use this technique in a limited way generally tend to place great emphasis on the opinions and decisions formulated during the actual face-to-face interview. Many agencies consider the employment interview so highly important that it becomes a part of the training program. The image generated during the interview of the applicant's personal status is interpreted by the interviewers and becomes a basic component of the applicant's evaluation report for employment as well as a focal point for his later training in the agency.[1]

Often a highly qualified, interested applicant becomes tense and may even "freeze" during an interview, unfortunately masking his true personality. Many supervisors, administrators, and personnel examiners have attempted to overcome the artificiality of the setting by later interviewing in different settings with a change in the complement of the interviewing team.

The Interview Process

For the benefit of the potential applicant, we must examine the nature of the interview process. If the applicant understands the roles of the participants in the setting and the purpose of the interview, perhaps some of the artificial stress will become minimized. One way to gain this perspective might be to look at the interview through the frames of reference held by the interviewer. That is, the applicant must determine what the interviewer is seeking to achieve during the interview; what goals, objectives, purposes, and reasons are inherent in the process from the viewpoint of interviewers in general. In essence, the object of the interview for the applicant becomes an opportunity for him to express his true self and thoughts rather than the distorted views of himself often conveyed in actual interviews.

---

[1] Adopted from a nonpublished internal interviewing policy formulated by Inspector Fred Schmidt (deceased) and Sergeant Alfred Gomez of the Detroit Police Department Scientific Bureau, 1969.

Stages of the Interview

Taking an overall view of the interviewing process is the most likely way to gain insights into the process. From this approach, one can observe four major divisions of the induction interview:

1. Initial contact.
2. Discussion.
3. Conclusion.
4. Evaluation.

Each of these divisions creates a major emphasis upon the entire process through the personal relationships generated during each aspect. Upon closer examination, each division has many subdivisions of importance.

Initial Contact. When initial contact occurs, several behavioral patterns develop between the participants in the setting. Early recognition of the participants' roles is critical to the success or failure of the later stages. Each actor must understand what is required of him and must try to understand the other individual's role.

Discussion. The second phase of the interview can be characterized as the information-gathering process. Questions, statements, and responses indicate the direction of the interview. Many agencies believe that this is the substance of the interview. However, this phase must be considered as a continuance of the whole personal relationship that developed during the initial contact.

Conclusion. The conclusion of the interview seems to be the end of the process to the applicant but, in actuality, it is not the end for the interviewer. The examiner must analyze the results obtained during the previous stages as well as develop a summary that will coincide with his interpretation of the individual applicant. He must formulate actions to be taken for further explorations into the background of the individual or else determine if one or more interviews with the potential candidate are needed.

Evaluation. After the other three phases are completed, a final evaluation must be made. The examiner must make a decision based upon the actions and reactions of the applicant during the entire process.

We can only identify two distinct divisions of the interview—initial contact and conclusion. But experienced interviewers can often distinguish the point at which they begin to conclude the interview, to form their tentative, and, in some cases, their final decisions about the employability of the person being examined. Often the examiner will recommend that further study be made by the unit that has responsibility for the final decision.

As impressions are received by the interviewer, he is judging the attributes of the candidate on a scale of standards formulated from his own education and experiences as an interviewer, considering always the standards within the particular employment area. The highly experienced interviewer can control and compensate for his own prejudices (viewing prejudices as dislikes and likes rather than in any ethnic or racial sense) so that he can formulate a decisive and accurate evaluation of the applicant's qualities and capabilities.

Reactions of the Interviewer
To minimize the possibility for individual bias, most interviewers adhere to guidelines that are impartial and objective. These guidelines, or standards for behavior and reference, usually pertain to observable and measurable characteristics of both participants in the interview. Some of the more predominant characteristics are nonverbal in nature. During the initial contact the examiner may consider the following:

1. How is the applicant's physical appearance?
2. Is he prepared to show his best side?
3. Does he look me in the eye?
4. Was that a firm handshake?
5. How was his response to my greeting?
6. Does he seem genuinely interested?
7. Is he overtense?
8. Is he overly relaxed?
9. Does he look the part for the job?

These reactions of the interviewer might seem too commonplace, but the questions seem to be operative in most interviewing situations. Many other tangible and nontangible questions of this nature are sought, and sometimes answered, at the beginning of the formal process. The beginning, as a definite part of the overall evaluation, is considered significant by Dr. Leonard Zunin, who discusses the responses of two persons meeting initially and the importance of the first four minutes of contact. "It is not an arbitrary interval. Rather, it is the average time demonstrated by careful observation, during which strangers in a social situation interact before they decide to part or continue their encounter."[2] The comments of Dr. Zunin seem to fit the interviewing process, which is actually the meeting of two or more strangers in a social situation that is highly formalized (by most agencies).

The Social Interaction
With this perspective in mind, one may feel that the interview as a social interactional situation similar to that of other social processes and interactions in our society. As the interviewer conducts the evaluatory process, he has some perfunctory goals or objectives to achieve, in addition to the goals that people have when they are desirous of meeting other people. These objectives may or may not be accomplished in a social or formal meeting, depending upon the early responses produced during the initial contact phase of the social interaction.

The interview or the social interaction may become a disaster, regardless of later repairment attempts by either party, if the initial contact period has created negative connotations or animosities. To be a successful interviewer, one must realize the severity and austerity of the interview from the applicant's perspective and try to minimize any negative qualities in the first contact. Spontaneous positive reactions of the interviewer or the applicant can do much to avoid the development of later hostilities.

Perhaps a more pertinent application of the foregoing can be gained by examining three human processes, not unique to interviewing but often evident in it. They are the perceptions, preconceptions, and previous experiences of the participants.

As an individual enters into the job interview area, he or she has some previously formulated ideas of what is about to happen. These concepts cannot always be transmitted verbally but may be expressed through other facets of communication. As the interview begins, the interviewed person projects some of his previously formed opinions, views, or attitudes into the situation in ways that incorporate (consciously or unconsciously) physical and verbal responses. These expressions often appear to be attitudes or attributes of the applicant but, in

---

[2] Leonard Zunin and N. Zunin, *Contact: The First Four Minutes* (Los Angeles: Nash, 1972), p. 8.

actuality, these preconceptions may be gained from other persons who have, knowingly or unknowingly, informed or advised him as to what will happen. Other people's reactions may become his fears and anticipations. Often, the information may be distorted, enlarged, or even erroneous. These distortions can inhibit the flow of information from either of the parties in the interview situation. If the applicant has negative preconceptions toward the process or the person, the success will be limited. Spontaneous responses will be less likely and generalized.

The applicant may perceive the interviewer as a symbolization of his future job, as an opportunity for the job, as an impersonal, somewhat neutral (employer-oriented) and highly powerful individual. At the same time, the experienced interviewer is trying to impart an attitude of interested impartiality and maintain a neutral but relaxed atmosphere to gain a higher degree of participation from the applicant.

Any previous experiences in an employment interview can, coupled with perception and preconception, benefit or restrict all parties engaged in the setting. Interviews experienced in the past by the applicant should be critically reviewed by the person as a means to suggest self-improvement for future situations. Some minor behavioral patterns can be recognized and either eliminated or reduced to acceptable levels by the individual. One may, by an honest and in-depth self-critique, improve and enhance one's own capabilities and develop desirable characteristics for employment.

Types of Questioning During the Interview

Open Questions. The question is worded to motivate the applicant to give one or more statements in response to the theme of the question. Questions that ask a person to describe, discuss, explain, and compare are examples of open questions commonly found in everyday conversation. They are used to obtain information of a wider range than is implied in the question.

Closed (limited) Questions. These are questions designed to evoke minimal and limited answers. Questions that ask for a specific type or form of response, such as who, what, where, and when, are closed in nature. They are used to obtain certain types of information that can be coded, compared, verified, and analyzed.

Blend Questions. These are a mixture of an open and a closed question. A choice or categories of choice are contained within the wording of the question, which seeks answers to several aspects of the topic, with the freedom to add additional responses.

Awareness of the Questions

The applicant and the interviewer should both be familiar with the basic format of questions in order to produce a more meaningful dialogue between them. If an open question is stated by one of the characters, then the respondent should be prepared to answer the question on an open basis. The same must be true of the other types of questions. However, the experienced interviewer must be able to control his selection of questions in order to produce an appropriate mixture of these questions to prevent the onset of lethargy or disinterest. Too many open questions may cause the applicant to "talk himself out," or an overabundance of closed questions may create the feeling of inferiority in the applicant.

Nonverbal Reactions

Successful interviewers often look between the questions to determine if they are developing any of the foregoing problems within the confines of the interviewer. The interviewer (and the applicant) must be cognizant of the nonverbal developments taking place during the situation. Although the nonverbal reactions may not be as definitive as the spoken words, the presence or absence of the nonverbal responses is an indication that something is abnormal. In our everyday communication with people, we offer more than just a verbalized form of information-giving. Each of us divulges information with our body through movements, attitudes, positions, and the like. However minimal or maximal the motion is, it remains a form of information that can prove to be of value in the interview. It may provide the impetus to continue the discourse from the initial contact.

Body communication and oral communication are appropriately termed linguistics-kinesics. One of the leaders in the field of kinesics has stated that Americans move in American English as well as speaking American English. From his studies of the relationships found between body and sound communications, he has found some correlations between the two. "Accumulated research is convincing that, while ethnic groups do display differential papakinesic behavior, there is, besides this (at least for Western European languages), a set of necessary and formal body motions that are tied directly to linguistic structure."[3] From this, it seems that the interviewer must not depend upon his own standards of what the body communication is saying, but upon his recognition that the person is communicating.

Promotional Interview
While most of the foregoing has been directed toward the employment interview, the accumulated data and information can be used and implemented in still another aspect of interviewing found within the criminal justice system; that is, the promotional interview to evaluate the capacity of individuals to function at a higher level of authority and responsibility. This interview must seek information other than that sought in the employment interview. But the basic interview process and its guidelines remain similar in scope and content. Its importance as a tool for evaluation of personal qualities of future supervisors is well recognized. It seeks out the qualities of leadership, the capability to communicate with others, insights into human nature, and responsiveness to the public, among other qualities that are not always readily recordable. The most obvious step is to conduct interviews whereby the interviewers may determine the potential for advancement.

New Trends in Interviewing

Many organizations have moved away from the formal, often staid, face-to-face interview in employment and promotional interviewing. The adoption of techniques from other fields of study has definitely provided some provocative aspects for interviewing criminal justice applicants.

One particular technique that holds great promise is an extract from the group therapy practices that are found in the social sciences. In group therapy, several persons are placed in a relaxed informal setting, and they discuss their situations, backgrounds, and experiences. In the employment setting, several methods are used. In one case, several

---

[3] R. L. Birdwhistell, *Kinesics and Context* (Philadelphia: University of Pennsylvania Press, 1970), p. 103.

applicants are invited into the organization for their employment reviews. They are placed together in the same room accompanied by a discussion leader and are encouraged to discuss their reasons for seeking this type of employment. The discussion leader attempts to draw out the comments of all members of the group and their experiences that might be applicable to the job under review.

Another method under consideration is that the applicant should meet with several of the employees who currently hold the same type of position sought by the applicant. At this time, the applicant is asked to participate in a discussion with the employees present. The latter are carefully selected for their abilities to communicate with others. They are asked to direct the discussion so that they can formulate opinions as to the applicant's capabilities and potential employable status. In this method, as in the former, the final decision is not made by the group, but their recommendations are carefully considered.

A relatively new method for employment interviewing is a situational, or simulation, type of study. This method requires some previously produced situational material, such as photographic slides and a projector. Real-life situations are photographed and selected for use in employment interviews. The applicant is asked to view the slides and discuss his reactions to them. He is asked what actions he would take if he encountered these situations. This type of approach enables the reviewer to evaluate the candidate upon predictable responses. In addition, it seems to motivate the applicant to react more freely and positively, since he has something concrete to react to. The situation chosen must be appropriate to the type of job and its qualifications. It must have direct application to the kind of performance expected from prospective employees.

Another form of personnel examination that has been employed in many areas of the country, but has not gained widespread adoption, is the specialized team approach to interviewing. The team would consist of a qualified individual from the social sciences (psychology, sociology, or other); a second member from the field of criminal justice (related to the position sought); and a member of the community where the position is to be filled.

In addition to the latter techniques, many agencies are now demanding a psychological examination for every candidate under review. For the most part these examinations are not part of the interview process per se, but they are a component of the overall employment process.

For future interviews, one can expect to find a greater diversity in each aspect of interviewing due to the intervention and adoption of suggestions offered from outside the fields of criminal justice. Further than the change in interviewing, applicants will also find a trend toward the adoption of more relevant requirements and qualifications in the fields of criminal justice.

Summary

The maze of the employment process can be generalized into the components common to most employment opportunities in the criminal justice agencies. These components are: (1) the formal application seeking factual background and current information, (2) a background investigation, (3) the medical examination, and (4) an interview with a representative of the potential employer. Each of these four steps is designed to screen out undesirable candidates as well as locate desirable candidates.

The first three aspects of the employment process leave the applicant little control over the outcome. But the interview does give the applicant some measure of control. It has four major divisions: (1) initial contact, (2) discussion, (3) conclusion, and (4) evaluation.

The interviewer uses three basic types of question. The first is an open question, worded to motivate the applicant to give one or more statements pertaining to the theme of the question as a response. The closed question is the second type, designed to evoke a minimal answer or response. The third is the blend question—a mixture of an open and a closed question. Successful interviewers often look between the questions to determine if they are developing any problems within the confines of the interview.

Many organizations are moving away from the formal interview. One particular technique that holds promise is an extract from group therapy practices. Another method calls for the applicant to meet with several other applicants and participate in a discussion with the employer present. A situational or simulation type of interview is also being experimented with. The team concept has been used in interviewing, but it has not gained widespread acceptance.

The influx of new ideas from areas outside the field of criminal justice will cause greater diversity in all areas of interviewing.

Student Checklist

1. Do you understand the job elements common to most criminal justice agencies, and how to go about determining your own eligibility?
2. Are you able to cite at least four areas to be researched during the background investigation?
3. Can you cite the four major stages of the interview process?
4. Are you able to cite at least five points of interest that the interviewer is looking for in an applicant?
5. Can you give at least two examples of open, closed, and blend questions?

Topics for Discussion

1. Discuss the purpose behind the interview process.
2. Outline the various stages during the interview process.
3. Discuss your opinions of new trends in interviewing.
4. Set up a mock interview and allow several students to be interviewed.

ANNOTATED BIBLIOGRAPHY

Baker, E. R. *Police Promotion Handbooks*. London: Butterworths, 1971. A British view of the techniques for advancement of police officers. Some concepts are very usable for persons other than those within the British criminal justice system.

Birdwhistell, Ray L. *Kinesics and Context*. Philadelphia: University of Pennsylvania Press, 1970. Essays on the communication process between words and body movements. An in-depth examination of the so-called body language from a scientific perspective.

Gordon, R. L. *Interviewing Strategy, Techniques and Tactics.* Homewood, Ill.: Dorsey, 1969. A sound textbook that covers many aspects of the interviewing process from a distinctively scientific perspective. In-depth views into the traits of respondents and interviewers are examined and explained. Methods for the successful employment of the techniques are suggested.

Hall, Edward T. *The Silent Language.* Garden City, N.Y.: Doubleday, 1973. Insights into the communication processes between persons of differing and similar backgrounds. Applicable to the interviewer who attempts to examine more than verbal answers.

Post, Richard, and Arthur Kingsbury. *Security Administration.* Springfield, Ill.: Charles C. Thomas, 1970. This book is directed toward another area of the criminal justice system, but it has some valid concepts relating to personnel interviewing and the security of the information obtained. The safeguarding of personnel information is highly necessary to protect the interviewing process.

Watson, Nelson A., ed. *Police and the Changing Community.* Washington, D.C.: I.A.C.P., 1965. Examination of the changes evolving within the existing systems are seen in this work. Some of the more important are found with regard to the employment, evaluation, and acceptance into the police system.

Wicks, Robert J., and Ernest H. Josephs. *Techniques in Interviewing for Law Enforcement and Corrections Personnel.* Springfield, Ill.: Charles C. Thomas, 1972. A programmed learning approach to interviewing that is recommended to the novice interviewer and the potential applicant alike. Although somewhat basic for the experienced interviewer, it may still contain the positive value for updating or refreshing his thoughts.

Zunin, Leonard, and Natalie Zunin. *Contact: The First Four Minutes.* Los Angeles: Nash, 1972. A book, written in the popular media style, that attempts to explain some aspects of human interaction based upon initial contacts. It strives to depict the processes that occur and some of the existing reasons for the results of initial contact. This book is recommended for any person who is planning on becoming the subject of a pre-employment interview.

Part Five

The Future

The study of this chapter will enable you to:

1. Explain the impetus that the LEAA provided for the criminal justice system?
2. Discuss project STAR, its objectives and benefits.
3. Discuss the expanding role of policewomen.
4. Cite at least four changes in correctional procedures.
5. Explain affirmative action programs.
6. Discuss several suggestions for judicial reform.
7. Cite the recommendations of the National Advisory Commission on Criminal Justice Standards and Goals.

15
Trends in the Administration of Justice System

Beginning in the mid-sixties attention to the criminal justice system became intensified. Prior to this, there was a reluctance on the part of many to openly criticize the criminal justice process, whose problems were evident and growing. Once the criticism started, it appeared as though the floodgates were opened. Problems were pointed out rapidly by society; some were real, some were imaginary. Nothing remained sacred. Efforts were made by some to radicalize the system, to abandon all that went on before.

The interest of the public has been focused, not only on police activities, but also on courts and corrections. The necessity for change has been dramatized in the voices of those in the public eye, by their challenge of current police, court, and corrections activities.

The Impetus

Some of the effort expended by the system has been a result of the findings of the President's Commission on Law Enforcement and the Administration of Justice. Although some members of the system thought this report was unfair, many progressive administrators have tried to isolate those recommendations with merit and to experiment with them.

Various chapters in this book have dealt with suggestions in specific areas. What is provided here is not intended to be a resume of the chapters, but an attempt to highlight a few of the trends in the justice process.

Some of the positive action that has taken place in the last few years has been the result of the Law Enforcement Assistance Administration. To say that the LEAA is entirely responsible for the ideas would be an error. However, federal moneys to local agencies have provided the fiscal aid necessary to develop some ideas that otherwise might not have been realized (Figure 15-1). And cooperative efforts between police, courts, and corrections have been manifested by their new interaction.

Many have challenged the LEAA program and its forerunner, the Office of Law Enforcement Assistance program, as being a waste of taxpayer funds. But there have been benefits from both programs. There has been the development of a planning capability for people involved in the entire system—a planned effort rather than one of response to crisis. If the federal dollars spent have achieved nothing more than getting the participants together, it is a tremendous plus for the entire process. It has been the Office of Law Enforcement Assistance and Law Enforcement Assistance Administration dollar programs that have produced some valuable studies. Some, such as project STAR, are still not complete.

Figure 15-1. The first videotaping of a criminal trial in the nation took place in November 1971; it was sponsored by the criminal bar in Michigan and financed by a grant from the LEAA. This is part of the national effort to streamline court procedures.

Project STAR

Project STAR (*S*ystems and *T*raining *A*nalysis of *R*equirements for Criminal Justice Systems Participants) was undertaken through a contract between the California Commission on *P*eace *O*fficer *S*tandards and *T*raining (POST) and the American Justice Institute. The project includes California, Michigan, New Jersey, and Texas criminal justice personnel. It is based on the assumption that better identification of job requirements and improvement in the performance of operational criminal justice personnel will increase the effectiveness of the criminal justice system.

The project involves a comprehensive research effort to define roles, functions, and objectives, as well as knowledge and skill requirements for operational criminal justice personnel. In addition, the project will involve the development of recruitment and selection criteria and the design and demonstration of education and training modules predicated upon the findings of the research.

Objectives

The project's objectives are to do the following: identify and describe the various roles of operational criminal justice personnel, identify major functions and formulate performance objectives for appropriate tasks; determine knowledge and skill requirements for operational criminal justice personnel, including police officers, probation or parole officers, custodial officers, prosecutors, defenders, and judges; formulate education and training recommendations related to these criminal justice personnel and the public; develop education and training modules that address those performance objectives not satisfied by existing education and training programs; demonstrate new or improved training modules in cooperation with local criminal justice agencies; and set forth implementation plans and procedures for a continuous assessment of knowledge and skill requirements, as well as changing job responsibilities for operational criminal justice personnel.

Personnel selection and training can be materially changed in the entire process with the exception of judicial selection. One small example can be shown in the police field. Presently, most police departments recruit all male sworn personnel from a single set of standards. This project could prove the feasibility as well as the advantages of various standards for selection of peace officer personnel, thereby drastically changing present selection procedures.

The training modules being developed in this project are based on empirical studies. Up until this time, most of the training in the criminal justice system has been based on "what we think we need to know." These new modules will not only make the participants more aware of what they need to know, but they will give them a real grasp of what they have learned. In addition, the modules can be used interchangeably by various elements of the system, easily adapted to the varying sophistication of the students.

Another benefit of STAR is that the criminal justice process will have its roles identified and clearly stated; something that many have talked about, some have undertaken, but none have accomplished. Once the roles are spelled out, selection of personnel can be made according to new criteria. This will have a profound impact on each subsection of the system. If duplication in roles can be eliminated and tasks assigned differently, the selection procedure will be of enormous significance. And when a person is employed in the system, there will be the need to provide a training package that not only prepares him for the direct assignment, but also provides cross-training in the entire system.

As STAR has developed, other activities have also been moving forward. Two programs that are receiving much attention are the employment of more females in the criminal justice system and the manner in which training and education is being delivered.

Policewomen and their Expanding Role

Police departments are taking a long, realistic look at their activities with the thought of employing more females. Simply stated, a police agency has sworn personnel that: respond to called-for services; patrol and inspect; provide traffic enforcement; and conduct and follow up investigation. Some agencies have sworn personnel that are involved in custodial operations and the service of civil process. When each of these are viewed objectively, very little can be seen that cannot be undertaken by females.

The most controversial assignment for women is in the response to

Figure 15-2. When each of the tasks of police departments are viewed objectively, very little can be seen that cannot be undertaken by females.

called-for services. Women argue that the vast majority of calls are not dangerous. There is also the question of hazard in the patrol function, to which the point is made that danger is minimal. Many of those arguing against the assignment of females to these functions point out the need for physical prowess in many circumstances, and the increased amount of abuse being directed toward the police, not necessarily physical. To counter this argument: when a female officer is present, people frequently act differently, with no need for physical prowess. Other duties can be accomplished by females with a minimum of danger. In some assignments, in larger agencies where sworn personnel specialize, females may bring a new dimension that may enhance the effectiveness of the police. Three specialties in the investigative field can be used as examples: crimes against property, such as burglaries; crimes against person (i.e., rape); and juvenile cases.

In corrections, some experimentation concerning increased job opportunities for women is taking place. The Department of Corrections in California is employing females to work as correctional officers in male institutions—in those areas that do not invade the privacy of the males. Whether or not this idea will be expanded in other sections of the country remains to be seen. However, it further demonstrates an expanded role for females. In the remainder of the correctional procedure, such as parole or probation, female participation has increased over the years. The assignment to courts does not provoke the controversy that it does in police and corrections. However, women can rightly object to a lack of assignment to the bench. But this is being changed as more women are being appointed and elected to this position.

Correctional Procedure

Corrections has received as much publicity in recent years as any part of the process. The discovery of improper treatment, lack of facilities, riots, and formation of prisoner and citizen groups have done much to spotlight the correctional situation. The attention noted here refers to those in custody, who are only one-third of those to be affected. Probation and parole have also attracted considerable criticism.

Changes in Correctional Procedures

Treatment programs in correctional institutions are being expanded. Some are experimental and quite controversial; others, although experimental, are more acceptable to society. In the general field of probation and parole there are diversion programs in which, rather than enter the person into the institutional program if found guilty, he may be diverted before trial into remedial programs to convert his behavior patterns. A probation subsidy program in California, which has been under fire since 1970, provides a payment to a jurisdiction to keep a person on probation rather than send him to a state prison. The controversy centers around the fact that payment is taken and the individual is kept in the community, and both are considered detrimental to society.

Halfway houses are being used in many areas to reintroduce an inmate to society. The inmate is released several weeks or months before his expected discharge from an institution to a "house" on the outside. The inmate gets employment, but is supervised in the house—halfway between custody and final release. Other treatment programs include weekend release and work furlough. The weekend program entails releasing an inmate near his final release date for a period of 48 to 72 hours to spend in his community. Work furlough is employed in many areas and has been extended to selected inmates where the risk is minimal. When an inmate meets given criteria, he maintains a job during the week, but he spends the remainder of his time in a custodial situation receiving further education and therapy. His wages are handled by the institution.

One of the major points of change in the field of corrections concerns its physical facilities. Most state and federal prisons built in the past have been large brick and mortar units housing many hundreds of inmates. These units have been described in many accounts over the past few years as breeding places for crime. Violence has broken out in numerous prisons because of overcrowded and dehumanizing conditions.

A concerted effort is now being made to reduce the size of the units or institutions and to deploy the units into the community. Some of the goals are that a unit should not house more than 200 persons, and that the housing be a vastly different configuration of buildings than the existing ones. Furthermore, the need for family and community involvement suggests that the units be located in the area in which the inmates normally reside. The contention is that the family and friends can help in the rehabilitative process, if the smaller units are in the community.

Rather than the traditional cell-block concept, more recent designs provide for fewer persons to be placed in the same close proximity to one another. The design also includes more space for varied programs, such as education, training, and counseling activities. The American Institute of Architects has taken an active role in the development of new designs after discussing the needs with progressive institutional administrators.

Figure 15-3. At the Ft. Worth, Texas co-correctional institution, men and women have separate housing facilities, but they share institutional activities, such as meals, counseling, education, recreation, and most training opportunities. This experimental program is an effort to normalize life in the institution as much as possible.

Conjugal visits (married inmates meeting in private with their spouses) is a program that has received wide attention outside of the United States and is now being promoted in this country. And programs in which either corrections personnel or volunteers transport families to institutions for visits are also in the experimental stage. These programs require more facilities, equipment, and personnel, but they will probably be more widely used in the future.

Educational programs—remedial, formal, or vocational will receive more attention. Each of these can be of benefit to those who are willing to accept and participate in the programs. The expectation is that they will reduce recidivism in violations of the law.

A revolution is taking place in educational techniques. These are gradually being applied to the training of criminal justice personnel. Multimedia is the catchphrase used to describe methods being used for the presentation of educational materials. Some of the multimedia programs have been in existence for years in business and industry and should be adapted to criminal justice. Videotape, 16mm film, 35mm film, tape recording, computers, and others should all be used for training in criminal justice. The future will bring to the participant individually tailored training modules by the use of these methods.

Affirmative Action

The Equal Employment Opportunities Act became law in 1965. Until March 1972, the provisions of the EEOA applied principally to private industry employers but, after that date, it became applicable to all public agencies within the United States. The federal agency responsible for the administration and enforcement of the Act is the Equal Employment Opportunity Commission.

Its purpose is to reinforce and secure the accepted personnel policy that all employment be made without regard to a person's race, color, religion, sex, or national origin. The EEOA specifies those actions that are discriminatory and unlawful, and it states procedures to insure compliance with the Act.

In the latter part of 1971, the Office of Federal Contract Compliance, the Equal Employment Opportunity Commission, and the Department of Labor adopted new regulations to develop and evaluate the good-faith effort required to transform programs from paper commitments to equal employment opportunity. The new regulations were to be known as Revised Order No. 4 or Affirmative Action Programs, and they were made applicable to any agency contracting with the federal government with an employee population of 50 or more.

An affirmative action program does not function in a social, economic, or political vacuum. It must, in order to be truly effective, have complete support from all segments of the government and community. In addition, such a program must reaffirm the EEOA policies and goals. In concert with the EEOA, an effective affirmative action program is intended to accomplish the following objectives: to maximize the participation of persons who continue to suffer the effects of discrimination—because of race, color, religion, sex, or national origin—in the employment process through an active affirmative action program; to have, as an ultimate goal, an employee population that fairly and objectively represents the labor market population with regard to race, color, religion, sex, and national origin; to reaffirm the commitment that the agencies' decisions regarding employment and promotion shall be made on the basis of merit and valid job-related factors; to eliminate all artificial and arbitrary barriers to employment and promotion; to demonstrate that the employment actions of the agency are made without regard to a person's race, color, religion, sex, or national origin; and to provide a systematic ongoing procedure to evaluate the agencies' effectiveness in accomplishing the above.

There are several major elements in any of the programs in a jurisdiction. The activities start with total commitment by the policy makers (legislators) and department heads of any jurisdiction. Classification is another element. This is the process of organizing jobs in a systematic manner to reflect similarities and differences in job title, duties, responsibilities, and employment qualifications in the form of class specifications. An accurate classification plan is used to: establish internal salary relationships; establish recruitment and selection criteria; analyze and develop training programs; establish career ladders; and assist in general administrative and budget processes. This is usually the responsibility of the personnel department.

Recruitment and selection are the major goals of the program. Recruitment includes those procedures used to attract applicants for employment: selection involves those procedures used to evaluate and select applicants for referral to the appointing department head. The personnel department, with assistance from the respective justice system agency, is normally responsible for the implementation of the recruitment and selection elements. After a person has been recruited, there is a need to appoint. The appointment process includes the offering of a position to an applicant and taking the necessary action for final processing. Department heads should accept the responsibility for the effective implementation of the affirmative action program for their agency. In the larger agencies the department head may select a responsible member of the management team to implement the program. The training process develops skills for improved performance through education and selected learning experiences. A personnel department can be responsible for the implementation of the training elements. Personnel rules and procedures should be developed for the jurisdiction; all personnel must be informed of their existence and meaning. There are normally two sets of rules and regulations, one for the entire jurisdiction, the other for the separate agencies. Each program should be evaluated to make sure that the objectives and goals are being met and that the program is viable.

Judicial Program

Largely because of a rapid population expansion and the development of a legalistic society, the workload of our judicial system has increased tremendously over the past few years. Unfortunately, developments and improvements in the day-to-day administrative functions of the courts have not kept pace with the rapid increase in workload. In concise terms, most courts need study, structural overhaul, and reform.

The court system has evolved over a period of many years, and the methods employed to deal with its problems have largely been piecemeal. There has been little systematic planning and development. In many jurisdictions, problems have not been dealt with effectively and, in some cases, they have not even been identified.

Attempts to improve the quality of criminal justice that ignore the courts, prosecutors, and defenders will fall short of their objectives. There is a need for future developments that will aid the entire process. The following items discussed briefly are only a few of many suggestions for judicial reform.

Reduction of Delay

The reduction of congestion and undesirable delay has a high priority, since it involves all levels of the judicial process. Also, because the courts must hear both civil and criminal cases, problems of civil delay are related to problems of criminal delay. Furthermore, the guarantees of a fair and speedy trial are more than a constitutional mandate; they are essential to effective criminal justice.

Calendar Management. The effective management of existing resources is essential to the reduction of delay. Calendar management experts and supporting staff could be established to provide the necessary expertise for dealing with complex calendar problems. Present calendaring practices should be examined to develop more effective procedures. A program to conduct a training conference on calendar management for court administrators and presiding judges would be a useful tool.

Continuances. The courts should develop rules or laws regarding continuances that will promote speedier trials. Stern enforcement of these requirements should reduce the number of continuances granted for frivolous or insubstantial reasons.

Training of Judges and Court Executives. The training of judges in the conduct of trials and administration of the courts should be enhanced. Continuing education of the judiciary is of critical importance to the improvement of courts, prosecution, and law reform. Training programs and conferences should be developed for court executives also, to aid in the development of a comprehensive body of court management theory, and of the standards, qualifications, and functions of court executives.

Using Technology. Judicial participants have been slow in adopting technological advances. Significant time is wasted in processing large amounts of paper through traditional methods: computerized case scheduling and calendaring systems could provide a speedier system for the court. This system would make it possible for the judge or administrator in charge of the calendar to monitor the flow of cases, measure cases against fixed standards or timetables for disposition, and assign priorities among cases. The system could allow identification of those cases that have not met time standards at various stages of the trial process, and thus facilitate the flow of cases.

A videotape examination of witnesses could be experimented with. This might reduce the court time spent examining witnesses; allow witnesses to testify at their convenience; and would eliminate the possibility of the jury hearing inadmissible testimony.

Electronic data-processing techniques could be developed for the operation of the courts. A study may produce a modular integrated court information system adaptable to use in small, medium, and large courts.

Other Recommendations. Additional items that may be developed are: court administrators for larger courts who would become involved with general management, personnel management, and data management; alternatives to grand jury and preliminary hearings that would be aimed at reducing the present unnecessary consumption of time; crime-charging standards to develop uniform police reporting and prosecutor charging, uniform citations, and pleading and practice forms; increased use of citation to district attorneys with informal, voluntary probation by the police; judicial workload studies and the development of standards; and not last in any regard—the legislative changes in existing law.

Two areas that are receiving great attention today that must be dealt with, both legislatively and judicially, are pretrial release programs and preventive detention. Pretrial release programs have done much to alleviate inequities in the bail system. These programs have conclusively proven their success, effectiveness, and value: they result in substantial human and monetary savings to the public and to local agencies. Preventive detention is a complex issue which must be considered realistically. The major problem is to codify the categories of persons to be detained by the court. These and other programs that have been described can be developed in the future to the benefit of the entire process and society.

National Advisory Commission on Criminal Justice Standards and Goals

This text has repeatedly referred to the studies funded by the federal government in the past 10 years. Specific reference has been made to the President's Commission on Law Enforcement and the Administration of Justice and to the experimental Office of Law Enforcement Assistance, the forerunner of the Law Enforcement Assistance Administration. Much of the material developed through the studies has been of great value for further development by the criminal justice participants. Other suggestions and recommendations have not received the attention they warranted. As a result of the varieties of the studies and the multiplicity of books released, many important recommendations were overlooked. There appeared to be a need to gather a group of experts in the field of criminal justice to discuss the wealth of material available and, in addition, to expand upon ideas or develop new ones so that they could make some firm recommendations to improve the process. A commission was formed to do this work, which was entitled The National Advisory Commission on Criminal Justice Standards and Goals. Their first release of information was made early in 1973. Since that time more work has been done by the Commission, and recommendations are being released as the work continues.

The ultimate goal of the Commission's work is to reduce crime through the combined effort of all in the criminal justice process, including federal, state, and local governments. The Commission did not undertake new research, rather it developed standards that take a fresh look at the process, unhampered by traditional practices that no longer apply. It further took the view that wherever policy, program, procedures, and law are in need of improvement or should be eliminated, the legislatures should make the necessary changes, and the agencies in the process should implement the changes.

As with any study where recommendations are made, the recommendations are subject to attack. And those who oppose several recommendations might try to discredit the entire work because of some opposition. The work of this Commission may be subject to this pitfall. There are many ideas put forth that should receive serious attention to upgrade the criminal justice process. Some of these recommendations will be enumerated as they relate to police, courts, corrections, and crime prevention.

Recommendations for the Police

Seven objectives were identified by those studying the police. They did not give priorities for their objectives nor for those specific items that can be developed as programs to tackle the objectives. The Commission called for immediate action to: fully develop the offender-apprehension potential of the criminal justice system; stimulate the police and the citizens to work together as a team; motivate those in the criminal justice system to work in unison; clearly determine and act on local crime problems; make the most of human resources; use technological advances to their fullest capacities; and fully develop the police response to special community needs. The Commission made numerous recommendations for implementation of each objective.

Offender-Apprehension Potential. To fully develop the offender-apprehension potential of the criminal justice systems, programs of crime prevention need to be implemented by police agencies. Volunteer neighborhood security can be developed where citizens mark personal property with identification numbers or call in suspicious acts taking place in their community, for example. Crime prevention through physical planning can be undertaken for citizens or businesses by using design ideas calculated to reduce the opportunity to commit crime.[1] Security standards can be enhanced by the enactment of necessary laws and ordinances.

Police and Citizen Teamwork. The objective to get the police and the people working together as a team could be met with programs that make the people aware of written police policy that deals with authority, law, misconduct of the police, and every aspect where the police and the public must work together. It would follow that the public would also be made aware of the police role in society.

Criminal Justice System Teamwork. Where the need exists to get the criminal justice system working together as a team, the police and all others in the process must communicate with one another. They must execute their roles to keep adults and juveniles from being enmeshed in the criminal justice process. Alcohol and drug abuse centers are examples of areas that require a tremendous team effort.

Other Recommendations. Some of the about 50 program recommendations are: the deployment of officers; use of communication equipment; command and control; developing specialists; resources development; combination of services; developing intelligence information; use of civilian personnel; personnel development; and the administration of promotions. Some agencies may argue that these are not new for them, but one must realize that the report addresses the entire police service in the United States.

Recommendations for the Courts

The subcommittee set forth the major components of the court procedure to include judiciary, prosecution, defense, and court administration. It viewed each component in terms of changes that could be implemented to reduce crime on a national scale. The committee developed programs for: screening; diversion; negotiated plea; the litigated case; sentencing; review of the trial court proceedings; the judiciary; the lower courts; court administration; the prosecutor; and the defense. Within these major items are 50 programs for the improvement of the total court's effort.

[1] See Oscar Newman, *Defensible Space: Crime Prevention Through Urban Design* (New York: Macmillan, 1972).

Screening. Screening is the action taken before formal entry into the process; diversion, after some of the formal action of the process has started. The subcommittee indicated that an accused should be screened out of the criminal justice process when the benefits gained from prosecution or diversion would be outweighed by the costs of such action. Screening standards should be developed so that prosecution and police have guidelines in as specific terms as possible so that they can identify the cases when a person would not be taken into custody.

Diversion. Diversion programs can be developed that would state the categories to be selected. No program should impair the impact that criminal punishment may have. The person subject to diversion must offer some hope of rehabilitation as a protection against the commission of further crimes.

Negotiated Pleas. A strong position was taken against plea bargaining, yet there is a need to develop some form of negotiated plea with uniform policies and practices. These standards or guidelines must take into consideration the impact of the plea on society, the offender, and his rehabilitation.

Sentencing. Sentencing of offenders is an important aspect of the process, crucial both to society and the defendant. The reaction of the defendant to a sentence can materially affect the outcome of a rehabilitation program. The feeling was expressed that juries should be removed from the sentencing procedure and that courts should be required to impose the sentences provided by statute.

Review of Proceedings. The committee sees the need for improvement for: unified proceedings in review; dispositional time in reviewing court decisions; further review at all levels in prior adjudication; and prior factual determination.

Judicial Selection. Judicial selection should be based on merit. Although this may seem obvious, the committee stated that selection procedures must be aggressive in seeking out the best qualified individuals to sit on the bench. In addition, after the selections are made, judges should be subject to discipline or removal from office for reasons that would interfere with the performance of their duties.

Other Recommendations. The subcommittee has made recommendations for: the unification of state court systems; state court administrators;

local and regional trial court administrators; case flow management; professional standards for prosecuting attorneys; public representation of convicted offenders; and workload and salaries for public defenders. All of these are worthy of study, development, and implementation for the benefit of the courts and society.

Recommendations for Corrections
Sixty-three recommendations covered all aspects of corrections. The emphasis was based on developing standards for: the rights of the offender; diversion; pretrial release and detention; sentencing; offender classification; corrections and the community; juvenile intake and detention; local adult institutions; probation; major institutions; parole; manpower; research and development, information and statistics; and statutory framework. Although some of the standards may seem minor, when the corrections procedure is viewed nationally, it becomes apparent that many rather simple or minor items have not been dealt with in a great many institutions or by correctional personnel.

One standard suggests that each correctional unit develop and implement policies and procedures that fulfill the right of persons under supervision to have free access to the court. People under supervision have the right to access to the following: challenge the legality of conviction or confinement; seek redress for illegal conditions or treatment while under control; seek remedies in connection with civil problems; and seek all remedies against any one individual or group that violates the person's constitutional or statutory rights. The access is also to be extended for the person to receive all legal services.

A number of standards are recommended that relate to the person in custody, for health, welfare, and the protection of his rights. They can be described in a few words and are self-explanatory: healthful surroundings, searches, rules of conduct, discipline, grievance procedures, exercise of religious beliefs, and access to the public.

This subcommittee also had suggestions for standards on the subjects of diversion, pretrial release, pretrial detention, and alternatives to arrest. Again, this points up the need for active communication between police, courts, and corrections, each of whom has attitudes based on different perspectives. All recognize the twofold responsibility of the rehabilitation of the offender and the protection of society, with a common interest in sentencing.

Classification teams or committees should be established to provide the offender with meaningful programs: often the program that an offender is placed in does more harm than good. There is a need to develop the criteria to be used by classification committees composed of both professionals and the community.

Since the community becomes involved in many areas, a plan for community-based alternatives to confinement could prove helpful. This plan could specify the services to be provided directly by the correctional unit and those provided through community resources. This requires that the correctional process establish a good working relationship with major social institutions and agencies in the community.

Other Areas of Recommendation. The committee also took into consideration the juvenile problems, and it suggested standards for the police, juvenile intake, and diversion programs. It also suggested the need for legislation in this general area to enable the court to establish organized intake services. Juvenile detention, another field of attention, became involved because of the need to renovate facilities to accommodate intake.

Other standards thought to be helpful were in areas such as: total correctional systems planning; state operation and control of local institutions; service of probation; planning new institutions; parole grant hearings; community services for parolees; recruitment of personnel; evaluation of corrections; and corrections legislation.

A subcommittee of the Commission dealt with community crime prevention. The suggestions covered the need to organize, implement, and manage everyone's effort to reduce crime, delinquency, and recidivism. Although this same theme ran through the recommendations on police, courts, and correction, the Commission felt that this area had sufficient impact to develop a special public committee to emphasize its importance.

Summary and Prospects for the Future

The 1960s brought the attention of the public to the criminal justice system. This public attention brought with it federal and state money for the system. This money allowed many different programs to be initiated. One such program is STAR.

Project STAR was undertaken through a contract between the California Council on Criminal Justice, the California Commission on Peace Officer Standards and Training, and the American Justice Institute. Project STAR is based on the assumption that a better identification of job requirements and an improvement in the performance of operational criminal justice personnel will increase the effectiveness of the criminal justice system. The project involves a comprehensive research effort to define roles, functions and objectives, as well as knowledge and skill requirements for operational criminal justice personnel. One program that is receiving attention in STAR is the employment of women in the entire criminal justice system.

Corrections has also received a great deal of publicity in recent years. A great many programs are now underway in the field of corrections. Work release, halfway houses, and other programs are constantly being viewed.

There is also a concerted effort being made to equalize employment opportunities. In concert with the EEOA, an effective affirmative action program has been started to provide for equal opportunity for employment for all.

The judiciary had been plagued by the same problems as the other branches of the criminal justice system. They suffer from a lack of training, insufficient manpower, and a lack of funds. However, programs are underway to correct some of these problems.

The National Advisory Commission on Criminal Justice Standards and Goals had as its objective the reduction of crime through a combined effort of all in the criminal justice process. The Commission did not effect new research, but viewed data already collected. They have released several recommendations with more to follow. These recommendations cover all phases of the criminal justice system.

This book in its entirety sets forth the tone of what needs to be done in the future. Each of the chapters makes suggestions for those in the criminal justice process. One recurrent theme throughout is the need within each subsection of the process to turn the process into a real system. This is probably the greatest single challenge. If each of the suggestions or recommendations of this book are viewed objectively, it should be obvious that a systems approach is needed, if many of the problems of the process are to be solved and eliminated. The future must develop personnel that are working together to make a system and personnel that are working with society to make it a system.

In an effort to deal with the challenge of crime in modern society, the process must develop and make use, as fully as possible, of modern scientific and technological advances. Of extreme importance is the need to develop data gathering and manipulation. A criminal justice information system that can provide comprehensive, up-to-date information on which policy, programs, procedures, and management decisions can be made for the entire process is a absolute necessity.

Everyone must realize their responsibility. The process can gear up, reduce delay, and perform hundreds of other activities, but society must reassert its emphasis on the individual's responsibility for his conduct and the conduct of others. If there is a refusal to obey there should be a certainty of punishment. Besides protecting the rights of the accused, we must remember the rights of the rest of society. Each person in our society has the right to expect to be able to live and work in safety without the threat against his person or property.

It is often said that the final goal of criminal justice is to reduce crime, delinquency, and recidivism. To ascertain the truth is the constitutional role of the courts, and they should be restored to this activity. Future participants in the system can arrest those practices that contribute to delay in the court, that abuse technicalities of the law, and that encourage lawlessness. These must be replaced by a method to assure equal, fair, speedy, and certain justice.

All of the suggestions mentioned in this book can be achieved: better law enforcement, efficient corrections, and certain justice can all be accomplished. Crime, delinquency, and recidivism can be greatly reduced without the system developing a "police state." Effective criminal justice guarantees individual freedom, and it will also provide domestic tranquility.

Student Checklist

1. Can you explain the impetus provided by the LEAA?
2. What are the objectives and benefits of project STAR?
3. In what ways will the role of policewomen expand?
4. What four proposed changes in correctional procedures seem most significant to you?

5. Do you understand the purposes of the affirmative action programs?
6. Can you cite several suggestions for judicial reform?
7. What are some of the areas of recommendation for the National Advisory Commission on Criminal Justice Standards and Goals?

Topics for Discussion

1. Discuss the impact of the results of the National Advisory Commission's recommendations.
2. Discuss the future role of women in the justice system.
3. How do you envision the criminal justice system of the future?
4. In which area do you see the greatest need for reform? Why?
5. What role would you like to have in the criminal justice system?

Glossary

Perhaps the fastest way to gain a general knowledge of a particular profession is to acquire an understanding of the terminology used. The criminal justice system uses many unique words and phrases in carrying out its duties. Many of the most frequently used terms will be defined in this terminology guide. It must be emphasized that the definitions presented here are not intended to be complete interpretations of the words. For a complete explanation, consult a law dictionary or a textbook on criminal justice terminology.

Notations

Abet
To encourage or advise another to commit
a crime. To aid by approval.

Accessory
One who aids or conceals a criminal so that he
may avoid arrest or punishment.

Acquit
To find a person not guilty of the crime charged.

Addict
Usually a person who is addicted to the taking
of narcotics in some form.

Admission
A statement by a defendant tending to prove
his guilt. Not a complete confession.

Adultery
Sexual intercourse by a married person with
one who is not a wife or husband.

glossary   359

Notations

Affidavit
A written statement made under oath.

Alias
A false or assumed name.

Alibi
The defense that the accused was in some place other than that where the crime was committed.

Alien
A subject of another government.

Alienist
A person who specializes in the study of mental diseases.

Ante Mortem
Before death.

Appeal
The transfer of a case to a higher court, in which it is asked that the decision of the lower court be altered or reversed.

Appellant
One who makes an appeal or who takes an appeal from one court to another.

Appellate Court
A court that has jurisdiction of review and appeal.

Notations

Arraignment
A court proceeding in which the defendant is informed of the charge against him, advised of his constitutional rights, and at which he may enter a plea or deposit bail.

Arrest
Detaining a person in a manner authorized by law, so that he may be brought before a court to answer charges of having committed a crime. Both peace officers and private persons may make the arrest.

Arson
Willfully burning property.

Assault
An unlawful attempt to physically hurt another person. If the person is actually struck, the act is called "battery."

Bail
Security, in the form of cash or bond, deposited with a court as a guarantee that the defendant, if released, will return to court at the time designated to stand trial.

Ballistics
The science of the study of bullets and firearms.

Barratry
The unlawful practice of initiating lawsuits or police complaints without just cause.

glossary

Notations

Battery
The unlawful use of force or violence against a person without his consent.

Bertillon System
A method of identifying criminals by body measurements and description. *See* **Portrait Parle.**

Bigamy
The crime of being married to two persons at the same time.

Blackmail
The extortion of money from a person through threats of accusation or exposure of an unfavorable nature.

Blue Laws
Rigid laws regulating activities on the Sabbath.

Bribery
The offering or accepting of any undue reward to or by a public official in order to influence his official actions.

Brief
A summary of the law pertaining to a case, which is prepared by the attorneys for submission to the judge. Useful in police work for case law reference.

Brothel
A house used for the purpose of prostitution.

Notations

Bunco
A type of theft perpetrated by the use of false or misleading representations.

Burglary
The crime of entering a building with the intent to steal or commit some felony. Not to be confused with robbery, which is a theft from the immediate presence of the victim through force or fear. In burglary, the victim is seldom present at the time.

Capital Crime
A crime punishable by death.

Caption and Asportation
Generally, to prosecute for theft, it is necessary that both taking (*caption*) and carrying away (*asportation*) be proved.

Certiorari (*writ of certiorari*)
An order issued by a higher court to a lower court directing that a case be transferred to the higher court for review or trial.

Change of Venue
A change of the place of trial in a criminal or civil proceeding.

Circumstantial Evidence
Evidence tending to prove a fact through a logical association of other facts, but without an actual witness to the act to be proven.

glossary

Notations

Citation
An official summons issued by a court or peace officer directing a person to appear before the court for some official action. Frequently referred to as a ticket.

Civil Action
A law suit to recover damages or correct some wrong between two parties. Does not usually involve a crime and is apart from a criminal action. A person may be convicted in a criminal court and also sued in a civil court for the same act. *Example*: A drunk driver may be sentenced to jail in a criminal proceeding and then sued in civil action by the owner of a car damaged by the drunk driver.

Commitment
An official court order directing that a person be taken to a jail, prison, hospital, or other location (usually a place of confinement).

Common Law
The basic, unwritten concepts of English and American law. In many states, there are no "common law crimes." For an act to be a crime, there must be a specific, written statute so declaring it.

Complaint
The formal accusation of crime presented to the court and which acts as the formal commencement of a criminal prosecution.

introduction to the administration of justice

Notations

Compounding a Crime
The unlawful act of accepting money or other reward for agreeing to refrain from prosecuting a crime—concealing it from the authorities or withholding evidence.

Compromising a Crime (misdemeanors only)
The proceeding by a court whereby a person charged with a misdemeanor may be discharged without prosecution upon payment of damages to the party injured.

Conspiracy
A secret combination or agreement between two or more persons to commit a criminal act.

Confession
A voluntary declaration admitting the commission of a crime.

Confidential Communication
Communications between a person and his attorney or clergyman, or between husband and wife, which may be legally concealed in court testimony.

Contempt of Court
Disobedience to the court by acting in opposition to the authority, justice, or dignity thereof. Punishable as a crime.

Conviction
The finding of a person guilty of a criminal charge.

glossary

Notations

Coroner
A county official whose principle duty is to determine the manner of death of any person.

Corpus Delicti
The complete set of elements necessary to constitute a particular crime.

Crime
An act committed or omitted in violation of a law forbidding or commanding it, for which a punishment is provided.

Criminal Action
A court proceeding instituted and prosecuted by the state for the punishment of crime. Not to be confused with civil action.

Criminal Procedure
The method prescribed by law for the apprehension, prosecution, and determination of punishment for persons who have committed crimes.

Criminology
The science that deals with crimes, their causes, and their prevention and punishment.

Defendant
The person sued or charged in a court action, whether criminal or civil.

Demurrer
A plea made to the court that the actions alleged in the complaint, even if true, do not constitute a crime.

Deposition
The written testimony of a person, who, for some reason, cannot be present at the trial.

District Attorney
A county official whose duties require him to act as attorney for the state in prosecution of criminal cases.

Double Jeopardy
The act of placing a person on trial a second time for a crime for which he has already been tried once (forbidden by criminal procedure).

Duces Tecum
A subpoena whereby a person is summoned to appear in court as a witness and to bring with him some piece of evidence (usually a written document).

Dying Declaration
A statement made by a dying person regarding the cause of his injuries. Acceptable evidence in a homicide prosecution. Based on the theory that a person about to die will be inclined to be truthful in any statements he makes.

Embezzlement
The crime of stealing property or money that has been entrusted to one's care.

glossary

Notations

Et Al.
And others. For example: "*People* v. *Jones*, et al." indicates that Jones and others are the defendants in a criminal case. This form is used to prevent repeating the names of all persons involved every time the case is referred to.

Evidence
Testimony, physical objects, documents, or any other means used to prove the truth of a fact at issue in a court proceeding.

Ex Post Facto
After the facts. Usually refers to a law that attempts to punish acts that were committed before it was passed.

Extortion
Similar to blackmail.

Extradition
The surrender by one state or nation to another, on its demand, of a person charged with a crime by the requesting state.

Felony
A major crime punishable by death or imprisonment in a state or federal prison. All other crimes are called misdemeanors.

Fence
A person who makes a business of purchasing or receiving stolen goods from criminals.

Notations

Fingerprints
A reproduction of the ridge formation on the outer joint of the fingers. Although a definite identification can be made using only one finger, it is usually necessary that the prints of all ten fingers be available for a successful search of fingerprint files.

Fine
The financial punishment levied against a lawbreaker that is paid to the government funds.

Forgery
Any of several crimes pertaining to the false making or alteration of any document with intent to defraud.

Former Jeopardy
Same as double jeopardy.

Fugitive
One who has fled from punishment or prosecution.

Grand Jury
A group of men and women whose duty it is to make inquiries and return recommendations regarding the operation of local government. They also receive and hear complaints in criminal cases, and if they find them sustained by evidence, present an indictment against the person charged. It is called a grand jury because it is composed of a greater number of jurors than a regular trial jury.

glossary **369**

Notations

Habeas Corpus (writ of)
A court order directing that a person who is in custody be brought before a court in order that an examination may be conducted to determine the legality of the confinement.

Habitual Criminal
Many states have statutes providing that a person convicted a certain number of times may be declared an habitual criminal and, therefore, unsuited for attempts for rehabilitation.
A person so declared may then be sentenced to life imprisonment for the protection of society.

Hearsay Evidence
Evidence that deals with what another person has been heard to say. This evidence is usually excluded in a trial.

Heroin
An opium derivative drug. It is a coarse white or gray powder that is taken hypodermically, orally, or by sniffing. It is completely outlawed for any purpose in the United States.

Homicide
The killing of a human being by another human being.
    Fratricide—killing of one's own brother
    Matricide—killing of one's own mother
    Infanticide—killing of a child
    Patricide—killing of one's own father
    Uxoricide—killing one's own wife

Impeachment
The process whereby a public official may be removed from office through judicial proceedings. Also, the discrediting of a witness in order to show that his testimony is probably false.

Indeterminate Sentence
A court or board-imposed sentence with neither minimum nor maximum limits.

Indictment
An accusation in writing, which is presented by the grand jury, charging a person with a crime.

Information
An accusation in writing, presented by a prosecuting official; i.e., district attorney or city attorney, charging a person with a crime.

Informant
One who supplies information leading to the apprehension of a criminal.

Injunction
A court order whereby a person is ordered to do, or restrained from doing, a particular thing. Not enforced by the police without an additional court order to that effect.

Inquest
An inquiry with a jury conducted by the coroner to establish the cause of death.

glossary

Notations

Intent
In general, there must be a concurrence between a person's acts and his intentions in order to constitute a crime. A person cannot be convicted of a crime if he committed the act involuntarily, without intending injury. If a person acts negligently, however, without regard for the rights of other people, this is sufficient in itself to establish criminal intent. Thus, the drag racer who kills an innocent party may be convicted of manslaughter even though he did not intend the death or injury of anyone.

Interrogation
The art of questioning or interviewing, particularly as applied to obtaining information from someone who is reluctant to cooperate. May apply to the questioning of witnesses, victims, suspects, or others. Requires the use of psychology, salesmanship, good judgment, and a knowledge of human nature. The use of physical force to obtain information has no legitimate place in modern law enforcement.

Jail
A place of confinement maintained by a local authority, usually for persons convicted of misdemeanors. The terms prison or penitentiary apply to such institutions operated by the state or federal government, usually for more serious offenses.

Judiciary
That branch of the government concerned with the administration of civil and criminal law.

introduction to the administration of justice

Notations

Jurisprudence
The science of laws.

Jury
A group of men and women whose duty it is to determine the guilt or innocence of persons charged with a crime.

Juvenile Court
Generally, a special court or department of another court that hears cases involving juveniles. Proceedings are less formal, and the primary objectives are rehabilitation and protection, rather than punishment.

Kleptomania
An abnormal desire to steal.

Larceny
Same as theft. The unlawful taking of the property of another. Divided into grand theft and petty theft. Grand theft includes the taking of money or goods in excess of $200; the theft of any item from the immediate possession of another; theft of an automobile of any value; the theft of certain domestic animals; and the theft of certain fruits, vegetables, and fowl over the value of $50. All other theft is petty theft.

Libel
The circulation of written matter that tends to discredit or injure the character of another. It is not necessary that the material be false.

glossary

Notations

The prime consideration is the motives under which it was issued. Slander is of the same nature except it is verbal rather than written. *Note*: There are few criminal prosecutions for libel or slander. It has become largely a civil matter.

Limitations, Statute of
The statutory time limit within which a criminal prosecution must be begun. For felonies, this is usually three years from the date the crime was committed. For misdemeanors it is one year. There are some crimes that have a longer time limit and a few, such as murder, that have no time limit.

Lynching
In popular usage, the killing of an accused criminal by a mob that has taken him from the authorities by force. Technically, it is the act of a group unlawfully taking a person from the custody of a peace officer for any purpose.

Magistrate
A judicial officer having authority to conduct trials and hearings in criminal and civil matters and to issue writs, orders, warrants of arrest, and other legal documents.

Maim
The crime of willfully disfiguring another.

Mala in Se and Mala Prohibita
A basic grouping of crimes according to the nature of the act. *Mala in se* means "bad in

itself" and refers to those crimes, such as murder, robbery, and rape, which are deemed to be wrong in almost all civilized societies. *Mala prohibita* means "bad by prohibition" and refers to those offenses, such as building and safety regulations and certain traffic violations, established by statute for the public convenience, which are not immoral or bad in themselves.

Mandamus, Writ of
An order issued by a court, directed to a government agency or to a lower court, commanding the performance of a particular act.

Mann Act
The federal statute relating to the interstate transportation of females for immoral purposes.

Manslaughter
The unlawful killing of a human being without premeditation or intent to take life.

Marijuana
A narcotic produced from the East Indian Hemp plant (*cannibis sativa*). The leaves and flowering tops are ground into a form resembling tobacco, but which is drier and coarser. It is then rolled into cigarettes and smoked.

Misdemeanor
A crime punishable by other than imprisonment in the state prison.

Notations

Modus Operandi
Literally, method of operation. Refers to the habit of criminals to continue to pursue a particular method of committing their crimes. Through study of a criminal's habits (or *modus operandi*), it is possible to link several crimes committed by the same person and even to determine where he can be expected to commit his next crime.

Murder
The unlawful, deliberate, or premeditated killing of a human being. It is not required that the premeditation be of any specific length of time. The instant of time necessary to form a specific intent to kill is sufficient.

Nolle Prosequi
A motion by the prosecuting attorney in which he declares that he will not prosecute a case. Used when extenuating circumstances in a case indicate that, although a crime has been committed, it is in the best interests of justice to forego prosecution.

Notary Public
A public officer authorized to administer oaths, witness signatures, and acknowledge the genuineness of documents.

Oath
Any form of attestation by which a person signifies that he is bound to perform a certain act truthfully and honestly. A person making a

false statement while under oath to tell the truth may be prosecuted for perjury.

Opium
A narcotic substance prepared from the juice of the original poppy. It is further refined to produce morphine, heroin, and other narcotics. Opium is normally found as a dark, sticky mass that is smoked in special pipes. Opium smoking is decreasing in the United States in favor of the much stronger derivative, heroin.

Ordinance
Term used to designate any law enacted by a local governmental legislative body.

Panel
A group of men and women summoned for jury duty. A panel of approximately 25 prospective jurors is examined by attorneys for both sides prior to the start of a case. Through this examination, 12 are selected to hear and decide the case.

Pardon
An act of grace, proceeding from the power entrusted with the execution of the laws, that exempts the individual on whom it is bestowed from the punishment the law inflicts for a crime he has committed.

Parole
The conditional release of a prisoner from jail prior to the completion of his sentence, usually

on the condition that he remain under the supervision of a parole officer.

Peace Officer
General term used to designate a member of any of the several agencies engaged in law enforcement.

Penal Code
A collection of statutes relating to crimes, punishment, and criminal procedures. This is the portion of the law most frequently used by police officers.

Perjury
The crime of knowingly giving false testimony in a judicial proceeding while under oath to tell the truth. Subornation of perjury is the crime of procuring or influencing someone else to commit perjury.

Plaintiff
In a civil action, the party initiating the suit. One who signs a complaint or causes a complaint to be signed. Other party to the suit is the defendant.

Plea
The answer that the defendant makes to the charges brought against him.

Pleadings
Written statements reciting the facts that show the plaintiff's cause for bringing the action and the defendant's grounds for defense to the

charges. These are prepared by the attorneys
for each party and are presented to the judge.

Policy
In gambling, a game in which bets are made
on numbers to be drawn in a lottery.

Portrait Parle (word picture)
Method of identification established by
Alphonse Bertillon wherein a description
of physical characteristics is used
to identify a person. This is one of the
identification methods used in America today.

Posse Comitatus
The authority of the sheriff to assemble all
able-bodied male inhabitants of the county to
assist in capturing a criminal, keeping the peace,
or otherwise defending the county. Refusal to
obey the summons is a criminal offense.

Post Mortem
After death. Refers to the examination of a
body after death. Also called an autopsy.

Precedent
A parallel case in the past that may be used as
an example to follow in deciding a present case.

Preliminary Hearing
An examination before a judge of a person
accused of a crime in order to determine if
there is sufficient evidence to warrant holding
the person for trial.

glossary

Notations

Prima Facie
"On its face" or "at first view." Refers to evidence that, at first appearance, seems to establish a particular fact, but that may be later contradicted by other evidence.

Principal
A person concerned in the commission of a crime, whether he directly commits the offense or aids in its commission. All principals to a crime are equally guilty; therefore, the driver who waits in the getaway car during a robbery is as equally guilty of murder as the accomplice inside the building who fires the fatal shot.

Private Person's Arrest
The authority granted to a private party to make an arrest under certain conditions. Sometimes referred to as a "citizen's arrest," although it is not limited only to citizens.

Privileged Communication
See **Confidential Communication.**

Probate Court
A court that establishes the legality of wills and administers the distribution of the estate of a deceased.

Probation
Allowing a person convicted of a criminal offense to go at large under the supervision of a probation officer rather than confining him

introduction to the administration of justice

to prison or jail. The probationer must comply with certain conditions set forth by the court and must be on good behavior. Failure to comply with these conditions will cause the probationer to be placed in jail to serve his sentence.

Proof
The establishment of a fact by evidence.

Prosecutor or Prosecuting Attorney
A public officer whose primary duty is to conduct criminal prosecutions as attorney in behalf of the state or people. The district attorney and city attorney are examples.

Prostitute
A woman who engages in sexual relations for hire.

Pyromania
An unnatural, overpowering attraction to fire.

Rape
Unlawful sexual intercourse with a woman against her will, usually accomplished by physical violence, but it may be committed when the woman is drunk, unconscious, feebleminded, or otherwise unable to resist. Statutory rape is where the female is under the age of eighteen, even though giving her consent to the act.

Notations

Recidivist
An habitual criminal.

Recognizance
Official recognition of some fact by a court. In criminal procedure, it applies to a person accused of an offense being released on his own recognizance without being required to post bail, on his promise to appear for trial. Employed where the accused is well known to be reputable or is charged with a minor offense.

Res Gestae
Things done. Facts and circumstances surrounding a particular act. Refers particularly to acts or exclamations overheard by a third party, which would be inadmissible in court under normal rules of evidence but which, because they occurred at the moment of the particular act in question, are admissible under the rules of *res gestae* evidence.

Resisting an Officer
Any person resisting, delaying, or obstructing a public officer in the discharge of his duties is guilty of a misdemeanor.

Return
A short account in writing made by an officer in respect to the manner in which he has executed a writ or a process.

Reversal
The setting aside or annulment of the decision of a lower court made by a higher court. *See* **Appeal**.

Notations

Rigor Mortis
The stiffening or rigidity of the muscles and joints of the body which sets in within a few hours after death.

Robbery
The unlawful taking of personal property in the possession of another, from his person or immediate presence, against his will, and accomplished by use of force or fear.

Search Warrant
An order to a peace officer, issued by a court, directing that a certain location be searched and that certain specifically described property, if found, be seized and delivered to the judge. A search warrant can be executed only by a peace officer and is valid for ten days from issue.

Seduction
The offense of inducing a woman to engage in sexual relations under a false promise of marriage.

Statute Law
A written law enacted and established by the legislative department of a government.

Stay of Execution
An order of a court postponing the carrying out of the penalty or other judgment of the court.

Stipulation
An agreement between opposing attorneys relating to certain portions of a case. Usually

glossary

refers to minor points in a case that are accepted without demanding proof in order to shorten the time of trial.

Subpoena
An order issued by a court commanding the attendance of witnesses in a case.
See **Duces Tecum.**

Summons
In a civil case, an order directed to the defendant giving notification that an action has been filed against him and giving instructions as to how and when he may answer the charges. Failure to answer the summons will result in the case being awarded to the plaintiff by default.

Supreme Court
Highest court of appeal, either state or federal.

Suspended Sentence and Judgment
Suspended sentence is where no sentence is pronounced by the court, and the offender is released after being found guilty on condition that he abide by certain rules laid down by the court, such as making restitution to the victim. Suspended judgment is where the offender is released as above after sentence has been pronounced. In either case, the offender may be returned to court at any time to be sentenced or, in the case of suspended judgment, have the sentence carried out.

Notations

Testimony
Oral evidence given by a witness under oath.

Theft
See **Larceny**.

Tort
A civil wrong. An invasion of the civil rights of an individual.

Transcript
A printed copy of a court record, including the verbatim testimony of witnesses.

Trauma
An injury to the body caused by external violence.

Trial
That step in the course of a judicial proceeding that determines the facts. A judicial examination in a court of justice. May be held before a judge and jury, or a judge alone.

Versus
(against). Abbreviated "vs." or "v."

Valid
Having full legal force and authority.

glossary

Notations

Waive
To surrender or renounce some privilege or right.

Warrant
A written order from a court or other competent authority, directed to a peace officer or other official, ordering the performance of a particular act, and affording the civil protection for the person executing the order. Examples are a warrant of arrest and a search warrant.

Witness
A person who has factual knowledge of a matter. One who testifies under oath.

Subject Index

Accusation, formal, 11
Adjudication, 19, 20
  by courts, 28, 42
Adjudicatory hearing, 19
Alcoholic offenders, 9
  juveniles, 180
American Bar Association (ABA), 266, 287, 289, 290, 305
American Correctional Association (ACA), 253, 266
American criminal justice system, see Criminal justice system
Appeals, 11, 14, 96, 230, 231, 232, 360
  courts of, 96, 231, 232
  formal, 231
  to U. S. Supreme Court, procedure of, 236, 237
Appellate courts, 98, 230, 231, 360
  state, 230, 231
    intermediate, 231
    lack of uniformity created by regionalization, 231
Appellate procedure, 231
Arraignment, 11, 12
Arrest, 8, 9, 11, 16, 197, 202, 250, 361
  citizens' powers of, 7, 380
  and constitutional rights, 9
  definition of, 8
  for felony, 8, 9
  illegal, 85, 174, 175, 178
  legal, 176
  for misdemeanor, 8, 9
  police, 7, 28, 37, 143, 181
  powers of police to, 8
  of suspected criminals, 139, 140
  warrant, 8, 9
Assigned-counsel system, 241
Attorney general, state, authorities and duties of, 239, 240
Attorney General, U. S., 79, 148
Auburn System of New York, 112, 115, 116, 127

Bailiff, 142, 143, 242
Bail system, 9, 10, 11, 361
  bond bail, 99
  bondsman in, 99

  role of, 10
  economic motivation for, 99
  effect on justice, 98-101
  inequities in, 10, 349
  money bail, 10, 99
  purpose of, 10
Barristers (trial lawyers), 105
Betts v. Brady, 316 U. S. 455 (1942), 99
Bill of Rights, 9, 30, 31, 241; see also Constitution, U. S.
Blacks and police, 84
Booking, 7, 9
British common law, see Common law
British judicial systems, 103, 105
Bureau of Narcotics and Dangerous Drugs, 80, 148
Burger, Warren, Chief Justice, 100

California Commission on Judicial Qualifications, 238, 239
California Commission on Peace Officer Standards and Training (POST), 301, 302, 303, 308, 309, 339
California Superior Court, 232, 233, 234
Capital crimes, 7, 99, 111, 363
  federal, 99
Capital punishment, 111
  controversy over, 117, 120
Central Intelligence Agency (CIA), 147
Certification, 236, 237
Cherry Hill in Philadelphia, 112, 113, 114, 115
Citation, 101, 198, 203
  increase use of, 348
  traffic, 211
Citizen, private, 7
  involvement in law enforcement, 224
Civil actions, 233, 234, 364
  civil filings and criminal filings, ratio compared, 233, 234
Civil courts, 94
Civil law, 102
  concept of law, difference between common law and, 102
Civil liberty, 285
Civil rights, 8
Civil rights movement, 84, 88
Civil service system, 82, 87, 142, 243

387

Code of Professional Responsibility, 289
Codes of Ethics, 284, 287-292
   Correctional Code of Ethics, 291, 292
   Judicial Code of Ethics, 290, 291
   Law Enforcement Code of Ethics, 287, 288
   Legal Code of Ethics, 289, 290
   Parole Officers Code of Ethics, 288
Common law, 28, 364
   British, 8, 101, 102
      historical significance of, 94
   concept of law, differences between civil law and, 102
Communications, importance of in policing, 198, 203-207
   forms of, 204
   telecommunications, 205, 206, 207
Community, involvement in rehabilitative process, 260, 343, 353
   -police relationship, 84, 135, 136, 173, 180, 190
Community-based corrections, concept of, 121
   criticisms of, 121
   reintegration of offender into the community as objectives, 261-265, 268-272, 291, 354
   treatment, 251, 261
   trend toward, 126, 127
Complaints, 11, 140
Confessions, 30, 365
   coerced, 174
Conformity, 65, 66, 68
Congress, U. S., 79, 96
Conjugal visitation, 344
Constable, 75, 76, 142, 143, 144
Constitution of the United States, 29, 30, 94, 95, 96, 97, 238, 239, 290
   Article III, 95, 96
   protection of, 31, 42
   see also Eighteenth; Eighth; Fifth; First; Fourteenth; Fourth; and Sixth Amendments
Constitutional rights, 9, 123, 124, 127, 173, 208, 285, 287, 292
   to counsel, 30
   to due process of law, 123, 127
   to a jury trial, 30, 31
   of majority, 31, 42
   of minority, 31, 42
   to privacy, 8
   to speedy trial, 100, 101
Constitutions, state, 94, 97
Conviction, 31, 202, 353, 365
Correctional Code of Ethics, 291, 292
Corrections system, 12, 13-15, 17, 18, 111-127, 249-277
   British influence of on, 111, 112
   classification in prison, 254-261
   community alternatives to, 268-272
   community and, 260, 261-265
   components of criminal justice system, 28, 42
   toward a consistent system of, 275, 276
   corrections personnel, 273-274, 344
      education and training for, 274, 306-307
      general characteristics of, 273-274
      professional status of, 286, 287, 292
      see also Criminal justice personnel
   corrections reform, trends toward, 342-345
   European influence on, 111, 113, 115
   future of, 274-275
   historical significance of, 111-117, 127
   institutionalization, 251
   parole, 249, 251, 261, 265-272; *see also* Parole
   presentence investigations, 251, 252, 253, 254-261
   probation, 249, 251, 261-265; *see also* Probation
   recommendations for, by National Advisory Commission on Criminal Justice Standards and Goals, 353-354
   religious influence of in nineteenth century, 116, 127
   treatment in prison, 254-261
      treatment techniques, 271-272
      various treatment models, 269-272
Corruption, in police, 74, 76, 78, 81, 82, 85, 87
   in public office, 40
Counsel, 20
   need for, 99, 173
Counseling, 124, 125
   group, 124, 125
   religious and psychiatric, in prison, 260
Court administrators, 242, 351, 352, 353
Court clerk, 242, 243, 303
Courts, of appeal, 96, 231
   appellate, 98
   circuit, 96
   civil, 94
   criminal, 94, 263
   district, 96, 231, 232
   federal, 10
   function of, penal or preventive, 106
   general characteristics of, 230-232
   general types of, constitutional, 94
      legislative, 94
   state, 99, 100
   trial, 11, 12, 98, 103, 230, 231, 233, 234

Court system, 9-13, 93-107
  components of criminal justice system, 28, 42
  court organization, 232-236, 243
  court personnel, *see* Criminal justice personnel
  court reform and reorganization, need for, 230, 235
    judges, selection of, 238, 239
    new direction in, 230, 235
    to simplify judicial structure, 98, 100
    trial delay problem, 101
  English origins of, 94
  federal, 94, 231
  historical development of, 93, 94, 229
  origins of from three sources, 94, 95
  recommendations for, by National Advisory Commission on Criminal Justice Standards and Goals, 351-353
  state, 94, 352, 353
    general characteristics of, three basic court functions characteristic to all states, 230
    historical and social differences among, 230
Crime, 7, 8, 14, 16, 365, 366
  capital, 7, 99, 111
  causation, 42, 47-68
    administrative and legislative theories, 48-51
    biophysical theories, 51-54
    contemporary concepts of, 65, 66, 67, 68
    crime as learned behavior, 57, 58
    environmental influences, 58-63
    psychoanalysis and crime, 63-65
    socioeconomic determinism, 54-57
  classification of, 40
  and the community, 120, 121
  control of, 36, 66, 76, 185, 249, 250
    and integrated policing, 187, 188
    police methods and, 180-183
    policing style and, 175, 176, 177, 178, 180
  definition of, legal, 25, 26, 42, 49, 50, 51, 66, 67
    sociological, 26, 27, 42, 49, 50, 51, 66
  deterrence, 49, 66, 181
  federal, 26, 79
  and growth of American cities, 76, 83
  Index Crimes, 32, 33, 34, 36, 40
  interconnected, 214, 215
  investigation of, 78, 198, 201, 208, 300
  laboratory, 208
  major, 174
  national trends of, 32-42
  official statistics of, 55, 59, 62
  organized, 40, 83, 200, 214, 215
  prevention of, 36, 66, 76, 134-136, 157, 162, 164, 197, 224, 349, 350, 351
  British definition of, 157
  contemporary concept of, 181
  social climate and, 134, 135
  property, 33, 34, 37, 54, 55, 58, 202
    police record-keeping system, 203
    see also Federal crime statistics
  reduction of, 209, 210
  repeat, probation and, 121
  slum conditions and, 81, 84
  specialized, 230
  types of, 32, 33, 40
  unreported, 250
  variables in, 41
  without victims, 26, 27, 215
  of violence, 32, 33, 34, 37, 54, 202
  white-collar, 40, 41, 50, 51, 55
Crime in the United States: Uniform Crime Reports, 28, 32
Criminal acts, 26, 29, 40, 47, 49, 50, 366
Criminal codes, 50, 74, 111
Criminal courts, 94, 263
Criminal justice personnel, 28, 29, 313, 315, 338-340
  corrections personnel, education and training for, 306-307
  court personnel, education and training for, 304
  education and training concepts of, 297-316, 344
    future trends in training, 313-314
    Modesto Regional Criminal Justice Training Center in California, 311, 312
    regional criminal justice training and resource system, 309, 310-312
    state standards councils, creation and expansion of, 307, 308, 309
  general employment process, 321-323
    employment interview, impact of, 321, 323
    the interviewer, 325, 326, 327, 328, 329
      reactions of, 326-327
      types of questions asked by, 328, 329
    interview process, nature and purpose of, 324, 325, 326, 327
    new trends in interviewing, 330-332
    promotional interview, 330
  professionalism in, 284, 287-292; *see also* Codes of Ethics
  professionalism throughout the system, importance of, 285-286, 292
    shortcomings of, 286, 287
  roles of, 298
Criminal justice system, 3-23

subject index   **389**

administration of justice in, 134; *see also* Justice
adversary system in, 13, 15
chronology of, 4, 5, 6
components of, 134, 164
constitutional factors supporting, 29-31
corrections, 12, 13-15, 17, 18, 28, 42
  and offenders in, percentage of, 250, 251
  primary functions of, 249-277
  see also Corrections system
courts, 9-13, 28, 42; *see also* Courts; Court system
friction within the system, 15-19, 20
  "people" problems, compositional differences, 15, 16
functions and responsibilities of, 29
juveniles in, 19-20
juvenile system, "people" problems in, 20.
  See also Juvenile court system; Juvenile delinquency
nonsystem approach of, 275
objectives of, 292
parole, 122; *see also* Parole
personnel, *see* Criminal justice personnel
police, 7-9, 15, 16, 17, 18, 28, 42. *See also* Police; Police system; and Policing styles
security, importance of in, 156-163; *see also* Security
sentencing practices, effect of on, 123
subsystems under, relationship with each other, 15-19, 203, 285, 286, 291
trends in the administration, 337-356
  affirmative action programs, 345-347
    recruitment and selection as major goals of, 346
  correctional procedures, changes in, 342-345
    conjugal visitation, 344
    educational programs, 344-345
    prisons, changes in physical facilities, 343
    rehabilitation, community involvement in, 343
  impetus provided by Law Enforcement Assistance Administration, 338
  judicial program, 347-349
  policewomen, expanding role of, 340-342
Criminalistics, 145, 151, 208
Criminal procedures, 93, 305
  rules of, 16
Criminal law, causes of crime and, 48, 50, 54
  procedural, 173, 174
    police role and, 174, 176, 177, 178
  source of, 49
  subordination of in legal education, 304, 305
  substantive, 173, 174
    police role and, 173, 174, 176, 177, 178
Criminals, 64, 74, 81, 134, 138, 214, 215, 268
  as an antisocial person, 50, 57, 58, 64, 65, 66, 67, 68
  apprehension of, 213, 300
  arrest of, 139, 140; *see also* Arrest
  dangerous, 201
  definition of, 50
  mobility of, 205
  numbers of in the United States, 250
  personalities of, 64, 65
  police handling of, 176, 177
  policewomen and apprehension of, 213
  theory of classes of, 51, 52, 53
  treatment and punishment of, major influences in nineteenth century, 114, 115, 116, 117
    in seventeenth and eighteenth centuries, 111, 112
Criminology, 300, 366
  future of, 48, 65-67; *see also* Crime, causation
  social control as new theories of, 68
Cross-examination of witnesses, 268
Custody, 98, 99, 100, 101
Customs Department, 80, 147

Due process of the law, 99, 233
  in parole hearings, 123, 127
Death penalty, 31, 99, 111, 112
  controversy over, 120
  incarceration as substitute for, 112
Defendants, 6, 11, 12, 13, 14, 17, 18, 101, 366
  indigent, 10, 99, 100
  presentence investigations, impact of, 251
Defense, 351
  quality of, 241
Defense attorneys, 6, 232, 251, 286, 304, 305
Defense counsel, 11, 12, 17, 18, 99, 100
Definite sentences, 122
Delinquency, *see* Juvenile delinquency
De nova, 231, 232
Department of Agriculture, 149
Department of Health, Education, and Welfare, 149
Department of the Interior, 149
Department of Justice, U. S., 79, 80, 148, 323
Department of Labor, 345
Department of the Treasury, 80, 147
Detectives, responsibility of, 197, 202
  role of, 6, 150, 300
Detention, 9, 353

preventive, 349
Determinism, 66, 68
　physical, 51, 52, 53, 54
　socioeconomic, in crime causation, 54-57
Discretion, of court, 122
　police, 172, 177, 179, 188-190
　police power of, 172
Dismissals, 240
Disposition, court, 250
　nonadjudicatory, 19
District attorney, 13, 100, 101, 349
District courts, 96, 232
　of appeal, 231
　state, 98
Diversion from justice system, 183, 342, 351, 352, 353
Double jeopardy, 30, 367
Drug Enforcement Administration, 80
Drugs, *see* Narcotics and dangerous drugs

Economic variables to crime, 56
Eighteenth Amendment to the Constitution, 82
　Prohibition, 82
Eighth Amendment to the Constitution, 31
Employment, preparation for, *see* Criminal justice personnel
Equal Employment Opportunity Commission, 345
Ervin Committee Senate Hearings, 201
Ethical conduct, canons of, 283-293
Evidence, 11, 51, 198, 201, 208, 232, 368
　examination of, 11
　illegally seized, 30
　presented in trials, 12
　search for, 202
　suppressing of, 11
Ex parte, 291

Fair trial, 15
Federal Bureau of Investigation (FBI), 26, 32, 36, 37, 38, 39, 42, 79, 83, 121, 148, 301
　crime statistics of, 40
　　and police departments, 38, 39, 40
　　see also Federal crime statistics
　fingerprint, 124
　jurisdiction of, 148
Federal courts, 10
Federal court system, 96
Federal crimes, 26, 79
Federal crime statistics, 32-42
　Crime Clock, 37
　crime increase or decrease, 33, 34, 40

Crime Index, 33, 34, 36, 38
crime rate, 33, 34
　area analysis, 36, 37, 59
　national, 34, 35
　by regional comparisons, 34, 36
　population and, 33, 37
　weaknesses of, 37, 38, 39, 40, 41
Federal judicial system, *see* Judicial system, federal
Federal law enforcement agencies, 79, 146-150
　Bureau of Narcotics and Dangerous Drugs, 80
　Central Intelligence Agency (CIA), 147
　comparison between local, state and, 80
　Customs Department, 80, 147
　Department of Justice, U. S., 79, 80, 147
　Department of the Treasury, 80, 147
　Drug Enforcement Administration, 90
　Executive Office of the President, 147
　Federal Bureau of Investigation, 79; *see also* Federal Bureau of Investigation
　Immigration and Naturalization Service, 80
　Internal Revenue Service, 79, 80, 147
　Law Enforcement Assistance Administration (LEAA), 80
　Postal Inspection Service, 79
　U. S. Secret Service, 79, 80, 147
Felonies, 25, 100, 103, 104, 120, 368
　arrest for, 8, 9
　court jurisdiction, 232, 233, 234
　definition of, 7
　as major category of crimes, 7, 12
Field interviews, 208, 209, 210
Fifth Amendment to the Constitution, 9, 30
Fines, 10, 117, 120, 262, 369
Fingerprint, 124, 144, 208, 369
Fire and safety agencies, 145
First Amendment to the Constitution, 30
Food and Drug Administration, 150
Fourteenth Amendment to the Constitution, 233
Fourth Amendment to the Constitution, 30
Frauds, 147
French judicial system, 103, 104, 105
Freud, Sigmund, 63
Furlough, 291
　work, 343
Furman v. *Georgia,* 92 S.Ct. 2726, 225 Ga. 253, 171 S.E. 2d 501 (1972), 31

Gambling, illegal, 200, 215
Gangs, street, 56, 57, 58, 179
Gideon v. *Wainwright,* 372 U. S. 335 (1963), 100, 241

subject index **391**

Grand jury, 11, 12, 103, 233, 369
    alternatives to, 348
    definition of, 11
    hearings, 233
Group counseling, 124, 125
Group therapy, 258, 259, 260

Halfway houses, 343
Homosexuality, 26, 27
Hoover, J. Edgar, 79, 121
Hurtaldo v. *California,* 110 U. S. 516 (1884), 233

Identification, 145, 202, 203
    identification agencies, 144, 145
Immigration and Naturalization Service, 80, 148
Immunity, 240
Imprisonment, 112, 251, 252, 266
    community-based alternative to, 261-265
    as form of corrections or punishment, 111, 117, 120, 121, 127
    public cost of, 125, 126, 127
    as substitute for death penalty, 112
    see also Corrections; Prison; and Prisoners
Indeterminate sentences, 116, 117, 122, 266, 371
Index Crimes, 32, 33, 40
    increases and decreases, 33, 34, 36, 40
    see also Federal crime statistics
Indictment, 11, 12, 233
    and information, difference between, 11
Indigent, 10, 99, 100
Inferior courts, 96, 230, 231, 233, 234-236
    civil actions in, 234
    common characteristics of, 235
    constitutional authority of, 95
    lack of uniformity in, 235
Information, 11, 12, 233
    and indictment, difference between, 11
Infractions, 25
Initial appearance, 9
Institutions, 7, 20, 93
    correctional, 117, 121, 249, 252, 253, 254, 255, 260, 342, 343, 344
    juvenile, 260, 261
    security concerns in, 253, 254
    social distance between staff and inmates in, 253
    definition of, 3, 5, 13
    friction of roles and goals among, 15-19, 20
    juvenile, 124
    mental, 234

penal, 3, 13-15
Institutionalization, 13, 127, 251-253
Intake, juvenile, 353
Intake hearing, 19
Interconnected crime, 214, 215
Intermediate appellate courts, 231
Internal Revenue Service, 79, 80, 147
    Alcohol and Tobacco Tax Division of, 145, 147
International Association of Chiefs of Police, 287, 309
Interrogation, 30, 181, 210, 372
Investigations, 214
    classification of, 202
    of crime, 78, 198, 201, 208, 300
    investigative services, general, 200, 201, 202
    presentence, 251, 252
Investigative agencies, 144-146

Jail, 7, 10, 11, 121, 122, 124, 372
    city, 25, 42
    county, 142
Judges, 6, 10, 14, 15, 16, 17, 28
    British, 105
    discretion of, in sentencing, 266
    education and training for, 303-306
    probation decision and, 120, 265, 266
    retirement, discipline, and removal of, 238, 239
    role of in court trial, 13
    selection of, 238, 239
        in foreign judicial systems, 104, 105
        Missouri plan, 238
    setting of bail, 98, 99
    Soviet, 105
    in Supreme Court, 95
Judicial Code of Ethics, 290, 291
Judicial system, court personnel, 237-243, 303-306
    attorney general, state, 239, 240
    court administrators, 242
    court clerk, 242, 243
    defense counsel, 241
    district attorneys and county prosecutors, 240
    justices, *see* Judges
    marshal or bailiff, 242
    federal, 236-237
        historical perspective, 95, 96
        foreign systems and American system compared, 101-105
            British judicial system and American, compared, 102, 103, 104, 105

392   subject index

judicial selection processes, significant differences in, 104-105
French judicial system and American, compared, 103, 104, 105
legal system of U. S. S. R. and American system compared, 103, 104
judicial reform, 98, 347-349
to promote speedy trial for reduction of delay, 347, 348
paraprofessionals, job responsibility of in judicial functions, 101
social inequities in, 98-101
state, 96-98
historical perspective of, 96-98
California, 96-98
judicial structure of, 97
lack of uniformity created by regionalization, 231, 235
three-tier system, 98, 230, 233, 235
inferior courts, 230, 231, 233, 234-236
problem of overlapping of jurisdictions, 230, 231, 233
state appellate courts, 230, 231, 232
trial courts of general jurisdiction, 230, 232
two-tier systems consisting of appellate and trial courts, new trend toward, 98, 230
Judiciary, 28, 263, 290, 291, 305, 306, 351, 372
criticisms of elective and appointive processes for, 238
Soviet, 105
Jurisdiction, 95
appellate, 230, 231
over civil actions, 234
correctional, 250
of courts, 230
general, 230, 231
of Federal Bureau of Investigation, 79, 148
of federal circuit court districts, 96
of inferior courts, 96, 234
lines in criminal activities, 214
overlapping, problem of, 26, 230, 231, 233
probate, 234
state police, 78
Jurists, 49
French, 105
Jury, 12, 13, 17, 373
selection of, 101
unanimity, 30, 31, 101
Jury trial, 12, 101, 229
right to, 30, 31
Justice, application of to American criminal justice system, 28, 29, 31, 134, 149, 190, 298, 304, 305, 306, 307
recommendations by National Advisory Commission on Criminal Justice Standards and Goals to improve, 349
security, importance of, 156-163
Justice courts, 235
Justice inequities, 98-101
within the system, 122
Juvenile court system, 19-20, 135, 373
alternatives to, 199, 200
intake, 353
jurisdiction over, 233
juvenile court, authority of, 233
in French judicial system, compared, 103
juvenile court laws, purpose of, 199
"people" problems in, 20
Juvenile delinquency, 7, 19-20, 124, 135, 142, 150, 199, 200, 232, 233, 262, 264
alcoholic offenders, 180
as learned behavior, 57, 58
physical determinism in, 51, 52, 53, 54
policing style and, 185
prevention of, 199
psychoanalysis of, 64
self-concept and, family as source of, 59, 62
slum conditions and, 59, 60, 61, 62
social class and, 56, 57
see also Crime, causation

Knapp Commission Report, 215, 216

Law, changing, 229, 230, 301
constitutional change, 234
Supreme Court, U. S. and, 237
changing society and, 28, 229, 230
civil, 102
code of, 93, 102
concept of, 101
Western European, 102
juvenile court, 199
martial, 146
parole, 266
practice of, 285, 289
purpose of, in a democracy, 27-29, 42, 49, 66, 67
and social belief, 49, 50
violation of, 140, 177, 179, 187, 234, 235
see also Crime
Law enforcement, citizen involvement in, 224
impact of private security on, see Security
new image of, 84
problem of, 83

subject index **393**

selective, 173, 177
training of, 83
trends and direction of, 223-225
women's role in, 211-214
Law enforcement agencies, federal, *see* Federal law enforcement agencies
functions and purposes, *see* Police, functions of
state, 143-146, 164
Law Enforcement Assistance Administration (LEAA), 80, 85, 148, 149, 156, 165, 311, 312, 323, 349
trends in administration of justice system, provided impetus, 337-338
Law Enforcement Education Program (LEEP), 149, 300
Law schools, lack of attention to criminal law, 304, 305
Lawyers, basic training standards for, 305
canons for professional conduct of, 289, 290
Legal Code of Ethics, 289, 290
Liberty, civil, 285
personal, protection of, 139
Liquor control boards and commissions, 145
London police force, 74, 76, 138
Lower courts, 230, 231, 233, 234; *see also* Inferior courts

Magistrates, 9, 103, 233, 304, 374
Majority rights, 31, 42
Mapp v. *Ohio,* 367 U.S. 643 (1961), 30
Marshal, U. S., 11, 79, 148, 149
functions of, 148, 149
role of, 143
Martial law, 146
Medical model, theory of criminal behavior, 67, 68
Mental illness, crime and, 63, 64, 65, 67; *see also* Crime, causation
Metropolitan Police Act, 74, 75, 87
Metropolitan Police Department of Washington, D. C., 201
Minority rights, 31, 42
Miranda decision, effect on rate of confessions, 30
Miranda Warning, 9, 10
Miranda v. *Arizona,* 384 U.S. 436 (1966), 9, 30
Misdemeanors, 25, 101, 103, 120, 375
arrest for, 8, 9
court jurisdiction, 232, 233, 234
definition of, 7
major category of crimes, 7, 12
right to counsel and, 100
Missouri Plan, *see* Judges

Mistrial, 13, 17
Motor vehicle divisions, 145

Narcotic addicts, 142, 148, 214
approaches to treatment of, 85
Narcotics and dangerous drugs, 200-201, 214
drugs, use of, 85, 122
National Advisory Commission on Civil Disorders, 84
National Advisory Commission on Criminal Justice Standards and Goals, 266, 275, 349-354
goal of the Commission's work, 349
recommendations for corrections, 353-354
recommendations for the courts, 351-353
recommendations for the police, 350-351
National Conference on Parole, 123
National Council on Crime and Delinquency, 266
National Crime Information Center (NCIC), 206
National Guard Units and State Militias, 145
National Security Council, 147
Negotiated pleas, 351, 352
New York City Police Department, 76, 78, 81, 136, 143, 220
historical contributions of to police system, 76, 78
Knapp Commission Report on, 215, 216
NYSIIS (communication system), 206
No bill, 12
Nonconformity, 65, 66, 68
Nonsystem, of criminal justice system, 275

Oaths, 93
Omnibus Crime Control and Safe Streets Act of 1968, 200
Ordinances, 25, 197, 377
Organized crime, 40, 83, 200, 214, 215
Organized Crime Control Act of 1970, 200

Paraprofessionals, job responsibility of in judicial functions, 101
Parole, 14, 15, 20, 29, 120, 121-123, 127, 249, 251, 261, 265-272, 353, 377
authority, 266
effectiveness and fairness of, 124, 267, 268
laws, 266
legalistic trend in, 123
parole hearings, 123, 127
representation at, 267, 268
rights to due process of law in, 123, 127, 267, 268

394   subject index

parole officers, 6, 125, 255, 272, 306
parole revocation, 125, 266, 267
personnel, professional status of, 286, 287, 292
practices, 122
prevention of crime and, 134-136, 164
and probation, differences between, 121, 122, 265, 266
purpose of, 123
and sentencing structure, 266
Parole boards, 121, 122, 123
decisions, 266, 267
Parolees, 15, 125, 266, 267
Parole Officers Code of Ethics, 288, 289
Pat-down search, 8, 209
Patrol, 78, 88, 197-198, 213, 299, 301
border, 148
highway, 144
officer, responsibilities of, 197, 198, 201, 202, 208, 209
policewomen in, 213, 214
preventive, 208, 209, 210
question of hazard in, 340, 341
Patrolmen, 6, 19, 20, 86, 138, 140, 150, 151, 152, 299
peace-officer role of police and, 177
Peace officers, 218, 340, 378
training programs for, 302
Peace Officer Standards and Training, California Commission on (POST), 301, 302, 303, 308, 309, 339
Peace Officers Research Association of California, 287
Penal codes, 26, 378
Penology, 254
modern, 113, 117-120
therapeutic ideology, 117
philosophy behind, 113, 117-120
punitive, 111-117
Personal recognizance, 10, 11, 94, 99
Philadelphia Prison Society, 112
Plainclothes, 201
Plea, 12
of guilty, 12
of insanity, 65
negotiated, 351, 352
of not guilty, 12
Plea bargaining, 18
court delay and, 100, 101
Police, 7-9, 15, 16, 17, 18
alienation, 209
arrests, *see* Arrest, police
authority and powers of, 8, 78, 151

misuse of, 85
civil service system in, 82, 87
community perceptions of, 84, 183-188
community-police relationships, 84, 135, 173, 180, 190
corruption in, 74, 76, 78, 81, 82, 85, 87
discretion, 172, 177, 179, 188-190
factors that influence police exercise of, 189
importance of, 189, 190
policing styles and, 177
discretionary power of, 172
education and training of, 82, 83, 84, 85, 88, 298-303, 339, 340, 342
California Commission on Peace Officer Standards and Training (POST), 301, 302, 303, 308, 309
differentiation between education and training, 298
educational requirements, controversy over, 298, 299
in-service training, 300, 301
postemployment and continuing education, emphasis on, 299, 301
recommendations by President's Commission on Law Enforcement and Administration of Justice, 298, 299, 300, 301, 305
see also Criminal justice personnel
European model of, 73, 74, 75
FBI crime statistics and, 38, 39, 40
functions of, 133-164
new concept of, 139-140, 164
versus traditional, 139
response to citizen complaints, 139, 140
traditional, 134-139, 164
preservation of order, 136-138, 164
prevention of crime, 134-136, 164
protection of personal liberty, 139
protection of person and property, 138-139
investigation of crime, 7, 8, 16, 78, 181, 197, 198, 199, 200, 208
investigation of police, 215, 216
isolation of from the community, 172, 176, 177, 190
methods used by, 180-183
negative methods, 180, 181, 184, 188
apprehension, 181
saturation, 181
positive methods, 180, 181, 183, 184, 188
deterrence, 49, 66, 181
education, 181, 182

subject index **395**

mediation, 183
   referral or diversion, 183; *see also* Diversion from justice system
and minorities, 84, 85, 88, 189
morality, 81, 82
new technology, impact of, 143
   use of, 78, 85, 135, 136, 203, 301
as objects of racial criticism, 84
professionalism in, 136, 139, 143, 144, 178, 187, 190
   efficiency versus effectiveness, 188, 203
   importance of, 297, 298
   new concept of, 84
   see also Criminal justice personnel; Police, educational and training of
professionalization of, 80, 83, 84, 85, 86
professional status of, 286, 287, 292
public attitudes and myths about, 6, 7
recommendations for, by National Advisory Commission on Criminal Justice Standards and Goals, 349
removing police from politics, 81, 82, 87
role of, 30, 80
   concept of, 172, 190, 299
   conflict in, 172-175
      adjustments to, 174, 175-180, 190; *see also* Policing styles, development of
      factors create, 173, 174, 175
      expectations for, community, 172, 173, 174, 175, 176, 180, 190
      legal, 174, 175, 176, 188, 190
      police organization, 174, 175, 177, 178, 185
   "social workers" versus "cops," 140
state, 143-146
violence, use of, 85, 176
Police system, 73-88
   components of criminal justice system, 28, 42
   development of, 76-80
      Boston Police Department, historical contributions of, 76
      Chicago Police Department, historical contributions of, 78, 81
      critical periods of, 80-86
      depression years, impact of on, 83
      New York City Police Department, historical contributions of, 76, 78
      Philadelphia Police Department, historical contributions of, 76
   English contributions to, 75, 87
   an era of change, 83-86
   federal-level, 79, 80; *see also* Federal law enforcement agency

historical significance of, 73-75
human relations aspects of, 84, 85
local control of, 73
minorities in, 85
origins of, 75-76
police agencies in America, 140-150, 164
   city, 143, 164
   country police, 141-143, 164
      and local, comparisons between, 144
   federal level, 141
   investigative agencies, 144-146
   levels of, 141
   organizational structure of, 152-156
   state, 143-146
police organization, characteristics, 150-156, 164
   criticisms of, organizational weaknesses in education and training, 156
   nature of, 150-152
   organizational principles, 151, 152
police personnel, 216-223
   education of, importance of, 222
   recruitment of, 217, 218
   selection process, 216, 218-222, 339, 340, 342
      physical fitness, 217, 218, 219
      qualification standards, 218
      recruit training and probation as part of, 221, 224
   training of, 221, 224
   see also Criminal justice personnel
police reform, 74, 76, 80
police services, 197-226
   line functions, 197-201
      juvenile, 199, 200
      patrol, 197-198, 213
      plainclothes, 201
      traffic enforcement, 198, 199, 211
      vice/narcotics, 200-201
   special investigative functions, 214-216
   staff and supportive functions, 202-208
      communications, 198, 203-207
      crime laboratory, 208
      field interviews, 208, 209
      investigative, 202
      record-keeping function, 203
policewoman in, role of, 211-214
   expanding role of, 340-342
political influences on, 185
promotion system in, 76
state-level, 78
Policing styles, 171-190

counselor role versus enforcer role, 184, 187, 188
development of, 174, 175-180, 190
Hopkins' "war theory" of crime control, 175, 176
integrated policing, balance between enforcer and counselor roles of, 184, 185, 187
law-enforcer role versus peace-officer role, 177, 178, 180
passive concept of, 184, 185, 187
passive-punitive cycle, 185
personalized policing, 174, 184, 185, 186, 187
punitive concept of, 184, 185, 187, 188
social-order role versus legal-actor role, 177, 178
Wilson's three policing styles, 178, 179, 180, 185, 187
POST, see Peace Officer Standards and Training, California Commission on
Postal inspectors, responsibility of, 79
Powell v. *Alabama,* 287 U. S. 45 (1932), 99, 241
Preliminary examination, 103, 233
Preliminary hearing, 9, 11, 233, 379
Presentence investigation, 251, 252, 254-261
President, Executive Office of the, 147
President's Commission on Law Enforcement and Administration of Justice, 29, 45, 106, 220
  recommendations for police reform, 85, 88, 90, 298, 299, 300, 301, 305
  Task Force on Corrections, 306, 307
  and trends in the administration of justice system, 337
Pretrial release, 98, 99, 100, 349, 353
Prison, 13, 112, 115, 116, 117, 121, 122, 124, 249, 252, 253
  changes in physical facilities of, 343
  classification and treatment in, 254-261
  inmate subculture, 253
  prison riots, 249, 252, 253, 342, 343
  state, 25, 42, 343
  types of in structure, 115, 116
Prisoners, 112, 115, 116, 117, 122, 124, 127, 142, 143, 197, 342
  classification of, 252, 254-261
    ideology behind, 122, 127
  handling of, 253
Private security, *see* Security
Probable cause, 8, 16, 30
Probate matters, 234, 380
Probation, 6, 13, 14, 17, 19, 20, 67, 120-121, 127, 380
  as community-based alternative to incarceration, 249, 251, 261-265
  court-based, argument against, 263
  historical background of, 120, 121
  juvenile, 262
  National Advisory Commission on Standards and Goals for Criminal Justice System, new direction proposed by, 264, 265, 353
  and parole, similarities and differences, 121, 122, 265, 266
  personnel, professional status of, 286, 287, 292
  presentence investigations and, 251, 252
  probation officers, 13, 14, 17, 262, 263, 264, 306
  within purview of executive branch, argument for, 263
  revocation, 264
  variations of, 120
Profession, definition of, 283, 285, 286, 292
  requisites of, 283-285, 286, 287; *see also* Codes of Ethics
Prohibition, violations of, 82, 85, 87
Project STAR (Systems and Training Analysis of Requirements for Criminal Justice Systems Participants), 338, 339-340, 354, 355
Property, crimes, 33, 34, 37
  protection of, 138, 139, 145
Prosecution, 13, 16, 17
Prosecutors, 6, 11, 12, 13, 15, 16, 100, 303, 381
  county, 240
  institutional friction between police and, 16, 17, 18
Prostitution, 27, 40, 200, 214, 215, 381
Psychotherapy, 255
Public defender system, 10, 13, 16, 305, 306
Public health regulatory agencies, 145
Punishment, 26, 67, 94, 111, 124, 176
  capital, 111, 117, 120
  cruel and unusual, 31
  policing style and, 181

Reasonable doubt, 18, 31
Recidivism, rates of, 124, 125
Recognizance, personal, 10, 11, 94, 382
Referees, 101
Referral, 183, 199, 200
Reformatory idea, 116, 117
Rehabilitation, 67, 106, 255, 258, 260, 273

subject index **397**

concepts of, 111, 115, 117, 127, 343; see also Parole, Probation
   effectiveness of, 125, 127
Release, 10, 11, 20, 94, 120, 121, 124, 125, 273, 291
   community pressure against, 122
   conditional, 14
   criteria of, 99
   final, 343
   mandatory, 266
   on parole, 123, 124, 125, 127
   pretrial, 98, 99, 100, 349
   on recognizance, 10, 11
   rehabilitation programs and, 260, 273
Remand, 31
Repeaters, see Recidivism
Rights, constitutional, see Constitutional rights
Riots, 84, 88, 189
   prison, 249, 252, 253, 342, 343

San Francisco Police Department, 213
Screening, 351, 352
Searches and seizures, 30
   illegal, 174, 175, 178
Secret Service, U. S., 79, 80, 147
Security, classifications of security forces, 159
   concept of, 157
   defined, 158
   governmental, 158
   impact of on law enforcement, 133
   importance of in administration of justice, 156-163
   national, 147
   proprietary, 158, 162, 163
   private security services, 157, 162, 163
   recommendations for improvement of, 163
   three basic processes to security endeavors, 162, 163
Self-incrimination, 9, 30
Sentences, 18
   consecutive, 266
   definite, 122
   execution of, 120
   indeterminate, 116, 117, 122, 266
   maximum, 266
   suspended, 120, 122
Sentencing, 12, 18, 106, 351, 352
   discretion of court in, 122
   effect of sentencing practices on criminal justice system, 123
   modern innovations in, 122, 123
   parole and, 266
   presentence investigations and, 251, 252

Seventh Amendment to the Constitution, 30
Sheriff, 11, 214, 215
   country, 141, 142, 164
   as early forms of policing, 75, 76, 78
   office of, 78, 141, 142
   training programs for, 302
Sixth Amendment to the Constitution, 241
Social control, as new theories of criminology, 68
   police system and, 75
   as purpose of laws, 49, 66, 67
Social inequities, see Justice inequities
Soviet court system, 103, 104, 105
Speedy trial, 100, 101, 347, 348
STAR, Project, 338, 339-340, 354, 355
Stare decisis, 102
State courts of general jurisdiction, 232
State district courts, 98
State judicial system, see Judicial system, state
State law enforcement agencies, 143-146, 164
State police, 144
Statutory limitations, 252
Stop-and-frisk, 8, 209
Subpoenas, 143, 197, 384
Supreme Court, U. S., 30, 120
   appeal procedure, 236, 237
   capital punishment ruling, 31
   composition of, 236
   judges in, numbers of, 95
   jurisdiction of, 236, 237
   justices of, 96, 236, 237
   on right to assistance to counsel, 99
   stop-and-frisk procedure, ruling on, 208, 209
Suspended sentence, 122

Taleaferro v. *Locke,* 182 CA 2nd 755 (1960), 240
Task Force on Corrections of the President's Commission on Law Enforcement and Administration of Justice, 306
Task Force Reports, 200, 220
Telecommunications, 205, 206, 207
Terry v. *Ohio,* (392 U.S. 1 (1968)), 208, 209
Testimony, 9, 135, 385
Therapy, 67, 255, 260, 272
   group, 258, 259, 260
Traffic enforcement, 136, 137, 142, 145, 150, 198, 199, 211
   citations (traffic), 211
   juvenile violations, 181
   officer, duties performed, 198, 199
   policewomen in, expanding role of, 340-342

selective law enforcement and, 171, 173, 174, 178, 179
state police in, role of, 144
Treatment, 67, 342, 343, 353
   community-based, *see* Community-based treatment
   group, 258, 259
   modern approach to offenders, 120-123
   in prison, 254-261, 264, 267
   strategies of, 269-271
Trial, 11, 12, 13, 14, 17, 18, 230, 233, 350, 351, 385
   criminal, 338
   de nova, 231, 232
   fair, 15
   jurisdiction of, 230
   jury, 12, 30, 31, 101, 229
   speedy, 101, 347, 348
   without jury, 12
Trial courts, 11, 12, 98, 103, 230, 231, 233, 234
True bill, 12

Undercover operations, 200, 201

Verdict, 12, 13, 17, 18, 101, 232
Vice, 200-201
Violence, 30
   crime of, *see* Crime, of violence

Waive, 101
Walnut Street Jail in Philadelphia, 112, 114
Warrants, 140, 197, 203
   of arrest, 143
   search, 30
Western Penitentiary in Pittsburgh, 112, 127
White-collar crime, 50, 51, 55
Wickersham Commission (National Commission on Law Observance and Enforcement), 82, 83
Wills, 234
Witness, 11, 100, 202, 290
   cross-examination of, 268
   against himself, *see* Self-incrimination
writ of certiorari, 142, 236, 237, 363

Youth Service Bureau (YSB), 135, 200